Teaching
Physical Education
for Learning

Teaching Physical Education for Learning

JUDITH E. RINK

University of South Carolina

SECOND EDITION

with 42 illustrations

 Mosby

St. Louis   Baltimore   Boston   Chicago   London   Philadelphia   Sydney   Toronto

Dedicated to Publishing Excellence

Editor-in-Chief: James M. Smith
Editor: Vicki Malinee
Developmental Editor: Cheryl Gelfand-Grant
Project Manager: Trish Tannian
Senior Production Editor: Betty Hazelwood
Designer: Julie Taugner
Production: Joan Herron

SECOND EDITION
Copyright © 1993 by Mosby–Year Book, Inc.
A Mosby imprint of Mosby–Year Book, Inc.

Previous edition copyrighted 1985.

Printed in the United States of America

Mosby–Year Book, Inc.
11830 Westline Industrial Drive
St. Louis, Missouri 63146

Library of Congress Cataloging in Publication Data
Rink, Judith.
    Teaching physical education for learning / Judith E. Rink. — 2nd
ed.
       p. cm.
    Includes bibliographical references and index.
    ISBN 0-8016-6744-5
    1. Physical education and training — Study and teaching.
2. Physical education for children—Study and teaching.   I. Title.
GV363.R55 1992   92-
34827
796'.07—dc20   CIP

      96 97 MS/DC 9 8 7 6 5 4 3

To Eleanor

Preface

THE purpose of this book is to help preservice teachers develop instructional skills necessary to teach physical education effectively. Teaching is a process, and because it is a process, teaching behavior is interactive and to a large degree context specific. Not only must teachers have the technical skills of teaching, they must also be able to use those skills appropriately for particular situations. A large part of this book is devoted to describing teaching functions, the skills that constitute those functions, and the principles that guide their selection and use. The goal is not the acquisition of discrete, effective teaching behavior, but effective, context-specific practice.

◆ CONTENT FEATURES

The text has been totally revised since the first edition, but it maintains a focus on learning as a primary purpose of physical education programs.

Chapter 1 orients the learner to the purposes of teaching physical education and the language of teaching, and teaching functions. New to this edition is the inclusion of the NASPE definition of the Physically Educated Individual, which is introduced in the first chapter and used throughout the text.

Chapter 2 focuses on factors that influence learning. Because this chapter develops ideas relative to practice conditions and the content to be learned to a much larger extent than many texts, it is suggested that all students use this chapter as a review of their motor learning and development course work.

Chapter 3 presents a summary of the latest research on effective teaching and the implications of this research for the practice of physical education. Since the publication of the first edition of this text, there has been a decline in process product research and an increase in qualitative research and research on teaching physical education.

Chapters 4, 5, 6, 7, 8, and 11 are reorganized and rewritten but are basically oriented to present the essential teaching functions of interactive teaching—how to design movement tasks and learning experiences, how to present information to learners, how to develop content, how to develop and maintain the learning environment, the teaching functions during activity, and planning and evaluating instruction. Chapter 7, which discusses developing and maintaining the learning environment, has been totally rewritten to reflect basically an authoritative perspective on management that has as its goal the development of student self-management. Several teaching strategies have been added to Chapter 9, including team teaching and cooperative learning.

Two new chapters appear in this edition. The first is a chapter on student motivation and personal growth (Chapter 10), and the second is a chapter on context-specific pedagogy (Chapter 12). Both of these chapters reflect current needs in our field—the first to be able to motivate learners and to contribute to their personal growth, and the second for teachers to deal with special populations in an inclusive way, as well as to have more knowledge of how to approach teaching particular content.

The last chapters, on observation and analysis of instruction (Chapter 13) and tools for the analysis of instruction (Chapter 14), have been revised and reorganized to reflect more current needs. Since the publication of the first edition of this text, several good books devoted exclusively to these topics have been introduced.

◆ ANCILLARY MATERIAL

A manual is available to instructors that suggests how to use this material for both preservice and inservice teachers. In addition, test questions and evaluation material is provided.

◆ ACKNOWLEDGMENTS

No project of this magnitude is ever completed alone. I will always be indebted to the many people I have worked with in the past who supported me and encouraged the development of these ideas. I am continuously grateful to my friends, colleagues, and students at the University of South Carolina for their support and for helping to create an environment of challenge and continuous growth.

Also, I would like to thank the reviewers, whose critical suggestions have been extremely helpful in the preparation of the second edition:

Margarite A. Arrighi
University of Maryland at College Park

David Claxton
Baylor University

J.L. Gusthart
University of Saskatchewan

Melissa Parker
University of North Dakota

Thomas Steen
University of North Dakota

Judith E. Rink

Contents in Brief

Contents

PART

I

◈◈◈◈◈◈◈◈◈◈◈◈◈◈◈◈◈◈◈◈◈◈◈◈◈◈◈◈◈◈◈◈◈◈◈

Understanding the Teaching / Learning Process

Teaching Physical Education: An Orientation

❖ ❖ ❖ ❖ ❖ ❖ ❖ ❖ ❖ ❖

OVERVIEW

Teaching can be viewed from many different perspectives. The perspective teachers take when they look at the teaching-learning process determines what they will look at in that process and how they will look at it. Perspectives are important because they cause the teacher to see things in certain ways.

This chapter establishes a perspective for this text. It is an overview on instruction from which other chapters in the text are developed.

❖ ❖ ❖ ❖ ❖ ❖ ❖ ❖ ❖ ❖

CONCEPTS

▪ **Teaching as a goal-oriented activity**
Types of goals
Establishing realistic goals
Choosing instructional processes to meet goals
Achieving goals through processes

▪ **Understanding the instructional process**
Prelesson and postlesson routines
Movement task–student response unit of analysis
Teaching functions
Management and content behavior

▪ **Becoming a professional teacher**
Value positions and beliefs in teaching
Personal characteristics of the teacher
Developing commitment

Most people who decide to teach physical education do so because they were good at it, enjoyed their experiences with sport and physical education, and like to work with people. These are good reasons to choose a profession. Because engaging in sport and physical activity is fun for most people, a misconception often exists that teaching physical education is easy, or at least easier than teaching any other content. Teaching can be exciting, rewarding, and fun, but when done effectively, it is not easy.

Teaching is a complex activity. Its goal is student learning. The teacher has primary responsibility for directing the teaching-learning process. When a student does not learn, often the teacher is responsible, and this is where teaching becomes so difficult. There are many different kinds of students and many different kinds of skills, knowledges, and values that teachers will want to teach. Teaching is not an exact science. Finding ways to reach objectives for learning with all students is a real challenge. Teachers design and redesign experiences for their students based on their pedagogic goals and their knowledge of the learner, the lesson content, and the teaching-learning process itself.

Teaching Physical Education for Learning is primarily a text on instructional processes and the teaching skills required to execute those processes effectively, that is, what teachers can do to help students learn what they want them to learn. Instruction is seen as a goal-oriented activity. This means that the process is meaningless unless it is designed with a clear goal regarding what the student will learn. Throughout this text readers will be asked to articulate what they want learners to acquire as a result of what they do as teachers. Instructional processes are specific to an intent. This means that the teacher selects an instructional process to best accomplish a specific purpose.

For instance, a teacher may decide to lead students through a problem-solving experience in balance to help them understand principles related to base of support. The teacher selects problem solving rather than telling because the teacher's objective is not just that students *know* the information but that they are able to use the information in their balance activities.

It is important for teachers to choose instructional processes appropriate to their goals. To do this, teachers must (1) have a clear idea of what they want students to be able to do, (2) understand the instructional environment in which they will be working, and (3) have the skills necessary, given their environment, to achieve their goals. This chapter is designed to explain the basic framework of the instructional process in physical education and to identify the skills needed to operate successfully within this framework.

◆ TEACHING AS A GOAL-ORIENTED ACTIVITY

Instruction is guided by a long-term plan for student outcomes called the **curriculum.** When curricular decisions are not made or used to guide instruction, the instructional process is like a car without a driver. For this reason curriculum and instruction are integrally related. Teaching as a goal-oriented activity begins at the curricular level.

Physical educators must explain and defend their role and program in the schools. Physical education programs are expensive in terms of the facilities, equipment, and personnel they require. Growing opportunities for students to participate in sport activities outside the schools, often with more success, have caused educators, administrators, and taxpayers to view with uncertainty the contributions of physical education programs to the overall education picture. Research done by physical educators on the attitudes of secondary students toward physical education (and the products and processes of physical education program) largely confirms the discrepancy between what physical educators promise and what they actually produce. Many physical education programs are simply not defensible.

No national curriculums exist in physical education, and there are few state or local curriculums to which physical educators are held accountable. Recent work by the National Association for Sport and Physical Education (NASPE) has begun to identify performance outcomes for physical education with their definition of the physically educated person (Box 1-1). According to this document, the following are characteristics of a physically educated person:

- Has sufficient skill to perform a variety of physical activities
- Does participate regularly in physical activity
- Is physically fit
- Knows the benefits, costs, risks, and obligations of physical activity involvements
- Values the role of regular physical activity in the maintenance of a healthy life-style

NASPE's work has helped to articulate the goals of the physical education field, but physical educators are largely left on their own when establishing goals and instructional programs. Lack of accountability has produced much diversity. It has given the creative teacher the opportunity to more nearly match programs to student needs. It has also resulted in many poor programs—programs that have no identifiable pedagogic goals or programs that bear no relation to their stated goals. If physical education is to attain credibility as a truly educational program, the relationships between curriculum and instruction must be clearly defined and programs must be oriented toward clearly stated goals.

BOX 1-1

NASPE Physical Education Program Outcomes For a Physically Educated Person

Has learned skills necessary to perform a variety of physical activities

1. Moves using concepts of body awareness, space awareness, effort, and relationships
2. Demonstrates competence in a variety of manipulative, locomotor, and nonlocomotor skills
3. Demonstrates competence in combinations of manipulative, locomotor, and nonlocomotor skills performed individually and with others
4. Demonstrates competence in many different forms of physical activity
5. Demonstrates proficiency in a few forms of physical activity
6. Has learned how to learn new skills

Does participate regularly in physical activity

7. Participates in health-enhancing physical activity at least three times a week
8. Selects and regularly participates in lifetime physical activities

Is physically fit

9. Assesses, achieves, and maintains physical fitness
10. Designs safe personal fitness programs in accordance with principles of training and conditioning

Knows the implications of and the benefits from involvement in physical activities

11. Identifies the benefits, costs, and obligations associated with regular participation in physical activity
12. Recognizes the risk and safety factors associated with regular participation in physical activity
13. Applies concepts and principles to the development of motor skills
14. Understands that wellness involves more than being physically fit
15. Knows the rules, strategies, and appropriate behaviors for selected physical activities
16. Recognizes that participation in physical activity can lead to multicultural and international understanding
17. Understands that physical activity provides the opportunity for enjoyment, self-expression, and communication

Values physical activity and its contributions to a healthful life-style

18. Appreciates the relationships with others that result from participation in physical activity
19. Respects the role that regular physical activity plays in the pursuit of lifelong health and well-being
20. Cherishes the feelings that result from regular participation in physical activity

Types of Goals

Educational program outcomes are commonly called **goals** when they refer to broad outcomes and **objectives** when they refer to more specific outcomes. Whereas curriculum objectives usually define what the student should achieve as result of an entire program, instructional objectives usually describe what the student should achieve as a result of a single lesson. Educational goals and objectives are used for both curriculum and instruction. They are usually classified under one of three interrelated categories according to the domain of learning that characterizes that particular goal or objective. The box on p. 5, which describes the NASPE outcomes project, shows differences in the kinds of outcomes specified.

Goals and objectives that deal with motor and physical abilities are termed **psychomotor** objectives. The NASPE outcomes related to motor skills and fitness are called psychomotor objectives. Psychomotor outcomes are the unique contribution of physical education to the education of the students. No other educational program emphasizes psychomotor objectives the way physical education does. They include motor skill objectives such as teaching fundamental skills (e.g., skipping, throwing, or rolling) or the complex skills required for sports (e.g., the basketball lay-up or back handspring). Psychomotor objectives also include fitness outcomes (e.g., arm strength, cardiorespiratory endurance, and flexibility). A psychomotor goal might be to play basketball at an intermediate level of ability.

The term **cognitive** refers to objectives that describe knowledge or ability levels in processing information. The NASPE outcome related to *knows* specifies the cognitive objectives important to physical education. Cognitive goals and objectives are intellectual and thinking related. They include outcomes related to knowledge students should have (e.g., how to develop joint flexibility) and outcomes related to problem solving and creativity or the transfer of knowledge from one situation to another (e.g., how to apply zone defense to a six-on-six soccer game).

Affective objectives describe student feelings, attitudes, values, and social behaviors. The NASPE outcome *values* specifies the values that students should attain as a result of a physical education program. The desire to have students value fitness and engage in activity on a regular basis is actually an affective goal. Objectives teachers have related to student feelings, attitudes, values and social behaviors are affective objectives.

Unlike sport programs outside the school, physical education also shares many cognitive and affective goals with all educational programs within a school. The teacher in physical education often has psychomotor, cognitive, and affective objectives in one lesson. Physical educators should help students to be thinking, caring, and sharing individuals. Lessons that in part teach waiting turns, fair play, independent learning skills, and positive self-regard all have objectives classified as affective.

Chapter 11, on planning, describes in detail how teachers can write goals and objectives for different purposes when planning both curriculum and instruction. At this point it is important simply to recognize that educational goals are concerned with each dimension of human development.

Establishing Realistic Goals

If the relationship between curriculum and instruction is to be maintained, the curriculum goals and objectives established must be appropriate to the instructional situation. *Instructional programs cannot be conducted in a manner consistent with established goals if the goals set are hopelessly unattainable.* Selecting realistic goals for a program is very difficult to do in physical education. The field has the potential to contribute in many ways to educational goals and objectives. Physical educators can use active learning and physical activity to make major contributions to all domains of learning. Designating realistic goals has been a major problem for many programs. Physical educators for the most part have tried to be all things to all people. As a result, they have tended to accomplish little. For example, a representative middle school curriculum guide for the eighth grade might list the following goals:

- Develop and maintain fitness
- Develop skills for participation in six team sports, four individual sports, gymnastics, and dance

- Teach students how to value themselves and inter-act with others in positive ways
- Teach students how to be independent learners and problem solvers
- Develop skills, attitudes, and knowledge related to participation in physical activity that will transfer to new skills and encourage lifetime par-ticipation

If students in this eighth grade have physical edu-cation class two times a week, it should be apparent that even the first goal of fitness is not attainable within the confines of the assigned class time. If the sport, gymnastics, and dance objectives are divided by the time normally available in a school year, the extent of the problem becomes apparent. Enough time simply is not available to successfully complete even the simplest of the stated goals. The goals listed in this curriculum are worthwhile—teachers should be setting their goals high. However, had the design-ers of this curriculum considered the instructional process needed to reach their goals, they would have realized that the goals stated were not attainable in the time allotted.

To attempt to meet all of these goals in one pro-gram can result only in accomplishing none of them, since the students need adequate time to experience any degree of success. The goals established for any program must be realistic to their setting, which often means that the teacher must choose between many worthwhile goals.

More realistic skill and fitness goals for this eighth grade setting might have included the fol-lowing:

- Students should be able to design personal goals for fitness with the help of the instructor and meet those goals by the end of the school year through a personal fitness program.
- Students should be able to attain an intermediate level of ability in one team sport and one individ-ual sport of their choice.
- Students should be able to participate successfully in at least one dance unit.

To meet these skill and fitness goals, the curricu-lum format and instructional processes, as well as the specific cognitive and affective goals, would have to change.

Choosing Instructional Processes to Meet Goals

Instructional experiences and processes are cho-sen intentionally to reach specific goals. Although more occurs in classes than is intended, teaching processes are designed to be specific to their desired learning outcomes. It is impossible to discuss what to do without discussing what the teacher hopes to accomplish.

One of the best examples of the specificity of teaching processes to desired outcomes occurs in the area of fitness. Fitness is developed only when certain criteria for work load, duration of activity, and inten-sity are met. The type of exercise is specific to the type of fitness desired (e.g., strength, muscular en-durance, flexibility, or cardiorespiratory endurance). The type of fitness is specific not only to the type of exercise, but also to a muscle group.

Criteria for teaching processes involved in learn-ing motor skills are not as neatly defined as those for fitness, but they are beginning to emerge in the literature. Open skills require different processes from closed skills. Teaching for transfer of learning from one skill to another requires a different pro-cess from teaching that does not intend transfer. All motor skill learning involves processes that require consideration of certain prerequisites for learning, such as the amount and type of information, prac-tice, and feedback that learners at different levels of development need.

Processes and criteria for meeting affective and cognitive objectives in physical education are not neatly packaged but are just as specific as those for other areas. Physical educators have traditionally assumed that if learners are engaged in creative experiences, creative learning is occurring. They have assumed that learners engaged in social inter-action with others are developing positive social interaction skills and that learners engaged in team sports will develop sportsmanship. Teachers have come to realize that merely engaging in an experi-ence that has the potential to make a positive contri-bution to affective or cognitive goals does not ensure that these goals are met. Learning experiences must be designed and developed for specific out-comes: what is not taught often is not learned.

Sportsmanship, independent learning skills, problem solving, positive social interaction, and the development of positive self-concepts require specific conditions and processes in which to develop. These goals should be designated, planned for, and taught, just as with other kinds of content goals.

Achieving Goals Through Processes

Teachers can achieve psychomotor goals and objectives directly by teaching movement content. Physical educators can teach basketball, jumping, dance, or swimming by providing carefully planned and conducted experiences in basketball, jumping, dance, or swimming. A more difficult question concerns how the educator teaches creativity, positive self-concept, positive social interaction skills, love of activity, or fair play.

Sometimes a teacher might put the primary emphasis of a lesson on developing student cooperative behavior or creativity. A teacher might also plan an entire lesson to teach a moral value or positively contribute to the self-concept of students. Most often these affective concerns are taught in conjunction with psychomotor or fitness skill development. The teacher chooses a way to develop the lesson with students so that more than a psychomotor emphasis becomes the focus of the lesson. This means that, although the primary content might be the basketball lay-up shot (and we design experiences to best teach the basketball lay-up shot), how the teacher goes about teaching this skill contributes a great deal to affective and cognitive goals. How students feel about basketball, themselves, and others, their knowledge of basketball, and their abilities to work independently, think creatively, and problem solve are all affected by the process by which the teacher chooses to teach the lay-up shot. If teaching the basketball lay-up were the only objective, teaching would be easy, or at least easier. I know, for instance, that if I could line up students near a basket and have them shoot the ball to the basket 100 times each class period, their lay-up skills would probably improve. However, I will have accomplished little if in the end they dislike class and will never play basketball unless they are forced to play. A teacher's goals must be more

inclusive. Although no teacher would intentionally teach for negative affect in class, in many classes affective goals are ignored. Teacher decision making in the instructional process is affected by the complex interrelationship between what to teach (*content*) and how to teach it (*process*). The two questions are not easily separated. The teaching process a teacher uses results in products many times not intended. Effective teachers choose processes because they are aware of the potential contributions of those processes to their goals.

Little research has been done that links different pedagogic processes to specific affective and cognitive outcomes. This is because of the difficulty of measuring such elusive and long-term products of instruction. Teachers, however, should be objective in assessing all the outcomes of their teaching. This necessarily includes affective and cognitive goals. Until teachers have a better understanding of the contribution of different instructional processes to these important outcomes, they must make informed decisions regarding teaching and carefully observe the products of these processes.

◆ UNDERSTANDING THE INSTRUCTIONAL PROCESS

It is helpful in designing and implementing successful instructional programs to understand instruction as a process that involves both teacher and students in a highly interrelated set of events. If someone asked what happened in gym class today, how would what the teacher and students did be described? An example of a high school class described in terms of observable events is shown in Box 1-2.

Not all physical education lessons fit the description given. However, many physical education lessons share aspects of this record. First, "getting ready" and "ending" routines frequently stand apart from the actual lesson of the day. There are identifiable times when the lesson begins in earnest and ends. Second, there is usually a recurring series of events in which the teacher presents a movement task to the students, the students respond to that task, and the teacher observes and tries to improve perfor-

BOX 1-2

Sample Secondary Lesson

- A bell rings. The students gradually come into the gym after changing clothes in the locker room.
- Some students remain on the fringes of the gym, talking with each other. Others begin playing with the balls.
- After a few minutes the teacher asks the students to form squads. One student from each squad checks attendance and preparation for class and then gives the squad card to the teacher.
- The teacher asks for student attention and gives an overview of the day's lesson. After the overview the teacher describes and demonstrates a new skill with another student. The teacher explains how the skill will be practiced and asks that students go to their area of the gym to practice. Students begin practicing.
- While students are practicing, the teacher observes the students' work, provides help to individuals, and occasionally stops the whole class to offer help on performance.
- The teacher asks one student to stop fooling around and get serious about the task.
- After students have had sufficient time for practice, the teacher calls the group together and asks the students to begin practicing the skill with a partner.
- The class puts the extra balls away, organizes into partners, and begins practicing the new task.
- The teacher resumes helping students with the task—sometimes individually and sometimes as a class.

FIGURE 1-1
Movement task–student response to task.

school. Elementary children usually do not change clothes for class, and taking attendance is not necessary. Lessons begin almost immediately. In instructional classes at the secondary level, however, teachers are required to perform tasks before class, such as checking attendance and determining whether the students are prepared for class. Usually this time is used also for announcements concerning after-school programs and events. In some cases, after-class routines include such duties as checking showers. Prelesson and postlesson routines should be accomplished in the least possible amount of time. Time used for these routines is time taken away from the actual lesson. If dressing and showering are necessary, time must be allotted for students to accomplish these tasks. If the tasks are not necessary, it is a waste of time to assign them.

Movement Task–Student Response Unit of Analysis

Instruction in physical education technically begins when "getting ready" routines end. After the set induction of a class in which the teacher orients the class to what is to happen in the class for the day and why, an identifiable series of events revolves about the interaction unit called the **movement task–student response.** This cycle of events is described in Figure 1-1.

mance. Third, two kinds of behavior and/or events are commonly present: (1) those that arrange or manage the environment in which the lesson is taught; and (2) those that work directly on the lesson content. Each of these aspects of instruction is described in the following pages.

Prelesson and Postlesson Routines

In most elementary classes, prelesson and postlesson routines are not as elaborate as in the secondary

The movement task. At the heart of the instructional process in physical education is the movement task. Movement tasks are motor activities assigned to the student that are related to the content of the lesson. The teacher directive to "practice the volleyball set to yourself until you can do it three times in a row without moving out of your place" is a movement task. "We're going to play keep-it-up in groups of six to see how long you can keep the volleyball up in the air using sets only" is also a movement task. Movement tasks are content. They are learning activities that are defined by the teacher either in an explicit or implicit way. An observer should be able to watch a physical education lesson and identify what "the teacher asked students to do." In lessons taught by effective teachers, students should be able to identify rather specifically what they should be working on at any point in the lesson.

Teachers design movement tasks as a progression of experiences to meet their objectives. Movement tasks do not necessarily have to be communicated directly by the teacher, although they usually are. Task cards and other media can communicate tasks.

Organizational arrangements. In group instruction, not only must tasks be communicated, but the arrangements for practicing the tasks must be communicated. Teachers must organize people, space, time (for practice), and equipment (when appropriate). They also should establish procedures for these organizational arrangements—how students will get equipment, how they will organize into groups, and how the space will be divided among students for practice.

Student response. After the teacher has given students the signal to begin working on a task, student practice or work with the task begins. Once the students have begun to practice the movement task, a major responsibility of the teacher is to observe and provide feedback to students on their performance, either individually or as a group. Initially when work begins on a task, the teacher is observing to see that the environment is safe, that students are working on the task, and that students have interpreted the task correctly. The teacher then must assess the responses

of the student to the task to determine an appropriate next teaching move.

Many teachers may find that as a result of their observations of student responses, they must restate or clarify the task, handle organizational or safety problems, motivate the students, and maintain on-task behavior during student response time. Teachers select the next step in the lesson after evaluating student performance on the previous task. Sometimes the next step is an entirely unrelated task (e.g., moving from the volleyball set to the serve), but most often the appropriate next step is to provide the students with additional information and an additional task focus to help them (1) improve the performance of the tasks they are currently working on, (2) increase the level of complexity or difficulty of the task, or (3) assess their ability in a self-testing or competitive situation. If a task with a new focus is assigned, the movement task–student response cycle begins again. This process is called **content development** and is discussed in Chapter 6.

Teaching Functions

Each instructional event in the sample secondary lesson (see Box 1-2, p. 9) can be described in terms of its contribution to the movement task (Box 1-3).

Because the movement tasks and the events (both direct and indirect) associated with it are so critical to the instructional process, many teaching skills are associated with this unit of interaction. We can begin to describe teaching behavior in terms of the function that teacher behavior performs in the teaching/learning process (Box 1-4).

The chapters of this text are organized primarily by the concept of teaching functions. Many of the chapters are designed to consider each of these teaching functions separately. The concept of teaching functions is a useful concept because it allows us to focus on the purpose of a teaching behavior rather than on the specific behavior itself. There are many appropriate ways teachers can effectively perform a teaching function. We cannot prescribe the specific way in which teachers should perform a function. Teachers must be free to choose how they will implement a lesson based on their pedagogic intent, their knowledge of the student, and their own skills

---

BOX 1-3

Contribution of Instructional Events to Movement Tasks

Teacher behavior	Contribution to the task
Gives an overview of the lesson	Develops a learning set and motivation for students to engage in the movement tasks of the lesson.
Describes a new skill	Helps students get a clear idea of the task and what they will be trying to do.
Describes how students will be practicing the skill	Arranges the environment for task (equipment, space, people).
Moves from student to student	Provides information on performance of the movement task and makes suggestions on how to improve performance.
Asks a student to stop fooling around	Maintains on-task behavior.

BOX 1-4

Teacher Functions in the Teaching/Learning Process

Identifying outcomes: Identify learning goals and objectives.

Planning: Design and sequence appropriate learning experiences and tasks to meet the identified goals.

Presenting Tasks: Present and communicate these tasks effectively so that students have a clear idea of what they are being asked to do and are motivated to do it.

Organizing and Managing the Learning Environment: Arrange and maintain an environment that maximally motivates student practice of the task.

Monitoring the Learning Environment: Provide students with feedback on their performance through accurate assessment of student performance in relation to a task.

Developing the Content: Modify and develop the task further based on student responses to the task.

Evaluating: Evaluate the effectiveness of the instructional process.

---

and characteristics. Although specific behaviors are not prescribed, criteria for these functions that are general principles can be established (e.g., a good task presentation lets the students understand task requirements, practice arrangements, and goals). Guidelines can also be established for specific situations (e.g., beginning learners are not able to use specific information on motor skills and must be provided with more holistic descriptions of the tasks to be performed). Guidelines and general principles are used appropriately when they are adapted to the specific context in which they are used.

When teachers perform teaching functions, they exhibit specific behaviors and employ specific methods (e.g., demonstration, explanation, task cards, or media). Even though specific behaviors or methods for individual teachers should not be prescribed, the

competency and appropriateness of teacher performance can be evaluated. Did the teacher describe or demonstrate the skill accurately? Was the level of presentation appropriate to the age and ability level of the students? At the level of specific behavior, guidelines of appropriateness and competency can again be established.

In summary, teachers must perform particular functions essential for effective instruction. They can perform these functions in many different ways and still be effective. We can evaluate the extent to which teachers adequatey perform a function and, to some extent, the adequately and appropriateness of their choice. Teachers decide what and how they will teach based on what they know, what they believe, and their own unique personality, skills, and interests. This text is designed to increase the teacher's acquaintance with the factors involved (and the criteria that need to be considered) in performing teacher functions appropriately and competently.

Management and Content Behavior

Some of the teacher functions just described are directly related to the content of the lesson; the purpose of others is to arrange and maintain a learning environment in which the content may be learned. Transactions directly related to lesson content are called **content behaviors;** those that arrange and maintain the learning environment are called **management behaviors.**

Content behavior contributes directly to the movement task. Management behavior contributes to the task only indirectly by creating the conditions for learning. Examples of both content and management behaviors from our sample secondary lesson (Box 1-2) follow:

Content Behaviors

- The teacher describes how the task is to be performed.
- Students engage in the task.
- The teacher helps students with the task.
- The teacher modifies and develops the original task.

Management Behaviors

- The teacher gives directions for arranging the equipment, people, and space before practice of the task begins.
- The students get the equipment and organize themselves into partners.
- The teacher asks a single student to stop fooling around.

Content behaviors are important because they directly address the essence of the physical education lesson—the content—and contribute directly to the intended lesson outcome. If the lesson content is a cartwheel, the teacher communicates information on the cartwheel, directs students to do tasks related to the cartwheel, gives students information on how they have performed the cartwheel, and makes suggestions to them on how to improve their performance.

Management behaviors are concerned with two types of problems: conduct and organization.

Teachers manage when they structure, direct, or reinforce the appropriate behavior of students, such as taking turns, following directions, or being supportive of their classmates. They also manage when they structure, direct, or reinforce arrangements for people, time, space, and equipment for the practice of a movement task. One kind of management deals with the *conduct* of students and another with the *organizational* arrangements for the class. The teacher who says "Walk, don't run" or "You're working very hard today" is dealing with conduct. The teacher who says "Get your rackets and go to a court" or "Everybody stop what they are doing" is dealing with organization.

Management behaviors are important because they create the learning environment. Teachers want a learning environment that will support the learning of lesson content. They also want a learning environment that contributes in a positive way to how the students feel about themselves, others, and the content of the lesson itself. No matter how good a teacher is at selecting appropriate tasks, explaining tasks, or providing appropriate feedback, it is all for nothing if the environment does not support the lesson's short- and long-term goals.

Directing content-related experiences and establishing and maintaining a learning environment (both with an eye to the student successfully achieving intended lesson outcomes) are the two most important functions of a teacher in the instructional process.

◆ BECOMING A PROFESSIONAL TEACHER
Value Positions and Beliefs in Teaching

Different teachers have different beliefs about teaching that affect how they teach. Beliefs in teaching commonly have their roots in theories of learning in psychology and philosophy and are concerned with issues related to what is most important for schools to teach and how people best learn. As a physical education teacher, you will have to decide how much of your program you want to devote to teaching students higher-level thinking skills, personal interaction skills, fitness, or movement skills. You will have to decide whether your job is to make learners fit or to give them the skills to make themselves fit, or a combination of these ideas. All of these decisions and many more like them are related to the idea of what is most important for schools to teach. They are largely curriculum decisions, but are also related to learning theory and how you think people best learn. Teaching theorists typically follow the lead of learning theory and those areas of psychology that attempt to explain human behavior. As a result, teaching is often conceptualized as being either behavioristic or humanistic in orientation.

Behavioristic and humanistic orientations to teaching differ significantly at the theoretic level. Behaviorists explain human behavior in terms of response to environmental contingencies that can to some extent be controlled by the teacher. Humanists think of behavior in terms of student personal control that should be developed by the teacher. When theoretic positions give way to actual practice, most educators fall somewhere between these two attitudes. It is often difficult in practice to tell where teacher guidance (humanism) ends and teacher shaping (behaviorism) begins.

Inherent in these views of teaching is a continual tension between beliefs that characterize the teaching process as manipulative and teacher directed and those that emphasize facilitation and a student-centered orientation (Table 1-1). Research is not likely to prove one of these views right and the other wrong, because at the heart of the question are the long-term products of education and the values of the individual teacher.

Contrasting ideologies are often helpful when discussing theories, but in actuality may do the practitioner a disservice. The practicing teacher has many kinds of goals that require different approaches for different students. Most teachers find themselves at different times using procedures borrowed from many different theories. *The important thing is that teachers choose procedures with an eye to their effect on both long- and short-term teaching goals.*

Sometimes contrasting theoretic positions make it difficult for teachers to get beyond the "I believe" stage. Beliefs are important in determining behavior. Beliefs uninformed by experience can inhibit growth. Teachers must be careful not to defend what they do (what processes they employ) solely in terms of a set of beliefs. Teachers must be willing to discard beliefs that are no longer useful when evidence to the contrary is present.

TABLE 1-1	Behaviorist and humanist orientations to teaching (extreme positions)	
Component of teaching/learning process	Behaviorist position	Humanist position
Role of teacher	Manipulator	Facilitator
Content to be learned	Academic knowledge of and skills concerning specific information	Long-term affective and cognitive goals; insight
Role of student	Noncreative, teacher-directed behavior in narrowly designed experiences	Creative, active involvement in broad-based experiences
Teaching process	Teacher centered; student behavior shaped through systematic, programmed linear progression lessons; student adapted to the lesson environment	Student centered; student behavior guided through broad-based experiences in which students design their own goals; learning environment adapted to individual student
Outcomes of teaching	Competence; mastery of lesson content	Feeling of self-fulfillment, individuality, and sharing with others

Teachers must be willing to learn new skills

Personal Characteristics of a Teacher

Each teacher is a unique individual with his or her own abilities, personality traits, and likes and dislikes. Educators that people think of as good teachers in their own experience are often very different individuals. Some are quiet and reserved, and others are more aggressive; some display their feelings quite clearly, and others are more subtle.

Personality and individual teacher characteristics influence the way teachers perform instructional functions. What is common to good teaching is that good teachers perform teaching functions in ways consistent with their goals, particular students, and teaching environments. As a general principle, learners need accurate, appropriate information on how to

perform the task required. Some teachers use student demonstration, some demonstrate themselves, some walk their students through a task, and some use media or verbal description effectively. The selection of how to give students this information is not as important as the appropriateness and accuracy of the information and the effectiveness of the communication.

Teachers will likewise motivate students in different ways. Some teachers write poems about how enjoyable the activity will be, some show films that show the end product, and some are so enthusiastic about the task that their enthusiasm infects the students. How the teacher chooses to motivate his or her students is less important than the fact that the students have been successfully motivated.

Teachers are free to be themselves *within* the structure of required instructional functions. Teachers are *not* free to say, "It's just not me to try to motivate students or provide feedback, to take time to communicate clearly, or to establish a productive learning environment." Other teachers may be able to tolerate high levels of off-task behavior or noise in their gymnasiums, but successful learning cannot occur under these conditions. The instructional functions described in Box 1-4 (p. 11) provide the minimal structure necessary for successful learning to occur.

Within the structure of these functions, teachers are free to use behaviors that satisfy personal concerns (e.g., a preference for a humanistic or a behavioristic approach) as long as these concerns facilitate the goal of education, which is successful learning. The effective delivery of instructional functions is not optional. These functions are necessary for successful learning and cannot be set aside for personal reasons. Attention to the psychomotor, affective, and cognitive goals of a lesson will facilitate the selection of techniques appropriate to the student and the situation, whatever the pedagogic orientation or personality the teacher chooses to use to enhance the learning process.

The chapters that follow in this part of the text are designed to fully explore the teacher functions described. Criteria are developed in terms of how the function must be performed if learning is to occur.

Developing Commitment

Teaching is an exciting and rewarding profession. Few other jobs afford the opportunity to impact the lives of so many in as significant a way as does teaching. Teaching is most of all a moral activity. Because you are a teacher and are in a position of power over children, sometimes what seems to you to be a very insignficant interaction with a child can have significant consequences for that child. As a teacher you will be making decisions about what is important for people to learn and how they should learn it. These decisions will influence others either positively or negatively.

Teaching is a profession, which means that in your preparation you should acquire the skills, attitudes, and values of those people who are successful teachers. Because teaching is a profession, you will have much freedom to function in your role. It is primarily your own values and your own willingness to continue to grow that will determine your ability to be a successful teacher and contribute to the lives of others.

Your growth as a teacher will be determined largely by the extent to which you profit from your own experiences, both as a teacher and as a student learning to be a teacher. The effective teacher and the teacher who continues to grow is most of all a reflective teacher. The reflective teacher does not just act. Reflective teachers ask many questions about what they are doing and why they are doing it. The reflective teacher chooses what to do based on much information gathering about what is going on in a teaching/learning situation. The reflective teacher bases decisions of what to do on goals, values, knowledges, and accurate information about learners. The more experienced you become as a teacher, the more information you will be able to use in your decision making and the more accurate you will be in identifying what is important.

You never really stop growing as a teacher. There is always more to learn and more to do. As soon as you think you have it all figured out, you will have an experience that lets you know that you do not. As a professional, you will be expected to continue to learn through your own experiences and by keeping up with what is going on in your field through workshops, conventions, and additional course work. Teaching is not a job, in the sense that you can leave it when the bell rings or school closes. Teaching is a commitment. Professionals are guided by a desire to serve and contribute to society, and to do this well often requires that teachers work at becoming good at what they do and take advantage of all the opportunities they have to be the best they can be.

SUMMARY

1. The goal of teaching is student learning.
2. Instruction is guided by curricular goals.
3. Goals and objectives are designed in three learning domains: psychomotor, cognitive, and affective.
4. Goals should be set realistically if they are to be useful.
5. Instructional processes are selected to meet specific instructional goals and objectives.
6. Many teaching outcomes are the result of not only what is taught (content), but how it is taught (process).
7. Physical education lessons revolve about an interaction unit called the **movement task–student response.**
8. Two kinds of events—content behaviors and management behaviors—occur in large group instruction. Content behaviors are those directly related to lesson content. Management behaviors arrange and maintain the learning environment.
9. The instructional functions teachers perform in a physical education setting are the following:
   - Identifying outcomes
   - Planning
   - Presenting tasks
   - Organizing and managing the learning environment
   - Monitoring the learning environment
   - Developing the content
   - Evaluating

CHECKING YOUR UNDERSTANDING

1. What is meant by the idea that teaching is a goal-oriented activity?
2. Into what categories are outcomes or goals in education usually divided?
3. What is meant by the idea that goals should be realistic?
4. Why is the process that teachers choose to use to teach content important?
5. Why is the movement task–student response unit of analysis so important in physical education?
6. What is the difference between management and content behavior? List three things teachers do that fall under each category.
7. What is the relationship between teaching functions and teaching skills? List two teaching functions teachers must perform, and describe two alternative behaviors teachers can choose to perform these functions.
8. What role do teacher value positions and beliefs play in how a teacher teaches?
9. Describe major differences between the behaviorist and humanist orientation to teaching.
10. What role does teacher personality play in teaching?

SUGGESTED READINGS

Combs A et al: *The professional education of teachers,* ed 2, Boston, 1974, Allyn & Bacon.

Gagne R: *The conditions of learning,* ed 3, New York, 1977, Holt, Rinehart & Winston.

Kolesnik WB: *Humanism and behaviorism in education,* Boston, 1975, Allyn & Bacon.

Maslow A: *Toward a psychology of being,* New York, 1962, Van Nostrand Reinhold.

Rogers C: *Freedom to learn,* Columbus, Ohio, 1969, Charles E. Merrill Publishing.

Simpson EL: *Humanistic education: an interpretation,* Cambridge, Mass, 1976, Ballinger Publishing.

Skinner BF: *The technology of teaching,* New York, 1968, Appleton-Century-Crofts.

Skinner BF: *Beyond freedom and dignity,* New York, 1971, Alfred A. Knopf.

Sulzer-Azaroff B, Mayer GR: *Applying behavior-analysis procedures with children and youth,* New York, 1976, Holt, Rinehart & Winston.

Factors That Influence Learning

❖ ❖ ❖ ❖ ❖ ❖ ❖ ❖ ❖ ❖
OVERVIEW

To design educational experiences for students that result in learning, teachers must understand the nature of learning and the factors that influence learning. Although a comprehensive theory is not available that would predict or explain learning or the lack of it in all situations, information is available that can provide direction for educators in working with students toward learning goals. General principles of learning are modified by characteristics of the learner and the content to be taught.

This chapter discusses the factors related to the nature and process of learning, the nature of the content to be taught, and the nature of the learner. Concepts have been selected because they are considered essential to the teaching/learning process in physical education.

❖ ❖ ❖ ❖ ❖ ❖ ❖ ❖ ❖ ❖
CONCEPTS

- **What is learning?**
- **How do people learn motor skills?**
- **Stages of learning motor skills**
- **Requirements for learning motor skills**
  Prequisites
  Clear idea of the task
  Motivational/attentional disposition to the skill
  Practice
  Feedback
- **The nature of motor skill goals**
  Open and closed skills
  Discrete, continuous, and serial skills

- **Issues of appropriateness in skill development and learning**
  Environmental conditions
  Learner abilities
- **Practice profiles and success rates**
  Whole or part
  Practice variability
- **Motivation and goal setting**
- **Transfer of learning**
  Bilateral transfer
  Intertask transfer
  Intratask transfer
- **Learner characteristics**
  Motor ability
  Intelligence and cognitive development

◆ WHAT IS LEARNING?

Learning is commonly thought to be a relatively permanent change in behavior resulting from experience and training and interacting with biological processes. One of the problems teachers have in directing learning processes and in assessing learning is that learning cannot be directly observed. Learning can only be inferred from a person's behavior or performance. Performance is observable, whereas learning is not. This creates difficulty for teachers, because sometimes students have learned and are not performing according to what they have learned and sometimes they have not really learned and perform as though they have learned. For example, a student may demonstrate a motor skill when you are observing him or her and may not be able to produce that skill in any consistent way again. Likewise, a student may be fatigued and not demonstrate a motor skill and may have actually learned the skill. That is why the idea of *consistent observable performance* in determining whether learning has taken place is important. If students cannot demonstrate an ability consistently, they probably have not learned it.

Teachers have another major problem related to learning when they try to design experiences for students to help students learn and then try to assess whether students have learned. Students may be able to identify a rule on a written test and may not be able to apply that rule when they are actually playing the game. They may be able to demonstrate a motor skill on a skill test, but they may not be able to use that skill in a game situation or may be able to use a skill in a game and may not be able to demonstrate proficiency in a skill test situation. To help explain this, educators talk about different levels of learning. Learning that takes place at a lower level may not be usable in a situation that demands a higher level of learning. In this text you will learn how to specify the level of learning you are trying to teach and how to design experiences that lead learners from lower levels of learning to higher levels of learning.

◆ HOW DO PEOPLE LEARN MOTOR SKILLS?

The unique contribution of physical education is the learning of motor skills for an active life-style. Although physical education teachers will teach children many cognitive ideas and skills and can also make a major contribution to student attitudes and values, motor skills that contribute to an active life-style are the unique contribution of our field. Although there are many ideas that are generic to all kinds of learning, regardless of whether what is to be learned is motor, cognitive, or attitudes and values, this chapter focuses primarily on how people learn motor skills.

Motor skills are acquired in many ways. Some skills, such as walking, are developmental skills that all children acquire as the result of a maturational readiness and environmental conditions that encourage their development. By the time children come to school, they can perform a large number of fundamental motor skills, all without the benefit of a physical education teacher. More specialized skills, such as sport skills, and the skillful use of fundamental patterns develop largely as a result of learning.

Learning can take place independent of an intent to influence its occurrence; that is, a teacher is not necessary for learning to take place. Children learn how to do many things, including developing more advanced motor skills, outside an instructional environment. They learn by interacting with their environment, experimenting, and imitating what they see other people do. Most children, however, will develop their motor skill potential more fully as the result of instruction. Instruction is characterized by a specific intent to influence learning in a particular direction.

Effective instruction in motor skills can take many forms. Most people think of instruction as a "telling" process. The teacher tells and demonstrates to students how to do something, and students try to do it the way they were told to do it. This type of instruction approaches the learning process rather **directly.** It is sometimes called **direct instruction,** and direct instruction can help people to learn motor skills. Teachers also have a variety of approaches to learning that may not be direct instruction that they can use to help students acquire motor skills. A more recent emphasis, but not a new emphasis, stresses the role of environmental design. This means that the teacher can *elicit* motor responses by designing the environment to bring out the skill. If students are ready, they will respond to the conditions of the task with an effective response. The teacher does not have to go through an analysis of the exact way the movement should be performed. The teacher who puts a target area on a mat or floor for people to jump to is encouraging specific movements without using a lengthy description of how that movement should be performed. The teacher who increases the height of the volleyball net encourages students to get under the ball.

Using an environmental design approach to skill learning requires that the teacher have a good grasp of task conditions and requirements and that he or she is able to design conditions appropriate for different learners. Students who learn in this manner do not necessarily process what they are doing at a conscious level. The motor response is a coordinated response of a dynamic system to both external (the environment) and internal (the abilities of the learner) conditions.

Although learning motor skills has many unique aspects, approaches to learning motor skills are, for the most part, consistent with general learning theories. Learning in physical education can be approached from a **behaviorist model, information processing model,** or **cognitive strategy model.** Each of these models look at the process of learning differently and therefore advocate different approaches to teaching.

A **behaviorist orientation** to learning stresses the role that the external environment plays in shaping behavior. The focus is on what the learner does that is observable. Behaviorists suggest that teachers should model good behavior and shape desired behavior by rewarding and positively reinforcing desired responses. Content is usually broken down into small parts the student can handle successfully, and more difficult material is added gradually, building on the success of the student.

Information processing stresses the importance of the internal cognitive processing of the learner. Information processors study the way in which learners select, use, interpret, and store information. Information processing theory suggests ways in which teachers can present information to learners so that learners attend to important ideas, draw meaning from what they attend to, and integrate what they have learned in useful ways.

Cognitive theorists have attended to more holistic perspectives on learning and are interested primarily in how people solve problems, create, learn how to learn, and, in general, transfer what they have learned. Cognitive strategy approaches to teaching stress problem solving, environmental approaches, and interactive models of teaching.

In physical education, teaching strategies that approach instruction from more of a behaviorist or information processing model are usually referred to as *direct instruction models.* More indirect strategies of instruction use principles of learning that have their roots in work being done in cognitive strategies.

The focus of this text is on learning that is facilitated through both direct instruction and more indirect ways to help students learn. There are times when the teacher wants students to deal with higher levels of learning, such as the development of problem-solving abilities, and wants to choose methods of instruction based on what is known from cognitive strategy about how to facilitate this kind of learning. There are also times when the teacher wants the student to master a motor skill in the most efficient way and wants to use direct instruction. The skilled teacher chooses an appropriate approach based on what he or she wants students to learn and the characteristics of the learner. Each of these approaches will be made more clear in Chapters 3 and 9.

BOX 2-1

Stages of Motor Learning

Cognitive stage

Learner uses information on how the skill is to be performed to develop an executive/motor plan for a movement skill.

Thought processes are heavily involved as learner consciously attends to the requirements of the whole idea of the skill and sequencing the pattern.

Student responses are characterized by a high degree of concentration on how to perform the skill. Learner is unable to manage small details of the movement or cope with adapting the movement to environmental changes.

Associative stage

Learner can begin to concentrate on the temporal patterning of the skill and the refinement of the mechanics of the skill.

For most complex skills, learner is in this stage a great deal of time. Learner at this stage can profit from feedback and can begin gradually to cope with external demands of the environment. All the attention of learner does not have to be on every aspect of the performance.

Automatic stage

The goal of motor learning is for the skill to be performed automatically. At this stage, learner does not have to give cognitive attention to the movement itself. Performance is consistent and can be adapted to the requirements of the environment, such as where to place the ball and defensive players in open skills.

From Fitts PM, Posner MI: *Human performance*, Belmont, Calif, 1967, Brooks/Cole Publishing.

◆ STAGES OF MOTOR LEARNING

A useful way to describe how a motor skill is learned by an individual was developed by Fitts and Posner (1967). According to them, a person actually goes through three stages before he or she can reproduce a skilled movement (Box 2-1).

The first phase is called the **cognitive** phase, because at this stage the learner is very heavily focused on processing how the movement should be performed. Sometimes beginning learners at this stage are observed with their tongue to the side of their mouth in heavy concentration on what they are doing or completely oblivious to what is happening around them as they try to sort out just what they must do to perform a movement. At this beginning level the learner is concentrating on getting the general idea of the skill and sequencing the skill.

The second phase of learning is called the **associative** phase. At this stage of the learning process, the learner can concentrate more on the dynamics of the skill: getting the timing of the skill and coordinating the movements of different parts of the skill to produce a smooth and refined action. Learners at this level often find themselves attending to different parts of the skill, such as the backswing in a tennis forehand or the hand position in the jump shot in basketball.

The third phase of learning a motor skill is called the **automatic** phase. At this point in learning the skill, the learner does not have to concentrate on the skill. The processing has been relegated to a lower brain center, which frees the individual to concentrate on other things. The movement response does not require the attention of the learner. Many movements of adults are at an automatic phase. Many of you can ride a bike, shoot a basket, run, or serve a volleyball without even thinking about where the parts of your body are or what they are doing. Skilled basketball players are not concentrating on how to do the lay-up shot; they are concentrating on how to get around the defensive players.

The stages of motor learning are significant ideas that should be part of the knowledge base for teachers of motor skills. First, they are important because they alert the teacher to the idea that higher levels of functioning in cognitive learning results in increased cognitive processing, whereas higher levels of learning in motor skill acquisition results in less cognitive processing. The objective of motor skill learning is to have learners not focused on their response. Students who have acquired high levels of ability in motor skills should not have to think about it. Students who have to think about how the skill is being performed cannot concentrate on what is happening around them; this is why skills often fall apart after learners practice in simple conditions and then are expected to use the skill in complex situations, such as a game.

Second, the stages of motor skill acquisition are important because they help the teacher define the needs of the learner at different stages. The teacher who knows what learners need can better meet those needs through the instructional process. Some of these associations between learner needs and the instructional process are described in Box 2-1.

If you are going to teach a skill directly to learners at the cognitive phase, you have identified that the learners need a clear idea of what they are trying to do. You also know that they are so highly involved cognitively, (1) you must reduce the information you give them to only the essentials to get them started, and (2) you are trying to sequence the pattern for them. Although it is not always possible to do, beginning learners should be given the whole idea of the skill when possible and should practice it as a whole if meaningful work on any of the parts of the skill is to take place at the associative phase. Teachers who provide accurate demonstrations and sequence verbal cues for the learner, such as "get set," "racket back," or "follow through," help the learners to organize their beginning attempts at a skill.

After beginning learners have developed some consistency with the pattern and have moved into the associative phase, they are more able to use additional information from the teacher on refining and coordinating aspects of the movement they are trying to learn. Work on such areas as timing, speed, force levels, direction, and hand position becomes meaningful. For complex skills, learners are in this phase for a long time and often return to it even after high levels of skill have been developed. The learner at this associative phase can work on one aspect or one part of the skill and still be able to perform other parts of the skill without much attention. Also, the learner at this stage can begin to concentrate on other things besides the skill, so the teacher can begin

gradually to increase the complexity of the practice conditions, for example, by adding other skills, players, or rules to the practice. Working through this phase requires much practice. Teachers can facilitate the practice by helping learners to focus on what is important in skills and by providing feedback to learners on how to improve.

The student at the automatic stage of learning a motor skill does not have to concentrate on the movement itself. This learner can focus energy on other areas, such as offensive and defensive situations in sports, the target in activities such as golf and archery, or the aesthetic feeling of the movement in dance. The learner at this point is skilled at that movement.

◆ REQUIREMENTS FOR LEARNING A MOTOR SKILL

If you are going to try to teach someone a motor skill directly, you must be alert to the idea of what people need in order to learn that skill. Most of these ideas will seem like common sense, but they are often violated in practice and are not as easy for a teacher to do as it would seem.

Prerequisites

The first idea is that for learners to learn a motor skill you are trying to teach them, they must have the prerequisites to learn that skill. Prerequisites for motor skills often involve already having mastered some easier related skills or abilities. Prerequisites also often involve having the physical abilities to do that skill, which for young children may be a maturational ability or something as simple as physical strength or flexibility. Prerequisite abilities are often not defined for the teacher, which makes it imperative that the teacher do a task analysis of a skill and engage in a consistent process of trying to determine why a student is not able to perform a skill. Learners may not be able to catch a ball in the air because their eyes have not matured to the point where they have the tracking skill. Learners who cannot learn a tennis serve may not be able to use an overhand pattern in any sport. Learners who cannot get a serve over a volleyball net or do a hip circle on a bar in gymnastics may not have the physical strength to do so. Practice can only lead to frustration, because the individual does not have the capability to do the skill regardless of the amount of practice. Learners should not be put in situations where they cannot succeed.

Clear Idea of the Task

If learners have the prerequisites, the next concern is, Do they have a clear idea of what they are trying to do? Most skill-learning problems occur because the learner is operating with false or incomplete information on what he or she is trying to do. The body can perform the skill, but the head has not given the body the right directions. Sometimes these directions are called **motor programs,** or an executive plan for the skill. Motor programs are a memory representation for a pattern of movement that is rather abstract and usually does not involve a specific movement performed by a specific set of muscles and limbs, but a pattern that is generalizable to a variety of responses. For example, you have a program for writing that is usually carried out with your hands holding an implement such as a pen or pencil. If, however, you were to write your name in the sand with your foot, you would still be able to read what you wrote. The motor program is an important idea because it emphasizes the highly cognitive role in motor skills. Most problems in learning a motor skill come from problems in the motor program the learner has been given or the way he or she has interpreted the motor program. Good instruction facilitates the acquisition of accurate motor programs.

Motivational/Attentional Disposition to the Skill

If students are to learn motor skills, they must be actively engaged in the learning process. Active engagement in learning is facilitated if students are motivated to learn. Motivation usually involves a disposition to engage in a particular behavior. Motivation is a critical aspect of learning because learning is an active process. For learning to occur, the individual must be actively engaged in the process. The critical component of learning is the active

processing by the learner of what is to be learned. Although it is possible to design situations that force the learner to actively process what he or she is doing without the learner actually being highly motivated to learn a skill, it is easier to design situations that will result in active processing of behavior if the learner is motivated to learn.

The notion of active processing is directly related to the cognitive aspects of motor skill acquisition. The motor plan is developed and refined by the learners actively processing what they are trying to do. The teacher is trying to get the learners to attend to what is important in the skill, to focus the learners' attention on critical aspects. The teacher designs practice situations that will facilitate the learners attending to what they are trying to do. Repetitive practice of the same movements ultimately leads to the learners no longer processing what they are trying to do, which decreases the potential for learning. Success also plays a major role in motivating learners and maintaining their attention on learning. Lack of success often decreases motivation, attention to the task, and therefore any potential for learning.

Practice

Once you have learned a cognitive fact, such as the capital of a country, chances are that if you take a test on your knowledge of that fact for 10 consecutive days, you will be able to reproduce that piece of information with 100% accuracy. After you have learned how to do a basketball free throw and you do 10 throws for 10 days in a row, chances are that you will not be able to reproduce that skill with 100% accuracy. Because motor skills are learned as motor programs that are more general and not specific to muscle groups, you are able to more easily adapt your movements to different situations, as well as perform skills with different muscle groups. But because motor programs are not learned as a specific set of instructions for a particular set of muscles, human motor performance is very inconsistent and variable. Practice of motor skills is essential for developing and refining the motor program and reducing the variability. Practice should be designed to facilitate processing of motor information and move the learner to the automatic stage of motor skill learning. More specific guidelines for practice are addressed in a separate section on practice later in this chapter.

Feedback

Motor learning theorists have often addressed the importance of the role of feedback in learning. Feedback is information the learner receives on performance. Feedback has been characterized as **knowledge of results** and **knowledge of performance.** Knowledge of results is usually associated with information on the outcome of the movement, such as whether the ball went into the basket. Knowledge of performance is usually information the learner receives on the execution of the movement, how the movement feels, or the form characteristics of the movement. Learners can obtain information on both knowledge of results and knowledge of performance internally from sensory information, such as auditory, visual, or kinesthetic, or through information they receive externally from others. They can feel the movement, see its results, or hear the results. They can also be provided this information from external sources, such as a teacher or observer. Figure 2-1 describes the effect of different kinds of knowledge of results and knowledge of performance on the learner. The most desirable situation is to have the learner execute a skill correctly and also accomplish the goal of the movement. It is frustrating to the learners when they think they have performed correctly and still have not been effective in accomplishing the goal. It is difficult for the teacher to encourage students to perform correctly if the students accomplish the goal of the movement when they have not performed correctly.

Externally provided feedback by the teacher has been thought of as a source of error detection. It has also been thought of as a source of reinforcement and motivation for the learner. What is important at this point is to recognize that in a teaching situation, particularly with large groups of learners, individual feedback to the learner for error detection may not be as important as the role feedback plays in monitoring group instruction to maintain motivation and reinforce the task focus. The role feedback plays in error detection in group learning situations has not been supported, in spite of the emphasis it receives as part of the teaching/learning process. Feedback will be discussed as part of the instructional process in Chapter 8.

◆ THE NATURE OF MOTOR SKILL GOALS

How a teacher goes about teaching motor skill objectives to a class is largely determined by the type of motor skills the teacher is trying to teach. Movement skills have been dichotomized using several different criteria, such as fine or gross motor skills; simple or complex; fundamental or specialized; continuous, discrete, or serial; self-paced or externally paced; and open or closed. All of these characteristics have implications for what to teach and how to teach it. This section addresses some of these characteristics.

Open and Closed Skills

According to Fitts (1962), skills can be placed on a continuum according to their self-paced or externally paced nature. Self-paced skills, such as a dive, golf swing, gymnastics move, and archery shot, are

Knowledge of performance
Was movement executed as planned?

	Yes	No
Knowledge of results Was goal accomplished? No	Do that again!	Surprise!
Yes	Change strategy or plan.	Change everything.

FIGURE 2-1
Evaluative feedback.

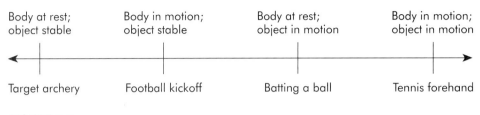

FIGURE 2-2
Continuum of self-paced and externally paced skills.

performed with the body and the object at rest before the execution of the skill. Nothing is moving in these situations. In other skills, such as kicking a football, batting a ball, and doing a forehand tennis stroke, the body or the object is moving, and these skills are identified as having characteristics of externally paced skills. In skills that are at one of the extreme ends of the self-paced/externally paced continuum, both the body and the object are moving. These ideas are illustrated in Figure 2-2.

Gentile (1972) modified Poulton's (1957) designation of open and closed skills for sports skills. Open skills are those skills regulated by variable or changing events in the environment. A lay-up shot in basketball is an open skill, because the environment is rarely the same from one time to another and is unfolding during performance. In basketball, for example, the angle of entry to the goal, the speed, the number of defenders, and the distance from which the shot is initiated change from one time to another. If a skill is closed, the environmental conditions are relatively stable from one situation to another. The basketball free throw is more of a closed skill, because environmental conditions, such as the distance to the basket, remain stable from one time to another. Figure 2-3 illustrates the nature of open and closed skills.

The ideas of self-paced/externally paced and closed/open skills are similar ideas but represent two different characteristics. Most skills that are self-paced are closed skills, and most skills that are open skills are externally paced. However, a skill can be self-paced, such as a golf putt, but yet have some

aspects of open skills, because the golfer does have to adapt performance to such situations as different lies and distances.

The important point here is that the instructional goal of these different kinds of skills is different. Skills that are self-paced and closed require the development of consistency in stable movement conditions. Skills that are primarily externally paced and open require that the individual be able to perform in complex external environments. Closed skills that are performed in a variable environment, such as the golf putt, require that the learner be able to adapt performance to changing external conditions. These different goals are best met by different kinds of progressions and instructional objectives. How the skill is presented, how it is developed, and how it is practiced are all affected by the nature of the skill.

The teacher will not want to practice closed skills in variable environments, and the teacher will not want to practice open skills for stability. If the skill is self-paced and closed, such as a gymnastics vault or many target activities like bowling, the teacher may initially make the skill easier, but ultimately, practice must take place in the exact environment in which the skill will be used. If the teacher is teaching a lay-up shot, the teacher may initially reduce the conditions by not using defenders and by slowing down the speed of the movement. Eventually, however, the skill must be practiced in gamelike conditions if it is to be performed in gamelike conditions. This means the teacher may gradually add defenders, other players, skills that precede and follow the lay-

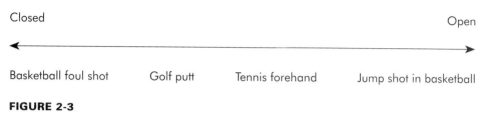

FIGURE 2-3
Nature of open and closed skills.

up, and practice doing the lay-up from different directions and distances from the basket.

Discrete, Continuous, and Serial Skills

Another useful dichotomy for teachers when they are thinking about the skills they are teaching describes the discrete, continuous, and serial nature of skills. Skills that are **discrete** are performed once, with a clear beginning and end. Their beginning or end is not governed by any movement preceding or following the skills. A javelin throw or vault in gymnastics is an example of a discrete skill. Different discrete skills that are put together in a series are usually called **serial skills.** Many motor skills, such as fielding a ball and then throwing it or dribbling and then passing a basketball, are serial skills. **Continuous skills** have arbitrary beginning and end points, such as basketball dribbling, swimming, and running. The teacher who wants to teach a discrete skill can focus on the beginning point and ending point of the movement and approach the skill as a closed situation (like the javelin throw). The teacher who wants to teach skills that will eventually be put into a serial relationship with other skills (such as the basketball dribble and pass or catching and then throwing a ball) must combine the skills early in a teaching progression and teach students how to prepare for the next skill during the previous one. For example, if you want students to catch a ground ball and then throw it, they will need help in how to place their feet and body so that they can come right up from the fielding situation into the throw.

All of these categorizations of movement skills used in physical education settings are important ideas that determine the goal of instruction for the teacher. The instructional section of this text will help you to plan instruction that is appropriate to the type of skill that you want to teach. At this point you will need to be able to characterize skills according to these characteristics.

◆ ISSUES OF APPROPRIATENESS IN SKILL DEVELOPMENT AND LEARNING

Most of the professional literature describes skills in terms of what a skill should look like when it is performed by a skilled person. Sport books describe how to dribble a soccer ball. Texts that focus on young children describe what a *mature* throw pattern should look like. This is useful information, but the ideas expressed in these sources are misleading in terms of identifying skill goals to be taught to different learners. What follows are several key ideas to consider when you are thinking about instructional objectives for motor skills.

Environmental Conditions Determine the Appropriate Process Characteristics of Most Skills

One of the first problems with using the descriptions of skills that are found in many textbooks as a guide for teaching a skill is that for all but closed skills in self-paced environments, the skill looks different and is adapted differently to different environments. Soccer dribbling looks different depending on whether you are closely guarded or not. If you are closely guarded, you will want to keep the ball close to you. If you are not closely guarded, you will want to move as fast as you can and therefore will keep the ball further in front of you. The overhand throw pattern looks like the one shown in the book only when the individual needs maximum force production in the skill and is not performing serial movements (a skill before the throw or after it). If you want to throw a short distance or need to be concerned about getting an object to a target area accurately or quickly, variations of the overhand throw pattern are *appropriate*. The wrong foot forward is appropriate for very short distances where accuracy is at a premium. If you are fielding a ball before you throw it, the skill looks different. The environmental conditions of a task are critical factors that determine the most appropriate way to perform a skill.

EXAMPLE: We recently tested students on their ability to use a drop shot in badminton. The students were effective in placing the shuttlecock where they wanted it. Their form did not reflect the full windup that they had been instructed to use. Upon reflection of why this might be so, it became clear that the windup is used in a game situation to disguise the fact that the drop shot is going to be used. In the testing situation there was no such need to disguise the shot and the additional movement served only to decrease accuracy.

Individuals Adapt How They Do a Skill to Their Own Abilities

Teachers face a second problem when using descriptions of skills found in sports books. Learners adapt the way a skill is performed to their own abilities. Sometimes when you are working with young children and even some beginning learners, you will find learners using immature patterns because that is where they are developmentally. They may not have the physical ability to perform differently because of maturational problems or because of physical characteristics. When faced with the task of getting a basketball up to a basket at a standard height, a young child will often use two hands and will perform in an underhand manner. Many 9-year-olds will still misjudge balls in flight because of lack of visual track-

ing maturity. A student not capable of handling the weight or length of a tennis racket will use two hands. We usually consider these approaches inappropriate skill responses because they do not match the description we have of the way the skill is supposed to be performed. Actually, the responses of these learners is quite appropriate for their abilities. The notion that students should be practicing skills at a mature level of performance is a relevant idea. If, however, the teacher wants the student to practice and learn a mature level of performance, the conditions of practice will have to be adapted for that individual to be able to perform at that level. This means that baskets must be lower, balls smaller and lighter, and rackets shorter and lighter if mature performance is to be developed.

The notion that learners adapt skills to their own abilities is also a valid observation for students who have abilities that allow them to reduce the skill to what we used to think was an immature performance. In skills that require much force production, teachers generally encourage the use of a mature pattern, such as rotation in the volleyball overhand serve. If, however, a student has the strength to get the ball over the net without using rotation, the student who uses block rotation may not be responding inappropriately for the conditions.

The issue of appropriateness is important for teachers. There are many implications of this idea for teaching, such as the following:

1. If a teacher asks a student to demonstrate a particular motor response, the teacher must be sure that the motor response is appropriate for that situation and that learner. It is not appropriate for a teacher to ask learners to use a full overhand throw pattern in a practice situation where students are a short distance from each other. Also, it is not appropriate for a teacher to expect a child who cannot handle the weight of an implement to be able to manipulate that implement in a mature way.

2. The teacher must design progressions that include combining skills and must focus on helping learners to make the transition from one skill to another. How do you stop the bas-

ketball dribble if you are going to pass? Shoot? How do you place your feet to field a ball if you are immediately going to throw to your right? Left? How do you go from a run into a two-foot takeoff? How do you come out of a forward roll if you are going to go right into an arabesque? All of these issues are part of progressions that begin to focus on the appropriateness issue.

Many learners will automatically adapt their performance to the conditions of a task, but many will not and will need help. Serial movements, open skills, and externally paced skills all require that the teacher be sensitive to the conditions of the task in terms of what the task requires and the appropriateness of the response to those conditions based on the abilities of the learner.

◆ PRACTICE PROFILES AND SUCCESS RATES

Nearly everyone accepts the idea that to learn motor skills, you must practice them. In general, a direct relationship exists between the amount of practice and the amount of learning, assuming the task is an appropriate task. In general, when students in our physical education classes do not learn, it is because they have not had enough practice time. Although motor skill learning is remembered much longer than other kinds of learning, learning motor skills takes time. Good teaching can facilitate that learning, particularly in the design of practice conditions.

What follows are some general principles that teachers must consider when designing practice for motor skills.

Whole or Part

One of the first decisions teachers must make in designing practice for learners is whether it is better to (1) break up a skill into its parts and practice one part at a time or (2) practice a skill as a whole. In general, it is better to practice a skill as a whole. The rhythm and timing of a skill is maintained better when the whole skill is practiced. There are times, however, when it is better to first practice the whole to give students the general idea of the skill and then

break down the skill into parts. When safety is an issue, such as a back handspring in gymnastics, or when the skill is very complex, such as the tennis serve, many teachers find that students learn the whole skill better if they have an opportunity to practice the parts. The more rhythmic the skill, the less appropriate practice of parts becomes. It is important to remember that unless safety is a real issue, learners should always be given an opportunity to get the feel for the whole skill before the skill is practiced in parts. From this framework, then, it can be concluded that there is a whole skill approach and there is a whole/part/whole skill approach. It is not often appropriate to use a part/whole approach.

Practice Variability

The manner in which teachers order and organize what is to be practiced for a given time period can affect learning. Practice variability refers to the idea of changing either the environmental conditions of practice or the skills involved in practice. Each of these ideas will be discussed.

Varying practice conditions. The kind of skill you want to teach determines to a large extent the amount of variability you want to have in practice. Variability of practice refers to the changing conditions of practice. The opposite of variability is drill and repetition of the same movement over and over for a long period of time. Practice can be organized so that many conditions are changing, such as changing the speeds, distances, and intent of practice.

In general, open skills should be practiced in variable conditions and closed skills should be practiced more repetitively in the same conditions (assuming a high level of student processing). Remember that open skills are those in which the ultimate learning goal is that the individual be able to adapt the skill to a variety of conditions (the basketball dribble) and the closed skill should be practiced to remove variability (bowling). Variability in practicing catching, for instance, can be added by changing the speed, distance, or direction the ball comes to the catcher or adding serial skills together, such as moving to receive the ball or throwing the ball after you catch it.

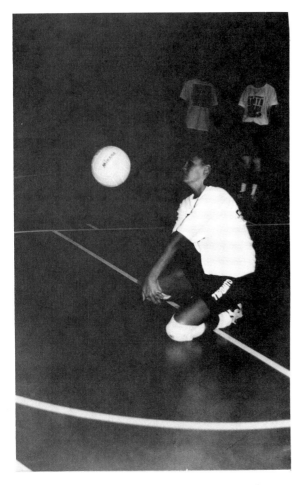

Learners must be able to do a skill under simple conditions before they can expect to perform under more difficult conditons.

A certain amount of variability exists in most practice situations, because performers are not consistent to begin with. Adding too much variability, such as too much distance to throw the ball, actually may change the skill the learner uses (toss to a full overhand throw pattern in the case of throwing) or may make the practice inappropriate for particular learners.

Variability of practice is a critical concept for open skill development. Teachers who practice open skills in closed drill-like practice situations are running the risk that the learner will not be able to adapt his or her performance. For instance, a student who has practiced the chest pass in basketball from the same distance and from the same position in the center of the body may not be able to pass quickly from other than the chest level.

Teachers may want to reduce conditions of open skills initially for beginning learners to almost closed conditions, such as practicing skills without a ball or with reduced speed or space. This is advisable while the learner is in the cognitive stage of learning the skill. The important idea here is that practice in these conditions should not be extensive and the learners should not be left at this stage of learning and this level of practice if they are to be able to use the skill.

Varying skills.   Some recent work in motor learning (Magill, 1989) suggests that if students practice more than one skill at a time, such as the long serve and short serve in badminton, they are more likely to learn both skills. This idea is based on a theory of contextual interference, which basically says that if you interfere with the rote characteristics of practice, you will encourage the learner to process the information more and therefore learn more. Although the phenomena of contextual interference are beyond the scope of this text, the idea here is that practicing one skill and then another skill, such as two different skills in random order, causes the learner to increase the level of processing and therefore increases the chance of learning. Rote repetition of the same skill decreases cognitive processing and therefore the amount of learning. Research is conflicting on how these concepts can best be applied. For the physical education teacher, several factors must be considered when making decisions about how many consecutive times learners should practice something before moving on. First, the beginning learners in the cognitive stage of learning are processing information because they must in order to execute a movement; little rote is involved in their repetitions. Second, to randomize practice of different skills, teachers may have to reduce the actual number of practice trials in a given period because of the management time required to switch from the practice of one skill to another (French, Rink, and Werner, 1990). Reducing actual practice may not be advisable. What this theory does stress is the importance of the learners processing what they are doing. Maintaining learner motivation and attention on what the learners are doing is critical. Unmotivated practice that comes from remaining on the same idea or task for extended periods is not supported.

Massed and Distributed Practice

The physical education teacher often must make decisions related to how long at one time students should practice a skill and how to distribute the practice over a unit of instruction. Although research in this area is limited (Magill, 1989), several ideas are significant for the teacher. Unfortunately, many units of instruction in physical education devote a day to the practice of a particular skill, such as the volleyball forearm pass, and then move on to another skill the next day, never returning to the forearm pass. Learners do not learn motor skills in this way. If the teacher has a 20- or 25-day unit in a sport, it is better for him or her to distribute practice of a skill over the unit and provide for practice of more than one skill a day after its introduction. This is called **distributed practice,** and although we don't know what the limits of this idea may be for what we do, we do know that distributed practice is better than massing the practice **(massed practice)** of a skill into a short amount of time. If we were to keep track of the number of times a first-grade student added 2 plus 2 over the year, we would find that adding 2 plus 2 would appear on student work sheets throughout the year. Repetition is a basic tenet of learning, and repetition over time ensures the development of skills.

Lessons that vary (1) the skills that are practiced and used and (2) the way in which skills are practiced have more potential to maintain student motivation for practice. Units that distribute the practice of a skill over time have a far greater potential to enhance learning. Yearly programs, particularly with young children whose abilities are changing at very rapid rates, have a greater potential to enhance skill development if the teacher revisits skills and ideas throughout the year.

◆ MOTIVATION AND GOAL SETTING

Although it is possible for a person to learn motor skills or other kinds of skills if he or she is not motivated to learn, learning is more likely to occur if the individual is motivated to learn. This is particularly true at the beginning stages of learning a motor skill when cognitive processing of the skill is greater. If students are not motivated to learn, it is likely that they will not process what they are doing to the degree that is needed for learning to occur. Motivated students approach a learning task positively and with great intensity. Students who are not motivated spend much of their time avoiding the task.

Motivation is a complex issue in the teaching/learning process. It is enhanced by good decision making on the part of the teacher as to what to teach and how to teach it. Learner motivation is also related to the success levels of the students, their experience with the content being taught, the social dynamics of the group they are in, and learner personality and aspiration level.

Every teacher would like to have an entire class of students who are internally motivated to do well. Students at this level are largely students who are able to grow and approach new experiences positively. Many students we work with in schools are not able to do this. Maslow (1962) would say that these students have not met some very basic physical needs and the need for safety, as well as the need for love, belongingness, and self-esteem. The more effectively a teacher can help students satisfy their basic needs, the more likely students are to function in ways that cause them to seek growth-producing experiences. Although it is not always possible to know what all students need, making the learning environment one that feels safe to individuals both physically and psychologically can go a long way in producing motivated learners.

Additional work done in the areas of attribution theory and locus of control can also provide some help for the teacher in understanding students and designing learning environments that encourage growth-producing behaviors and motivated students. Attribution theory is concerned primarily with questions related to what people attribute their success or failure. Chapter

10 discusses in greater detail issues related to motivation and learning in physical education classes.

◆ TRANSFER OF LEARNING

The concept of transfer of learning refers to the influence of having learned one skill or ability on learning other skills and abilities. That influence can be positive, negative, or no influence. Transfer can take many forms. When what you learn with one hand or foot transfers to the other hand or foot, it is called **bilateral transfer.** When what you learn in one skill or task transfers to another skill or task, it is called **intertask transfer.** When what you learn from practice of a skill in one condition transfers to practice of that task in another condition, it is called **intratask transfer.**

Transfer of learning is important to teachers because the way the teacher designs curriculum, the way the teacher sequences the practice of skills, and the way the teacher presents tasks to learners can all influence transfer of learning. The teacher will want to maximize the positive transfer of learning and minimize the negative transfer of learning.

Bilateral Transfer

It is commonly accepted that practice with one limb will affect practice with the other; that is, if you learn to dribble a basketball or soccer ball with one hand or foot, learning will transfer to the other hand or foot. Although the limb you practiced with will show the greater gain, both limbs will show gain. Because physical education teachers deal with the learning of complex motor skills that sometimes need to be performed by both limbs, teachers often ask whether the skill should be learned with both limbs and, if so, should practice with the dominant limb or nondominant limb be first. Most of the research supports the idea that for many reasons, learners should practice first with the dominant limb. Only after a reasonable level of proficiency is acquired should the teacher introduce practice with the nondominant limb.

Intertask Transfer

The influence of learning one skill first before trying to learn another skill is measured by the amount of time it takes to learn the second after having learned the first. If it takes less time to learn the second skill because the first one has already been learned, there is said to be a positive transfer from one skill to another. Although many of our assumptions about the positive transfer of one skill to another are handed down in terms of conventional wisdom rather than research efforts, it is commonly accepted that learning of fundamental skills, such as throwing, kicking, and jumping, should precede learning more specialized and complex sport skills, because there is a positive transfer from one to the other. The effect of transfer is largely determined by the number of component parts in one task that are similar to the other. The tennis serve, for instance, has many characteristics of the overhand throw pattern. The volleyball spike requires the learner to take a few steps into a two-foot vertical jump before striking the ball. If the learner already has become proficient in running and jumping with a two-foot takeoff, you would expect a positive transfer, from having learned these fundamental patterns, to the more specialized skill of the volleyball spike. Physical education curriculum should be based on an easy-to-more-difficult transfer of learning between skills.

Intratask Transfer

When the teacher develops progressions for teaching skills that go from easy to difficult or simple to more complex, the teacher is hoping that there will be a transfer from the practice at one level to the practice at another level. As discussed in the issues related to whether to teach the whole task or to break it down into parts first, there are many times when because of safety, the complex nature of the skill, or the complex nature of the way the skill is used in a game, the teacher will have to design a progression that goes from simple to complex. Teachers can determine if their progressions are successful by determining the extent to which practice in one situation transfers to the other. For instance, if students practice dribbling a soccer ball and shooting the ball into the goal in a practice situation, will they be able to do that in the game situation you put them in? If not, there has been no transfer and the teacher will have to either find another way of practicing or add some other kind of practice that more nearly approaches the game situation. If the teacher designs a way to practice the toss in tennis, but when the whole skill is put together, there is no evidence that students can toss the ball correctly and then hit it, there has been no transfer from the practice of the toss to using the toss to serve the tennis ball.

Designing an effective curriculum and progressions for learning depend on the ability of the teacher to monitor carefully their effectiveness in terms of transfer. Transfer can also be facilitated if the teacher keeps in mind some general principles that will facilitate transfer:

1. *The more the practice situation resembles the game situation or the final task, the more likely transfer will occur.*

   This means that ultimately the teacher will have to analyze game situations and add components of the game situation to the practice situation. How to do this is discussed in detail in Chapters 6 and 12.

2. *The more a skill is learned, the more likely there will be a positive transfer to the game situation.*

   This means that skills take a long time to learn. The more time devoted to what you want to transfer, the more likely that transfer will occur. Sometimes skills or abilities do not transfer because students have not learned them to begin with.

3. *Transfer can be facilitated by the teacher encouraging students to use information they already know and abilities they already have and making task expectations clear.*

   This means that the teacher can encourage transfer by making the components of a task clear to learners; cognitively making the connection between skills, such as "this is like..."; and giving concrete examples of concepts that the teacher wants students to generalize from one skill to another. These ideas are discussed in detail in Chapter 5, where task presentation ideas are developed, and in Chapter 12, where the idea of teaching concepts for transfer is developed.

◆ LEARNER CHARACTERISTICS
Motor Ability

One of the first observations that a beginning teacher of physical education makes as he or she tries to teach a group of learners a physical task is that any typical physical education class is usually made up of learners with great differences in ability. Unfortunately, too many physical education teachers assume that because a learner cannot do something when it is initially presented, the learner is incapable of learning. Teachers too often take their cue from students who have already done a skill or who do not need instruction. If a student does not learn, often it is because the teacher is not teaching. Although teachers formerly talked about the idea of general motor ability, it is more commonly accepted now to talk about the idea of there being a set of motor abilities related to specific skills (Thomas and Halliwell, 1976). These specific capacities are related to physical abilities, such as gross body coordination, static and dynamic balance, strength of particular muscle groups, and eye/foot coordination. The importance of each capacity depends on the skill that is to be learned. It is also generally accepted that although the limits of these abilities are most likely set genetically (given at birth), their development is influenced by experience; that is, probably not everyone is capable of being an Olympic performer in a sport, but most people are capable of developing their abilities to the extent that participation in the sport can be both successful and enjoyable. Many people who physical education teachers considered "motor morons" as students are successfully engaged as adults in tennis, golf, racquetball, and other sports.

It is important that teachers do not "tag" students in their classes as being capable or not capable of learning. This is true for many reasons. First, there is not a strong relationship between who learns a skill the fastest and who will ultimately be better at a skill. Second, teachers who communicate either positive or negative feelings to the student about what they are capable of doing can significantly affect learning. A third factor is related to working with children. Children who are older or mature earlier have increased abilities in many motor capacities that do not necessarily represent their potential. It is where they are at the time. Some students may be incapable of learning what teachers present because what teachers present is not appropriate for the students' stage of development. These same children who are developmentally not as mature as their classmates may in fact have more potential. If they are turned off to activities and skills at an early age, they may never reach that potential.

Intelligence and Cognitive Development

Many teachers have wanted to draw relationships between movement abilities and intelligence of the learner. It is not true that students with high academic ability are also good at motor skills or that students with low academic ability are poor at them. Students of low academic ability may not learn in the same way as more academically-oriented students and may need to be taught differently, but no direct relationship exists between motor ability and intelligence.

Several developmental factors related to cognitive functioning are critical concepts to teachers who are choosing how to approach teaching learners at different cognitive levels of development. The first of these is related to Piaget's levels of cognitive development. Although a complete description of Piaget's levels of functioning is beyond the scope of this text, it is wise to remember that children do not think in the same way that adults do. Adults can use scientific thinking. They can deal with "if...., then" relationships between ideas and can use abstract ideas. The very young child the teacher is likely to encounter in an elementary school (from kindergarten to Grade 2) does not necessarily think in a logical way. Children in this stage of development do not recognize points of view other than their own. I am reminded of an experience with a kindergarten child who was moving around the gymnasium pushing others out of his way. When the child was asked why he was doing this, he simply replied, "Because they are in my way."

Children who are 7 to 11 years of age are moving into what is called the **stage of concrete operations.** Children at this level of development can begin to order relationships between things and ideas and

begin to reflect on their own behavior. Children at this stage can begin to think logically and handle causal relationships. Some evidence exists that learners with little experience in a content area may operate at a concrete level of operations regardless of their age.

Teachers who work with students of elementary school age and students who have little experience with a content area should keep learning active and concrete. Teachers should limit problem-solving activities and attempts to deal abstractly with ideas with which students have not had a great deal of experience. As students get older and as they become more experienced with content, work that is more abstract in nature is appropriate.

SUMMARY

1. Learning is a relatively permanent change in behavior resulting from experience and training and interacting with biological factors.
2. Motor learning is largely consistent with other types of learning, except that the goal of learning is to reduce the level of processing.
3. Learning takes place in three phases—cognitive, associative, and automatic.
4. To learn a motor skill, learners must have the prerequisite, have a clear idea of the task, be motivated, have opportunity for practice, and have feedback on their performance.
5. Motor skills can be open, closed, discrete, continuous, or serial.
6. An appropriate movement response depends on the conditions of the task and the ability of the learner.
7. Skills that are high in complexity and organization may be better learned if they are taught in parts. In general, it is better to practice skills as a whole if possible.
8. Open skills should be practiced in variable conditions; closed skills in less variable conditions.
9. In general, practice should be distributed over time for more learning.
10. Motivation increases the potential for learning.
11. In general, skills transfer from one limb to another.

12. Skill-to-skill transfer depends on the similarity between skills: the more similar the skills, the more likely the transfer.
13. Most learners are capable of developing motor skills to the extent that participation is enjoyable and successful.

CHECKING YOUR UNDERSTANDING

1. Describe what a student would look like who is in different stages of learning a motor skill.
2. What are the requirements for learning a motor skill? What do each of these requirements mean for the teacher of motor skills?
3. What is the difference between the way closed skills, open skills, discrete skills, and serial skills should be taught.
4. What is meant by the idea that the student always chooses an appropriate response?
5. Describe how a teacher might elicit the following skills: a standing broad jump, a tight tuck in a forward roll, and getting under the ball in a volleyball set.
6. Describe three skills that might be better taught as a whole and three that might be better taught in a whole-part progression.
7. Describe how a teacher can facilitate transfer from one skill to a similar skill.
8. What role does cognition play in learning a motor skill?

REFERENCES

Fitts PM: *Factors in complex skill training.* In Glaser R, editor: *Training research and education,* Pittsburgh, 1962, University of Pittsburgh Press.

Fitts PM, Posner MI: *Human performance,* Belmont, Calif, 1967, Brooks/Cole Publishing.

French K, Rink J, Werner P: Effects of contextual interference on retention of three volleyball skills, *Perceptual and Motor Skills* 71:179-186, 1990.

Gentile AM: A working model of skill acquisition with application to teaching, *Quest* 27:3-23, 1972.

Magill RA: *Motor learning:concepts and applications,* Dubuque, Iowa, 1989, Wm C Brown Group.

Maslow A: *Toward a psychology of being,* New York, 1962, Van Nostrand Reinhold.

Poulton EC: On prediction in skilled movement, *Psychol Bull* 54:467-478, 1957.

Thomas JR, Halliwell W: Individual differences in motor skill acquisition, *J Motor Behav* 8: 89-99, 1976.

SUGGESTED READINGS

Schmidt RA: *Motor control and learning: a behavioral emphasis,* ed 2, Champaign, Ill, 1987, Human Kinetics Publishers.

Shea C, Kohl R: Specificity and variability of practice, *Res Q Exercise Sport* 67(2): 169-177, 1990.

Stallings LM: *Motor learning: from theory to practice,* St. Louis, 1982, Mosby–Year Book.

Research on Teaching Physical Education

❖ ❖ ❖ ❖ ❖ ❖ ❖ ❖ ❖ ❖

OVERVIEW

When this text was first published, research on teaching in physical education was in a neophyte stage of development. Since then, research on teaching in education in general has grown significantly and research on teaching physical education has established itself as a legitimate pursuit in the acquisition of knowledge.

The purpose of this chapter is to review from an historical perspective the research on teaching and to identify the major ideas contributing to our knowledge of research on teaching physical education and their implications. This chapter is included because (1) the significant findings of research on teaching have been used as a basis for this text and (2) the kinds of questions researchers ask about teaching are not so different from the questions that teachers should be asking about what they do on a daily basis.

❖ ❖ ❖ ❖ ❖ ❖ ❖ ❖ ❖ ❖

CONCEPTS

- **The search for principled practice**
- **Understanding research**
  Variables involved in studying teaching
  Ability to generalize data
- **Research on teaching: historical perspective**
- **Critical variables related to teaching**

◆ THE SEARCH FOR PRINCIPLED PRACTICE

The purpose of research on teaching is to inform practice. Many people, including teachers, view teaching as based primarily on the teacher's personality and philosophy and not open to scientific inquiry. A second orientation discounting research on teaching regards teaching as so complex that it cannot be studied in a way that can guide practice. Teaching *is* complex. Doyle (1984) describes the nature of the classroom environment in terms of several factors:

Multidimensionality Choices for teachers are never simple. Classes have many people gathered in one space who all have different needs and different agendas. When a teacher makes a decision to accommodate one need or teaching goal, other needs are affected.

Immediacy Events in a classroom happen at a rapid pace. Teachers must make decisions quickly and with little time to reflect on what should be done. Effective teachers can handle a wide variety of events occurring at the same time and still maintain the momentum and flow of lessons.

Unpredictability Classroom events take unexpected turns and are frequently interrupted. Because what happens is a joint venture among many people, events cannot be predicted.

Publicness Classroom events are acted out in public. What the teacher decides to do affects an entire class.

History Classes have a history. How a group of students responds on any one day is likely to be a function of what they have done in the past, as well as a function of present conditions (e.g., holidays, rain).

Because teaching is complex, any principles or rules of teaching that are established by research are said to be situational; that is, the rule applies in a particular set of circumstances. Effective teachers are actually teachers who make the best decisions after considering all the factors in a situation—they use principles of practice situationally. Research on teaching can help the teacher to understand some of those factors involved in decision making by providing a knowledge base for teaching. Because situations are different and because sometimes a teacher is faced with a choice between two conflicting principles, research cannot prescribe practice.

When people read research findings, they tend to either accept what is said as truth or approach findings in a completely cynical fashion. Neither of these approaches is constructive in helping to understand or apply the meaning of the results of research. Teaching, like any human endeavor, is a complex process. Researchers can deal with only a limited number of the factors involved at any one time. For any practitioner to be confident in research findings, evidence must be accumulated from many studies with similar perspectives using the same and different settings.

An attempt has been made in the presentation of research in this chapter to separate research findings from the inferences drawn from this research. Physical educators should become critical in their judgments of the implications of research for their field. As the results of the studies contained in this chapter are read, the following should be kept in mind:

- Despite the fact that teaching is one of the oldest professions, teaching research is a very young field. Educators experience an explosion of information every day, and much of this research is conflicting. Generalizations of data can be confirmed only by conducting many similar studies in many different teaching situations.

- Quantitative research makes a judgment about the value of products achieved. When achievement is attained in one area, such as psychomotor skills development, teachers must remain alert to other results as well, including attitudes, knowledge, social development, and more longterm goals.

- The biggest single predictor of achievement is the student's ability as he or she enters an instructional environment. Teachers do make a difference, but the teacher's contribution accounts for only 15% to 25% of the difference in performance at the end of instruction. Over many years of schooling this difference is practically significant. In any single study the difference in achievement among teachers will not be great.

◆ UNDERSTANDING RESEARCH
Variables Involved in Studying Teaching

The word *variable* has been defined in this book as a factor related to the teaching-learning process that can vary from one situation to another. Variables are what researchers study; they are presumed to have some relationship to the phenomenon under investigation.

Dunkin and Biddle (1974) developed a model for the study of teaching that has provided researchers with a useful framework for discussing relationships and variables in the teaching-learning process. This model is presented in Box 3-1 to help the reader understand the scope of research on teaching and how what is studied is related to a wider picture of the teaching/learning process. The model divides the

---

BOX 3-1

Study of Teaching Model

Presage variables

Presage variables concern the characteristics of teachers that may be examined for their effects on the teaching process—thus teacher formative experiences, teacher training experiences, and teacher properties. *

In the study of teaching in physical education, researchers might include a host of variables, including the teacher's age, sex, physical condition, knowledge of the subject matter, ability to demonstrate, educational background, motives, and attitudes. Any characteristic or property the teacher brings to a teaching experience is a presage variable.

Context variables

Context variables concern the conditions to which the teacher must adjust—characteristics of the environment about which teachers, school administrators, and teacher educators can do very little. *

Context variables in physical education include the student's skill level, attitude toward physical education, socioeconomic status (SES), and IQ; the size of the gymnasium or field; the amount and type of equipment available; the community; and the curriculum. Context variables include all student properties and characteristics, environmental characteristics, and school and community characteristics. The subject matter of the lesson and teacher objectives are also included in this definition of context variables.

Process variables

Process variables concern the actual activities of classroom teaching—what teachers and students do in the classroom. *

Process variables in the gymnasium include such variables as the amount of time students spend doing tasks, how students respond to teacher directions, and any characteristic of teaching behavior (e.g., feedback, cues for performance, directions, evaluations, or efforts to individualize). Process variables include teacher behavior, pupil behavior, and the interaction between the two.

Product variables

Product variables concern the outcomes of teaching—those changes that come about in pupils as a result of their involvement in classroom activities with teachers and other pupils. *

Product outcomes can be psychomotor (development of physical abilities), affective (social, emotional, and attitudinal changes), or cognitive (development of knowledge and thinking processes). Product outcomes can also be long term or short term. Some product outcomes in physical education are level of performance on a motor skill test, attitude toward a specific activity or the self as a mover, knowledge of an activity, and level of physical fitness. Product variables can be intended outcomes of teaching or unanticipated results.

From Dunkin MJ, Biddle B: *The study of teaching,* New York, 1974, Holt, Rinehart & Winston.

variables involved in teaching into presage, context, process, and product variables. In the box, Duncan and Biddle's original definitions are used to describe these variables, and examples are taken from physical education.

■   ■   ■

The Dunkin-Biddle model is useful for discussing both teaching in general and teaching research. The model can be used to examine relationships between presage variables, process variables, and/or product variables and the relationships between context variables, process variables, and/or product variables. It can also be used to talk about relationships between one process variable and another (process-process) or one product variable and another (product-product). Some examples of research questions on teaching physical education that will help clarify these relationships are shown in Table 3-1.

Ability to Generalize Data

The ability to generalize data refers simply to whether the results of a study done in one setting, such as an elementary school physical education setting, transfer to other settings, such as high school or middle school settings. The question of the ability to generalize data is important when research is being interpreted. It is not only the age level of students that is important. The content that is taught, the char-

acteristics of different students, the physical environment, the teacher's goals, and many other factors all can affect the teaching-learning process in different ways. Thus what is effective in one setting may not be in others.

A large portion of the research base physical educators have on teaching comes directly from research done in classroom settings. The problem with basing physical education directions on classroom research is one of generalizing the results from one setting to another. Research done in physical education has been consistent largely with classroom research, indicating that classroom research does, for the most part, generalize to a physical education setting.

The next section reviews the research in classroom teaching from an historical perspective. The overview is meant to emphasize the difficulty of research in teaching and the many false starts experienced in the search for important relationships in the teaching/learning process. A later section discusses those variables critical to physical education. Because of space limitations, both sections are selective and do not include some significant and important research. Selection was based on variables that have received significant attention in the research literature and that seem to have reached a level of conclusion. Implications have been stated strongly for the sake of clarity, even though the

TABLE 3-1	**Research questions on teaching physical education**
Research question	**Variable relationship**
Do the students of teachers who can demonstrate perform more skillfully?	Presage-product
Do teachers who ask more questions achieve more cognitive knowledge skills in their students?	Process-product
Do teachers help students who are skilled more than they help students who are unskilled?	Process-context
Do students who have more experience in a skill achieve more?	Context-product
Do teachers who positively reinforce student on-task behavior have fewer discipline problems?	Process-process
Do women teachers display more enthusiasm than men do in their teaching?	Presage-process

research in these areas may not warrant such clarity at this time.

◆ RESEARCH ON TEACHING: HISTORICAL PERSPECTIVE

Research on teaching began in the 1940s as an attempt to link presage variables (teacher characteristics) with effective teaching. This research was basically a blind search for universal qualities of good teaching.

Most of this early research was poorly conducted because it relied on high-inference scales of effectiveness that were not developed with any supported link with product outcomes (Dunkin and Biddle, 1974). Usually, rating scales based on someone's judgment about whether a teacher was good or bad were used. Unfortunately, many teachers are still evaluated using these types of scales. The results of most studies to determine characteristics teachers bring to teaching have not identified any specific trait that predicts effectiveness (Dunkin and Biddle, 1974).

During the latter part of the 1950s and well into the 1960s, research was dominated by process-process studies, particularly studies that investigated classroom climate. These studies reflected a large commitment to progressive education, as evidenced by the variables chosen for investigation (e.g., teacher warmth, use of student ideas, and student talk). Flanders Interaction Analysis System (FIAS) (Flanders, 1960) for recording the verbal interaction patterns of teachers and students in the classroom was employed extensively at that time. It used the following 10 categories to study teacher and student behavior:

Indirect influence
- Acceptance of feelings
- Praise or encouragement
- Acceptance or use of student ideas
- Question asking

Direct influence
- Lecturing
- Direction giving
- Criticism or justification of authority
- Student talk (response)
- Student talk (initiated)
- Silence or confusion

Many studies were conducted during those years to study the constructs of indirectness, teacher praise, warmth, acceptance of pupil ideas, and criticism.

Out of this era of research came several findings.
- Teachers were found to be basically direct
- Some support was established for the idea that indirect behavior has a curvilinear relationship with student achievement (i.e., the positive effect decreases after reaching a certain level).
- Classrooms are not warm or cold, but more neutral in tone.
- Teacher criticism has a negative relationship with student achievement.

Several conclusions came out of this block of research.
- Teacher behavior can be reliably observed.
- Teachers can be taught to be more indirect if this is held as a value commitment.
- Concepts in research must be defined clearly, context relationships must be considered, and designs of studies should go beyond simplistic descriptions of process.

Classroom management was studied by Kounin (1977) during this period. Kounin attempted to answer the question of what teachers do who are most effective in handling classroom management problems. Kounin did much to identify specific variables relative to classroom management. The behavior most strongly correlated with effective classroom management was "withitness." "Withitness" is the ability of the teacher to know what is going on in the classroom and to target behavior accurately and with good timing.

One of the most significant reviews of research of this period was done by Rosenshine and Furst (1971). Rosenshine and Furst reviewed 50 process-product studies and attempted to relate the variables used in those studies and the results. Although they received much criticism for taking liberties with relationships between variables that perhaps were too different to be combined, they identified five process variables that showed much promise in terms of research support and six others with some support. Variables that showed no support from the research were also identified. This synthesis did much to redi-rect research efforts and to provide direction in deter-mining where to look for relationships between teacher behavior and teaching outcomes. The vari-ables identified by Rosenshine and Furst's synthesis of early research are shown in Box 3-2.

Many of the variables identified in this synthesis became important in later research efforts that con-sidered student characteristics and other context vari-ables. The addition of context variables to the analy-sis, as well as efforts to combine similar studies for greater statistical power, shed new light on this important initial work.

The research conducted during the 1960s and early 1970s continued to search for generic teaching behaviors effective in all contexts. Unfortunately, for every study that showed a relationship with a variable, there seemed to be one that showed no rela-tionship with the same variable. These conflicting results can probably be attributed to variables that had little promise and to a statistical washout across contexts (i.e., variables that had different effects in different contexts).

During the 1970s, research began to turn in the direction of context-specific variables. The socioeco-nomic status (SES) of students, their ages, the sub-ject matter to be taught, and teacher objectives were all shown to make a difference in what constitutes effective teaching behavior. Frequency counts of teacher behavior were also thought to be misleading. Researchers began to describe patterns of behavior and put together behaviors that establish a single construct, such as task orientation, that could be described by many different teaching behaviors.

With the advent of the 1970s came a major break-through in the study of teaching behavior. Several large, well-financed, and well-conducted studies of teacher effectiveness were done at the elementary grade level in reading and mathematics instruction (Brophy and Evertson, 1974; Good and Grouws, 1975; McDonald and Elias, 1976; Soar and Soar, 1972; Stallings and Kaskowitz, 1974). The focus of this research was to identify patterns of teacher behavior and to analyze results in terms of situation-specific variables. Findings across studies consis-tently described a set of teaching variables that

---

BOX 3-2

Process Variables as They Relate to Product Outcomes

Variables having the most promise for a rela-tionship with product outcomes

Clarity of presentation (including organization)*
Enthusiasm (including movement, gesture, and voice inflection)
Variability (including various levels of discourse, various levels of tasks, and a variety of materials and techniques)
Task orientation (including businesslike manner and achievement orientation of the teacher)
Student opportunity to learn (including time student has with materials)

Variables having some promise for a relation-ship with product outcomes

Teacher use of student ideas (including behaviors such as acknowledging the student's idea, modi-fying the student's idea, and praising)
Criticism with negative affect (including disap-proval and rejecting behavior)
Teacher use of structuring comments (including use of "what" and "where" versus "how" and "why" and employment of those comments believed to be associated with convergent and divergent thinking)
Perceived difficulty of the course (including strict-ness in demanding high standards and challenge)
Probing (including getting students to elaborate on their responses)

Variables having little or no promise for a rela-tionship with product outcomes

Praise
Warmth
Flexibility
Type of question
Teacher talk
Student participation
Number of teacher/student interactions
Teacher time spent on class participation
Teacher experience
Teacher knowledge of subject area

*This variable has been defined conceptually and behav-iorally in later studies done by Kennedy et al. (1978)

researchers could point to and say, "Teachers who teach reading and mathematics well do this." Because the variables investigated as part of these research studies remain important and primary variables in present research on teaching, they are discussed as part of the next section, which identifies major variables important to teaching physical education.

What most of the process-product studies of the 1960s and 1970s found was that teachers who used what is called **direct instruction** were more effective in producing student learning gains in subject matter that was highly structured and could be hierarchized in terms of a learning progression. Direct instruction was characterized by the following:

- A task-oriented but relaxed environment
- The selection of clear instructional goals and materials and a highly active monitoring of student progress toward these goals
- Structured learning activities
- Immediate, academically oriented feedback

Highly active teaching, focused learning, and student accountability are inherent in the idea of direct instruction. With the identification of such a strong relationship between teaching and learning, direct instruction became almost a synonym for good teaching, and in some areas it remains almost a blueprint for practice, in spite of the cautions acknowledged by most of the research community.

Almost before all the data were in that demonstrated the strength of the idea of direct instruction, identification of its limitations began. Direct instruction may not be the best way to teach some students some things. When the subject matter requires student problem solving or higher-order thinking skills and when the subject matter is not highly structured, direct instruction may not be the teaching strategy of choice. Educators also cautioned that the limited responsibility given to the learner in direct instruction may produce other results that are undesirable, particularly in programs where the student is spending an entire day with teachers who use few other teaching strategies.

Several methodological changes in the way research was conducted characterized the 1980s.

These changes were primarily the result of asking different questions about teaching. First, researchers started to be disillusioned with the search for single variables and teaching behaviors that were related to student learning. Much of the research that came out of the process-product studies of the 1970s did have a positive influence on practice, but this positive influence was also accompanied by unanticipated negative results as well. Many educators took the results of this research and abused it by assuming every teacher in every situation should be using direct instruction. This "one size fits all" mentality was the impetus to a different line of research, which began to focus on context. In abandoning the search for the silver bullet, research started to identify how good teaching changed with different subject matters, different students, and different goals. Likewise, in abandoning the search for what effective teachers do that could be correlated with learning, researchers focused their attention on understanding what is happening in teaching. Instead of "number crunching" to establish relationships between single teaching behaviors and student learning, research was directed toward understanding teaching. Researchers sought to understand teaching from the perspectives of the participants (e.g., What are students and teachers experiencing? How do they think and feel about what they are experiencing?) and from the perspective of different content to be learned. For these kinds of questions a different type of research methodology was needed, which is commonly called *naturalistic inquiry* or *qualitative research.*

Qualitative research not only asks different questions, but it answers those questions in different ways. Interviews and extensive observations in field settings are the primary tools of the qualitative researcher. The qualitative researcher does not necessarily go into a situation looking for a teaching variable, but rather, allows what is important to emerge from the data. A great deal of current research in education is qualitative in nature. As a result of this research, we have very rich descriptions of teaching and learning that have helped us to understand context and the complex nature of the teaching and learning processes that take place in the schools.

◆ CRITICAL VARIABLES RELATED TO TEACHING

The rest of this chapter is devoted to describing the important ideas about effective teaching that have come from research on teaching. For the most part, research on teaching physical education has followed the lead of educational research. Both research on teaching and research on teaching physical education are discussed.

Academic Learning Time

The amount of time the learner spends at an appropriate level of difficulty with the content to be learned is the single most critical instructional variable related to student learning. This means that the student who spends more time practicing in physical education at an appropriate level of practice will learn more than a student who does not, all other factors being equal. This idea has been identified as academic learning time (ALT).

Supporting evidence for academic learning time comes from both large, well-conducted studies in classroom research (Berliner and Rosenshine, 1987; Brophy, 1979b; McDonald and Elias, 1976) and research conducted in physical education. Metzler (1979) and Siedentop, Tousignant, and Parker (1982) took the ALT construct used in the classroom setting and designed an instrument to be used in physical education (ALT-PE). ALT-PE measures the amount of time individual students actually work with physical education content at an appropriate level of difficulty. Appropriate level of difficulty is defined as a level with a high success rate. It is based on classroom findings that high success rate is a significant factor in determining appropriateness (Brophy, 1979b; Metzler, 1979).

Even when the additional criterion of appropriate level of difficulty is not added, much of the earlier descriptive work done in physical education does not reflect favorably relative to the amount of time students are actually engaged in motor activities in physical education. Only about one third of the time allotted to physical education is actually spent in motor activity (Costello, 1977; Pieron, 1980b). Newer descriptive studies in physical education using ALT-PE have similarly found that students are engaged at an appropriate level of difficulty only about one third of the time allotted for a physical education lesson (Godbout, Brunelle, and Tousignant, 1983; Metzler, 1979).

A direct relationship of ALT-PE with student achievement in physical education has not been established. Silverman (1991) investigated the relationship of ALT-PE to student learning and found that although the relationship is not as strong as anticipated, a relationship exists between high levels of motor-appropriate behavior and student learning. The notion that students learn more when engaged for longer times with the content at an appropriate level is a reasonable concept. Defining an appropriate

Quality practice is a key to learning.

level of engagement is a major problem for physical education. The original studies done in the classroom on ALT defined appropriate engagement in the content in a very content-specific way. ALT-PE (Metzler,1979; Siedentop, Tousignant and Parker, 1982) defined the construct for physical education in terms of general categories of motor-appropriate responses. Metzler, DePaepe, and Reif (1985) later determined that academic learning time should be based on a judgment of whether the student has a reasonable potential for completing a motor task successfully. Several factors are involved when considering the issue of what is appropriate practice.

Success rate.   Classroom research has assumed that a reasonable success rate for learning should approach 80%, and that is what Siedentop (1991) recommends for physical education. It is the author's experience that many motor responses are far more variable than cognitive responses and that a reasonable success rate for physical education varies with the nature of the activity. For most target activities, which require a great deal of eye/hand or eye/foot control, such as shooting a basket, archery, soccer, or golf, a reasonable success rate is closer to 50% for many beginning learners. For those activities that are primarily body management activities, such as a gymnastics move, dance, or locomotor skill, the appropriate success rate is higher. The teacher should decide what a reasonably skilled performer can expect to demonstrate in regard to success level and then adjust that success level accordingly. With practice, people become more consistent at a motor skill, but rarely can they perform consistently with 100% or even high degrees of success in some motor responses.

Contribution to the learning goal. A second factor related to appropriate practice is the potential contribution of the practice to what the teacher is trying to teach. If the teacher is trying to teach students how to set a volleyball and the extent of the practice is setting the ball from a soft toss from a partner, it is unlikely that students will be able to use the set in a game situation without additional practice from served balls. A student who never gets the ball in a basketball game is unlikely to learn the game of basketball, regardless of how appropriate his response may be for the situation. If the task the teacher has selected is inappropriate for the learning goal, it is unlikely that success at the task will be related to final learning.

Quality of practice. A third factor related to the notion of appropriate practice is the quality of that practice. Regardless of the success level of students at a task, if they are practicing a skill incorrectly, it is unlikely that they will learn the proper way to perform that skill. Not just practice, but *quality* practice has the greater potential to contribute to learning (Ashy, Lee, and Landin, 1988; Buck, Harrison, and Bryce, 1991; Goldberger and Gerney, 1990; Silverman, 1985). A second aspect of the quality of practice, more difficult to measure, is the degree of engagement of the learner. Rote practice with little cognitive engagement is not likely to be effective (Magill, 1989).

Teacher Use of Time

Related to the idea of academic learning time is the idea of how teachers use their time in physical education. If we take the idea that engaging students with the content at an appropriate level of difficulty is a fundamental principle of teaching, it follows that whatever the teacher does to support this engagement is appropriate and whatever the teacher does that reduces the amount of time students actually spend engaged at an appropriate level is not appropriate. This means that a judgment must be made as to whether the teacher is contributing or not contributing to learning by using time for purposes other than student practice.

Much of the emphasis on getting teachers in physical education to increase allocated time for student practice came from studies of physical education describing the amount of time most teachers allocated to student activity. Only about one third of the time allocated to physical education is actually spent in student activity (Costello, 1977; Pieron, 1980b). Newer studies using ALT-PE as the criteria also report a very small amount of time spent in appropriate practice (Godbout, Brunelle, and Tousignant, 1983; Metzler, 1989).

When investigators looked at how teachers were spending time, they discovered that much time was actually being wasted because of poor organization and management, as well as by just talking to students about what to do and how to do it. Students were standing around waiting for turns or spending much of their time just listening. Increasing activity time has become a major objective for many teachers because of the direct relationship of practice to learning.

The notion of increasing the amount of practice time in a physical education class is one of those general principles that should be applied with a full understanding of its intent. The misuse of this idea can affect other teaching functions and other educational goals. In general, the teacher will want to have maximum activity time, but there are times when the following situations exist and should be considered:

1. Time working on developing a good learning environment is time well spent.
2. Teaching routines will actually increase practice time in later lessons.
3. The teacher needs to take more time in a task presentation so the students can practice with a clear idea of what they are trying to do.
4. The teacher should observe when everyone is not moving at the same time in order to provide better feedback, establish accountability, or assess student performance.
5. Safety is an issue, and maximum activity would not be safe.
6. The teacher wants to work on affective goals that may require students interacting among themselves or with the teacher.

Teacher Management

A direct relationship exists between the teacher's skills as a manager and student learning. This means that you *cannot* be an effective teacher until you are first an effective manager.

Teacher management has come to be a term that is reserved for almost everything the teacher does that is not directly related to the content to be taught. In physical education, management is usually intended to mean both the manner and ability of the teacher to maintain appropriate behavior and the manner in which the teacher organizes a class. Management is important because good managers can solicit and maintain student engagement in the content and because poor managers use too much class time in management, which takes away from time with the content. Many interrelationships exist between content and management in teaching situations. What the teacher does in one of these areas affects the other. For instance, a teacher who has chosen a good learning experience but cannot get the attention or cooperation of the students cannot be successful. Likewise, a teacher who has perfect control will lose that control if the content is not appropriate.

Doyle (1984) refers to the idea of classroom management as being a problem of maintaining order. Order in this context means that students are doing what they are supposed to be doing for a particular time in the school day. Order is maintained in classrooms when students choose to cooperate by minimally not misbehaving; they may not be engaged in learning, but they are minimally not misbehaving.

The earliest work done on management was done by Kounin (1977). Kounin described three characteristics of the good manager: (1) the ability to know what is going on and to target behavior accurately and with good timing ("withitness"), (2) the ability to give specific feedback on behavior ("desist clarity"), and (3) the ability to handle several things simultaneously with a smooth, uninterrupted flow of events ("overlappingness").

Ornstein and Levine (1981) identified certain behaviors as being effective in decreasing the occurrence of inattentive and disruptive behavior (Box 3-3). Gage (1978) would add to this the importance of keeping to a minumum the time spent giving directions and organizing.

One difficulty teachers have is managing learning environments of large groups of students with very diverse needs. Some evidence exists that, even in the primary grades, children can be taught self-management skills that enable them to take increasing responsibility for planning and modifying the school environment without the constant direction of the teacher (Wang, 1979).

Long-term studies of effective managers at the elementary school, junior high school, and high school levels have shown clearly that effective management is a long-term, not a short-term, process. Box 3-4 presents Sanford and Evertson's description (1981) of what effective and ineffective managers did at the beginning of and throughout the year.

A more comprehensive review of research on classroom management was conducted by Soar and Soar (1979). Most of the early research on classroom management has been confirmed by later studies.

Soar and Soar identified three areas of management: management of pupil behavior, management of learning tasks, and student thinking. Management of behavior included ideas such as the physical move-

---

BOX 3-3

Effective Behaviors in Decreasing the Occurrence of Inattentive and Disruptive Behavior

Signal interference   Employing eye contact, hand gestures, and other teacher behaviors that reduce inattentive behavior

Proximity control   Touching or standing near the disruptive student while communicating that the teacher is concerned but not upset

Tension release   Using humor, which releases tension in the classroom

Support from routine   Using schedules, assignments, and general class practices that provide a class routine

Removal of seductive materials   Removing athletic equipment, outside reading, or other materials that encourage inattentive or disruptive behavior

Antiseptic removal   Asking a child who is disruptive to get a drink of water or run an errand

From Ornstein A, Levine D: Teacher behavior research: overview and outlook, *Phi Delta Kappan,* pp 592-596, April 1981.

BOX 3-4

Effective and Ineffective Teaching Practices

Teaching rules and procedures   Orientation and comprehensive rule setting accounted for almost one third of the first 5 days of school for some teachers and was continued during the first few weeks. Ineffective teachers spent less time on rules and were not clear on consequences. In elementary schools this time seemed to be consistently important. In junior high school classes composed of higher-SES students, it did not seem to be as critical.

Consistent enforcement and feedback   Effective teachers consistently enforced rules and reexplained the rationale for rules. The ineffective teachers ignored many and enforced few of what were designated as rules.

Clarity   Effective teachers presented clear directions and instructions in logical, step-by-step sequences at an appropriate level of vocabulary.

Knowledge and understanding of students   Effective teachers presented material at an appropriate level for students.

Student accountability for their work   Effective teachers held students accountable for their work, whereas ineffective teachers did not.

Time use   Effective teachers seldom had "dead time" when students were just waiting in their classes. Ineffective teachers had more dead time.

Standards for student behavior   Students in the classes of effective teachers were usually quiet and on task.

Maintenance of leadership role   Effective teachers maintained charge of all the students at all times. Ineffective teachers had periods in which students were just "let go."

From Sanford JP, Evertson CM: Classroom management in a low-SES junior high: three case studies, *J Teacher Ed* 32(1):34-38, 1981.

ment of students, socialization, and fluidity of groupings. Management of learning tasks was defined as the degree of control exercised by the teacher over the choice and conduct of learning tasks. Management of thinking processes encompassed pupil freedom to explore ideas and the cognitive level of interaction in the classroom between the teacher and the student. The results of this synthesis of studies led Soar and Soar to conclude the following:

- *Management of pupil behavior.* The teacher should limit pupil freedom to move about, to form subgroups, and to socialize. Unless a teacher has established a minimum of structure, relatively strong interactions that are not functional for pupil learning are likely to occur.
- *Management of learning tasks.* Learning tasks should be selected and directed primarily by teachers.
- *Management of thinking.* Some degree of pupil freedom, within the context of a teacher involvement that maintains focus, is related to student gain. Higher-complexity tasks require a greater degree of student freedom, but there is some indication that high--cognitive level interaction is dysfunctional with young students.

Efforts have been made to interpret research findings on management for the practicing teacher. The Classroom Organization and Effective Teacher's Project (COET) at the University of Texas (Evertson et al., 1981) resulted in a tested manual for organizing and managing the elementary school classroom. The manual itself is extensive and emphasizes the crucial need to (1) anticipate and plan rules and procedures ahead of time (including consequences), (2) teach rules and procedures clearly, and (3) consistently reinforce teacher expectations.

Research in physical education has proceeded under the assumption that teachers of physical education want to increase the amount of time students are actually engaged appropriately in motor activity (ALT-PE). Two dimensions of management have the potential to decrease this time: (1) organizational procedures (the time required to organize and the specific arrangements for equipment grouping, space, and time) and (2) time spent handling behavior and conduct problems of students. In a very real sense, management and ALT interact with each other. There are other reasons that students are not attentively engaged in motor activity, such as inappropriate task selection, but poor management seems to be a major source of off-task behavior and decreased ALT. Most authors on the analysis of teaching in physical education pay a great deal of attention to management behaviors of teachers (Anderson, 1980; Siedentop, 1991). Considerable evidence exists that physical education teachers spend far too much time in management activities (Metzler, 1989). Many of the characteristics of effective management in the classroom hold true for the physical education environment, including the following:

Clear expectations for behavior

Clarity of task presentation and organizational procedures

Consistency in enforcing expectations

Businesslike manner of class

Degree of structure conducive to the characteristics of the content and the task

The use of signals to start and stop activity, appropriate task pacing, and the frequent use of demonstration are added dimensions of the physical education environment that seem important to good management (Werner & Rink, 1989).

Direct and Indirect Instruction

As was discussed in the historical overview, the concept of direct instruction received early, strong, and continuous support as an effective way to teach. Direct instruction is characterized by the following:

- Learning activities sequenced in small, hierarchical chunks
- A task-oriented environment
- The selection of clear instructional goals and materials
- High teacher monitoring of those goals
- Structured learning activities
- Immediate academic-oriented feedback

In studies involved in teaching reading and mathematics at the elementary school level, the concept of direct instruction emerged as one of the strongest variables related to student achievement. Many educators have grasped the idea of direct instruction as being the "best" way to teach. Further reviews of the research literature caution that the subject matter, broader goals, and student characteristics all play major roles in deciding whether to use direct instruction or more open instructional procedures (Peterson, 1979; Stallings & Stipek, 1986).

When achievement of basic skills is the goal, research indicates that direct instruction does have the edge over more learner-centered or open environments (Peterson, 1979). When creativity, abstract thinking, and student independence are considered, however, more open approaches hold the edge (Peterson, 1979). Student characteristics and the nature of the content seem to be critical variables that must be considered when choosing between direct or indirect approaches to teaching. Content that requires more higher-order thinking and creativity is best taught using more indirect methods. Low-ability students, as well as those students who are unmotivated, unsociable, and nonconforming, seem to perform better in more structured environments characteristic of direct instruction. High-ability, motivated, sociable, and conforming students perform better in more unstructured environments (Bennett et al., 1976; Solomon and Kendall, 1976). Work done by Anderson and Scott (1978) also suggests the importance of the effect of teaching method on students with different characteristics. Regardless of aptitude, students tend to demonstrate more task-relevant behavior when methods with "two-way" communication are used (e.g., classroom discourse and seat work rather then lecturing, audiovisual materials, or group work).

Direct instruction has been contrasted with indirect instruction. Whereas the content of direct instruction is usually content that is hierarchical in nature that can be divided into small pieces to be presented one at a time, the content most appropriate for indirect instruction tends to be more abstract. Problem solving and creative experiences, cooperative learning experiences, and discussion, for example, all lend themselves to the use of indirect instruction. Indirect instruction is more difficult to describe. Learning outcomes in indirect instruction may not be as clear. The teacher may assume that by providing a rich learning experience, students will gain different things from the experience. The teacher may structure the experience more loosely so that the student has more responsibility in the learning process and so that the direction of the lesson may not be as precisely planned. The teacher is more likely to go with the flow of the lesson rather than use a step-by-step, preplanned progression. In indirect instruction the teacher may assume that students can work more independently with the content and do not need a high degree of supervision.

Process-product research in teaching physical education has largely substantiated the use of direct instruction for motor skill acquisition (French et al., 1990, 1991; Gusthart and Springings, 1989; Metzler, 1989; Rink et al.,1992; Silverman, 1985; Silverman, 1991; Werner and Rink, 1989). In most of these studies, the more the instruction that students received was consistent with the characteristics of direct instruction, the more the students learned. There is little research in physical education that looks at products of learning that would be more appropriate to indirect instruction. Physical educators must make decisions regarding the appropriateness of direct instruction for their subject matter. The decision of whether to use direct instruction or indirect instruction has at times been made to be a philosophical issue. Actually, the decision of whether to use direct instruction or indirect instruction is an issue related to objectives and curriculum goals and the characteristics of the learner. In physical education, teachers must decide what it is they want students to learn. If the teacher wants students to be able to do a specific motor skill, direct instruction is the most effective and efficient approach to teaching that skill. Indirect instruction usually takes more time and is not as direct and efficient a way to teach. If the teacher wants students to learn why a skill is performed in a certain manner, the teacher may choose a more problem-solving approach to teaching the skill. If the teacher has curriculum goals that relate to higher-order thinking processes, group interaction skills, or independent learning, the teacher will not want to structure every learning experience using direct instruction. Choosing when to use direct instruction and when to use indirect instruction is one of the major decisions the teacher must make in planning instruction.

Expectancy Effects

Expectancy effects deal with the relationship between teacher expectations for student behavior, the characteristics of the student, and the actual achievement of the student. Following the work of Rosenthal and Jacobson (1968) and Brophy and Good (1974), many physical educators have devoted their research efforts to investigating these relationships.

What is clear from classroom research is that students achieve more when teachers believe that they can achieve. Often student achievement and teacher expectations for achievement are closely related (Kranz, Weber, and Fishall, 1970; Martinek, 1981; Martinek, Crowe, and Rejeski, 1982; Martinek and Karper, 1981; Martinek and Karper, 1982; Martinek, Zaichowsky, and Cheffers, 1977; Rosenthal and Jacobson, 1968). Martinek and Karper (1982) hypothesized that a mediating link between teacher expectations and student achievement in physical education might be the teacher's perception of student effort. This means that what teachers expect students to achieve is largely determined by the teachers' perception of how hard students try.

Teacher expectations and the amount and type of attention they give students are also related to the characteristics of students. Students whom teachers like, high achievers, and boys seem to command more teacher help and attention than students whom teachers do not like, low achievers, and girls (Allard, 1979; Brophy and Good, 1974, 1986; Crowe, 1979). A study by Cousineau and Luke (1990) found a significant relationship between teacher expectations and academic learning time of students.

It is not surprising that students do not learn when teachers do not expect them to. Physical edu-

cators must continuously monitor their own expectations for students. A lack of teacher expectation for learning is a critical impediment in the physical education field. Many teachers do not expect students to learn because they do not think students want to learn or are capable of learning. In either case, the result is the same. Although low expectations are sometimes justified, teacher expectation is largely an attitude and many times is a self-fulfilling prophecy.

Another aspect of expectancy effects is the preferential treatment given to some students over other students. It is likely that there are significant trends related to the attention teachers give students who are high achievers, less deviant, and more attractive. Some teachers may give preferential treatment to students with other characteristics (e.g., female, quiet, or on-task students). What is clear is that teachers should become conscious of how they treat different students.

Emotional Climate

As discussed, research on emotional climate was one of the first areas of the teaching process to be investigated by researchers. Teacher warmth and indirectness, as well as the amount of student participation in classroom discourse, were investigated extensively. More sophisticated analyses of these early studies have shown a consistently low but positive relationship between teacher affect and student achievement at the elementary school level (Gage, 1978) and a slightly higher relationship at the secondary level (Soar and Soar, 1972).

To date, research indicates that the emotional climate of effective classrooms is basically neutral. Much research indicates the negative relationship of teacher criticism to student achievement (particularly for low-SES students) but does not indicate that high teacher affect is related to student gain (Gage, 1978; Soar and Soar, 1979).

Teacher-student interaction has been included in much of the literature on climate, with an emphasis on the relationship between teacher talk and student talk. Classrooms are very much teacher dominated. Increased student talk does not seem to be related to increased gains in achievement (Duncan and Biddle, 1974). There is some indication that student dialogue is more important in the secondary schools, where more discussion and interaction strategies are used, than in the elementary schools.

Work in physical education has consistently described a highly soliciting (directing to act) environment that is predominantly teacher controlled (Anderson, 1980; Rink, 1979). Relationships of teacher affect to student gain in physical education have yet to be established. Because little verbal interaction occurs between students and teachers in the physical education environment, teacher affect is best determined by observing the constructs of management and teacher reactions to the movement responses of students. Classroom research indicates that neutral and slightly warm environments are the most effective; there is no reason to believe that this finding cannot be applied to physical education. Criticism that is negatively affective is to be avoided.

Teacher Feedback

Teacher feedback as used here includes a variety of teacher reactions to student behavior, such as teacher praise, correction, and affirmation of correct response. Classroom researchers have concentrated a great deal of effort on the idea of teacher praise as a positive response to students that includes positive teacher affect. The conclusions of this research are summarized well in Box 3-5.

Praise is not always reinforcing and can actually decrease motivation rather than increase it. This is particularly true in situations where a person has previously been performing the behavior for its intrinsic value.

Most researchers support the notion that students need knowledge of results or statements on the correctness or incorrectness of student responses. However, they state that, for the most part, students assume they are correct unless told otherwise (Brophy, 1981). Praise and criticism go beyond simple knowledge of results. Criticism with negative affect should be avoided, and praise should be used

---

BOX 3-5

Guidelines for Appropriate Teacher Praise

- The teacher should praise genuine progress or accomplishment. (Quality, credibility, and the individualized nature of the accomplishment are more important than quantity.)
- The teacher should praise students when the students may not realize their accomplishment.
- The teacher should praise students who respond well to praise.
- Praise should be informative or appreciative, but not controlling. (The focus should be on task-relevant aspects, not on pleasing the teacher.)
- Praise should be contingent on objective accomplishment.
- Praise should be specific.
- Praise should show variety and other signs of credibility.
- Praise should be natural rather than theatrical or intrusive.
- Most praise should be private.
- Praise should be individualized.
- Praise should attribute success to effort and ability.
- Praise should attribute effort expenditure to intrinsic motivation.

From Brophy J: On praising effectively, *Educ Digest*, pp 16-19, Jan 1982.

---

with attention to the guidelines listed in Box 3-5.

On the basis of motor learning research and theory, physical educators have assumed that information on performance is an essential ingredient of effective instruction in physical education. The initial work in describing feedback patterns in physical education was done by Tobey (1974), who found that most teachers give general praise and specific criticism. (In more recent work this factor is not considered criticism, but corrective feedback.) In work done at the University of Liege, Pieron (1980a) found a significant difference in the response of students to master teachers and student teachers. A greater proportion of feedback from master teachers was followed by a modification of student performance.

Few teacher effectiveness studies have been done in physical education that link characteristics of teacher feedback with student learning. Yerg's study (1978) of beginning teachers teaching the cartwheel did not show a difference in the amount or specificity of feedback given by effective and less effective teachers. Pieron's study (1981) of beginning teachers teaching the handstand-rollout to college students found more effective teachers to be more specific in their feedback. A recent study by Rickard (1991) investigated the immediate responses of students to teacher feedback and found that low-ability students tended to increase their practice success after teacher feedback, but high-ability students slightly decreased their practice success. No direct relationships between student learning and teacher feedback have been established.

It is not surprising that a direct relationship between teacher feedback and student learning has not been identified. It is unreasonable to expect a single teaching behavior to predict learning. In physical education, as in other settings, teacher feedback serves several functions. Teacher feedback is for most learners (especially young learners) motivating. Teacher feedback also serves to maintain on-task behavior. A study by van der Mars (1989) found that teacher praise could reduce the off-task behavior of second grade students. Most teachers assume that it is necessary to give learners information on their performance, whether affirming what they are doing or correcting problems they are having. It is unlikely that the teacher will be able to interact with many students for a long enough period of time to provide effective corrective information on performance in large physical education classes.

Brophy (1982) raised a large and important issue in his discussion of teacher praise when he talked about extrinsic and intrinsic motivation and teacher domination through affective praise. Teachers can control the behavior of many students by giving or withdrawing personal affect for student behavior. Many teachers, particularly those who work with young children, have capitalized on this tool for control. Statements beginning with "I like the way..." are frequently heard in both classrooms and gymnasiums throughout the country. The issue of control is not likely to ever be fully resolved. Teachers should consider the following two factors.

- *The age of the student.* In terms of moral development, young primary students determine right from wrong largely by reflecting the behavior of important others (e.g., teachers or parents). Any teacher approval is likely to be construed as such and is a valuable educational tool when used appropriately.
- *The intrinsic or extrinsic motivation of the student.* Teachers may very well have to individualize the affect nature of the feedback they give students. For students who are not intrinsically motivated, positive teacher affect may be needed.

Implicit Curriculum

Curriculum is what students actually experience in school. A growing body of research has investigated levels of curriculum operating in classrooms and gymnasiums that are not what a teacher plans, specifically states, or shares with students. There are many labels for these other things that students actually learn from their experiences in schools. Sometimes this curriculum is called *covert, hidden,* or *null.* This text refers to it as the *implicit curriculum* (Dodds, 1983). An example of an implicit curriculum in operation is the message some teachers send to girls that they are not expected to be as accomplished as boys.

Dodds (1983) reviewed the research in this area and concluded the following:

- Students learn many more things than their teachers intend, and the impact of the implicit curriculum frequently overpowers that of the explicit curriculum proclaimed by teachers.
- Students may be receiving conflicting messages about what is important in physical education.

Understanding the hidden agenda may help explain why programs are not effective.

- Negotiations between teachers and students constituting the functional curriculum seem to mediate the effects on student learning of all nonfunctional curricula.
- Teachers learn as readily from students as the reverse.
- Teachers are amazingly unaware and unconscious of the nonexplicit curricula being played out in their physical education classes.

A body of knowledge is being gathered on how the implicit curriculum functions in physical education settings. Griffin (1983, 1984, 1985) identified five participation patterns into which middle school girls sorted themselves regardless of the efforts of the teacher to get all to participate in a high level. Wang (1977) reported how elementary schoolchildren learned to behave differently in their physical education class according to their gender, race, skill level, and socioeconomic level. Kollen (1981) reported that secondary students regard physical education as boring, alienating, and meaningless.

Just as teachers influence students, students are capable of shaping and maintaining specific teacher behaviors (Sherman and Cormier, 1974). Students negotiate downward the demands of tasks in the gymnasium (Tousignant, 1982), and they respond in ways in which teachers are totally unaware. Silverman (1982) reported how different students respond differently to different teacher interactions.

Within each setting in which a physical education class is conducted, many variables are operating that influence what teachers and students actually experience. Some of these variables are unique to a setting, and some have just remained undetected by the physical educator. Some of these variables contribute to the effectiveness of the teacher, and some undermine any teacher intent.

Physical education teachers need to be aware of the factors influencing their instruction. They can do this by taking time to study what is really going on in their gymnasiums and by investigating the meaning behind both teacher and student behaviors. Physical education classes in which the implicit curriculum and the explicit curriculum are closely related are more effective.

Teacher Enthusiasm

Teacher enthusiasm was identified initially as an important variable in teacher effectiveness (Rosenshine & Furst, 1971). Since the early work done with this variable, teacher enthusiasm has been deemed more important in secondary school classroom environments than in elementary school environments (Brophy, 1979a). One important reason for this might well be that at the secondary level, a greater need exists for motivation and an increase in class verbal discussion rather than independent work. What is clear from intervention research on teacher enthusiasm in the classroom and physical education is that teachers can learn to be enthusiastic (Collins, 1978; Locke and Woods, 1982; Rolider, 1979).

Clarity

Teacher clarity was identified early as being a significant variable in effective teaching and continues to be supported as a key variable in teacher effectiveness (Dunkin, 1984). In research efforts, teacher clarity has been operationally defined in different ways. Basically, teacher clarity includes the following teacher behaviors (Kennedy et al., 1978; Land, 1981):

- Gives explanations students understand
- Teaches step by step
- Describes the work to be done and how to do it
- Gives specific details
- Works examples and explains them
- Stresses difficult points
- Prepares students for what they will be doing next

In physical education, clarity is a major part of the development of the instrument "Qualitative Measures of Teaching Performance Scale" (QMTPS) (Rink and Werner, 1989). The QMTPS identifies teacher clarity and several other characteristics of task presentation, including demonstration and use of cues. In a study done with jumping and landing skills of second grade children, teacher performance on the constructs of this instrument were found to be related to student achievement (Werner and Rink, 1989).

The Role of Content

Content-specific pedagogy is one of the most critical and most recent variables to be studied. Whereas general pedagogical skills of the teacher are those that apply and are useful across content areas, content-specific pedagogy are those skills necessary to teach particular learners specific content (Marks, 1990; Person, 1988; Shulman, 1987). Knowledge of the content itself is not enough. The teacher's ability to relate and transform the content for particular learners was identifed in qualitative studies investigating expert teachers of specific content.

Content Development

Several researchers of the instructional process in physical education have studied the way in which teachers develop the content of physical education through the instructional process. Content development is the process through which teachers lead the learner to accomplish an objective. It is clear that there is no development toward any intended psychomotor outcome in many lessons in physical education (Rink, 1979). When a psychomotor outcome is intended, many physical educators move rapidly from the practice of skills in very simple environments to game play in very complex environments. Earls (1982) studied the more immediate effects of teacher tasks on student responses in the younger grades and concluded that much of what teachers ask students to do as lessons progress "causes a regression in the level of movement patterns exhibited by students."

More specific work using the construct of extension (progression) in several studies on teaching volleyball supports the idea that breaking down complex skills into more manageable parts facilitates learning (French, Rink, and Werner, 1990; French et al., 1991; Rink et al., 1992). Students who were given a progression of simple-to-complex conditions of practice learned more in these studies than the students who practiced the final test for the same amount of time. A second aspect of content development relates to the use of refinement tasks given to the entire class as a focus for their work. Some evidence exists that the use of refinement tasks facilitates learning (Masser, 1985) particularly when coupled with appropriate progressions (Rink et al., 1992).

Several studies have compared skill gains of students when allowed to play the game. A growing body of consistent research supports the idea that students do not improve their skill when they play the game (Buck and Harrison, 1990; French and Thomas, 1987; Parker and O'Sullivan, 1983).

How Teachers See Students

How teachers perceive students is critical to what students learn and how they feel about what they learn. Expert teachers are able to identify and translate individual differences into the pedagogical implications of those differences. They are able to view differences not as a problem but as context for designing and conducting instruction. These differences have been recognized not only in respect to planning for differences in academic ability, but also in adjustments teachers make to student characteristics, such as social class, culture, gender, and biological differences (Paine, 1989; Shulman, 1989).

How Students See Themselves

One of the strongest predictors of student success is how students feel about their potential for success (Wittrock, 1986). Many researchers believe that the student is the mediator of instruction. This means that the effectiveness of instruction depends on how well the instruction matches the specific needs of a particular student. Although research into student thinking and responses is relatively new, this line of investigation is likely to be a rich source for understanding the effectiveness of what the teacher does.

Grouping Students

Teachers have many options for grouping students, including homogeneous (all students with a similar characteristic), heterogeneous (students with different levels of same characteristic), peer group, cooperative learning, or individualized. Although student grouping is a widely used and significant variable in teaching physical education, the effects of student grouping have yet to be studied by researchers in physical education. The following review is from classroom research.

In many classes that are heterogeneous in terms of ability, teachers tend to want to form smaller homogeneous groups so that instruction can more nearly match student abilities. Several factors must be considered when teachers choose to work with groups of students, rather than the whole class. First, the teacher must develop management skills that ensure that students can work productively with groups, and if the teacher's attention is going to be with one group, other students must also be able to work productively. Second, if the teacher groups by ability, these groups must be flexible so that the same students are not always in the low group. Third, teachers may want to consider presenting a task or problem for the whole class and using group work for review, practice, or drill (Slavin, 1987; Ward, 1987).

Cooperative learning has been shown to positively affect students, both academically and socially, when conducted by teachers who are well trained in its use. Cooperative learning is a group strategy that is designed to encourage students to work together to accomplish a goal and to utilize all the talents and members of the group (Slavin 1987; Wood, 1987).

SUMMARY

1. Research can inform practice by establishing principles of teaching, which should be used situationally.
2. The study of teaching can be organized according to the relationships between presage, context, process, and product variables.
3. Initial efforts in the 1940s to study teaching were primarily efforts to link presage variables with effective teachers. Effective teachers were described using rating scales. The results were disappointing.
4. Research efforts of the 1950s and 1960s were primarily directed toward establishing relationships between process variables. Much descrip-

tive information was gathered, but few relationships were established between the process and the products of teaching. As a result of this period of research, the variables identified as having the most promise for relationships with product outcomes were clarity of presentation, teacher enthusiasm, variability, task orientation, and student opportunity to learn.

5. In the 1970s researchers began turning toward context-specific variables. Several large and well-financed studies converged in the subject areas of elementary school reading and mathematics and reported findings consistent with each other. The major variables of academic learning time (ALT) and direct instruction were identified as having a significant relationship to student learning in the areas of mathematics and reading. Other more specific variables were identified as being context specific.
6. Research in the 1980s focused primarily on understanding teaching from the perspective of the teacher and the learner. This era of research has primarily utilized qualitative research methods.
7. ALT and student achievement are highly correlated. Practice in physical education must be appropriate to the learning goal, successful for the student, and of high enough quality to be related to learning.
8. Good management skills of the teacher are essential to effective teaching.
9. Direct instruction, as a holistic concept, is highly correlated with student achievement in the areas of elementary school reading and mathematics and seems to be the best choice of teaching methodology when basic skills are the content to be learned and when learners need more structure.
10. Teacher expectation for student learning can significantly affect student achievement and the way in which students are treated during instruction.
11. A slightly warm, emotional climate seems to be the most effective.
12. Teacher feedback serves to motivate students and keep students on task. The teacher's ability to provide one-on-one corrective feedback in large physical education classes is limited.

13. An implicit curriculum operates in physical education that may contribute to or undermine teacher goals.
14. Teacher enthusiasm and teacher clarity are related to student learning.
15. When teachers use step-by-step progressions and refine student performance of motor skills, students learn more. When students just play the game, they do not learn skills.

CHECKING YOUR UNDERSTANDING

1. What is the difference between qualitative and quantitative research?
2. What does the idea of "principled practice" mean?
3. List five presage, product, context, and process variables specific to physical education.
4. What is meant by the ability to generalize data?
5. Why was early research in teaching unsuccessful in producing major variables that were associated with effective teaching?
6. Describe five teaching variables that research has shown to be directly associated with effective teaching.
7. For each of the variables you have listed above, describe what a physical education teacher would do that is associated with that variable.
8. What is the implicit curriculum? Why is it important?

REFERENCES

Allard R: A need to look at dyadic interactions. In American Alliance for Health, Physical Education, and Recreation: *Research consortium symposium papers: teaching behavior and women in sports*, vol 2, book 1, Washington, DC, 1979, American Alliance for Health, Physical Education, and Recreation.

Anderson L, Scott C: The relationship among teaching methods, student characteristics, and student involvement in learning, *J Teacher Ed* 29(3): 52-57, 1978.

Anderson W: *Analysis of teaching physical education*, St. Louis, 1980, Mosby–Year Book.

Ashy M, Lee A, Landin D: Relationship of practice using correct technique to achievement in a motor skill, *J Teaching Phys Ed* 7(2):115-120, 1988.

Bennett N et al: *Teaching styles and pupil progress*, Cambridge, Mass, 1976, Harvard University Press.

Berliner DC, Rosenshine BV, editors: *Talks to teachers*, New York, 1987, Random House.

Brophy J: Teacher behavior and its effects, *J Educ Psychol* 71(6):733-750, 1979a.

Brophy J: Teacher behavior and student learning, *Educ Leadership* 37(1):33-38, 1979b.

Brophy J: Teacher praise: a functional analysis, *Rev Educ Res* 51(1):5-32, 1981.

Brophy J: On praising effectively, *Educ Digest*, pp 16-19, Jan 1982.

Brophy J, Evertson C: *Process product correlations in the Texas teacher effectiveness study: final report*, Austin, Tex, 1974, University of Texas, Research and Development Center for Teacher Education.

Brophy J, Good T: *Teacher-student relationships: causes and consequences*, New York, 1974, Holt, Rinehart & Winston.

Buck M, Harrison J: An analysis of game play in volleyball, *J Teaching Phys Ed* 10(1):38-48, 1990.

Buck M, Harrison J, Bryce G: An analysis of learning trials and their relationship to achievement, *J Teaching Phys Ed* 10:134-152, 1991.

Collins M: Effects of enthusiasm training on pre-service elementary teachers, *J Teacher Ed* 29(1):53-57, 1978.

Costello JA: *A descriptive analysis of student behavior in elementary school physical education classes*, unpublished doctoral dissertation, New York, 1977, Columbia University.

Cousineau W, Luke M: Relationships between teacher expectations and academic learning time in sixth grade physical education basketball classes, *J Teaching Phys Ed* 9:262-271, 1990.

Crowe P: An observational study of teachers' expectancy effects and their mediating mechanisms. In American Alliance for Health, Physical Education, and Recreation. *Research consortium symposium papers: teaching behavior and women in sport*, vol 2, book 1, Washington, DC, 1979, American Alliance for Health, Physical Education, and Recreation.

Dodds P: *Consciousness raising in curriculum: a teacher's model for analysis*. Paper presented at the Third Physical Education Curriculum Theory Conference, Athens, Ga, February 10-12, 1983.

Doyle W: Classroom organization and management. In Wittrock M, editor: *Handbook of research on teaching*, ed 3, New York, 1984, MacMillan Publishing.

Dunkin M, Biddle B: *The study of teaching*, New York, 1974, Holt, Rinehart & Winston.

Earls N: *Research on the immediate effects of instructional variables*. Paper presented at the Committee on Institutional Cooperation Big Ten Symposium; Research on Teaching in Physical Education, West Lafayette, Ind, November 12-13, 1982.

Evertson CM et al: *Organizing and managing the elementary school*, Austin, Tex, 1981, University of Texas, Research and Development Center for Teacher Education.

Flanders N: *Interaction analysis in the classroom: a manual for observers*, Minneapolis, 1960, University of Minnesota Press.

French KE, Rink JE, Werner PH: Effects of contextual interference on retention of three volleyball skills, *Percept Motor Skills* 71:179-186, 1990.

French K, Thomas G: The relation of knowledge development to children's basketball performance, *J Sport Psychol* 9:15-32, 1987.

French K et al: The effects of practice progressions on learning two volleyball skills, *J Teaching Phys Ed* 10(3):261-275, 1991.

Gage NL: The yield of research on teaching, *Phi Delta Kappan*, pp 230-235, Nov 1978.

Godbout P, Brunelle J, Tousignant M: Academic learning time in elementary and secondary physical education, *Res Q Exercise Sport* 54(1):11-19, 1983.

Goldberger M, Gerney P: Effects of learner use of practice time on skill acquisition, *J Teaching Phys* Ed 10:84-95, 1990.

Good T, Grouws D: *Process-product relationships in fourth grade mathematics classrooms: final report of National Institute of Education grant (NE-G-00-0123)*, Columbia, Mo, Oct 1975, University of Missouri.

Griffin P: *Gymnastics is a girl's thing: student participation and interaction patterns in middle school gymnastics classes.* Paper presented at the Committee on Institutional Cooperation Big Ten Symposium: Research on Teaching in Physical Education, West Lafayette, Ind, November 12-13, 1983.

Griffin P: Girl's participation patterns in a middle school team sports unit, *J Teaching Phys Ed* 4(1):30-38, 1984.

Griffin PS: Boys participation styles in a middle school physical education team sports unit, *J Teaching Phys Ed* 4:100-110, 1985.

Gusthart J, Sprigings E: Student learning as a measure of teacher effectiveness, *J Teaching Phys Ed* 8(4):298-311, 1989.

Hoffman SJ: *Observing and reporting on learner responses: the teacher as a reliable feedback agent.* In Gedvilas LI, Kneer M, editors: Proceedings of the National Association for Physical Education of College Women and the National College Physical Education Association for Men National Conference, Florida, January 6-9, 1977a.

Kennedy J et al: Additional investigations into the nature of teacher clarity, *J Educ Res* 72(2):3-10, 1978.

Kollen B: *The experience of movement in physical education: a phenomonology*, doctoral dissertation, 1981, University of Michigan, University Microfilms No. 81-16272.

Kounin J: *Discipline and group management in classrooms*, Melbourne, Fla, 1977, RE Krieger Publishing.

Kranz P, Weber W, Fishall K: *The relationships between teacher perception of pupils and teacher behavior toward those pupils.* Paper presented at the annual meeting of the American Educational Research Association, 1970.

Land M: Combined effect of two teacher clarity variables on student achievement, *J Exper Ed* 50(1):14-17, 1981.

Locke L, Woods S: Teacher enthusiasm, *J Teaching Phys Ed* 1(3):3-14, 1982.

Magill RA: *Motor learning*: concepts and applications, Dubuque, Iowa, 1989, Wm C Brown.

Marks R: Pedagogical content knowledge: from a mathmatical case to a modifed conception, *J Teacher Ed* 41(3):3-11, 1990.

Martinek P: Pygmalion in the gym: a model for the communication of teacher expectations in physical education, *Res Q Exercise Sport* 51(1):58-67, 1981.

Martinek T, Crowe P, Rejeski W: *Pygmalion in the gym: causes and effects of expectations in teaching and coaching,* West Point, NY, 1982, Leisure Press.

Martinek T, Karper W: Teachers' expectations for handicapped and non-handicapped children in mainstreamed physical education classes, *Percept Motor Skills* 53:327-330, 1981.

Martinek T, Karper W: Canonical relationships among motor ability, expression of effort, teacher expectations and dyadic interactions in elementary age children, *J Teaching Phys Ed* 2(1):26-39, 1982.

Martinek T, Zaichowsky L, Cheffers J: Decision-making in elementary children: effects on motor skills and self-concept, *Res Q Exercise Sport* 48(2):349-357, 1977.

Masser L: The effect of refinement on student achievement in a fundamental motor skill in grades K-6, *J Teaching Phys Ed* 6(2):174-182, 1985.

McDonald F, Elias P: *The effects of teacher performance on student learning: beginning teacher evaluation study—phase II final report, v*ol 1, Princeton, NJ, 1976, Educational Testing Service.

Metzler M: *The measurement of academic learning time in physical education,* doctoral dissertation, 1979, The Ohio State University, University Microfilms No. 8009314.

Metzler M: A review of research on time in sport pedagogy, *J Teaching Phys Ed* 8:87-103, 1989.

Metzler M, DePaepe J, Reif G: Alternative technologies for measuring academic learning time in physical education, J *Teaching Phys Ed* 6(4):271-285, 1985.

Ornstein A, Levine D: Teacher behavior research: overview and outlook, *Phi Delta Kappan,* pp 592-596, April 1981.

Paine L: *Orientation toward diversity: What do prospective teachers bring?* (Research Rep. No.89-9) E. Lansing, MI, 1989, National Center for Research on Teacher Education.

Parker M, O'Sullivan M: Modifying ALT-PE for game play contexts and other reflections, *J Teaching Phys Ed,* pp 8-10, Summer Monograph, 1983.

Peterson P: Direct instruction: effective for what and for whom? *Educ Leadership,* pp 46-48l, Oct 1979a.

Peterson P: Direct instruction reconsidered. In Peterson P, Walberg H, editors: *Research on teaching: concepts, findings and implications, B*erkeley, Calif, 1979b, McCutchan Publishing.

Peterson P: Teachers' and students' cognitional knowledge for teaching and learning, *Educ Researcher 15*(5):5-14, 1988.

Pieron M: *From interaction analysis to research on teaching effectiveness: an overview of studies from the University of Liege.* Paper presented at The Ohio State University, Columbus, November 1980a.

Pieron M: Pupils' activities, time on task and behaviors in high school physical education teaching, *Federation International d'Education Physique Bulletin* 50(3/4):62-68, 1980b.

Pieron M: *Research on teacher change: effectiveness of teaching a psychomotor task study in a micro-teaching setting.* Paper presented at the American Alliance for Health, Physical Education, Recreation, and Dance National Convention, Boston, April 13-17, 1981.

Rickard L: The short-term relationship of teacher feedback and student practice, *J Teaching Phys Ed* 10:275-285, 1991.

Rink J: *Development of an observation system for content development in physical education,* unpublished doctoral dissertation, 1979, The Ohio State University.

Rink J et al: The influence of content development on the effectiveness of instruction, *J Teaching Phys Ed* 11:139, 1992.

Rink J, Werner P: Qualitative measures of teaching performance scale (QMTPS). In Darst P, Zakrajsek D, Mancini V, editors: *Analyzing physical education and sport instruction,* ed 2, Champaign, Ill, 1989, Human Kinetics Publishers.

Rolider A: *The effects of enthusiasm training on the subsequent behavior of physical education teachers,* unpublished doctoral dissertation, 1979, The Ohio State University.

Rosenshine B, Furst F: Research in teacher performance criteria. In Smith B, editor: *Research in teacher education,* Englewood Cliffs, NJ, 1971, Prentice-Hall.

Rosenshine B, Berak V: Content, time and direct instruction. In Person P, Walberg H, editors: *Research on teaching: concepts, findings and implications,* Berkeley, Calif, 1979, McCutchan Publishing.

Rosenthal RB, Jacobson L: Pygmalion in the classroom. New York, 1968, Holt, Rinehart & Winston.

Sanford JP, Evertson CM: Classroom management in a low S.E.S. junior high: three case studies, *J Teacher Ed* 32(1):34-38, 1981.

Sherman T, Cormier W: An investigation of the influence of student behavior on teacher behavior, *J Appl Behav Analysis* 7(2):11-21, 1974.

Shulman L: Knowledge and teaching: foundations of the new reform, *Harvard Educ Rev* 57(1):1-22, 1987.

Shulman L: Blue freeways: traveling the alternate route with big-city teacher trainees, *J Teacher Ed* 40:2-8, 1989.

Siedentop D: *Developing teaching skills in physical education,* ed 3, Palo Alto, Calif, 1991, Mayfield Publishing.

Siedentop D, Tousignant M, Parker M: *Academic learning time-physical education: 1982 revision coding manual,* Columbus, Ohio, 1982, The Ohio State University, College of Education, School of Health, Physical Education & Recreation.

Silverman S: T*he relationship among student achievement, student engagement, and selected student characteristics,* doctoral dissertation, 1982, University of Massachusetts, University Microfilms No. DA-3219849.

Silverman S: Relationship of engagement and practice trials to student achievement, *J Teaching Phys Ed* 5:13-21, 1985.

Silverman S: Research on teaching in physical education: review and commentary, *Res Q Exercise Sport* 62(4):352-364, 1991.

Slavin R: Ability grouping and its alternative: Must we track? *American Educator* 11(2):32-36, 1987.

Soar R, Soar RM: An empirical analysis of selected follow-through programs: an example of a process approach to evaluation. In Gordon IJ, editor: *Early childhood evaluation: seventy-first yearbook of National Society for the Study of Education,* part 2, Chicago, 1972, University of Chicago Press.

Soar R, Soar RM: Emotional climate and management. In Peterson P, Walberg H, editors: *Research on teaching: concepts, findings and implications,* Berkeley, Calif, 1979, McCutchan Publishing.

Solomon D, Kendall A: Individual characteristics and children's performance in "open" and "traditional" classroom settings, J *Educ Psychol* 68: 613-625, 1976.

Stallings J, Kaskowitz D: *Follow through classroom observation evaluation, 1972-1973.* Office of Education contract (OEC-08522480-4633[100]), Menlo Park, Calif, 1974, Stanford Research Institute.

Stallings J, Stipek D: Research on early childhood and elementary school teaching programs. In Wittrock MC, editor: *Handbook of research on teaching,* ed 3, New York, 1986, Macmillan.

Tobey C: *A descriptive analysis of the occurrence of augmented feedback in physical education classes,* unpublished doctoral dissertation, New York, 1974, Columbia University, Teachers College.

Tousignant M: *Analysis of the occurrence of augmented feedback in physical education classes,* unpublished doctoral dissertation, Columbus, 1982, The Ohio State University.

van der Mars H: Effects of specific verbal praise on off-task behavior of second grade students in physical education, J *Teaching Phys Ed* 8(2):162-169, 1989.

Wang B: *An ethnography of a physical education class: an experiment in integrated living,* unpublished doctoral dissertation, Greensboro, NC, 1977, University of North Carolina.

Wang M: Implications for effective use of instruction and learning time, *Educ Horizons,* pp 169-173, Summer 1979.

Ward B: *Instructional grouping in the classroom; school improvement research series close up no. 2,* Portland Ore, 1987, Northwest Educational Research Lab, ERIC Document Reproduction Service No. ED 291 147.

Werner P, Rink J: Case studies of teacher effectiveness in physical education, *J Teaching Phys Ed* 4:280-297, 1989.

Wittrock M: Students' thought processes. In Wittrock MC, editor: *Handbook of research on teaching,* ed 3, New York, 1986, Macmillan Publishing.

Wood K: Fostering cooperative learning in middle and secondary school classrooms, *J Reading* 31(1):10-19, 1987.

Yerg B: Identifying teacher behavior correlates of pupil achievement. In American Alliance for Health, Physical Education, and Recreation: *Research consortium symposium papers: teaching behavior and sport history,* vol 1, book 1, Washington, DC, 1978, American Alliance for Health, Physical Education, and Recreation.

SUGGESTED READINGS

Good T, editor: *The Elementary School Journal Special Issue: Research on Teaching* 83(4):1983.

Wittrock M, editor: *Handbook of research on teaching,* New York, 1984, McMillan Publishing.

❖❖❖

Effective Teaching Skills

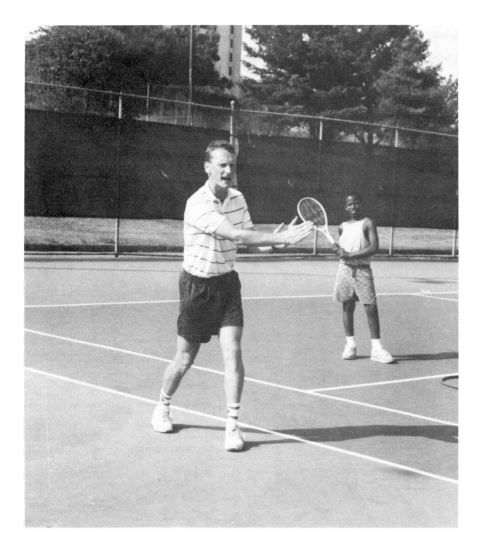

Designing Movement
Experiences and Tasks

❖ ❖ ❖ ❖ ❖ ❖ ❖ ❖ ❖ ❖

OVERVIEW

This chapter is designed to provide several frameworks to help you understand the nature of the content of physical education, criteria for translating this content into learning experiences, and the nature of teacher movement tasks that are selected to develop learning experiences. The frameworks presented in this chapter will become important concepts used in the development of teaching skills in the chapters that follow.

❖ ❖ ❖ ❖ ❖ ❖ ❖ ❖ ❖ ❖

CONCEPTS

▪ **Understanding the content of physical education**
  Movement concepts

▪ **Criteria for a learning experience**

▪ **Designing the movement task**
  Content dimension of movement tasks
  Goal-setting dimension of the task
  Organizational arrangements of the task

◆ UNDERSTANDING THE CONTENT OF PHYSICAL EDUCATION

Physical education programs have the same concerns relative to the domains of learning as do other educational programs: psychomotor, affective, and cognitive. The primary and unique contribution of our field is in the psychomotor area, which is usually divided into goals relative to fitness and motor skill acquisition. This section looks at the types of motor skill content that are critical to physical education. Teachers who have the development of fitness as an objective must attend to the principles that govern the development of fitness. Fitting fitness into the physical education program is the subject of Chapter 12. The intent of this section is to help you understand the nature of what you will be teaching so that you can more appropriately design and conduct learning experiences for students that have the potential to promote learning.

Motor Skills

Motor skill acquisition is a primary responsibility of the physical educator. Although much that is related to fitness is shared by programs that address health concerns in the school, physical educators have the unique responsibility of developing motor skills. The goal in teaching motor skills is the development of skillful performance for participation.

One of the first questions teachers should ask themselves about the motor skill content they want to teach is, "What does it mean to be skilled with this content?" If asked what it means to be a skilled bowler, almost everyone will respond with the same idea: a skilled bowler (1) can knock down all of the pins most of the time with one ball and (2) can knock down any that are missed with the second ball. If asked what a skilled bowler looks like, everyone will respond by describing from a mechanical perspective the action of bowling a strike (i.e., the position of the body and the steps taken at different parts of the action). If a third question is asked about how the bowler had to adjust the skill to the conditions of the game, responses will contain information on strategies for spare bowling.

Each of the responses to these questions will describe only a part of the concept of skillfulness in bowling. Together they form a more complete picture of what is involved in being skilled in bowling. They describe the quality of **effectiveness,** the quality of **efficiency,** and the quality of **adaptation.** All three are part of what is meant by skillfulness.

The quality of **effectiveness** is the essence of goal-oriented, or objective, movement. A basketball free throw is effective if it goes in the basket. An archer is effective if the arrows hit the center of the target. A defense is effective if the offense is prevented from scoring. Motor skills are effective if they accomplish their purpose.

The quality of **efficiency** describes the performance itself. A skill is performed efficiently when the action itself is mechanically correct for a given performer and situation. There are "best" ways of performing many skills. Sometimes a way becomes the "best" because most people have been consistently successful performing in that way. Recent changes in styles of performance in some sports substantiate that we are always in search of better ways and that all people (especially children) may not perform efficiently in the same way. There is more than one mechanically efficient way. Although it is possible to be effective performing in a mechanically incorrect way (e.g., stepping with the wrong foot on an overhand throw), it is difficult for most people to be effective consistently in an incorrect way.

The quality of **adaptation** describes the ability of the performer to adjust to conditions surrounding performance. The quality of adaptation is critical to skills where changes in conditions are continuous during performance (e.g., the basketball lay-ups, the forehand stroke in tennis, the football pass).

If asked what a skilled basketball dribbler looks like, a person might arrive at the responses presented in Box 4-1. The responses described for the skill of dribbling a basketball are more complex than those described for bowling. The basketball dribble is very much an open skill because the conditions under

> **BOX 4-1**
>
> ### Characteristics of a Skilled Basketball Dribbler
>
> **Effective**
>
> Keeps the ball away from the defense
> Uses the dribble to put the team in a better scoring position
>
> **Efficient**
>
> Uses pads of fingers and wrist action
> Keeps ball close and slightly to the side of the dribbling hand when stationary and out in front when traveling with more speed
> Keeps knees flexed when stationary
>
> **Adaptable**
>
> Varies *direction* of dribble appropriately for an offensive or defensive situation
> Varies *speed* of dribble appropriately for an offensive or defensive situation
> Varies *level* of dribble appropriately for an offensive or defensive situation
> Chooses appropriate time to dribble in relation to the pass
> Places body between ball and opponent

which the skill is performed are changing. The responses described for the skill of bowling are less complex, and bowling approaches an almost totally closed skill because conditions remain the same. In bowling, the only adaptation the performer must make is to the pin setup on the second ball.

In some skills, such as swimming and competitive gymnastics, efficient performance is a primary goal and almost always determines effectiveness. Adaptation is not a primary concern. In other skills, adaptation is more important than efficiency. Knowing the intent and nature of the content is essential to make decisions about how that content should be taught. Physical educators teach many different kinds of skills with different intents and descriptions of skillfullness. These skills can be divided into the categories of closed skills, closed

skills used in different environments, and open skills. Table 4-1 defines these areas and gives examples of each. The divisions between these groups are not always clear, but they help teachers think about the specific teaching implications inherent in their nature. Each will be discussed separately.

Closed skills. As identified in Chapter 2, Singer (1982) credits Poulton (1957) with the concept of closed and open skills. A closed skill is a skill that is performed in a fixed environment. A fixed environment means that conditions surrounding the performer during performance do not change. When performing a closed skill, performers can concentrate on self-pacing the skill (doing it on their own time) and using feedback from within their own bodies to guide their actions. Although theoretic differences probably exist between the terms, closed skills are most often self-paced skills. Examples of more closed skills are bowling, archery, darts, the foul shot in basketball, and the serve in volleyball or tennis.

Skilled performance in closed skills requires *efficiency* and *consistency* of response. The skill should be performed in the same way each time. The skilled learner relies on kinesthetic feedback (located in the joints and muscles) to provide information on how the skill is performed. Like all motor skills, closed skills eventually become automatic at highly skilled levels of performance.

Teaching a closed skill requires that the practice conditions and the manner in which the movement is performed be the same each time. Teachers do not want variation or a change in conditions that affect the movement itself. Although highly skilled athletes want to vary conditions associated with practice, such as sites of practice, speed and direction of wind, floor surfaces, and noise levels, in general, practice conditions that affect the movement itself should remain the same. Teachers want to develop closed skills through repetition in consistent environments. They will want to help the learner establish an efficient performance and then gain consistency with that pattern. As the learner advances, the teacher will want to help the student

TABLE 4-1	Classifying motor skills	
Classification of content	**Definition**	**Examples**
Closed skills	The environmental conditions surrounding performance of the skill stay the same during performance.	Tennis serve Bowling for strikes Volleyball serve Basketball free throw
Closed skills in differing environments	The environmental conditons surrounding performance of the skill stay the same during performance, but the performer may be asked to perform in different environments.	Bowling for spares Archery Golf Educational gynmastics
Open skills	The skill is performed in changing environments.	Tennis forehand Basketball lay-up Soccer dribble

focus on developing a kinesthetic awareness of the skill so that it can be self-corrected.

Much controversy exists over whether closed skills should be taught as a whole action or in parts. If the skill is one that is complex, parts of the skill may be taught separately. Teachers should be cautioned that in many instances the rhythm of a movement, particularly a flowing movement, is destroyed when parts are practiced in excess and then combined. The whole movement is different from the parts combined: preparation for a successive move occurs during the previous move in most complex skills. The practice of parts should not be carried on at great length. Where possible, skills should be taught as a whole. It is easier to insert practice of parts into the whole at a later date than to practice parts and then put them into a whole.

Closed skills require great efficiency of performance to be effective. Closed skills require little or no adaptation of performance, since conditions under which the skill is performed are, for all practical purposes, the same.

Closed skills in different environments. Some basically closed, self-paced skills require performer adaptation to different, but not changing, environments. Spare bowling requires adjustments of a basically closed skill to differing pin setups. Golf requires adjustment to different clubs, distances from the hole, and surfaces. These kinds of skills are referred to as closed skills in different environments.

Skilled performance in closed skills that must be adapted to different environments requires that the skill first be learned under less complex conditions and then practiced in a variety of environments and conditions to which the skill must be applied. The idea of adaptation of performance is added to the idea of consistency of performance as the learner adjusts the skill to differing conditions. Sometimes the ability of adaptation is referred to as *versatility* (Barrett, 1977).

When specific closed skills are used in different environments, they can be taught as a closed skill first. Practice in differing environments is then added. Whether the skill should be practiced in parts again depends on its complexity and flow quality. Successful adaptation of a skill requires opportunity to practice the skill in different environments (e.g., trying for spares in bowling, hitting from sand traps in golf).

Open skills.   An open skill is performed in an environment that is changing during performance. Examples of open skills are hitting the tennis forehand, dribbling a basketball, catching a baseball, and responding to a partner in dance. Open skills are usually externally paced (timing is controlled by the environment) and rely heavily on the ability of the performer to rapidly process perceptual (primarily visual) cues. Skilled performers can interpret the environment and can adjust the skill to changing conditions.

Some disagreement exists as to whether open skills should first be learned as closed skills. Open skills do require that the skill first be learned under the simplest of conditions. Sometimes this means reducing the nature of the skill to a more closed condition (e.g., batting off a tee instead of using a pitched ball or dribbling without a defender in basketball). Because open skills require the performer to attend to perceptual cues (e.g., the oncoming ball or other players), there is no guarantee that the student who can perform a skill in the closed environment will be able to perform the skill in an open environment. Practice conditions for open skills should never be left in closed environments for long periods.

An example from a high school girls' basketball team illustrates the danger of practicing open skills for long periods in a closed environment. In this instance, one of the team's players had a need to bring every ball to a chest pass position before passing it. This allowed defensive players to tie up the ball and severely limited the player's speed in getting off a quick pass. Although it is difficult to establish a cause-and-effect relationship between the player's passing skills and the way in which she learned passing, it is reasonable to conclude that she practiced passing in a relatively closed skill manner (i.e., she

always used a chest pass). The player thus did not choose the level or kind of pass appropriate to the situation, but brought the ball to a chest pass position regardless.

Two factors are involved in the performance of an open skill: (1) the performer must choose the correct response; and (2) the performer must be able to execute that response efficiently and effectively. To do this, practice situations must be variable. The job of the teacher is to reduce the complexity of the perceptual field in early stages of learning and then help the student adapt as complexity is gradually added.

◆ CRITERIA FOR A LEARNING EXPERIENCE

To teach motor skills or concepts to learners, teachers must design learning experiences that lead the learners from where they are to the desired objectives and goals. One of the most critical functions a teacher performs in an instructional setting is the design of learning experiences and the movement tasks that constitute them. The learning experience delivers the content to the learner. It structures and gives focus to student responses. It is at the level of the learning experience that the teacher determines the student's role in the process of learning.

Teachers have many options in the design of learning experiences and movement tasks. For example, the questions in Box 4-2 only begin to sort out the alternatives for teaching the headstand.

Learning experiences can be designed to individualize the content for the learner, to give learners a decision-making role, or to focus student responses on a psychomotor, affective, or cognitive process. Teachers choose one way of designing a learning experience over others, based on the specific nature of the content, their objectives for a lesson, their broader program goals, the characteristics of their students, and the facilities and equipment of their specific environment.

A learning experience is that part of an instructional lesson used to develop a particular set of stu-

---

> **BOX 4-2**
>
> ### Content Decisions
>
> ---
>
> Should the teacher demonstrate the skill, walk students through the skill one step at a time, or teach concepts about base of support and have students apply them to a balance using the head and hands?
>
> Should all students be doing the headstand? What other arrangements for ability levels can and should be made?
>
> What kind of learning environment does the teacher want for practice? Should the practice be fun, task oriented, or relaxed?
>
> Should the student focus be maintaining balance? Showing extension and a clear body shape? Both?
>
> Should students know why the hands and head are placed the way they are?
>
> How should students be grouped for practice of the headstand? Should they practice in small groups, individually, or with a partner? Who chooses groups and with what criteria?

dent outcomes. In this text the term **learning experience** is defined as *a set of instructional conditions and events that gives structure to student experience and is related to a particular set of teacher objectives.*

If the teacher is trying to teach partners how to dribble a soccer ball against a defensive player, the teacher might have several tasks related to this learning experience, including the following:

- Two offense and one defensive player without a goal
- Half speed without a goal
- Full speed without a goal
- Using the fake in the above
- Focusing on the player without the ball
- Full speed—count number of passes
- Full speed—with a goal

The teacher would design more than one task to reach the learning goal related to passing against a defensive player. How to develop the content to

establish viable progressions of tasks is discussed in Chapter 6.

Each of the tasks related to the learning experience of passing against a defensive player can be described in many ways, including the following:

- What the nature of the content was for the task
- What the nature of the goal was for each of the tasks
- How students were organized for the activity
- How the space was arranged
- What kind and how much equipment was used
- What the teacher did during activity
- How much time the class and each student spent in activity

The decisions teachers make in regard to these questions and others determine the potential of the learning experience to contribute to reaching learning objectives, as well as the potential of the experience to contribute to different domains of learning.

In this section, four essential criteria for the design of a learning experience are presented. These criteria should act as a first screen in sifting out instructional experiences that have the potential to facilitate learning from those that do not. The criteria are a blend of professional knowledge, beliefs, and attitudes concerning what is important in what teachers do with their students in physical education.

Teachers are guided in what they do by their knowledge, beliefs, and attitudes. The answers to such questions as "Would the teacher consider checkers appropriate content?" "Would the teacher line up half the class in front of one basket for a task?" "Does the teacher consider the role of the student merely to duplicate what the teacher shows?" and "Does the teacher consider student ability levels in teaching?" are all determined by the teacher's knowledge of, beliefs about, and attitudes toward the content of physical education and learning. Although it may not be possible for every learning experience the teacher designs to meet each of these criteria, it is desirable that the teacher strive to meet these criteria. Teachers who are effective and provide well-rounded educational programs for students meet these criteria more often than not.

Criterion One

The first criterion for learning experience design is that *the learning experience must have the potential to improve the motor performance/activity skills of students.*

This criterion makes clear a commitment to provide students with skills for an active life-style as the unique purpose of the instructional physical education program. It is not meant to exclude from physical education those activities that contribute to developing an active life-style but may not require complex motor skills. It is meant to exclude from programs experiences that do nothing but engage students in movement or play activities with no learning goal. Teachers must design experiences for students with the intent to provide a learning experience. Unless an experience has the potential to contribute to student learning and development in this way, it is not considered a valid physical education instructional experience.

The implications of this criterion should be clear. The teacher does not play games just because they are fun. The teacher does not teach reading through the use of movement experiences during time designated for physical education unless the psychomotor objective is an equally valid learning experience. The teacher does not plan lessons merely to engage students in motor activity or to provide a social experience. The criterion is not merely that students be engaged in an activity that involves balls or balance or coordination, but that the activity actually has the potential to improve performance.

In my experiences in the public schools, I have had many opportunities to discuss this criterion with practicing teachers. I have talked to elementary teachers who feel their job is merely to expose students to skills that they are not yet ready to learn. I have spoken with middle school and junior high school teachers who feel their main responsibility is to introduce and expose students to as many skills as they can. Finally, I have encountered many senior high school teachers who believe their job is simply to let students play. The following questions then remain:

- Who has the responsibility to actually teach motor and activity skills to students?
- Who has the responsibility to improve the physical potential of students?

To say that students suffer from overexposure is an understatement.

Interrelated variables. There are times when teachers will want to focus on affective or cognitive goals in the design of learning experiences. Cooperative games is an example of programs specifically designed to use activity to focus on affective concerns. Also, much has been written about physical education experiences integrated with other academic subjects, as well as developing cognitive goals in physical education. The position taken in this text is that these goals are important but it is possible to use the content of physical education to develop these goals without having to create content that has no potential to contribute to physical education's unique goal.

Criterion Two

The second criterion for learning experience design is that *the learning experience must provide maximal activity or practice time for all students at an appropriate level of ability.*

This criterion is not only a managerial concern, but a content decision as well. If the teacher's objective is ball-handling skills (more specifically, throwing and catching), then circle games in the elementary school, relay or squad formations in the high school, and many other so-called lead-up activities would not provide maximal potential for practice time. Most throwing and catching skill development requires practice by no more than one or two people.

Practice time is perhaps the single most critical element in the learning of a motor skill or the development of fitness. Maximal practice time can be obtained by identifying the minimal number of students in an organizational arrangement necessary to develop a psychomotor skill and then designing experiences using the smallest number of students possible. Maximizing practice time should be a primary concern in the design of a learning experience.

Interrelated variables. There are several valid reasons a teacher may choose to design a learning experience that does not maximize activity, including the following:

- Limited equipment or space
- Lack of independent working skills of students
- Need to limit the observational field to provide more accurate feedback
- A primary objective that is intended to develop social interactive skills

Limited equipment and limited space for an activity are valid reasons for restricting practice time if the activity is deemed critical to a program and no alternative organizational arrangements or equipment is available. However, in many instances, teachers who value maximal participation can find alternatives.

Another valid reason a teacher may choose not to maximize practice time is the students' inability to work independent of direct teacher supervision and to remain active at the same time. Unfortunately, this is often used as a cop-out for a teacher's failure to help students work in a more self-paced manner. Nevertheless, when all students are not active at the same time, the experience becomes more structured and may be easier for some teachers to handle. A word of caution: idle students are a primary cause of behavior problems in a gymnasium, and many times arrangements that decrease activity also increase management problems.

The third reason a teacher may not want to maximize practice time is so that the teacher can minimize the observational field (i.e., what the teacher must attend to) to provide more accurate feedback. If only a few students are moving at a time, the teacher can attend to those students better and therefore provide more accurate feedback. This situation also causes students to be performers in front of their peers. Teachers should carefully consider whether students are advanced enough to be affected positively rather than negatively by performance in front of others.

Criterion Three

The third criterion for learning experience design is that *the learning experience must be appropriate for the experiential level of all students.*

Students profit from a learning experience when it is appropriate to their level of ability. Students who cannot take weight on their hands can practice handstands for a full instructional period and still not be able to do a handstand. Teachers thus must design learning experiences that challenge students yet are within reach of all students in a class.

Error rate is a useful concept in determining whether the level of an experience is appropriate for students. If students are successful every time they try a movement, it can probably be assumed that the task is not challenging to the students. On the other hand, if students are never successful with a task, the task is probably beyond the ability of the students. In classroom research, an 80% success rate is deemed appropriate. For many physical education activities, a very high rate of success is probably appropriate for the teacher to aim for. In some activities, 80% success is too high (e.g., basketball free throw shooting). The teacher must consider the nature of the activity and what a skilled person would consider successful and then adjust this downward for a beginning learner.

The idea that students should be allowed to progress at their own rate is also included in the concept of appropriate level of ability. Even a task that is initially appropriate for all students quickly becomes inappropriate for everyone, simply because students learn at different rates (e.g., when learning a new skill, students initially may start at the same level of ability, but some learn more quickly than others). By moving on regardless of the needs of students who have not accomplished previous goals or by holding students back because other students are not ready, teachers make the task inappropriate for some students.

One of the most challenging teaching skills is to design a learning experience that permits each student to function at an appropriate level. This concept is sometimes called **individualization.** When individualization is taken to the point where the specific needs of each individual are considered in the design of an experience, this concept is often called **personalization.**

Criterion Four

The final criterion for a learning experience is that *the learning experience should have the potential to integrate psychomotor, affective, and cognitive educational goals whenever possible.*

Students are people, and each person functions as a whole. In one sense it is impossible to perform an intended motor skill without an affective or cognitive component, since people feel, think, act, and relate at all times in some way. People tend to repeat those activities at which they are successful and to avoid those at which they are not. The goals of physical education cannot be attained unless students are ultimately successful at what they are asked to do.

Physical educators also share affective and cognitive concerns for development with all other curricular programs. Students should be developing positive self-concepts. They should be learning how to relate to others in positive ways, how to exercise good judgment when making decisions, how to learn, how to express feelings, how to set personal goals and work toward their completion, and how to function in a democratically oriented society. Probably many more affective and cognitive goals should be part of this list. What is important here is to recognize that a physical educator must be concerned with more than the development of physical skills.

In physical education, the teacher's unique purpose is psychomotor development, but experiences can be designed to contribute to all areas of development without lessening the psychomotor intent. The following examples illustrate this point:

Psychomotor experience only. The teacher tells students to work on moving under a volleyball to get height on the hit.

Cognitive and psychomotor experience. The teacher asks students to find out what they have to do to get a high arch on a volleyball hit.

Affective, cognitive, and psychomotor experience. The teacher asks students to observe each other hitting and to decide together what must be done to get a high arch on the ball.

The last experience in this series is a richer experience than the other two because it involves students in affective and cognitive, as well as psychomotor, ways. Teachers do not want to and cannot make everything they do with students a rich experience. Nevertheless, the total learning experience should reflect a concern for affective and cognitive development. Careful thought should be given to ways in which each task can be made richer in its potential to contribute to all phases of development.

■   ■   ■

These four criteria should serve as a guide for the teacher in selecting and designing appropriate learning experiences. Although the criteria are easy to state and define, they are very difficult to apply. As is shown in the next section, the teacher can actually manipulate different dimensions of the task to meet these criteria.

◆ DESIGNING THE MOVEMENT TASK

Movement tasks are the specific movement experiences that constitute learning experiences in physical education. Movement tasks are what students do that are related to the content. When students are involved in a movement task, they are involved in content with a specific intent and are organized in some way to engage in the task. There is a what, a why, and a how to a movement task. Teachers do not just say, "Go practice basketball dribbling." If the teacher does not describe how dribbling will be practiced in a group instructional setting and the intent of that practice, the experience lacks focus.

Movement tasks have a content dimension, a goal orientation, and an organizational dimension that provide the needed focus:

- *The content of the task* is the movement content with which the students are asked to work.
- The *goal orientation of the task* describes the qualitative, or goal, aspect of the movement experience.
- The *organization of the task* is concerned with arrangements of time, space, people, and equipment, all of which are designed to facilitate work on the task.

Consider the examples of movement tasks that are presented in Box 4-3.

In some lesson situations, organizational arrangements for tasks are implicit in a situation because of previous experiences or established procedures. They are always present in some form, whether they are implicit or made explicit by the teacher.

What is important to note here is that each of these dimensions of the task is a critical aspect of task design. As important parts of the task itself, they can be manipulated by the teacher to achieve different goals and different objectives.

Content Dimension of Movement Tasks

The content dimension of the movement task describes for the learner the substance of the task (e.g., pass the ball to a partner or play softball). The choice of content is primarily a curricular decision based on the unit of study and lesson objectives. Teachers decide on a progression of experiences that lead the learners from where they are to where the teachers want them to be with the content. Once these decisions are made, however, teachers must further decide (1) the amount of decision making students will have in the choice of content itself and (2) the affective and cognitive involvement of the learner in each task. Teachers rarely make these decisions for a whole lesson. Each task is a unique decision for the teacher.

Teachers select the content of a task because they think that having students experience that content is important to a learning goal. As stated in Chapter 1, if you have no goals, it really does not matter what tasks you provide learners. The selection of the content of a task is easier if the teacher's goals are clear. As a beginning teacher, the content you are to teach will probably be selected for you. In this case, you will have to determine the best task to use to develop that content with a given set of learners.

Most of the learning experiences teachers present will be related to learning motor skills. The teacher will select a skill to teach and then will develop a learning experience to improve learner performance in that skill. Sequencing content is dis-

cussed in Chapter 6 on content development. Designing learning experiences to meet other goals is also discussed in Chapter 6.

Goal-Setting Dimension of the Task

Goal setting involves communicating to the learner the intent of a task and student practice. Most teachers assume the intent, or purpose, is to "learn" a skill or concept, but learners cannot acquire proficiency in short periods of practice for one task. Instead, they acquire proficiency in stages. For instance, an initial goal for students in learning to field a ball might be just to get their body situated

---

BOX 4-3

Examples of Movement Tasks

Example 1

The student and a partner practice the overhead set. The student sees how long the ball can be kept going between the two partners at a high level. If the ball falls to a low level, the student catches it and starts again.

Content: Practice overhead set.

Goal orientation: Number of consecutive passes without losing control.

Organization: Practice with a partner (no other arrangements explicit).

Example 2

The students play three-on-three basketball without baskets. To score, the students catch the ball across the end line after a minimum of three passes. The students keep the passes quick and move to a space to receive a pass. Each group of six students uses one fourth of the court from the wall to the bleachers.

Content: Play three-on-three game with no baskets; pass and move to receive a pass.

Goal orientation: Use quick passes and move into a space to receive a pass.

Organization: Play in groups of six on one fourth of a basketball court using one ball per group.

in the proper fielding position. Later goals might involve the position of the glove or what to do after the ball is in the glove. Teachers can manipulate the goal orientation of tasks to assure success by setting short-term goals en route to proficiency.

Teachers often explain a skill and then have the students start to practice or work on a task without the benefit of a goal for practice. For example, assume that the teacher has worked on the toss in a tennis serve and has explained the critical cues involved in the tennis toss. To set a useful goal for practice, the teacher might say, "Toss the ball until you can get it to land in the same spot consistently." The practice then has purpose. Teacher goals can also be set for practice involving skills that do not have easily identifiable results or that do not result in movement responses that are the same for all students. For example, the teacher can say, "Practice the backward roll until you don't have to stop the movement to let your head come through" or "Find all the ways you can think of to balance using three parts of the body as a base." These tasks provide a goal rather than just an intent to move. It is also possible for goals to be both individualized and personalized for the student. When teachers individualize or personalize goals, they are accommodating individual differences in students. Goal setting helps learners focus their work and realistically evaluate their progress. Goal setting also helps the teacher with analysis, observation, and evaluation of student responses in preparation for a new task focus.

The goal orientation of the task cannot be assumed unless stated by the teacher. Teacher responsibilities include not only telling students what task to do but also informing them how to do the task and indicating the goal toward which the task contributes. Statements such as the following help by giving the learner a goal and a qualitative emphasis in practice:

- "Work to get the transitions smooth."
- "Stay at the dribble until you can bounce the ball five times without looking at it."
- "Don't worry about accuracy yet, but work toward getting a full swing and hard hit."

- "Stay with the toss until you get the ball to fall consistently in one spot."
- "Choose a specific goal for your practice today so that you can evaluate your work at the end of the period.

An intent for good performance is communicated in these tasks. The teacher is sharing the purposes for which the tasks are designed, which gives the learners a focus in their practice.

More specific and narrower focuses of tasks will make the goal orientation clearer. The refining task, which asks the learner to focus on but one or two aspects of the movement (e.g., "Make your body shape much clearer"), provides a clear goal for students when efficiency of performance is what the teacher has identified as most important. More specific and narrower focuses of this kind also sequence learning cues for students one at a time. Students, particularly beginning learners, cannot assimilate a lot of information about movement at one time. The teacher can sequence goals for performance so that major ideas of good performance can be handled first and then performance can be polished.

When students are ready to test the effectiveness of their performance, a task with an application focus provides a clear goal. Application tasks can be designed as self-testing experiences or competitive experiences against others. The following examples have been reworded to illustrate the design of an application task and to clarify the goal orientation:

- "See how long it takes you before you can get your roll so smooth that you don't have to stop to let your head through."
- "Work until you can hit the ball 7 out of 10 times in the same spot without losing control."
- "Count how many ways you can find to balance on three parts of your body."

A warning: There is a danger in designing tasks of a self-testing nature too soon. The student focus is taken off the quality of movement in highly competitive tasks, even those of a self-testing nature. Beginning tasks should help the learner focus on the intent of the whole movement and not just on the effectiveness of it.

Tasks that involve group responses, such as

"Design an aerobic dance sequence in groups of four students," also should have a clear goal. In this instance the teacher should establish how students are to work, what a good sequence would look like, and what good group work would look like.

◆ ORGANIZATIONAL ARRANGEMENTS FOR TASKS

In group instruction, teachers must make decisions about the following:

- Whether students will work on a task alone or with a partner or group
- Where students will work on the task
- What equipment they will use
- How long they will practice

These decisions are organizational in nature. They arrange the environment for the content of the task. How the teacher arranges the environment is important, not only to the content of the movement task itself, but also to the potential of that experience to contribute positively to other program goals and objectives. Environment arrangements are instructional arrangements for people, time, equipment, and space. Sometimes these arrangements are explicit in a task, and sometimes they are implicit. They should always be purposefully designed. The teacher arranges people, time, space, and equipment to accomplish specific objectives. Teachers should not underestimate the importance of environmental arrangements in the facilitation of learning. Hough et al. (1975) define instruction as "the process of arranging human, material, and temporal resources with the intent of facilitating one's own learning of others." It is obvious that arranging environments for learning and instruction is part of if not the same process.

Arranging People

In physical education, arrangements for people include decisions concerned with the number of students in a group, the number of students active within each group, and the criteria the teacher uses to group the students.

Group size. Group size and opportunity for learning are integrally related. It is often useful to consider the following categories when determining how students are functioning within a class:

- Individual
- Partner
- Small group (3 to 6)
- Large group (7 or more)
- Whole class

In each of the units just mentioned, one student or all students within a single group can be active. For example, relays are usually a small group activity, but only one student is active at a time. The game of keep-it-up in volleyball is a small group activity with all students active.

Teachers should base the decision of how many students to include in a group primarily on the answer to the question, "How many students are necessary to engage in this task?" Some skills or experiences require more than one or two people to a group (e.g., offensive and defensive game experience cannot be gained by working alone). However, many teachers group students into larger units than necessary to practice a task. As a result, students are forced to share equipment and wait for turns. Sometimes limited space or equipment forces teachers to have less than total activity. Sometimes students who cannot respond productively in a total activity environment need to be arranged in organizational formats that allow for greater teacher monitoring. And sometimes teachers will want to give students roles in a group other than being physically active, such as observing. Again, it should be stressed that teachers should seek out alternatives to inactivity and work toward an environment that permits all students to be active.

Criteria for grouping. Criteria for grouping determine the basis on which students are put in groups. Unfortunately, most physical educators group primarily by chance, using no criteria. Grouping is a powerful tool that a teacher can use to influence the learning process, yet students are still chosen for teams by first selecting captains and letting the captains battle it out for the best and worst players.

Consider the situation in which 25 students are in

class at five different levels of ability in a particular activity. Assume that the unit is a basketball unit and that the students at levels one and two are ready for a five-on-five game using regulation rules. The students at levels four and five are able to handle only very modified situations. The class is coed, with no more than the usual number of social antagonists in the group. How would you handle this situation?

Level of Ability	Number of Students
One *(High)*	5
Two	5
Three	5
Four	5
Five *(Low)*	5

The immediate response of most beginning teachers to this situation is to create five teams with one student from each ability level. The first criterion for a learning experience, as described at the beginning of this chapter, is that the experience be appropriate for the student. Grouping five different ability levels on one team, regardless of game design, makes the experience inappropriate for a majority of students. The rationale given for such a decision is usually that the less-skilled players will learn from the more-skilled players. The students most likely will learn, but probably not much about basketball. It is sometimes desirable for students with greater skill to be placed in situations where they have to adapt to the abilities of less-skilled students. And in some situations, students with less abilty profit from being with students with more ability. However, in this situation, being criticized for not passing the ball to someone who loses possession every time is probably an unpleasant learning situation for even the most cooperative student. What are the alternatives? How can this situation be handled?

Although research findings are mixed on the value of ability grouping, this criterion remains one of the most desirable for skill acquisition. Teachers can ability group for the same or different tasks. Teachers can leave the choice to students, or they can make it themselves. Students will tend to ability group themselves when given the choice. Unless the students'

choice is socially nonproductive, teachers should strongly consider this alternative. Heterogeneous (mixed ability level) grouping can work well, especially in peer teaching situations and cooperative learning (see Chapter 9). However, teachers should avoid as much as possible the continuous use of heterogeneous groups for competitive situations in which the range of different skill abilities is great. Other alternative criteria for grouping may include the following:

- *Gender.* Grouping by gender is not a desirable choice in today's culture and should be avoided under most circumstances unless contact activities are involved.
- *Ethnicity.* If ethnic problems or an ethnic imbalance occurs in a class, serious consideration should be given to having ethnically balanced groups that are preestablished by the teacher.
- *Interest.* When alternative tasks are to be presented, teachers should seriously consider allowing students to choose tasks by interest.
- *Social compatibility.* Many times teachers have to separate students who cannot work together productively and regroup them for productive social relationships.
- *Size.* It is sometimes important for students to work with others of equal or unequal size. Support activities and combative activities are examples of when consideration should be given to size. It is sometimes advisable to use size as a criterion for grouping when height is a decided advantage or disadvantage.
- *Chance.* Sometimes it makes no difference how students are grouped. Clever teachers have found many ways to create random groups other than the time-consuming "count-off" method. Some of these include grouping by colors of clothing, birthdays, or colors of eyes. If teachers want to produce an experience that allows students to work with others with whom they ordinarily might not choose to work, chance may provide a good criterion for grouping.

Arranging Time

The time aspect of task design concerns the length of time students will spend in practicing a task and the responsibility for pacing responses to the task. Time is an important aspect of structure and can be used by the teacher to create more productive learning environments.

Task time.   Few teachers, even experienced ones, can predict beforehand exactly how much time students will need to work on a movement task before shifting the focus of the task. In some teaching strategies (see Chapter 9), the teacher must make this decision ahead of time. Having to make this decision in advance makes time allocation more difficult, particularly because there is no good way to anticipate how much time students will need or can spend productively before the teacher must refocus students.

The decision of when to refocus students on a new task or when to change the task is based largely on what the teacher sees happening with student responses. *Teachers should not let practice deteriorate into unproductive responses.* There is a limit to both the physical capabilities permitting continued practice and the interest of even the most motivated student. However, sufficient time must be provided for a student to gain some consistency of response. Many effective teachers will stop work short of deteriorating responses and provide a short transition period to focus on evaluation. This evaluation may result in continuing the same task or switching to a new focus using the same material.

Pacing responses to tasks.   When tasks are student paced, the teacher gives a task and the students begin and end a task in their own time. When tasks are teacher paced, students begin and usually end each movement on a teacher signal. Sometimes signals are verbal, and sometimes a whistle, drum, or clap of the hands is used. Teachers who count out exercises or cue or walk students through the practice of a skill are presenting tasks in a teacher-paced manner. When a task is teacher paced, all students are performing the task at the same time and in the same rhythm. Deciding whether a task is to be student paced or teacher paced should be determined by the type of skill the teacher wants the student to develop (open or closed) and the level of difficulty of the task. Teacher pacing of

tasks may be more appropriate to skills that are more closed in nature.

When teachers pace the task, they can select appropriate cues, and students are more likely to be "with" the teacher and not off task. Teacher pacing allows the teacher to attend to the speed and other dynamics of the movement. For many years, teachers of dance have practiced the use of teacher voice and rhythm instruments to assure proper dynamics in a response. Teachers of bowling who walk students through the cues "push out, swing back, bend, and release" are teacher pacing the initial practice of the skill. Some excellent teachers of sports skills have helped students' first attempts at skills by communicating the rhythm and dynamics of the skill through teacher voice and pacing.

Teacher pacing can help the student remember the sequence of cues used for a skill, because the student is using the cues immediately and not waiting until all the information has been given. Retention of cues can help the student form an accurate motor plan when teacher pacing is removed. Teacher pacing at the early stages of a complex skill may be of some benefit, particularly if the skill is a closed skill. However, teacher pacing for open skills destroys the desirable quality of unpredictability and should be removed quickly if used at all (Singer, 1980).

Arranging Space

The arrangements teachers make for the use of space are important and can determine whether the intent and potential of a task can be fulfilled. These arrangements are determined in part by the answers to the following questions:

- What area is going to be defined as the practice area?
- How is the practice area to be partitioned for students?
- What organization of people in the space will be used?

Defining the practice area.   Teachers must initially define the area of the field or gymnasium that will be considered the practice area. Teachers who neglect to establish clear practice areas probably will need to recall students from remote areas of a play-

Organization of people and equipment can facilitate learning.

ing field or from the side of the gymnasiums, where the students are leaning against walls or hanging on apparatus.

Practice areas can be defined with natural boundaries or with the help of markers of some sort. The selection of a work area is dictated largely by the nature of the movement content. Some skills need a great deal of space, and some need less space. Striking activities, when control is a problem, are better practiced against a wall when inside, because ball retrieval and safety are strong considerations.

How much space teachers allow for tasks in many cases determines both the way in which the task can be performed and its safety. In manipulative skills, the skill requirements for force production and absorption are determined largely by the size of the space. If a student and a partner have one quarter of a tennis court for their striking work with paddles, their practice of forehand striking skills will be far different from if they have a whole court. Volleyball is a different game when played on a regulation court from when played on a smaller, modified court.

Experienced teachers of young children learn

another space consideration, but they somehow forget to share it with beginning teachers: that is, large open spaces are disconcerting to the very young child. Sometimes a large gymnasium is very scary. Partitioning that space into smaller spaces until children feel secure in that environment is sometimes necessary. Psychologically, the smaller space makes the individual feel more secure. It also helps the teacher establish a more productive group learning environment, since group membership is more keenly felt in the smaller space. Chairs, traffic cones, or boxes are useful to divide space when large barriers are not available.

Partitioning practice areas. Partitioning practice areas involves deciding how to break up the play area for the use of students. The teacher's inclination is either to reduce the amount of space available to each student so that all may be active or to reduce the space and minimize the force or speed used in some activities. Sometimes, however, it is necessary to give students some opportunity to experience the effects of a larger space on their movement. This is particularly true in game areas, where force production and redirection are crucial. It should be considered also in dance and gymnastics tasks. The challenge is to allow some students the opportunity to use larger spaces and at the same time provide meaningful tasks for those who do not have use of the larger space.

The size of the space also is an important organizational decision, because teachers can manipulate the size of the space to reduce or extend the complexity or difficulty of a task, either for the class or for individuals. The need for large space must be balanced with the need for maximal activity. I once observed a high school floor hockey class of 40 students in which 12 students were playing and 28 were sitting out. The value of that experience for any of the students was indeed questionable.

Organizing people in space. The organization of people in space concerns the spatial formation of people in the play area. Figure 4-1 describes some of the more popular arrangements for people. The present emphasis on maximal participation in physical education classes has made the use of lines, squads, and circles of people less popular than it once was. Much time was lost getting people into these formations, and many of these formations were used to restrict the number of people active at any one time.

The scattered formation is a useful organizational arrangement of people when all individuals are going to be active at one time and when the task does not require other spatial arrangements. Telling students to quickly find a place to work readies students for activity without extensive time spent in organization; also, it uses all the play area available. Having other students around them, all working at the same time, is probably less confusing to the students than it is for the teacher. The scattered formation also eliminates the situation where one student watches another perform. This can be an asset when working with beginning learners.

The problem with the scattered formation is that the teacher cannot observe students as easily as in formal formations. Students can get "lost" in the crowd easily unless teachers circulate and make it a point to be aware of the total group. At times, teach-

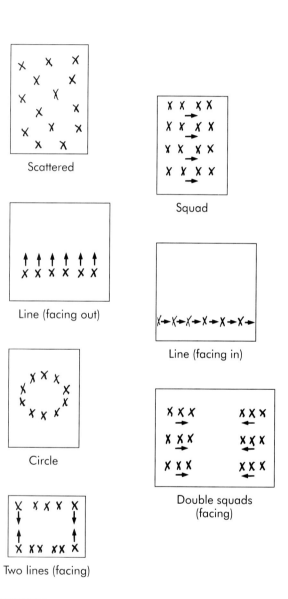

FIGURE 4-1

Organizational arrangements of people in space.

ers will want students in more formal organizations. Task presentations that are teacher paced (e.g., dance steps) are more successful if everyone is facing the same direction. The practice of striking or throwing skills, either with partners or against a wall, is safer if missed balls do not interfere with other students. Teachers will want to consider front-facing lines for these activities.

Group games usually have their own organizational formats. Teachers are cautioned to be alert in selecting games that have high rates of student activity. Highly organized formations for skill practice usually require much time to get students organized and often are unnecessary for the skills practiced. It is not uncommon to see a teacher take 7 minutes to get students into a practice situation that lasts 3 minutes.

Arranging Equipment

Procurement and arrangement of equipment are also critical determinants in the potential ability of motor task to accomplish its objectives. For most situations, particularly in the games and sports areas, it is ideal to have one piece of equipment for each student or, in the case of specialized equipment, for every two students. Teachers should try to avoid a situation where the arrangements for people and space are dictated by the amount of equipment available. Very few children in an ordinary classroom share texts, papers, or pencils. They should not be expected to share equipment when one piece of equipment for each learner is appropriate.

Included in decisions about equipment is determining whether to provide all students with exactly the same equipment (e.g., the same size, weight, or shape ball, the same rhythm instruments in dance, the same arrangements of apparatus, the same height net). As with decisions regarding space, the arrangement of equipment can change or modify the tasks. Higher nets in volleyball encourage getting under the ball to play it; lower nets make the spike more attainable for shorter or less-skilled players. Some combinations of gymnastics apparatus encourage traveling in one direction, whereas other combinations of equipment encourage a change in direction. The size

and weight of manipulative equipment can often determine whether younger and less-skilled students can be successful in performing a skill in an efficient way. Nothing is sacred about regulation-size equipment. If the equipment needs to be modified, teachers should seriously consider modifying it, even on an individual basis. The choice and arrangement of equipment is not just an organizational detail, but a critical factor of task design.

◆ STUDENT DECISION MAKING IN ENVIRONMENTAL ARRANGEMENTS

A critical concern in the design of movement tasks is the amount of student involvement in the learning process. Students can often be part of the decision-making process when environmental factors are discussed. They may make decisions for themselves or may be helped to make a group decision. Consider the possibilities that are presented in Box 4-4 for stu-

---

BOX 4-4

Possibilities for Student Choice Relating to Environmental Arrangements of Tasks

People

Who to work with
How to choose who to work with
How many to work with

Time

When to start a movement
How much time to spend on a selected task before moving to a new task

Space

Where to work
How much space to work in
Where the boundaries are to be placed

Equipment

What kind of equipment to use
How to arrange the equipment
What adjustments to make to the equipment

dent choice relating to environmental arrangements of a task.

When teachers make all the decisions relative to environmental arrangements, task content, and criteria for performance, the task is highly teacher structured. When teachers begin to share these decisions with students, tasks become less teacher structured. Many beginning teachers assume that task structure is an all-or-nothing proposition. This is not true. Teachers need to learn to add and remove structure as needed in particular learning experiences.

Although it is true that some students cannot and perhaps will not ever work productively in more unstructured environments, the concept of structure does not solely depend on the developed independent learning skills of students. Any learners inexperienced in an area of work will need more structure until a repertoire of correct responses for a situation can be developed. Appropriate decision making is a skill with carryover value from one area of work in the gymnasium to another. However, it is not independent of experience with the content.

The following example illustrates the importance of environmental arrangements in task design.

Example: A teacher of third grade students has worked with students extensively in the games area. During one of her class periods, she has students choose their own partners, move to an area of the gymnasium, choose a ball from within a range of choices, and work on a task involving throwing and catching. The students are able to work in this area without the need for long organizational periods during which they get partners or equipment. The teacher finds it unnecessary to use lines or more formal arrangements for the use of space. However, during next class period, the teacher introduces some work in creative dance. The teacher introduces the idea of pathways in space with different body parts. She explains what a pathway is and sends the students off into their own space to practice. The students do not work productively. Within a few seconds, very little work is taking place that can be described as productive.

The teacher's problem in the second class period is one of structure. The task was a new one to the students and very different from any experiences the students had encountered before. The students did not have a complete enough idea of appropriate responses to the task to be able to work independently with the content. The students in this situation could have profited from some initial experiences in which the teacher did the following:

- Choose the body part to be used
- Paced the task with verbal cues or instrument support
- Limited movement to personal space

The teacher could have then gradually removed aspects of the structure before encouraging students to work independently with the task.

The question of whether to highly structure tasks or whether to encourage student decision making is again a curricular decision. Students involved in the process are more likely to learn more than just psychomotor skills than those who are uninvolved in the process. When arrangements show some flexibility, they can potentially be made more appropriate for individuals. Some evidence exists that highly structured, teacher-dominated environments may be more efficient in producing more narrowly defined learning (Good, 1979). Highly structured environments will generally involve much time spent in organizational kinds of behaviors.

Teachers should operate at all points on this continuum, depending on what is appropriate for their objectives. The need for structure depends on the student's competence and confidence with the task and independent learning skills. Students should not be placed in unstructured environments unless they can work productively in those environments. Students learn few skills in decision making when allowed to drift aimlessly in undirected freedom. If students cannot direct themselves, teachers should add structure and very gradually remove that structure as students are capable of handling a less-structured environment. Teaching decision making and student independence implies a gradual development of these skills.

SUMMARY

1. Skillfulness in motor activity can be described in terms of the effectiveness of performance, the efficiency of performance, and the adaptive nature of performance.

2. Effective performance accomplishes its goal. Performance is efficient if the action is performed in a mechanically correct form for a given performer and situation. The quality of adaptation is the ability of the performer to adjust to conditions surrounding performance.

3. The motor skill content of physical education can be divided into the categories of closed skills, closed skills in differing environments, and open skills.

   - Closed skills are those in which the environment in which the skill is performed stays the same during performance. Practice conditions and the manner in which the movement is performed should be the same each time.

   - Closed skills in differing environments are performed in predictable environments, but the environment may change from one performance to another. Closed skills in differing environments are practiced in the least difficult environment first, and then opportunities are provided to teach learners to adapt to different environments.

   - Open skills are performed in environments that are changing during performance. Practice conditions must build complexity and variability of conditions.

4. A learning experience is a set of instructional conditions and events that gives structure to student experience and is related to a particular set of teacher objectives.

5. Four criteria should act as an initial screen in the design of learning experiences: the learning experience must have the potential to improve the motor performance of students; it must provide maximal activity or practice time for all stu-

dents; it must be appropriate for the experiential level of all students; and it must have the potential to integrate psychomotor, affective, and cognitive educational goals whenever possible.

6. The movement task is what teachers ask students to do that is movement content.

7. Movement tasks have three components: a content dimension (the movement content of the task); a goal orientation (the expected goal of practice or performance); and an organizational dimension (the conditions under which the content will be experienced).

8. Students can be involved in the choice of content. Tasks that provide for little student choice in content are called **limited tasks.** As more student choice is made possible, tasks become more unlimited. The teacher's choice of content and student ability largely dictate how and when tasks can be made more unlimited.

9. Affective involvement of students in a movement task is developed through both the design of the task and the appropriateness of the task for the individual learner. A positive effect is achieved through competence and confidence with the content and the social and emotional involvement of the learner in the task itself.

10. The goal-setting component of the task involves communicating the short-term intent of student practice and should be built into every task.

11. Environmental arrangements are the instructional arrangements for people, time, equipment, and space. Environmental arrangements are purposefully designed to accomplish specific learning outcomes.

12. The arrangements for people include the number of students in a group, the number of students active within a group, and the criteria for grouping.

13. The time aspect of task design has two considerations: how the task will be paced (teacher paced or student paced) and how much time is allowed for a task before a change in the focus is made.

14. Spatial arrangements include defining the play area and organizing people in the defined play area.
15. Equipment arrangements include decisions concerning how much equipment to provide students, what kind of equipment to use, and how to arrange the equipment.
16. When teachers make all the decisions relative to environmental arrangements and content, the task is highly structured. When students are permitted to make some of the decisions, the task is less structured. Deciding when to add and remove structure is part of the decision-making process in teaching.

CHECKING YOUR UNDERSTANDING

1. Describe the effectiveness, efficiency, and adaptability aspects of skillfulness for the basketball lay-up shot or the tennis forehand.
2. Develop a list of 20 physical education skills and classify each as either closed skill, closed skill in different environment, or open skill.
3. What guidelines should a teacher follow when teaching closed skills? Open skills? Closed skills in different environments?
4. For each of the four criteria for a learning experience, give an example and a nonexample from a physical education setting.
5. Write a sequence of related movement tasks for the development of a motor skill. For each task, label the content, organizational dimensions, and goal orientation of the task. When organizational dimensions are implicit in the experience, indicate in brackets what they are.
6. List five tasks in the same content area that move from minimal student content choice to maximal student content choice.
7. Four different ways to involve students in content decisions were presented. List each and provide an example using the same content area.
8. List four affective objectives you might have for a physical education lesson. For each objective, design a movement task that potentially could contribute to the objective.

9. Design a four-on-four basketball experience that includes one of the following concepts: the ability to encourage a teammate in a positive fashion, the ability to settle disputes over calls in a rational way, the ability to win or lose graciously, or the ability to use the ability of all members of the team.
10. On what basis do teachers decide how many students should be in a group?
11. What are the advantages and disadvantages of grouping by skill level?
12. How do teachers decide when to move on to the next task?
13. What is the difference between student-paced responses to tasks and teacher-paced responses? What are the advantages and disadvantages of each?
14. How can the spatial arrangements of a task influence student responses to the task?
15. What are the advantages and disadvantages of the scattered formation? Give an example of movement tasks that might appropriately use lines, circles, facing lines, and double squads as the organization of people in space.
16. On what basis do teachers make the decision to modify equipment?
17. What decisions can students make in the organizational arrangements of an experience? What criterion does the teacher use to transfer these decisions to students?

REFERENCES

Bain L: Status of curriculum theory in physical education, *J Phys Ed Recr* 49(3):25-26, 1978.

Barrett K: Games teaching: adaptable skills, versatile players, *J Phys Ed Recr* 47(7):21-24, 1977.

Good T: Teacher effectiveness in the elementary school, *J Teacher Ed* 30(2):52-54, 1979.

Hough JB et al: *What is instruction?* Draft Paper 1. Unpublished manuscript, The Ohio State University, Faculty of Curriculum and Foundations, 1975.

Kneer M, editor: *Basic stuff series,* National Association for Sport and Physical Education, Reston, Va, 1981, American Alliance for Health, Physical Education, Recreation, and Dance.

Logsdon B et al: *Physical education for children: a focus on the teaching process,* Philadelphia, 1984, Lea & Febiger.

Merrill DM, editor: *Instructional design: readings,* Englewood Cliffs, NJ, 1971, Prentice-Hall.

Poulton EC: On prediction in skilled movement, *Psychological Bulletin* 54:467-478, 1978.

Singer R: *Motor learning and human performance,* ed 3, New York, 1980, Macmillan Publishing.

Singer RN: *The learning of motor skills,* New York, 1982, Macmillan Publishing.

SUGGESTED READINGS

Allen D: *Joy, pleasure, and satisfaction in moving: affective consideration in curriculum design.* Paper presented at the American Alliance for Health, Physical Education, Recreation, and Dance National Convention, Houston, April 26, 1982.

Carr NP, editor: *Basic stuff, Series II,* Reston, VA, 1987, AAHPERD Publications.

Falls H, Baylor A, Dishman R: *Essentials of fitness,* Philadelphia, 1980, WB Saunders.

Getchell B: *Physical fitness: a way of life.* New York, 1983, John Wiley & Sons.

Hough JB: An observation system for the analysis of classroom instruction. In Amidon E, Hugh J, editors: *Interaction analysis: theory research and application,* Reading, Mass, 1967, Addison-Wesley Publishing.

Mauldon E, Redfern H: *Games teaching: a new approach for the primary school,* London, 1969, Macdonald & Evans.

Seidel B et al: *Sports skills: a conceptual approach to meaningful movmement,* Dubuque, Iowa, 1980, Wm C Brown Publishers.

Thorpe R, Bunker D: Landmarks in our way to teaching for understanding. In *Rethinking games teaching,* Loughborough, 1986, University of Technology.

Werner P: Teaching games: a tactical perspective, *J Phys Ed Recr Dance*, March, 97-101, 1989.

Task Presentation

OVERVIEW

Most learning experiences are delivered to the learner via the presentation of tasks for student engagement with the content. The movement task asks the learner to engage motorically with the content. One of the most important skills a teacher can develop is the ability to present movement tasks to learners in a way that facilitates the formation of an accurate motor plan and motivates students to want to engage in the task. The purpose of this chapter is to discuss the qualities of a good task presentation. Although managerial and organizational issues relative to task presentation are discussed, a major part of the chapter is devoted to developing clear task presentations and selecting and organizing learning cues. Learning cues are considered a major factor in determining the initial success of the learner with the content.

CONCEPTS

- **Getting the attention of the learner**
  Noisy, distracting environments
  Student preoccupation with other
    environmental factors
  Inability to hear or see
  Inefficient use of time

- **Improving the clarity of communication**

- **Choosing a way to communicate**
  Verbal communication
  Demonstration
  Media materials

- **Selecting and organizing learning cues**
  Accuracy of cues
  Critical nature of cues and brevity
  Appropriateness of cues to learner's
    age and stage of learning
  Selection of cues for different kinds
    of content
  Organization of learning cues for
    learners

- **Separating the content and organizational aspects of tasks**

EVERYONE has had opportunities to observe or attend a class in which the teacher was able to elicit good student performance. With good teaching, students are engaged at a high level with the content and are performing skillfully in a very short time. Likewise, most people have experienced a class in which the teacher muffed the task presentation and spent the rest of the time correcting communication errors. Sometimes learners do not know what to do because they are not listening, but most of the time students do not know what to do because the teacher is not selective or clear enough in presenting the tasks. When it comes to movement tasks, communication is the name of the game. The ability to present clear tasks that have the potential to facilitate learning requires preparation and practice.

Regardless of the type of content inherent in a task, the presentation of a task is always an exercise in communication. On some occasions, teachers can merely name or quickly describe what they want learners to do and simply assume that the learners have had experience with tasks that call for similar responses. In most teaching, however, this assumption cannot be made. This chapter, therefore, pays special attention to ideas that relate to the presentation of tasks having some aspect of unfamiliarity to the student. In Box 5-1 (below) is an example of a task presentation.

BOX 5-1

Example of Task Presentation

Liz is beginning a unit in striking with paddles with her fourth grade students. When the students walk into the gymnasium, they immediately spy the paddles separated into several piles and spaced throughout the gym. They immediately want to know if they are "going to get to do that today."

Liz has the students gather in the center of the gymnasium as a normal procedure. When the last child has sat down, Liz, in a normal tone of voice, says, "May I have your attention." She waits a few seconds for everybody's eyes to be on her and begins.

"Today we are going to start a unit on striking with paddles. We will be working on this unit for the next few weeks. What sports do you know that use rackets? *(Students give some examples)*.

I have a video tape prepared that shows different sports that use rackets. When the sports are shown, I am going to stop the tape and see how many you can recognize.

(Teacher shows prepared video tape of tennis, racquetball, badminton, deck tennis, and squash and leads the students to identify the name of the sport.) How many of you have ever played these sports before? Which ones do you think you would like?

All of these sports require that you have some control of the paddle and the object—you must make the object go where you want it to go. We are going to start today to get some control of these paddles and foam balls.

When I say 'go,' I would like for you to pick up a ball and paddle at one of the locations around the gym—find a space you can work in—and show me you are ready to begin. GO. *(Students complete organizational task.)*

When I say to start practicing, we are going to try to bounce the ball down in our own space. *(Teacher demonstrates bouncing the ball down, attending to keeping a forward stride position, bent knees, and flat racket face in the demonstration.)* What you are trying to do is to maintain enough control of the ball so that you don't have to travel out of your own space and so that you can keep the ball going. *(Teacher demonstrates what 'out of control' is.)* Who can show me what control means? *(Teacher asks a student to demonstrate the task.)* Okay, that was pretty good control—the ball kept going, and you didn't have to move too far out of your own space. Everyone stand up and see if you can keep your ball in control in your own space, tapping it downward."

◆ GETTING THE ATTENTION OF THE LEARNER

It seems almost unnecessary to point out that students must be attentive to benefit from any task presentation. Unfortunately, throughout the gymnasiums of this country, teachers are trying to communicate by talking over or outshouting students in an environment that is not supportive of any kind of communication. The best task presentation in the world is worthless unless the teacher has the attention of the students.

Many conditions contribute to why students are not attentive when tasks are presented. Although the teacher may not have control over some of these conditions, the teacher *can* prevent many of the causes of inattention. The following section explores some of the reasons a teacher may not have student attention and discusses some ways a teacher can exert more control over student attention.

Noisy, Distracting Environments

Students cannot be attentive to teacher presentations if the environment is noisy or distracting. If the noise comes from the class itself, teachers should not try to compete. Shouting over a noisy class when the teacher has asked for attention may be effective once or perhaps even twice, but it quickly loses its effectiveness. A whistle is useful in large play areas but should not be relied on as a substitute for a learning environment that is not conducive to learning. Many teachers find that the whistle in smaller play areas is unnecessary and creates an undesired atmosphere. Students can be taught to respond to a signal or a teacher call for attention.

If you find that you are not easily getting the attention of your students, it may be that you need to take the time to establish a procedure or signal. You will need to make clear your intentions and practice with students responding to a signal until it is clear that the expectation is for quiet and attention. Teachers should not proceed until they have the attention of the students.

Distractions over which the teacher has less control are more difficult. In situations in which two classes are sharing a facility, workmen are changing light bulbs, dogs are on the field, or airplanes are fly-

ing overhead, the teacher must try to remove the distraction when possible and cope creatively when all else fails. One way in which teachers can minimize the effects of distractions is to bring the students into a smaller group, closer to the teacher, with the students facing away from the distraction. A teacher who says, "I know it's hard to listen when workers are up on the roof, but let's try," is also likely to be successful in soliciting student attention.

Student Preoccupation with Other Environmental Factors

Many times students are not attentive because their attention is engaged by other people or other articles in the environment. Teachers who work with young children have a hard time competing with objects the children may have in their hands (e.g., balls, ropes, bean bags) or with nearby equipment (e.g., mats, bars, nets). Teachers can set up class procedures to eliminate some of these problems by giving students something to do with the objects (e.g., telling the students to place the bean bag on the floor in front of them). When young children have had sufficient time to explore the qualities of these objects, the children can be expected to hold them without trying to get the beans out of the bean bag or picking at the foam of the ball.

Teachers can solve many attention problems by having children rest away from mats, equipment, and walls as a routine procedure. If students are not working with partners or as a group, they should not be resting near others. Standard procedures that teachers take time to structure and reinforce will eliminate many problems in the long run.

The attention of older students can be requested. Older students should be expected to be able to ignore distractions in the environment. If the teacher consistently holds the students' attention despite the influence of external factors, a strong chance exists that internal causes of inattention will be controlled as well.

Inability to Hear or See

Many times teachers do not have students' attention because the students cannot hear or see what is going on. Because of the time wasted, many teachers are reluctant to call students in from large play areas to some central point for a task presentation. This is acceptable in situations where all the students can hear, the material is brief, and the concepts with which the students are being asked to work are not new. However, if any of these conditions do *not* exist, teachers can save productive work time by calling students in to a smaller area so that the task can be properly communicated.

Another commonly occurring problem that teachers must address, particularly in outdoor settings, is that students' vision is impaired because of glare from the sun. Sometimes students will complain, but usually they will just struggle with limited vision. Teachers should always position students so that they are sitting with their back to the sun.

Inefficient Use of Time

Teachers may find that they have student attention initially and then gradually lose it. Many times this is because the learning experiences that teachers have designed fail to meet one or more of the criteria for a learning experience discussed in Chapter 4. Often attention wanes because teachers take 5 minutes to do what could be done in 1 minute or because teachers use verbal discourse rather than activity.

Teachers of young children must recognize that these children have short attention spans to begin with and even shorter attention spans in a gymnasium that invites activity. The secret to effective task presentation is brevity. Young children are motivated to move, and if teachers have much to communicate, they will have better results doing it through activity and short transitions between activity periods.

Older students' longer attention spans do not excuse inefficient task presentation. Older students will tolerate more inefficiency, but that does not mean they are attending. These students may not express their lack of interest overtly, but they will simply tune out the teacher. The amount of information, particularly new information, that people can attend to at any one time is very limited. Teachers of older students must spend more time in communicating material and in motivating students, but long verbal discourses are again to be avoided in favor of shorter, more frequent breaks in activity.

◆ IMPROVING THE CLARITY OF COMMUNICATION

A teacher has been clear when learner intent in responding to a task is the same as teacher intent. Many factors determine whether the students will do what the teacher expects them to do when they are requested to engage in a learning task. The teacher may have no control of some of these factors. In many cases the teacher can improve the probability that students will engage in the task appropriately if the task is presented with attention to the factors that we know improve attention and communication. The clarity of a presentation is often helped by using some of the following guidelines when presenting material.

Orient the Learner (Set Induction)

People feel more comfortable if they know in advance what they will be doing and, in some cases, why they will be doing it. Teachers should seriously consider giving learners information in advance on what they will be doing. This allows students to relate parts of lessons to a larger whole.

EXAMPLE: "Today we will be focusing our lesson on the transition from fielding the ball to throwing the ball. This will be important in game play so that you can make a smooth transition and quickly throw the ball where you want it to go. We will work first with a partner at a closer distance and then begin to increase the distance and add a target area to throw to."

Sequence the Presentation in Logical Order

Putting material in a logical order facilitates communication. Sometimes in physical education it is logical to present the most important part of an action first. Thus the teacher does not necessarily present the parts of the action in chronological sequence. Examples are (1) teaching the chorus in a folk dance first and (2) teaching the contact phase of a striking action first. Some teachers have been successful in presenting the major part of the action first (e.g., the takeoff and shot against the backboard for the basketball lay-up; the striking action without the

Personalize the Presentation

Referring to the experience of a student or to the experience of the teacher is helpful in communication. Phrases such as "When I tried to..." or "Johnny has had a lot of experience with..." help the learner identify with the material being presented. Teachers personalize in a lesson when they refer directly to the experiences of participants.

Repeat Things Difficult to Understand

Many teachers assume that students will understand material after it is explained just once. Repetition is useful, particularly repetition that takes a slightly different approach. Planned repetition of essential cues just before students begin work on a task is very helpful in effective communication. Repetition of significant information is important also after students have had an opportunity to try new skills or when skills are practiced on more than one day.

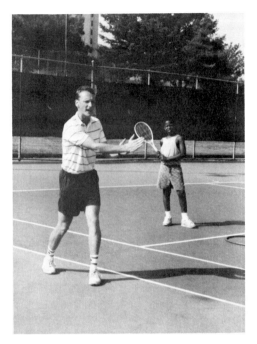

Teachers must decide whether they need to call students in to present a task.

Draw on the Personal Experience of Students

Showing students how the activity they are preparing to do is similar to or different from other skills they have learned can help students use the new information more effectively. "The floater serve is like the overhand throw pattern, except there is no follow-through" is an example of drawing on past experience. Transfer of learning is also facilitated through teacher attempts to bridge past experience and new experience, such as, "You remember that last week we worked on including techniques to improve upper arm strength in your warm-up routines. Today we are going to explore ways to develop abdominal strength so that we may add these exercises to your routines. The principles that govern how strength is developed will be the same."

back swing in tennis). This is called **backward chaining** and may be more logical and meaningful than beginning with preparatory aspects of skills. Usually, however, order is sequenced chronologically, with the beginning of a movement presented first.

Give Examples and Nonexamples

Many important ideas relating to movement, particularly the qualitative aspects of movement, are more fully understood when both examples and nonexamples are given. For instance, to know what a soft landing is, the learner needs to know what a hard landing is. Similarly, traveling is more fully understood in terms of what traveling is not, and full extension is more easily understood in terms of what full extension is not. The use of both examples and nonexamples in teaching such concepts is helpful.

Check for Understanding

Teachers need feedback from students regarding whether students have understood teacher instructions. Many teachers do not discover that students have not understood a set of instructions until the students try to act on the information they were given. Teachers can avoid wasting a great deal of time if, before the students begin work on a task, the teachers ask them questions to determine their understanding or ask them to demonstrate what they learned from the teacher's instructions. When teachers take the time to do this, they generally find that they were not communicating as well as they thought.

Present Material Dynamically

Voice inflection, nonverbal behavior, and timing can do much to enhance communication. Loudness contrasted with softness, high-pitched inflection contrasted with low-pitched inflection, and quick delivery contrasted with slow delivery will catch students' attention. Teachers need not be public speakers, but they should know how to use voice dynamics when needed to make communication clearer.

Box 5-2 summarizes the methods that are effective in improving communication.

◆ CHOOSING A WAY TO COMMUNICATE

A second critical aspect of task presentation is selecting a means of communication. Teachers may choose to present a task verbally or to use demonstration and/or other visual materials. Similarly, they may choose to communicate what is to be learned verbally or to guide the learner through the entire exercise or series of directed experiences. As with other instructional decisions, the characteristics of the learners and of the content must determine which method will be best.

Verbal Communication

If learners are experienced with a skill or activity and know its language label, verbal directions should be sufficient. Caution should be used, however, because teachers generally assume too much understanding on the part of a learner. Because of their own familiarity with the material, teachers who study movement terminology or who use the same terminology in five different class periods a day tend to assume that students understand after they have been

"told" something once or twice. Teachers often think they have done a good job of verbal communication, but they need only ask students what was meant by a communication (a check for understanding) to gain enormous insight into the difficulty of describing movement in abstract terms. It should be remem-

---

BOX 5-2

Improving Communication

Orient the learner (set induction)

Alert the learner to what he or she will be doing, how, and why.

Use a logical sequence

Present material in chronological order unless there is a good reason to do otherwise.

Use examples and nonexamples

Many concepts are best understood if the learner is helped to understand not only what the concept is, but what it is not.

Personalize the presentation

Use students' names and personal experiences of the teacher and students in the class.

Repeat things difficult to understand

Repetition of important ideas during the initial presentation, after students have had an opportunity to engage in the task, and when tasks are continued on other days improves clarity.

Draw on personal experience of learners

Bridge the gap from old experiences to new material by showing the learner how things relate; this improves communication and increases the potential for transfer.

Check for understanding

Ask students what you meant or ask students to demonstrate what they are trying to do.

Present material dynamically

Students are more attentive if voice inflection (volume, pitch, tone, speed of delivery) is not always the same.

The use of humor can create interest in a task.

bered that the younger the student, the more the student is functioning at a concrete level with regard to verbal material. Therefore a teacher will be less able to rely on verbal communication unaided by demonstration.

Demonstration

In physical education, visual communications most often take the form of demonstrations. Used in conjunction with verbal explanations, they provide the learner with two sources of information. A discussion of guidelines for the use of demonstration in physical education follows.

Accuracy. Students will attempt to reproduce the movement they see. No matter how much an important point is emphasized verbally, many students will attend primarily to the visual demonstration for information. The demonstration therefore should be accurate. Teachers tend to only partially go through the action of a movement skill or task or to demonstrate a skill out of the context in which the students will be using it. At some point, students

need to see the whole action performed at correct speed and in context. Students will also gain more accurate information from a demonstration if they see it performed at more than one angle.

Student demonstrations. If students are capable of demonstrating accurately, they should do so rather than the teacher unless the performance would put students in an undesirable situation with their peers. When students demonstrate, the teacher can focus the attention of the observers on important aspects of the performance.

Use of proper organizational format for practicing tasks. If the task to be practiced stipulates a specialized organizational format (e.g., standing across a net from a partner or working in groups of three), the demonstration should use the same organizational format that will be required in practice. Many teachers who give good skill demonstrations are still unsuccessful in getting students to understand what is expected because they have failed to include the organizational format for the practice of the task. Good task presentations use demonstrations to communicate both the skill and the organizational format of the practice.

Usefulness when creativity, problem solving, and expressiveness are task goals. Many teachers who set creative responses, expressiveness, or problem-solving processes as task goals are reluctant to use demonstration in presenting the task. They are concerned that if demonstration is used, the spontaneity of student response will be impaired. Indeed, spontaneity will be hurt if the teacher demonstrates only one response to a task and asks that it be copied or if a teacher presents a problem having only one solution and then demonstrates that solution. However, tasks that require expressiveness, creative responses, or solutions to movement problems can use demonstration successfully to communicate to the learners the *kind* of response expected. If a teacher wants expressiveness, the teacher needs to communicate the *concept* with which the students are to work by giving examples of responses within that concept. If a teacher asks students to solve a movement problem that has only one solution, the principle or idea with which the students are to work can be demonstrated. For example, the teacher could demonstrate a few examples of contrasting quick and slow movements with a partner.

Tasks that seek variety, expressiveness, or problem solving should not result in a student's futile search for what the assignment is. Beginning learners of all ages depend on visual cues. The need for demonstration should not be taken lightly. The need for accuracy of demonstration is critical. The clarity of a task is enhanced by demonstration and examples of the concept being developed. The teacher can encourage students to seek their own responses within a framework clearly understood by all.

Emphasis on important information about a skill. For students to get the most from a demonstration, the teacher must guide their observations. The critical aspects of a skill or task should be highlighted verbally and, if possible, visually through freezing the action at critical points or verbally overemphasizing important aspects of the skill. For example, if a teacher is going to teach a back handspring, three points should be emphasized before the actual execution of the movement: (1) starting in the sit position with a straight back, (2) subsequently losing balance backward, and (3) thrusting the arms and legs.

Provision of information on why a skill is performed a certain way. Some learners will be able to remember the visual and verbal cues of a skill better if they are provided with information regarding why a skill is performed in a certain way. The badminton serve, for instance, is performed with a low back swing and follow-through because the rule says that the shuttlecock cannot be contacted above the waist. The influence of a rule or the principles of movement efficiency on an action often help learners pay attention to important cues. This kind of information is useful but should not turn an efficient task presentation into a lecture on the skill. Information should be provided only where it is critical to understanding the skill.

Checking student understanding after a demonstration. Before teachers have students practice a skill, teachers should check the students' understanding of what they have observed. This can be done by asking questions after an observation or by asking students to demonstrate what they are trying to do. It can be done also by asking students to look for particularly important points during the observation and checking their understanding afterward.

Box 5-3 summarizes the qualities of a good demonstration.

Media Materials

Because the videocassette recorder (VCR) is standard equipment in most homes and is becoming a more essential part of the equipment of gymnasiums, teachers have access to a wide variety of visual media in their content area. These materials can be used to motivate students and give students a perspective on the "whole." Knowing what games look like when they are played well helps students to know what they are working toward and therefore makes practice more meaningful.

BOX 5-3

Qualities of a Good Demonstration

- Information is accurate.
- Demonstration is performed by student if possible.
- Teacher uses organizational format students will use for practice.
- Important information is emphasized.
- Information is provided on why a skill is performed in a certain way.
- Student understanding is checked.

An increasing supply of commercially produced pictures, films, charts, and loop films and video tapes also are available to physical educators. As visual aids to communicating a skill, these materials have the advantage of being professionally produced. In addition, the teacher has some assurance that the models provided are good ones. These materials can also be repeated in slow motion if desired. Such materials tend to motivate a television-age audience and allow the teacher to observe both the demonstration and the student response.

One disadvantage of using commercially produced visual materials that attempt to show how a skill is performed is that the materials may not be appropriate for the particular group of learners with whom a teacher is working. Material above or below a learner's ability may not be valuable. Much commercially produced material with dialogue gives learners more information than they need for one skill. The sound tracks of such material will probably be more valuable if they are not used in the initial presentation of a movement skill or idea but are saved until the learners can make better use of more specific information.

To use visual materials well, the teacher should preview these materials, use them for a specific purpose, and set up the equipment for their use in advance. Student time should not be consumed with teacher preparations. Teachers should not abandon their role as teachers to be projectionists. Setting up and taking down the equipment should occur outside

the instructional period. These materials are very useful instructional tools, and teachers should seriously consider using them and adapting their use to the specific needs of their learners.

◆ SELECTING AND ORGANIZING LEARNING CUES

A third aspect of task presentation is the teacher's selection and organization of learning cues. A **learning cue** is a word or phrase that identifies and communicates to a performer the critical features of a movement skill or task. If the teacher is going to teach the floater serve to a volleyball class who has learned the regular overhead serve, the following information might be useful in helping the students understand the skill:

- The action of the floater serve starts like the regular overhead serve.
- Contact is made with an open hand straight through the ball.
- The action used is a punching action with little or no follow-through.

Each point would be considered a critical feature of the skill. Teachers can facilitate the cognitive process needed to establish an accurate motor plan for a skill by determining critical features of that skill and selecting a learning cue that can be used to represent that critical feature (Box 5-4).

In designing the learning cues for the smash, the teacher decided that the "get set" cue could be taught as a package. Actually, the first four critical features have to do with the "get set" position, which can be practiced apart from the execution and follow through.

Selecting good cues is important for all learners, but is absolutely essential for the beginning learner. This is because motor performance and cognition are interdependent, especially in the early stages of learning.

Good cues have several characteristics. They are (1) accurate, (2) critical to the task being presented, (3) few in number, and (4) appropriate to the learner's age and stage of learning. Cues presented to learners should be reduced to key words and orga-

---

BOX 5-4

Learning Cue

Definition

A word or phrase that efficiently communicates as much information about a critical feature as possible.

Example
Critical features of a tennis overhead smash

- Position yourself where the ball will be coming down (the ball should be in front and slightly to the right)
- Bend your knees
- Position the racket head behind you at about head level
- Shift your weight to the back foot
- Point your hand or finger at the ball
- Swing the racket upward and forward with an extended arm at contact

Learning cue for critical features

- Get set
- Point and shift
- Swing up and forward

---

nized with the specific learner in mind. What the teacher focuses the learner on is critical and largely determines the ability of the task to elicit the desired outcome.

Accuracy of Cues

Teachers must know their subject matter to select accurate cues. What the teacher focuses the learner on can make the difference between student success and student failure in performance. Physical educators are often called on to teach activities with which they have no experience. Resources are available to help familiarize teachers with almost any activity they may be asked to teach. If you will make a list of the critical features of a skill from a textbook, you will then be able to reduce those critical features to important learning cues. Many inexperienced teachers remain ignorant because they fail to consult appropriate resources and prepare themselves to teach the lesson.

A research team at the University of South Carolina asked four different physical education specialists to teach jumping and landing skills to one of their second grade classes. The ability of the students was tested before and after six lessons taught by each teacher. Only one of the four teachers had accurately identified the learning cues for the skills involved. The performance of the students reflected this accuracy. The more effective teacher had used reference material to correctly identify what was important in the skill being taught (Werner and Rink, 1989).

The ability to select critical cues that are accurate and can elicit the desired response from students is developed through preparation and practice. With experience, teachers will become selective in choosing critical cues for a movement skill or concept.

Critical Nature of Cues and Brevity

Learners cannot use a great deal of information on the specifics of a movement response. The cues the teacher selects should be chosen because they are critical to the performance. For the overhand serve, the following description might be written by a beginning teacher:

- The performer stands in an open stride position with his or her side to the intended direction of the object being thrown. The foot forward should be opposite to the throwing arm.
- The back swing of the throw is initiated by rotating back at the hips and shoulders. The arm movement is led with the elbow, which is about shoulder level. The hand drops back at the close of the back swing as the weight is transferred to the back foot.
- The forward motion of the throw is initiated with an elbow lead and trunk rotation forward. The momentum of the throw is released sequentially through the shoulder, elbow, and wrist with a quick, sudden action leading to weight transfer onto the forward foot and a follow-through in front of the body.

How much do students need to know? It is obvious that few students initially would gain much from all that information. It would be better to assume the ready position for the skill and then select only three cues for the action as follows:

1. "Keep your elbow high and lean forward."
2. "Step to the opposite foot."
3. "Put your hand out and snap on throw."

Selecting critical cues is important to giving learners good, accurate pictures of what they are trying to do. One teacher asked an 8-year-old to tell the rest of the class how to throw a ball. The youngster replied, "I just l-e-a-n back and let 'er fly." Physical educators might all take a lesson from that child.

For complex skills, some cues are especially important. Most of the time these cues involve locating the body in space at critical points in the action. The stance, the back swing, and the follow-through are usually critical points for manipulative tasks. Breaking down most body actions into preparation, execution, and follow-through helps divide actions into manageable parts. Picture these three phases for the cartwheel, bowling, and the forward roll.

Words that help students understand the type of action desired (e.g., snap, punch, push, press) often are useful in designing cues. Sometimes these words are referred to as **summary cues** because they are single words that capture a quality or critical feature of the movement. These types of words give the learner a description of the time quality (e.g., quick or sustained) and weight quality (e.g., strong or light) of the action. In skills such as the basketball lay-up, it is important to know that the ball is *placed* up to the basket and not *thrown* up. Striking activities are primarily quick actions requiring muscular tension just before contact. In sports such as field hockey, some actions are hits (with a back swing) and some are pushes (no back swing). In gymnastics, a walkover is a continuous application of force, whereas a round-off is an explosive action. Cues that describe the action can help the learner get a more accurate picture of what to do.

The selection of cues is just as critical for task presentations that use an environmental design approach.

EXAMPLES:

- The teacher is teaching the overhand throw pattern and has decided to use a high target and the cue "hit the wall above the line as hard as you can" without giving the learners any more information on how the overhand throw is performed.
- The teacher has decided to encourage students to get under the ball when using a volleyball overhead pass by having them set the ball into a basket or large hoop placed at least 10 feet high. The teacher uses the cue "get the ball into the basket," with full knowledge that to be successful, the student must get under the ball.

In these examples the cues do not focus the learner on how to do the movement. Rather, the learner's attention is focused on the intent of the movement, under the assumption that to be effective, the learner must also do the skill correctly.

Appropriateness of Cues to Learner's Skill Level and Age

Selecting cues to present to learners involves making judgments about the ages and levels of ability of the learners. Both of these learner characteristics significantly affect the kinds of cues selected and the manner in which they are communicated.

Skill level of the learner. Although most young learners are beginners, some are not; although some older students are advanced, most are not. Thus teachers in physical education will be working primarily with beginners in their classes. As learners become more proficient in their movement skills, they can profit from a different kind of learning cue. Teachers must learn to adjust their cues to the proficiency levels of the learner.

Beginning learners. Beginning learners are at a cognitive stage of learning a motor skill. The intent in selecting cues is to give the learner the "whole idea" of the skill or the "gross action" of the skill in as few words as possible. It is not until after the learner has had some experience with the skill that he or she can use more specific information on how to do it. In one sense, that is why environmental design for many skills is effective for the beginning learner. Too much analysis destroys the response. Demonstration at this level is also critical to communicate the whole idea.

Advanced learners. Once learners have passed the initial cognitive stage of learning, they move into the associative stage. At this stage they are expected to be able to concentrate on more specific aspects of the skill. However, the details, like the original cues, should be kept selective and ordered by importance. As always, the cues should be appropriate for the level of proficiency of the learner. When working with more advanced learners, teachers should avoid the temptation of trying to correct at once everything that is wrong. It should be remembered that even an advanced learner cannot attend to large numbers of cues at one time. With the advanced learner, process-oriented cues are used rather than "gross framework" cues, but the cues must be limited in number all the same.

Age of the learner. Students of different ages have different learning characteristics that should be considered in the selection and organization of learning cues. Although great differences exist between individual students of the same age, recognizing the age characteristics of learners in terms of their ability to profit from different kinds of cues can guide the teacher's efforts.

Young learners. Two problems should be remembered when working with young learners. The first is that they have less movement experience to bring to a new skill and therefore cannot call up large chains of previously established motor responses. It is possible that a young learner will be putting together most of the parts of a complex chain for the first time instead of just combining them in a new way, as an older learner would. The second problem associated with young learners is their undeveloped verbal skills. Most of the terms used in physical education textbooks to analyze skills have little meaning for young learners. The abstract nature of most language used for movement description is not appropriate for learners functioning at very concrete levels of abstraction.

Cue selection for young learners at the beginning stages in learning a skill, particularly a complex skill, can take several forms. It should be remembered that young learners are adept at mimic behavior; they are able to reproduce whole actions with surprising accuracy merely by seeing the action. Therefore demonstrations that are accurate and overemphasize the critical cues often are useful. Freezing a movement at its critical points to create a visual picture also is very helpful.

A second strategy useful with young learners is focusing the learner initially on the whole action and what it should produce, rather than presenting a process analysis of what is happening in the action. Teachers who want to emphasize getting power in a jump can focus learners on "jumping as high as you can" rather than on "bending at the hips and knees and ankles and using the arms to drive up to full extension." Another way to elicit the jump might be to use the cue "jump to a complete stretch in the air." The cues used in these examples help the learner to form a visual picture of the whole action.

Environmental design is particularly useful for the young learner. Responses can be elicited by creating an environment requiring the correct response. Overhand throwing patterns are better elicited using the cue "throw as hard as you can" in conjunction with a high target placed just within maximal throwing distance of the student. Tight forward rolls are elicited by short spaces between equipment or by the cue "roll as slowly as you can."

Young learners can focus on refining cues after experience with the gross action. At this point, the whole response does not need their attention and they are able to attend to more specific cues in future performance. If students are still not performing the gross action with consistency, the teacher must go back and find cues that will communicate to learners the intent of the task. If some consistency in performance has been attained, the teacher can move on to focus the learners on what is happening in different aspects of performance to refine the learner's response. However, the number of cues given to the learner must always be few, accurate, and at a next stage in refinement. Observation of many effective teachers with young children has shown that the focus of follow-up refining tasks is very narrow.

Older learners. Many times older learners already have an idea of their ability to succeed or fail with a task based on their past performance with the same or a related task. If the learner has not been successful with the task in the past, motivation to learn it again in the present may be decreased. Additionally, movement responses needed for successful performance may have been learned and practiced incorrectly for a long time. Changing established patterns is very difficult.

However, older learners have increased ability to profit from verbal communication. Many words meaningless to young learners may be used with older learners. An older learner can call up chains of motor responses without paying attention to every aspect of the response. Previous experiences with similar motor responses help the older learner select the right cues from a movement environment.

Many teachers continue to "overload" the information-processing system, particularly of older learners, by presenting far too many cues to performance. The phrase "paralysis by analysis" rings true here. A useful exercise for teachers is to reduce the number of initial cues they present to a maximum of four and then see if they can list which cues they think are going to be needed at higher levels of task refinement. Older learners in many school situations may not have acquired fundamental ability; therefore the teacher cannot count on these being present. For students who have not been successful in the past, the teacher must take care to design tasks that assure success in a reasonable amount of time. Although it is possible to learn even rather complex skills through a completely random process of trial and error, one job of the teacher is to shorten the time it takes to learn. Teachers can do this if they select cues wisely and attend to the limited information-processing abilities of students. Older learners have different problems and different resources, but a beginning learner, whether young or old, is still a beginning learner. Many of the approaches described previously for the younger learner are appropriate for an older learner who is a beginner.

Selection of Cues for Different Kinds of Content

The type of learning cues used by the teacher should vary with the kind of content being presented

and the specific task. Content may be a closed skill, an open skill, or a movement concept. When establishing progressions for each of these content areas, the teacher will use a variety of tasks requiring different kinds of cues. Three types of cues are presented in Box 5-5.

These three types of cues are largely representative of the different kinds of motor content we teach in physical education. Discussion of cues for closed skills, open skills, and movement concepts follows.

Cues for closed skills. Most people's mental image of teaching physical education is usually that of a teacher explaining and/or demonstrating a movement to be reproduced by the learner. The teacher's role in such situations is to translate movement into verbal and visual pictures for the learner in ways that organize cues and facilitate the student's development of a motor plan. The student's role is to reproduce the desired response.

BOX 5-5

Cues for Different Kinds of Content

Cue for the response

Gives the learner information on the process of the movement.
Task: Chest pass to a stationary partner.
Example: Place your feet in a forward stride position.

Cue for adjustment of the response

Gives the learner information on how to adjust a movement response to a different condition.
Task: Dribbling a basketball against a defensive player.
Example: When being closely guarded, keep the dribble close to your body.

Cue for the use of a response

Gives the learner information on how to use a movement in a particular situation.
Task: Passing a basketball to a player on the move against defense.
Example: Pass the ball ahead of the moving receiver; get rid of the ball quickly; pass the ball from the level at which it is received.

The selection of cues for closed skills consists largely of cues for the response that create visual pictures of the critical elements of the skill. When working with closed skills, many effective teachers demonstrate a movement by freezing critical spatial aspects of the movement and drawing attention to body-space relationships and to the movement processes that move the body from one position to the next. The phrase "scratch your back" is an effective cue, used to describe the position of the racket head before the forward swing in the tennis serve.

Teachers can facilitate the accurate reproduction of closed skills by vividly sequencing the action of the skill with a few descriptive terms. If the teacher can use these cues in a way that also communicates the dynamic qualities of the movement (including the rhythmic quality of the movement), the motor plan of the student is likely to be more accurate. An example of rhythmic sequences is the cue "hand-hand-foot-foot" used for the cartwheel. Many skills can be sequenced rhythmically to provide another dimension that adds accuracy to the learner's motor plan.

Cues for open skills. The specific kind of response for an open skill changes with the environment in which the skill is performed (e.g., dribbling a soccer ball is never quite the same in all conditions). Most teachers begin by teaching an open skill in a closed way. Teachers will often reduce the complexity of the environment for the beginning learner almost to the point of that necessary in practicing a closed skill (e.g., demonstrating how a skill will be performed without using the ball; practicing batting using a batting tee; practicing a lay-up shot from the same spot without any interference). When practice of an open skill approximates closed skill practice, cues can be similar to those given for closed skills. However, practice should not remain in closed skill conditions for a long period of time.

When an open skill is practiced in a changing environment, the type of cues needed changes from cues about the performance of the response itself to cues concerned with adjusting the response to meet changes in the environment. The cues used should

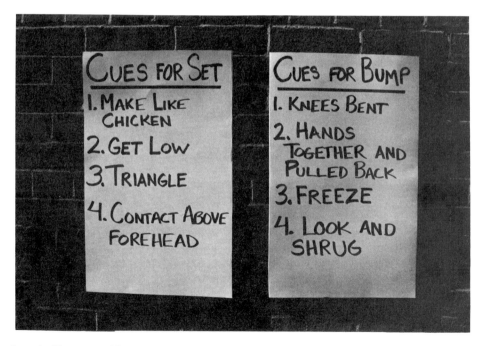

Cues facilitate cognitive understanding of a skill. (Photo by Michael Gelfand-Grant.)

reflect the specific environmental conditions to which the learner is being introduced.

EXAMPLE: The throw pattern in a baseball game changes according to how the throw needs to be made, how quickly the throw needs to be made, and the direction of the throw relative to receiving the ball.

As each of the conditions just mentioned are introduced, the learner should be focused on how to appropriately make the change in the throw pattern to be successful.

Critical to open skills are cues that are primarily perceptual in nature—cues that guide the learner not in the performance of the movement action itself, but in the appropriate selection of an action for the given situation. The ability to perform the action required as an appropriate response is assumed by the time learners get to complex environments.

The changes in the type of cue that becomes useful in complex environments are illustrated in Table 5-1, which describes the development of the basketball dribble through four stages of skill development.

If the cues used for the sample task provided are studied, a change from cues for how to execute the dribble to cues for how to use the dribble in increasingly complex game situations can be seen.

The information learners receive in the form of cues should be the content of teacher feedback to learners on their performance. If teachers must continually focus students on cues more appropriate to earlier stages of skill development, the lesson they are currently teaching may be too difficult. In such cases, it would be wise to return to earlier stages of skill development.

EXAMPLE: If students are playing two-on-two in basketball and the teacher's feedback is still on how to execute the dribble or how to execute the pass, students are probably not ready for two-on-two basketball. The cues for two-on-two basketball should primarily involve strategies and what to do in offensive and defensive relationships.

Cues for movement concepts. The kinds of tasks presented in the development of movement concepts are so varied that precise guidelines are dif-

TABLE 5-1   Changes in the appropriateness of cues for the basketball dribble

Stages in games play development	Sample task	Appropriate cues
One	Dribble the ball at different levels in your own space. Travel with the ball in different directions.	Use pads of fingers and push ball down to produce force. Change contact point on ball to produce different directions.
Two	Dribble the ball to a wall, pass it, receive it, and continue dribbling to a new wall; stay moving the whole time.	Pass at an angle to a wall to lead the ball so that it can be received on the move. Make smooth transitions between dribbling and passing, passing and receiving, and receiving and dribbling.
Three	Play one-on-one offense against defense with offense dribbling and defense trying to touch the ball.	Keep body between ball and the receiver. Change hands. Maintain eye contact with the defense.
Four	Play four-on-four full court basketball.	Do not dribble if a teammate is open ahead. Use the dribble to allow a teammate to get open.

ficult to specify. Two common types of tasks used in developing concepts are illustrated in Box 5-6.

When teachers ask students to choose a response within a concept, they usually attach limitations to the students' choices. These limitations serve as cues to guide the students in selecting appropriate responses. In the examples given for choosing a response, the limitation in the first task is "three parts of your body." In the second task the limitation is "changing your direction." The limitations that the learner must attend to as cues when selecting a sequence must be few in number. It is not uncommon to hear elementary physical education teachers ask students to change their level, direction, and speed as they travel. Students, even adults, cannot attend to this number of cues.

When teachers ask students to apply principles to a movement response or to discover principles from their movement responses, cues should function to give the learner a strategy for solving the problem. In the examples given for applying a concept, the teacher has asked students to focus on the transfer of weight from the back foot to the front foot in the tennis forehand. A useful cue for the students might be to "focus on where your weight is after you have finished your swing." In the second task, a useful strategy for designing a defense might be to "try placing your defensive players at different spots under the goal."

In both examples it is necessary for students to know the concept words being used before being asked to work with them. Ideas such as balance, travel, weight, and strategy for defense must be clearly defined.

Organization of Learning Cues for Learners

Students are more likely to be able to use cues if the cues are organized sequentially for them. Complex tasks that require more description are presented more clearly if the teacher takes as a cue a descriptive phrase, reduces it to a single word, and then sequences the cue words for the learner. When teachers do this, they are using summary cues. The following examples of the sequencing of summary cues for different kinds of tasks illustrate their use:

> *Bowling:* "push away-extend-swing back"
> *Rising and sinking:* "rise turning-sink twisting"
> *Traveling and balancing:* "travel-balance-travel"
> *Floater serve:* "toss-back-extend-stop"

The use of summary cues allows the learner to practice the order of complex skills without having to remember lengthy descriptions of how each phase of the movement should be done. Most teachers learn through trial and error which words are most effective in eliciting desired movement responses from students. Perhaps someday, experienced and effective teachers can share in more formal ways what has worked for them. Meanwhile, inexperienced teachers should spend time preparing and designing word cues for students and putting them into a summary sequence.

A teacher trying to get young children to achieve flight off a piece of apparatus and land with a soft landing might have several alternative word cues. Initially, the teacher might consider action words such as "jump" and "land." These words sequence

---

BOX 5-6

Common Tasks Used in Developing Concepts

Choose a movement response within a concept
Example tasks

- Balance on three parts of your body.
- Travel in different ways changing direction.
- Design three exercises for developing hamstring flexibility.

Problem solving to determine movement principles
Example tasks

- Where should the weight be when you finish the forehand stroke?
- Design a strategy for defending the goal rather than the player.
- Determine the best stance for a ready position in a sport.
- Determine where to contact a ball to put different kinds of spin on the ball.

the action, but they do not cue the leader to the *quality* of the movement desired. Alternative cues to "jump" and "land" are "spring-extend-squash." These cues, put in sequence, communicate a great deal more.

Summary cues do several things for learners and the teacher. They highlight the significant aspects of a movement, which helps learners remember and form visual pictures of what they are trying to do. They sequence actions for learners and can also provide a rhythmic cue if chosen carefully and expressed dynamically. Summary cues can serve also as observation cues for the teacher and establish a common language for teacher feedback.

Summary cues summarize information that was presented to the learner at another time. The cues are effective only if they are meaningful to the learner and have the same meaning for both learner and teacher.

◆ SEQUENCING THE CONTENT AND ORGANIZATIONAL ASPECTS OF TASKS

How the teacher orders the content and organizational aspects of the task can determine how successful the student response to the task will be. The presentation of tasks usually involves information concerning (1) what task is to be performed (including the goal orientation) and (2) the organizational arrangements for the way the task will be practiced. Teachers have a tendency to mix these two types of information in their task presentations. This is confusing for the students. Task clarity is enhanced if these two kinds of information are not confused in the presentation.

EXAMPLE: A PROBLEM TASK PRESENTATION: "Today we are going to work on fielding ground balls. We are going to work with partners. When you field a ground ball, you have to make sure that you get your body behind the ball in the proper position. If the ball gets by you, it is going to go over that hill over there."

In this example the teacher started with identifying the skill to be practiced and then gave the organi-

zational arrangements. As soon as the idea of partners was introduced, it is likely that only a few students heard anything else. At that point they would be either shuffling around to find a partner or trying to anticipate how the teacher was going to choose partners.

When tasks have an involved management component, teachers may need to separate the management aspect of the task from the content aspect of the task. Beginning teachers and teachers working for the first time with students should not expect students to be able to handle too much too soon. Teachers can structure a complex task by giving the *management directions* first and waiting until the students have complied before giving the *content dimension* of the task, as in the example below:

- "We are going to work with partners and a ball. When I say 'go' I want you to sit next to a partner in a good work space." *The teacher waits until students have a partner and are listening.*
- "One of you will walk over and get a ball and sit back down with your partner." *The teacher waits until students have complied with the organizational task.*
- "We are going to work on passing a ball to a moving receiver...."

With time, many groups of students can handle both organizational tasks simultaneously. If they cannot, the teacher must break down the organizational tasks. Organizational directions do not always have to be given before the content is explained. Separating organizational directions from the content part of a task presentation is useful if students will anticipate that they will have a choice of partner or equipment.

If the organization for practice is critical to how the task is performed, the organizational arrangements should be described and be part of the demonstration. For example, if the teacher pairs a student with a student partner, with one student on one side of the volleyball net and the other on the other side, and asks him or her to toss the ball over the net to the partner, who will try to set it back to the tosser, the student will need to know that the ball is coming over the net from a toss. Few groups of learners can handle having the organizational aspects and content aspects of tasks mixed in the teacher's presentation.

In tasks that involve an extensive management dimension (e.g., getting in groups of three, selecting a ball, and working on passing the ball while moving continuously), the management aspect (getting in groups and selecting a ball) will usually need to be preceded by the cue "When I say go,...." to prevent students from beginning the organizational dimension of the task before they have fully comprehended the content dimension. The value of signals or cues to begin should not be underestimated, even with older learners. Teachers' descriptions of what to do are often communicated in language associated with an expected response, but teachers do not want that response until they are finished giving their instructions. Young children and people with whom teachers have not worked previously in a learning situation may not be sure when a response is expected. Alerting learners to the idea that a signal will be given ("When I say go,....") and using signals ("Go!") makes intention clearer.

When new material is being presented, the directive "Now go and do this" usually involves a summary of the explanation (e.g., "When you get your ball, take it to a wall and begin striking it to the wall with at least four different parts of your body."). The assumption is that the specific details of the skill have already been explained. Thus the teacher is simply summarizing the directive. This summary is necessary and many times is used in conjunction with the type of summary cues mentioned earlier in this chapter. The summary helps fix in the students' minds exactly what they will be working on and the order in which the parts of the task will be performed. The summary should also include the goal orientation of the task. Teachers who want to check the students' understanding of directives should ask the students what they are going to work on.

Box 5-7 provides the teacher a checklist of the characteristics of a good task presentation. Good teachers cannot always be as clear as they want to be. However, with practice, teachers can make clarity in task presentation a part of their teaching repertoire.

BOX 5-7

Teacher Checklist for Task Presentation

1. Do I have the *attention* of the students?
2. Have I included a *set induction* for the beginning of the class?
3. Is my presentation *sequenced in logical order*?
4. Have I presented both *examples and nonexamples*?
5. Have I *personalized* my remarks?
6. Have I *repeated* things that are difficult to understand?
7. Have I related new material to *previous experience*?
8. Have I *checked for student understanding*?
9. Is my presentation *dynamic*?
10. Does my *demonstration*:
    Reflect accuracy?
    Utilize students?
    Use proper organizational aspects of practice?
    Emphasize important information?
    Provide information on why a skill is performed a certain way?
11. If I am using *media*, have I *prepared in advance*?
12. Are my *learning cues*:
    Accurate?
    Appropriate for the content?
    Appropriate for the age and ability of the learner?
    Condensed to effective word cues?
    Summarized and sequenced?
13. Have I *separated the organization and content* aspects of my presentation?

SUMMARY

1. Students must be attentive if they are to profit from a task presentation.
2. Clarity of communication is assisted by attending to the factors that aid communication between people.
3. Verbal communication, demonstration, and the use of media materials are the most common forms of

task communication. Each has its advantages and should be used with attention to guidelines for its effectiveness.

4. Critical features of a skill are selected to be the most important information on how to do a skill.

5. A learning cue is a word or phrase given to a performer that identifies and communicates the critical feature of a movement skill or task. Good cues are accurate, critical to the task being presented, few in number, and appropriate to both the age of the learner and the stage of learning.

6. Cues that sequence the action and communicate not only the action but also the movement quality of the action assist the learner in developing a more accurate plan for the task.

7. Organizational aspects of a task should be separated from the content dimensions of a task.

REFERENCE

Werner P, Rink J: Case studies of teacher effectiveness in physical education, *J Teaching Phys Ed* 4:280-297, 1989.

SUGGESTED READINGS

Briggs LJ, editor: *Instructional design*, Englewood Cliffs, NJ, 1977, Prentice-Hall.

Landers DM: How, when, and where to use demonstrations, *J Phys Ed Recr* 49(1):65-67, 1978.

Levin T, Long R: *Effective instruction*, Washington, DC, 1981, Association for Supervision and Curriculum Development.

Rink J, Werner P: Qualitative measures of teaching performance scale (QMPTS). In Darst P, Zakrajsek D, Mancini V, editors: *Analyzing physical education and sport instruction*, ed 2, Champaign, IL, 1989, Human Kinetics Publishers.

CHECKING YOUR UNDERSTANDING

1. What are some major causes of student inattention? How can the teacher best prevent inattention?

2. What are some things teachers can do to improve communication with learners in task presentation?

3. What are guidelines for using demonstration effectively?

4. What are the advantages and disadvantages of media materials?

5. What are the characteristics of good learning cues? Design a set of learning cues you would use with young beginning learners for a closed skill, open skill, and movement concept. Design a set of learning cues you could use for an older advanced learner using the same skills as above.

6. What focus can be used if young students doing a vertical jump are not getting adequate flexion, are not using their arms as much as they could, and are not getting full extension? Why would this focus be effective?

7. What are organizational signals? Where are they most necessary in a physical education class?

Content Analysis and Development

❖ ❖ ❖ ❖ ❖ ❖ ❖ ❖ ❖ ❖

OVERVIEW

One characteristic that distinguishes the expert from the novice teacher is the ability of the expert to relate and transform the content for the learner. To do this, the teacher needs a knowledge of the content and a knowledge of general pedagogical skills, but the teacher also needs a knowledge of how to actually best teach particular content. This is called content pedagogical knowledge (Shulman, 1987), and this work emphasizes the critical role that content and knowing how to best teach content plays in the teaching/learning process. This chapter establishes skills in content analysis and development as essential content pedagogical skills of the teacher.

❖ ❖ ❖ ❖ ❖ ❖ ❖ ❖ ❖ ❖

CONCEPTS

- **Planning for content development: the developmental analysis**
  Extension
  Application
  Refinement

- **Guidelines for developing different kinds of content**
  Developing closed skills
  Developing closed skills performed
    in different environments
  Developing open skills
  Developing movement concepts

O NE of the essential content pedagogical skills is the ability of the teacher to break down the content and sequence it into appropriate learning experiences. Chapter 1 establishes the movement task and the student response to that task as the primary interactive unit in physical education classes; Chapter 5 describes how tasks can be presented to learners. However, movement tasks are not delivered unrelated to each other. Teachers use progressions of tasks to lead the learner from beginning levels to more advanced levels with the content. Teachers establish progressions of content based on their instructional objectives, their knowledge of the nature of content and ability to analyze that content, and their assessment of student needs in relation to the content. *Sequencing movement tasks in a manner that has the potential to facilitate learning is the*

nature of content development. Consider the scenario presented in Box 6-1.

You will notice that in this lesson there are many movement task–student response units. You will also notice that the tasks used in this lesson have some relationship to each other. The actual lesson content is taught through a process that takes the learner from one level of performance to another level of performance through a carefully designed sequence of tasks. This process is called *content development.* The way in which teachers develop content can best be described in terms of teacher content moves from the beginning of a lesson to the end of a lesson. Good content development has the following characteristics:

It sequences learning experiences from simple to complex or from easy to hard.

BOX 6-1

Sequencing Movement Tasks in Softball Lesson

Fred is a third grade physical education teacher who is beginning a unit on softball and will focus the lesson on fielding skills. After he orients his class to the day's lesson, Fred presents the following task to the group:

"Stand about 20 feet from your partner and slowly roll the ball to your partner. Show me what you think would be the best way to field the ball and roll it back."

After the students have had sufficient time to try different ways, Fred calls the group back in and asks for volunteers to resolve the problem. Several students who have played Little League baseball identify a standard fielding position. Fred remarks that these students have had some experience in baseball and thanks them for their demonstration. He asks the class, "Why do you think this is the best way?" and students respond that it prevents balls from going through the legs.

Fred presents appropriate cues for the fielding position and then has the entire class practice the appropriate position without the ball. He then asks them

to quickly move up to a "pretend ball" and get in position on his command; then he asks the students to do it in their own time.

Fred notices that although many of the students are getting their body into position, many of them are neglecting to get their glove down on the ground. He stops the class and says, "You are doing a super job of getting your body into position; now let's focus on getting that glove all the way down." He demonstrates the skill again, emphasizing in the demonstration getting his glove down.

Fred follows these initial experiences with the following tasks:

"Send the ball to your partner's right or left so that he has to move a few steps."

"What is the best way to move your feet to get to you right or left quickly? Let's work on that."

"When you feel that you are ready, move back a few steps from your partner so that the ball can come a little fast."

"See how many you and your partner can field in a minute without letting the ball get past you."

It focuses the learner on achieving good performance.

It provides opportunities to apply skills.

- **Establish a progression (extension)**

Sequencing learning experiences from simple to complex or from easy to hard is sometimes called **progression**. Teachers start at a less difficult or less complex point and gradually add complexity and difficulty. Sometimes the teacher does not add difficulty or complexity. Sometimes the teacher must reduce complexity even more. A few of the ideas Fred used in the lesson described in Box 6-1 follow:

From no ball to ball

From close distance to far distance

From a ball coming directly to the receiver to one in which the receiver had to move

From no emphasis on speed to an emphasis on speed

This development of content is called **intratask** development because the skill or task the teacher was working on was the same task. Fred was merely sequencing the conditions of the task. Sometimes teachers change tasks altogether in a lesson that includes more than one skill, such as fielding and batting. This kind of development is called **intertask** development because the skills or tasks are different. Teachers actually establish lessons, units, and yearly program plans based on their knowledge of both intertask and intratask development. The actual tasks that manipulate the level of complexity or difficulty to previous tasks are called **extension tasks**.

- **Demonstrate a concern for quality of performance (refinement)**

The second characteristic of good teacher development of motor skills content is the communication to students of a concern for the quality of student performance. Concern for quality of student performance can be exhibited by teacher feedback to the class or individual students about how they are performing. It is also exhibited very clearly by teachers when they stop student practice and focus students on achieving particular movement qualities. When Fred called the class in because he observed that the students were not getting their glove on the ground to field the ground balls and when he focused the class to go off and practice getting the glove on the ground, he was demonstrating a concern for quality. He was refining performance. These types of tasks will be known as **refining tasks.** The following are other examples of refining tasks:

"Now work to get your landing as soft as you can."

"Make sure your weight is transferred to that forward foot after your stroke."

Refining tasks can have a powerful impact on student performance when the teacher keeps the focus of improvement narrow and when students are held accountable for actually working within the focus of the refining task. Accountability in this case means that if the teacher does not see students working with the focus of the task, the teacher calls the students in once more and reemphasizes that focus.

- **Give students an opportunity to apply their skills (application)**

The third characteristic of good content development involves the way in which teachers integrate opportunities for students to apply their skills. In most skill learning, students are asked to focus their attention on how they are moving. This is the efficiency component of motor skills. Although the teacher may be interested in good form, students are largely interested in doing something with a movement. Eventually, students will be asked to apply their skills to experiences in which they will be focused on factors other than how they are moving. This is the effectiveness component of motor skills. A competitive game, for instance, focuses on the goal of the game (i.e., how to score—not how to move to score). Dance experiences focus on the expression of the movement.

Effective progressions provide opportunities for students to use their developing skills in application experiences throughout the development of their skills. Teachers do not wait until all the skills of basketball are "learned" and then have the students play a full game of basketball. The teachers include basketball-like game and self-testing experiences throughout skill learning.

Students can test their skill effectiveness at almost any stage of the progression if the application experiences use the level of skills that students have learned and not more advanced skills. We will call tasks that provide students with opportunities to apply their skills **application tasks**. In our example lesson, Fred used an application task when he asked the students to see how many times they could field the ball in a minute without letting the ball get by them. Beginning basketball dribblers can test their ability to keep the ball going without losing control or their ability to keep the ball from their partner. The skill is not being used in the basketball game, but it is being applied. Application experiences are added when students are both confident and competent with a particular level of a skill.

In an actual lesson the teacher's development of content can be seen through an analysis of the kind of tasks that are presented. The development of content is achieved through the integration of all three of the teacher moves just described: (1) extension—the gradual progression of difficulty and complexity; (2) refinement—a concern for the quality of student performance; and (3) application—the integration of application experiences. Together, the three teacher moves constitute the progression through which the teacher develops the content. They have been labeled and defined for discussion purposes as follows:

- **Extension**. A teacher move that communicates a concern for changing the complexity or difficulty of student performance.
- **Refinement**. A teacher move that communicates a concern for the quality of student performance.
- **Application**. A teacher move that communicates a concern for moving the student focus from how to do the movement to how to use the movement.

Although all teacher content behaviors contribute to these processes, the movement task the teacher gives the student (e.g., "Bounce the ball 10 consecu-tive times in the same spot without moving" or "Today we are going to play softball") is the most obvious and most critical way in which progression is established. Figure 6-1 illustrates a progression of tasks for a study done at the University of South Carolina on a middle school volleyball unit (Rink, 1985). Each of the points on the graph represent a new task the teacher has presented. The tasks are graphed according to their type. The only term in this progression not yet discussed is **informing**, which is the teacher's first introduction of a new skill and therefore not a progressive intratask move. An informing task is the initial task in a sequence for a lesson. The figure describes how three different teachers developed the content of their volleyball unit through movement tasks over the first 4 days of the unit. It should be clear that the development used by Teacher A was much more gradual, which means that students practiced the overhead set in many more different conditions than Teacher C. Teacher A also used application and refining tasks throughout the progression.

Content development is important. At a very general level, it is a measure of the clarity of teacher goals and an intent to teach for student learning. It distinguishes the intent to merely provide activity for students and the intent for students to learn. At a more specific level, it is a measure of the teacher's ability to blend concerns for the progression of conditions of practice, the quality of performance, and the integration of application experiences. The presence of extension indicates a desire on the part of the teacher to sequence experiences—to build toward more complex and difficult forms. The presence of refinement indicates a concern for quality—the teacher does not just let students get through a movement experience, but insists that the skill is done well. The presence of application indicates a desire to help the students use the skills they develop while learning how to perform the skills well.

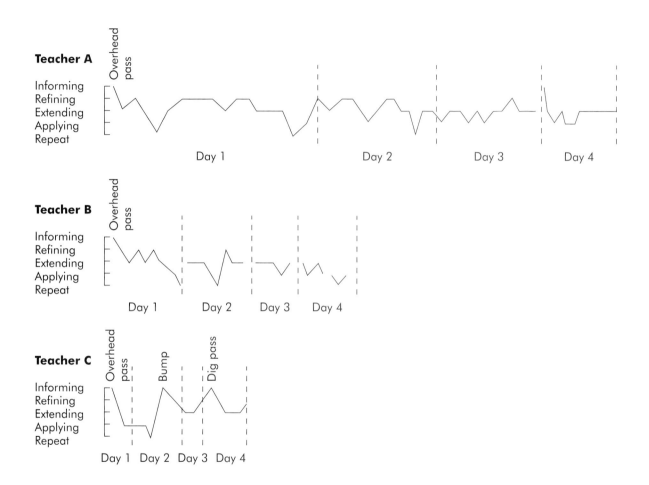

FIGURE 6-1
Content development through the task focus.

◆ PLANNING FOR CONTENT DEVELOPMENT: THE DEVELOPMENTAL ANALYSIS

Adequate development of content during the teaching process can be facilitated by teacher planning. In the past, teachers learned to develop appropriate sequences of experiences for learners primarily through a process of trial and error and through insightful perspective on the content itself. The process of selecting sequences of experiences is facilitated if teachers in their planning do a **developmental analysis** of the content they are teaching. A developmental analysis of the content is a chart of content development that uses three columns, as presented in Table 6-1.

The developmental analysis breaks the content down into its component parts—extension, refinement, and application. The developmental analysis gives structure to the teacher's ability to provide appropriate, progressive sequences of experiences. It helps the teacher to identify the characteristics of good performance for an experience and to integrate appropriate application experiences. The developmental analysis begins with identifying the extension aspects of skill development.

Extension

A developmental analysis of content begins with the extension column. At this point the teacher decides (1) how to reduce the complexity and difficulty of content for learners and (2) how to order the parts that will be added to create a sequence, or chain, of experiences. The teacher must first think through

factors that add complexity and difficulty to a learning experience and then sequence experiences in a progressive order. Many factors can be manipulated to change the complexity or difficulty of motor performance. The following factors have been selected for discussion and are summarized in Box 6-2:

- Practice of parts
- Modification of equipment
- Spatial arrangements for practice
- Focus of intent of performance
- Number of people involved in performance
- Conditions of performance
- Number of skills or actions combined
- Expansion of number of different responses
- Establishment of sequences of experience

Practice of parts. Teachers can often reduce the difficulty of beginning stages of learning skills by breaking a whole action into parts and practicing the parts before the whole is put together. Most instruction in square or folk dance is done this way. The teacher begins with a small part of the dance and then adds other parts of the dance, combining parts until the whole dance is learned. Similarly, the tennis serve can be learned by first practicing the toss of the ball without the racket, then the swing without the ball, and then both the toss and the swing together with or without the ball.

When skills are complex, there is a real advantage to reducing the skill to its parts. When skills are not complex or when breaking the skill into parts would destroy the rhythm of the skill, practice of parts in beginning stages is contraindicated.

Teachers will also want to consider the idea of

TABLE 6-1	*Developmental analysis of content*	
Beginning skill: Teacher describes the initial skill to be learned.		
Extension	**Refinement**	**Application**
A task that adds complexity or difficulty to the prior task	Qualitative aspect of the extension task	A competitive, self-testing, or performance focus

backward chaining, or beginning the practice of parts with the last part in the chain. Backward chaining is useful for many complex skills. Practicing the main action first, before the preliminary action of a skill, can give more meaning to the parts leading to the main action. Examples of backward chaining include the tennis serve progression that begins with the last part of the striking action (hitting the ball from a racket position behind the back); the bowling or basketball lay-up progression that eliminates the approach; the folk dance progression that begins with the chorus; and the shot put progression that begins with putting action (rather than the steps into the action).

When teachers choose to present a skill to learners in parts, it is critical that students first have an opportunity to practice the whole skill if possible, or when not possible, to see the whole skill performed. Many teachers who break down skills for students neglect to give students a feel for the whole action before they break the skill down. Practice of parts is not meaningful if there is not some idea of the whole.

Modification of equipment. One of the most useful ways to reduce the difficulty or complexity of performance in learning skills is to modify the equipment or its arrangement. Skills that directly manipulate objects, such as putting the shot, throwing a

---

BOX 6-2

Summary of Extension: Common Methods of Extending the Movement Task

Breaking down a skill into parts
Example:

- Practice the takeoff and placement of the ball in the lay-up shot in basketball.
- Practice dropping the ball for a courtesy serve in tennis or racket skills.

Modifying equipment
Example:

- Begin with a light ball and increase the weight of the ball in volleyball.
- Reduce the size of rackets initially and then increase the size and weight of the rackets for racket sports.

Making the space larger or smaller
Example:

- In a chasing game, decrease the space to make it easier for the tagger.
- In two-on-one soccer, increase the space to make it easier for the offense.
- Increase the force requirements for a throwing or striking skill by increasing the space.

Changing the goal (intent) of practice
Example:

- Practice the tennis serve to get a feel for the rhythm and then practice to get the ball in the court.

- Practice batting to get a hit and then practice to place the ball in different locations.

Adding or decreasing the number of people
Example:

- Practice dance steps first by youself and then with a partner.
- Practice two-on-one in soccer and then two-on-two. (Note two offense vs. one defense is easier than two-on-two.)

Combining two skills
Example:

- Practice shooting in basketball and then practice dribbling and shooting.
- Practice a forward roll and then practice a forward roll into a headstand.

Expanding the number of different examples of a concept
Example:

- From task of "Show me what a balance is" to "Show me three different ways to balance."
- Design three exercises to improve back flexibility.

Self-testing activities motivate competent learners. (Courtesy SIUE Photo.)

football, or passing a volleyball, are many times more easily learned with equipment of reduced size or weight. Skills that use implements are likewise more easily learned when skis, clubs, or rackets are shorter or lighter. This is particularly true for younger learners, who may not be able to learn an efficient movement pattern with equipment disproportionate to their size. It is also helpful for beginners of any age to use equipment that permits earlier efficiency of performance. As discussed in Chapter 2, students will choose an appropriate response for the conditions and their own abilities. A good rule of thumb is that if the equipment encourages less than mature and efficient patterns, changing the equipment should be seriously considered.

Equipment arrangements that can be modified in a learning environment include lowering or raising volleyball nets to encourage particular skills, lowering baskets for younger learners, and increasing the size of targets or goal areas to encourage success at beginning levels of development. Gymnastics equipment can be modified in height, and in educational gymnastics the arrangement of groups of equipment in relation to each other can be manipulated to control difficulty.

Spatial arrangements for practice. Teachers can establish a progression of difficulty through spatial arrangements. The level of difficulty in skills involving throwing, catching, or striking projectiles is increased or decreased by manipulating the distance, and therefore the force requirements, of the skills. Skills involving moving with others in space, such as dribbling a basketball, are increased in difficulty when space is reduced. When establishing progressions, the effects of reducing or expanding the spatial arrangements for experiences throughout the progression must be considered.

When planning progressions for the development of sport skills, it is also helpful to consider game requirements. The forearm pass in volleyball must eventually be done from a serve that comes from the other side of the court. Practicing the forearm pass from a short toss of a partner may be helpful initially, but unless the teacher increases the space between the partners and eventually uses a thrown or hit ball from a distance, the student cannot be expected to be able to use a forearm pass from the volleyball serve. With large numbers of students there is a tendency to reduce the space allocated for practice. Because the amount of space that objects cover and the force of the objects are so integrally related and because the goal is for students eventually to be able to either produce or receive objects with force, progressions must be designed to increase the amount of space and the amount of force required.

Focus of intent of performance. At any point in a progression of experiences, difficulty can be extended or reduced by manipulating the instructions for the intent of performance. This will later be referred to as the *goal orientation* of the task. The practice of batting, for example, changes considerably when the focus shifts from just hitting the ball to placing the ball in a specified area or to hitting balls of different trajectories. Running for practice of form changes considerably when running for speed becomes the intent. Throwing in track and field changes when distance becomes the intent. Teachers can manipulate student intent in the design of experiences and their progressions.

Number of people involved in performance. Many skills initially are practiced by individuals but eventually will be used with others in a more complex activity. Practicing a skill individually is almost always easier than practicing it with others. As soon as other participants are added, the skill is out of the complete control of the individual, and individuals must begin to adapt to one another. For example, practicing tennis strokes alone by using a ball machine to serve the ball eliminates the variation that comes when another person serves the ball. Practicing a dance step first without a partner eliminates the need to relate the movement to the partner while the step pattern is being learned.

Many skills are difficult to practice individually, such as catching at the beginning stages. For this skill, learners eventually need balls coming to them, and walls create too much force. In cases such as this, partners are necessary for individual practice.

In most progressions, other people are added to develop relationship skills (both cooperative and competitive) in the use of a motor skill. Most team sports involve both competitive and cooperative relationships with others. These relationships are built gradually by adding people one by one to a progression. Volleyball or most net activities can begin with relationships between two people and advance very gradually to relationships of two-on-two, three-on-three, four-on-four, and so on. Basketball and field activities can be developed by using similar progressions. Obviously, spatial arrangements must increase to accommodate greater numbers of participants. The idea of gradually adding people to whom the individual must relate should also be considered in gymnastics. Educational gymnastics and traditional stunts and tumbling units use group work, but working with others in these areas is difficult and should progress gradually.

BOX 6-3

Example of poor progression

The teacher begins class with a demonstration of the overhead set in volleyball. After practicing the hand position while seated, students are divided into groups of six. Each group is asked to form a circle. Students are told to practice setting the ball to the person next to them around the circle. The students do not experience any degree of success in this skill. They are unable to pass the ball to the person next to them because they have to receive the ball from one direction and then pass it in another direction. The condition of practice is too difficult because students have not had an opportunity to first send the ball in the same direction from which it is received.

Conditions of performance. Conditions of performance that increase or decrease the level of difficulty of content are largely content specific. The teacher will have to think through ways to make the content more and less difficult. A situation in which the conditions of performance are *not* anticipated adequately is described in Box 6-3.

In most manipulative patterns (e.g., throwing, catching, striking), the following conditions of performance can be modified to increase or decrease the difficulty of practice:

Less difficult	More difficult
▪ Low speed	▪ High speed
▪ Low force	▪ High force
▪ Stationary sender	▪ Moving sender
▪ Stationary receiver	▪ Moving receiver
▪ Movement forward	▪ Movement backward or sideways
▪ Medium level of trajectory	▪ High or low level of trajectory

The difficulty of an experience can be increased or decreased by manipulating the *rules* of many sport activities. Rules are conditions of practice that limit performance. They limit how individual skills are performed and how people interact with each other. Rules that are safety considerations (e.g., the height of the hockey stick) should be included from the beginning. Teachers should also ask themselves if not applying a rule will cause bad practice habits that cannot be easily changed. When safety or practice habits are not problems, it can be helpful not to apply a rule that complicates initial learning. When and to what degree the traveling rule is added to basketball dribbling or illegal hits are called in volleyball can be manipulated as part of a progression.

Game rules most certainly can be adapted and should be modified. *A good rule to follow is that if a rule or other aspect of a game destroys the continuous nature of play, modifying that element should be considered.* Good examples of this are eliminating the serve in beginning tennis or volleyball and making other arrangements for foul shots in basketball.

Music is a condition of performance that plays a critical role in dance progressions. When music is added and the speed of the music are important decisions that affect progression. Skills are more easily learned initially without music, and in the case of fast rhythms, they are more easily learned at slower speeds.

Number of skills or actions combined.

Many perspectives on progressions of skills stop with the individual skill and move directly into competitive uses of the skill in complex situations. The full development of a skill must include combining that skill with other skills with which it will be used. Students do not just shoot baskets in basketball—they dribble and shoot, or they receive a pass and shoot. Students do not just set a volleyball—they set a volleyball and move into another defensive or offensive position. Teachers must consider how skills will be used and prepare learners for the variety of ways in which the skill will be performed with other skills. If students will have to dribble and shoot or receive a pass, dribble, and pass, they should have the opportunity to practice all possible combinations of skills in less complex environments before they are expected to combine all of these skills in complex situations.

Expansion of number of different responses.

In progressions of concept teaching, an eventual goal is for the students to transfer their knowledge of a concept to new experiences. Progression of experiences will move from experiences that help students to define the concept to experiences that expand the number of appropriate responses and ask students to apply what they have learned to new experiences. Initial experiences must help the student define the concept, and later experiences in a progression must expand the number of ways in which the concept is applied. Still later experiences will ask the students to select and refine their responses. When the teacher asks for different responses, the complexity of response is increased. A teacher who first defines for students what the word *balance* means and then asks students to find as many different balances as they can is expanding the concept for students. A teacher who defines for students the type of exercise necessary to produce cardiorespiratory endurance and then asks students to find two types of exercise to achieve cardiorespiratory endurance is expanding the concept for students. Guidelines for these types of progressions are discussed in Chapter 12.

Establishment of sequences of experiences.

Sequencing experiences for students is not easy. Teachers must think through the content itself and make decisions about how the content can best be sequenced for a particular group of learners. The extension column of a developmental analysis describes the sequence the teacher has chosen to use with a particular group of learners. Examples of sequences of extension for the tennis serve and the basketball dribble are presented in Boxes 6-4 and 6-5 (p. 110). Inherent in each of these sequences are many of the ideas for gradually building in complexity and difficulty that have been discussed.

In the development of these skills you will notice many examples of ways to build in progressions. You will also notice many examples of both intratask and intertask development.

Once the teacher has established a sequence building in complexity and difficulty, he or she must give some thought to identifying the qualities of good performance for each of the extensions of tasks provided. This is the refinement aspect of the developmental analysis and is discussed next.

Refinement

The refinement column of the developmental analysis answers the question "What does it mean to perform the experience well?" For each experience listed in the extension column of a developmental analysis of content, a dimension of quality is described in the refinement column. Box 6-6 (p. 111) uses the tennis serve to illustrate the relationships between the extension column and the refinement column. The teacher in this example identifies what is important about the movement characteristics of the performer of each of the extension experiences provided: the teacher has established **cues** for each task identified as an extension task. The refinement column is concerned primarily with cues for how to do the skill (form characteristics). In many cases this will be so, but there are times when cues for the response are not what is most important.

Consider the example from the basketball dribble progression in Box 6-7 (p. 112). In this case the refinement column is not concerned with how the basketball dribble is performed, but with how the player adjusts the dribble to the conditions of a defensive player. As discussed in Chapter 5, this is a cue for an adjustment of the response. Because this is a later stage in the progression, the technique of dribbling is assumed to have been developed; the attention thus is put on how to *use* the dribble.

The refinement column serves the following purposes in planning progressions for students:

- Identifies cues the teacher can use for the presentation of tasks
- Focuses the teacher on what to observe in performance
- Provides information to use in teacher feedback to students

---

BOX 6-4

The Tennis Serve (Right-handed Player)

Extension	Refinement	Application
Practice grip.		
Practice stance.		
Practice toss.		
Toss and strike ball with an open hand from "scratch your back" position; stand a few feet from net and serve ball over net.		
Toss and strike ball with a racket from "scratch your back: position; choke up on racket; stand at midcourt and serve ball over net.		
Change sides of court.		
Stand farther back; slide grip down; strike ball from "scratch your back" position; serve ball over net.		
Stand at baseline; add backswing; use normal grip; serve ball over net.		

In an actual lesson, after the teacher presents a task to the class, he or she looks for the information in the refinement column. If the teacher does not see good performance as identified by the cues in the refinement column, the teacher has several choices:

- Correct performance individually if problems are not widespread
- Make the task easier if it is too difficult
- Stop the class and focus the entire class on a cue that will improve performance (the refinement task)

BOX 6-5

The Basketball Dribble

Extension	Refinement	Application
Dribble a ball in personal space.		
Dribble continuously without losing control.		
Change level.		
Move the ball to different parts of personal space.		
Change hands.		
Dribble while looking someplace else.		
Travel with the ball in general space.		
Travel slowly.		
Change direction (forward, backward, and sideways).		
Change speed.		
Stop and start quickly.		
Change levels.		
Keep ball close and then far away.		
Travel in smaller shared space while increasing speed.		
Dribble and pass the ball.		
Dribble, send ball to the wall, pick up the ball, and continue dribbling.		
Dribble and pass to a partner.		
Dribble and pass while moving in same direction at slow speed.		
Dribble and pass while moving in same direction at increased speed.		
Dribble and pass while traveling in different directions in a confined area.		
Maintain possession against a defensive player.		
Another student tries to force a loss of control.		
Another student tries to gain possession of the ball.		
Maintain possession with a partner against one defensive player.		
Play with no line of direction (deep-away situation).		
Add directional goal.		
Add traveling rule.		

NOTE: There is a choice of ball size and weight.

It is not easy to complete the refinement column of a developmental analysis because most physical educators cannot know everything they need to about every skill that they teach. However, excellent books are available that describe how skills are performed, and these can be very useful to both beginning and experienced teachers. It is helpful, but not sufficient, for physical educators to be able to perform skills themselves. Teachers must also be able to describe good performance at different stages of the develop-

---

BOX 6-6

The Tennis Serve (Right-handed Player)

Extension	Refinement	Application
Practice grip.	Hold racket head like a knife and use continental grip (halfway between eastern forehand and backhand). Spread fingers. Hold racket firmly.	
Practice stance.	Stand 2 to 4 feet from center mark. Use throwing stance. Keep front toe 2 inches behind service line at 45-degree angle. Check shoulder width.	
Practice toss.	Push ball into air. Check height above extended racket. Ball should drop 1 foot to right of front toe.	
Toss and strike ball with an open hand from "scratch your back" position; stand a few feet from net and serve over net.	Keep elbow parallel to ground Hand should brush over head. Use pads of fingers, not palm.	
Toss and strike ball with a racket from "scratch your back" position; choke up on racket; stand at midcourt and serve ball over net.	Loosen grip on racket. Maintain grip. Contact ball at full extension.	
Change sides of court.	Maintain form.	
Stand farther back; slide grip down; strike ball from "scratch your back" position; serve ball over net.	Hit out on ball, not down.	
Stand at baseline; add backswing; use normal grip; serve ball over net.	Break wrist. Maintain grip. Keep continuity of backswing and striking action.	

BOX 6-7

Basketball Dribble (Maintaining Possession Against a Defensive Player)

Extension	Refinement	Application
Another student tries to force loss of control.	Place body between ball and defense.	
Another student tries to gain possession of the ball.	Keep ball low and close.	
	Anticipate move of defensive player.	
	Change speed when appropriate.	

---

ment of content. Teachers must prepare. As you teach skills to students, you will improve at sequencing tasks and focusing students on what is important if you will evaluate your success.

When teachers have filled in the extension and refinement columns of the analysis, they are ready to consider planning for ways in which experiences can be provided to help the learner apply skills. Application is discussed in the next section.

Application

The application column of the developmental analysis describes experiences that can help the students apply their developed skills to situations that shift the focus from *how to move* to *how to use the movement*. The application column completes the developmental analysis. Boxes 6-8, 6-9 (pp. 115-116), and 6-10 (p. 117) are complete developmental analyses for the tennis serve, the basketball dribble, and the movement concept of force reduction.

Application experiences are usually, but not necessarily, competitive experiences. Application tasks redirect the learner's focus from *how to do the skill* to *accomplishing a goal using the skill*. The following are examples of application tasks:

- **Self-testing (individual or partner)**
  Learners are encouraged to test their mastery of a skill (e.g., see how many, how quick, how far).
  Example:
  "How many times can you toss and catch without dropping it?"
  "How far can you stand from the wall and still hit the wall?"

- **Self-testing (group)**
  A group of learners are encouraged to test their mastery of a skill.
  Example:
  "How long can you keep the volleyball up in the air without letting it hit the floor?"
  "How many times can your court pass the volleyball over the net using at least two passes on each side?"

- **Competitive**
  Activities are played against others with varying degrees of complexity.
  Example:
  One vs. one basketball
  Eleven vs. eleven soccer

The effects of the application focus.

Application experiences are a powerful focus. *No matter what additional focuses teachers may give an experience, the application focus will dominate most of the time*. Application experiences change the learner's focus from *how the movement is performed* to *the goal of the skill*. For this reason, students should be both competent and confident with the content before their abilities are tested. When beginners who have been working on dribbling skills in basketball are asked to use that skill in a relay race for speed, ball control decreases significantly, no matter how much the teacher reminds the students to control what they are doing. The students are not yet competent in the skill.

Competitive focuses can improve the performance of students who have achieved a degree of compe-

BOX 6-8

The Tennis Serve (Right-handed Performer)

Extension	Refinement	Application
Practice grip.	Hold racket head like a knife and use continental grip (halfway between eastern forehand and backhand). Spread fingers. Hold racket firmly.	Close eyes and attempt to pick up racket and assume proper grip.
Practice stance	Stand 2 to 4 feet from center mark. Use throwing stance. Keep front toe 2 inches behind service line at 45-degree angle. Check shoulder width.	Assume proper stance from all four serving positions.
Practice toss.	Push ball into air. Check height above extended racket. Ball should drop 1 foot to right of front toe.	Practice until five tosses in a row land consistently in proper place on the court.
Toss and strike ball with an open hand from "scratch your back" position; stand a few feet from net and serve ball over net.	Keep elbow parallel to ground. Hand should brush over head. Use pads of fingers, not palm.	Practice until three hits clear the net in a row.
Toss and strike ball with a racket from "scratch your back" position; choke up on racket; stand at midcourt and serve ball over net.	Loosen grip on racket. Maintain grip. Contact ball at full extension.	Practice until three hits in a row clear the net and ball lands within service court. Same as above.
Change sides of court.	Maintain form.	Same as above.
Stand farther back; slide grip down; strike ball from "scratch your back" position; serve ball over net.	Hit out on ball, not down.	Same as above.
Stand at baseline; add backswing; use normal grip; serve ball over net.	Break wrist. Maintain grip. Continuity of backswing and striking action.	

Continued .

The Tennis Serve (Right-handed Performer)—cont'd

Discussion: The teacher in this skill has identified the following variables to manipulate the complexity and difficulty of the serve:

    Racket or no racket

    Length of grip on racket

    Whole striking action and parts

    Distance served over net

    Target of serve

    Right or left court target

Each of these variables is manipulated in the progression. Each level of experience in the extension column also has associated qualitative cues, which appear in the refinement column, and appropriate application experiences.

---

tence and confidence with content. They can decrease the level of performance of students who have not. For these latter students, competitive focuses are likely to be discouraging rather than motivating.

Application experiences should be congruent with the level of extension and refinement in a progression. The following example illustrates a progression of experiences for students that uses an application task that is not appropriate for the level of extension or refinement developed:

- Practice forearm volleyball pass with a partner from an easy toss.
- Without a net, practice forearm pass from a partner's toss, moving forward, backward, or sideways to receive it.
- Practice forearm pass to set up overhead set for the partner from a toss.
- Use the forearm pass in a game of volleyball.

The teacher who planned this progression began by considering the conditions that made the forearm pass difficult. The teacher decided that the initial toss should be easy and that the performer should not have to move. The second experience encourages the performer to move, and the third experience focuses on what to do with the forearm pass. These are important considerations in developing this skill, but the progression does not go far enough. Because several critical elements are left out of the practice of the forearm pass before a full game is played, it can be predicted that students will not be able to use the pass successfully in the full game situation. Most

critically, students will be given no experience with receiving balls coming forcefully over the net. This experience could have been gained if the ball had been served or simply tossed over the net. Even if all other game conditions (e.g., number of people on a court; choosing the bump or overhead set) are practiced, this single condition alone will prohibit success with the use of the skill.

The developmental analysis can serve as a check to see if the application experiences in the progression are appropriate for the level of development of the content. Application experiences in sport activities should be spaced throughout a progression of experiences and not be reserved for the end of a progression. They should also use the level of skill development that the learner has experienced in a noncompetitive focus. Teachers can consider achievement level when designing these experiences for students and can also transfer some of that responsibility and choice to students.

What Content Development Looks Like in a Real Lesson

This chapter began with a scenario describing a teacher named Fred teaching fielding skills. It might be useful to go back to Fred's lesson to see if you can determine what you think Fred's developmental analysis of the fielding skill might look like. In his lesson Fred used extending tasks, refining tasks, and application tasks. It is unlikely that Fred used all the extension tasks or application tasks he had listed or that he shared with the students all of the cues he

BOX 6-9

The Basketball Dribble

Extension	Refinement	Application
Dribble a ball in personal space. Dribble continuously without losing control. Change level. Move the ball to different parts of personal space. Change hands. Dribble while looking someplace else.	Flex knees. Maintain low body position. Keep head up. Keep ball toward dribbling side. Push ball to the floor with fingers.	Dribble the ball as many times in a row as possible while (1) looking at ball, (2) changing hands, and (3) not looking at ball.
Travel with the ball in general space. Travel slowly. Change direction (forward, backward, and sideways). Change speed. Stop and start quickly . Change levels. Keep ball close and then far away. Travel in smaller shared space while increasing speed.	Change angle of rebound with speed. Keep ball out in front of body with speed. Change angle of body to upright with speed. Be aware of others (eye contact off ball). Look for spaces to move into.	Move as fast as possible without losing control of the ball. Touch as many different lines in the gym with the ball as possible in 30 seconds. Play frozen taggers game (half the class is spaced out as frozen obstacles trying to tag ball).
Dribble and pass the ball. Dribble, send ball to the wall, pick up the ball, and continue dribbling. Dribble and pass to a partner. Dribble and pass while moving in same direction at slow speed. Dribble and pass while moving in same direction at increased speed. Dribble and pass while traveling in different directions in a confined area.	Make smooth transition from dribble to pass and pass to dribble. Send ball to the wall at an angle and speed that will allow continuous traveling. Pass ahead of moving partner. Maintain awareness of partner during dribble. Use the pivot to change direction in stopped position.	Go to as many different walls as possible in 1 minute without losing control.
Maintain possession against a defensive player. Another student tries to force a loss of control. Another student tries to gain possession of the ball.	Place body between ball and defense. Keep ball low and close. Anticipate move of defensive player. Change speed when appropriate.	Maintain possession as long as possible without stopping the dribble or losing control. Give defense a point every time they touch the ball in 1 minute.

Continued .

The Basketball Dribble —cont'd

Extension	Refinement	Application
Maintain possession with a partner against one defensive player.	Dribble when defense is in a position to block pass and pass when pass is open.	Keep control of the ball with partner as long as possible.
Play with no line of direction (keep-away situation).	Make quick passes.	Start at one end of a space and try to move the ball
Add directional goal.	Move into empty spaces to receive pass.	down to the opposite side to score a point (minimum of three passes without loss of control)
Add traveling rule.	Defensively force a bad pass.	

Discussion: The teacher in this analysis has identified three phases of skill development for the dribble. The first phase is practice of ball control responses. The second phase is practice using the dribble with another skill, with other players. The third phase uses the dribble in competitive relationships with others. The following variables were established as being part of the complexity and difficulty of the skill:

Weight and size of ball
Level of dribble
Direction of ball around personal space
Dominant or nondominant hand
Stationary or moving player
Relationship to another offensive player
Relationship to a single defensive player
Relationship to offensive and defensive players at same time
Directional or nondirectional goal
Direction of locomotion
Speed of movement
Distance of ball from the body
Number of people active in one space
Combinations with other skills
Traveling rule

NOTE: There is a choice of ball size and weight.

---

had identified in the refinement column for each of the tasks. Because teachers base what they do in an actual lesson on the needs of learners at the time, several ideas regarding content development and the use of the developmental analysis in teaching should be kept in mind.

No set sequence of extending, refining, and application. After teachers do a developmental analysis of the content and present the initial task, they decide what to do based on what they see. Possible actions are presented in Box 6-11 (p. 118).

Teachers skilled at developing motor skills with students blend these "teacher moves" into their lesson appropriately. At times, beginning teachers who gain some insight into the complexity of the process used to develop content have remarked, "Well, that's coaching!" The point is that good coaching is good teaching. Good coaches are actually good teachers.

BOX 6-10

Force Reduction: Manipulative Objects

Extension	Refinement	Application
Toss a ball into the air and receive it so that it makes no noise in the hands	Reach to receive Move down with object until the force is reduced.	Toss ball as high as possible and still receive it with "soft hands."
Identify concept (force is reduced by giving with it).	Create maximal distance to receive the force.	Come as close to the floor as possible before stopping the ball.
Receive thrown balls of different types (e.g., footballs, basketballs, softballs).	Place body parts directly behind object to receive the force.	Go as long as possible with partner without any sounds being made by hands.
Receive self-tossed balls.	Adjust hand placement to the level of the ball and shape of object.	Go as far away as possible from partner and still maintain quality of catch.
Receive balls from different directions.	Move to get behind object.	
Receive balls from increasing distances and force levels.		
Receive balls while both stationary and moving.	Anticipate where ball will land.	
Receive manipulatable objects with implements (e.g., scoops, lacrosse sticks, hockey sticks, bats).	Same as all of above with the adjustment of an implement.	Same as all of above with the adjustment of an implement.
Receive objects at increasing distances and force levels from a partner.		
Receive objects both while stationary and moving.		

◆ GUIDELINES FOR DEVELOPING DIFFERENT KINDS OF CONTENT

The preceding sections developed general concepts for use across content areas. In the next section, ideas for the development of different kinds of content are more specificallly explored. Chapter 5 identifies a classification for three different kinds of motor skill content: (1) closed skills, (2) closed skills in differing environments, and (3) open skills. Each of these categories is unique in its learning intent and

---

BOX 6-11

Options for Teachers Based on Observed Learner Needs

Restate the task
  When it is obvious that the learners did not understand or choose not to work within the limits of the task.

Skip steps in the progression
  When the task is too easy.

Reduce the difficulty or complexity of the original task
  When learners are having little success.

Use a refining task
  When learners are not exhibiting the performance cues identified in the refinement column for a task.

Use an extending task, planned or unplanned
  When learners are ready to increase or decrease the complexity of the skill.

Use an application task
  When learners are confident and competent enough with the task presented

---

therefore requires a different approach to the development of learning outcomes. In this part of the chapter some implications of the unique nature of the content for the design of a development analysis are discussed.

Developing Closed Skills

The intent of the development of closed skills is to produce consistent and efficient performance in a defined environment. However, skills can rarely be practiced at the beginning stages of learning the way they will eventually be used. Thus teachers must make many decisions regarding progression and development of a skill.

Prerequisites to learning
- *Establish prerequisites.*
- *Modify the skill or equipment to ensure success.*

Prerequisites for learning closed skills usually include both physical abilities (e.g., strength, flexibility) and motor abilities. Physical abilities are impor-

tant factors in gymnastics skills. Students who do not have the abdominal strength or arm strength necessary for a hip circle on the uneven bars or a swing on the parallel bars will not be successful to any degree with these skills until their physical abilities are developed.

Motor ability is an important factor in manipulative patterns with objects. Students who have developed strong throwing patterns are in a better position to learn striking patterns than those who have not. Students who have developed strong locomotor patterns will be able to call on these patterns when needed to move to or with objects. Motor ability is a function of both experience and maturation.

Teachers who have to teach closed skills to students who do not have the prerequisite abilities must establish these abilities, modify the skill or equipment to permit success, make provisions to teach a different skill, or provide different experiences. Teachers should ask themselves if learning the skill at that particular time is important. Programs for young children and handicapped students should be carefully selected for skills important at a particular stage of learning. Although it probably is possible to eventually teach any skill to any student, teachers must consider a particular student's stage of development. Teachers must decide whether the skill learned warrants the time spent and whether the time can be best spent on other skills that can be learned more efficiently or on other experiences that provide a developmental base for motor learning.

Whole-Part question
- *Teach the whole whenever possible.*
- *Break the skill down into parts after providing students an opportunity to see or practice the whole.*

Teachers of closed skills must decide whether to teach a skill as a whole action or to break it into parts. This decision is often called the *whole-part dilemma.* Closed skills should be taught as a whole if possible. The rhythm of the movement performed in parts is often not the same as the rhythm of the whole. One part of a movement is actually preparation for another part. There is no guarantee that a student who can perform each part separately will be successful with the whole. A golf swing is a good

Beginners need an opportunity to work at a low level of complexity with a skill. (Courtesy SIUE Photo.)

example of a highly rhythmic skill that is destroyed if broken into parts.

Nevertheless, it may be desirable to teach complex skills, such as the tennis serve, in parts. Even under these conditions, however, many learning theorists recommend that the student be given an opportunity to work with the whole action before working with parts. The progression then becomes a whole-part-whole progression.

Teaching a skill as a whole does not preclude teachers from focusing students on parts. In fact, the refinement column of the development analysis in this case becomes a critical aspect of progression. Because learners will not be able to attend to all that they should at one time, the teacher orders what the students will be asked to focus on in the refinement column, even though the practice conditions remain the same. A good example of this is in practicing the golf swing. Even though the students may be doing the whole swing, the teacher can establish a progression of what is important to focus on first, such as

the role of the hips and left arm, head, etc..

There are no set answers to the whole-part question. Each skill is in a way unique. The complexity and rhythmic nature of the skill should help serve as guidelines for when to break the skill apart and when to teach it as a whole.

Modifying equipment

- *When it is the equipment that is making success difficult, modify the equipment.*

When teaching closed skills, if the conditions of performance are reduced, teachers must decide whether learning can occur more rapidly and more successfully by modifying the equipment. In most cases, students will profit from modified equipment when it is the equipment itself that is making success difficult. Clubs or rackets that are too long or too heavy; balls that are too hard, too heavy, too small, or too large; or goals that are too small, too high, or too far all make success difficult for the beginning learner.

If the learner must modify the pattern of the skill to be effective with regulation equipment, the equipment should definitely be modified. Such is the case with young students who must shoot underhand to do a free throw with high baskets or who must use two hands on a projectile when the skill actually calls for only one hand. The equipment should be modified in these cases, since it is not suitable for the age or level of skill of the student.

Many beginning students do not have the prerequisite physical abilities to manipulate or use regulation-size equipment. Beginners can profit from shots that are light, bowling balls that are light, bows with a low pull weight, or hurdles that are low. Equipment can also be modified to eliminate the fear aspects of regulation equipment for beginners (e.g., a rope can be added to the high bar; rope hurdles can be used instead of wood; soft balls can replace hard balls).

Changing Conditions of Practice

- *Change the conditions of practice to ensure success and build difficulty gradually.*
- *When working on the form of the movement, remove knowledge of results.*

Closed skills will eventually be performed in stable conditions, and extensive practice in the "real" environment will ultimately have to occur. Teachers can reduce initial practice conditions to ensure success or can focus the practice on efficiency rather than effectiveness.

As long as the conditions of practice do not destroy the integrity of the skill, they may be changed to ensure success. Serving lines in volleyball, tennis, or other target skills can be moved up initially to decrease the force production needed for success.

Teachers should also consider removing student knowledge of results from the environment in initial practices. Removing knowledge of results means not letting students see whether their action was effective. If students are not permitted access to knowledge of results, it is easier to get them to refine their performance and to focus on the critical kinesthetic cues aspect of closed skills. Bowling pins can be removed and golf swings or archery shots can be aimed into a net to eliminate knowledge of results.

Establishing progression of intent
- *Modify the goal (intent) of performance to ensure success.*

Most closed skills have a definite performance goal. Manipulative skills (e.g., bowling, golf, archery) usually are target oriented. Nonmanipulative skills (e.g., dance, swimming, diving, gymnastics) have a form goal. Self-testing skills (e.g., high jump, javelin, hurdles) have an effectiveness goal.

Beginners should not be held to the same standards of accuracy, form, or effectiveness that surround the performance of the skill at advanced levels. Goals for effectiveness and efficiency should be reduced for the beginner and gradually increased as ability increases. These goals should be part of the teacher's planning and should be included when the developmental analysis of the content is done. Beginning bowlers can strive initially to keep the ball in the alley. Beginning tennis servers can attempt to get the ball over the net or can hit into the fence. The skill is performed as a whole, but the goal of practice changes with ability, thus allowing success to be built into the progression.

Accuracy versus force production
- *High degrees of accuracy should be required only after force production abilities have been established.*

Many closed skills of a manipulative nature are accuracy oriented (e.g., basketball free throws, tennis serves, bowling, archery, golf). In such a progression, teachers must decide when to stress accuracy and when to stress force production. Motor-learning work in this area suggests that force production should be emphasized first. High degrees of accuracy should become the focus of practice only after some degree of consistency of form has been established. Teachers who stress accuracy too soon force students to modify their form, because the students have not reached high enough levels of control to experience success at being accurate. An example of this occurs frequently in the tennis serve. Many students can accurately serve the ball with a "chop" stroke instead of the full tennis serve. Students will use the "chop" stroke if they are asked for high degrees of accuracy, because they cannot be accurate with the full tennis serve.

Teachers are often reluctant to allow students to practice skills with maximum force production. This is because of managerial and organizational difficulties involved in giving students enough space to let objects fly out of control. However, there is very little transfer from skills practiced with little force to those practiced using maximum force. If the skill requires force production, it is unlikely to be learned without having opportunities to use maximum force.

Environmental design
- *Design the environment to elicit a response when possible.*

Environmental design is a useful way to establish progression for learners at beginning stages, since verbal communication is not as critical. Equipment or a learning environment can be arranged to promote learning. This is called **environmental design**. An example of environmental design is putting a stick out in front of a student practicing the front dive to encourage the student to jump *up* first, not *down*. Another example is placing targets on a tennis fence at the height where the ball is to be hit to provide a guide for learning. A tennis teacher can use environmental design to teach the rhythm of the serve by having students swing a sock with a ball in it. If students break the rhythm, the ball loses its centrifugal force.

There are many ways to encourage learning difficult skills through environmental design. Teachers can develop the ability to design environments to promote skill learning by asking themselves, "How can I put students in a situation that will *bring out* a particular movement?"

Developing Closed Skills Performed in Different Environments

- *Introduce the skill in the simplest environment and extend practice into all types of the environment used in the activity.*
- *Alert the learners to the types of modifications they may need to make in their performance for different environments.*

Closed skills in different environments are developed in ways similar to those used for closed skills. Skills used in different environments will eventually have to be practiced in those different environments. The basic pattern of the skill, such as bowling, a golf swing, or a forward roll in Olympic gymnastics, is modified when the environment changes. These patterns should be established with some consistency under simpler conditions before more complex conditions are introduced, such as bowling for spares, hitting a golf ball out of a sand trap, or doing a forward roll on the balance beam.

When planning for later progressions in skills that will be used in different environments, teachers should include many different practice environments. The specific modifications the learner will need to make in the basic pattern should be part of the refinement column of the developmental analysis. Differences between these modifications and the basic pattern will need to be communicated to the learner through teacher cues (e.g., instructing a student to descend on the ball for a golf shot in tall grass) or through problem-solving experiences that help the learner identify how the pattern changes under new conditions. Box 6-12 (pp. 122-123) presents an example of a developmental analysis for a closed skill used in different environments.

Developing Open Skills

Progressions of experiences for open skills should be developed with the intent of helping performers adapt skills to the complex changing environment under which the skills will be performed. To develop useful progressions of experiences for open skills, teachers must do a thorough analysis of the ways in which these skills will be used in the open environment.

Most open skills used in physical education are skills used in game situations. Thus the teacher must be able to identify quite specifically how a skill is used in a game. Analyses of what learners must be able to do to use both the volleyball overhead set and the tennis forehand in a game situation follow.

Volleyball Overhead Set
  - The player must be able to set a ball:
    Coming from different directions
    To different directions
    Coming to and from different force levels and trajectories
    By moving in different directions
    From a stationary position
    Coming from a serve or a forearm pass
  - The player must be able to decide:
    When the appropriate time is to use the set in relation to the forearm pass
    When the ball is his or her own responsibility
    Where to set the ball

Tennis Forehand
  - The player must be able to strike the ball with a forehand stroke:
    Coming from different directions
    To different directions
    Coming from different levels
    To different levels
    Coming with different amounts of force
    Coming with different amounts of spin
    By moving in different directions to contact the ball
    From any position on the court
    To any position on the court
  - The player must be able to decide:
    Where spatially to place the ball in the opponent's court
    When it is appropriate to use the forehand stroke
    When to put different kinds of spin on the ball

BOX 6-12

The Golf Swing in Different Environments (Right-handed Performer)

Extension	Refinement	Application
Get the ball out of tall grass and sand.	Use a descending, punchlike blow, not a long takeaway. Open iron a few degrees at address. Maintain firm grip. In sand do not contact ball but contact sand behind ball. Skim club head through sand and float the ball out. Close the club face to knife through heavy sand. Position ball opposite left hand. Pull left side back from target line. Use a short backswing (down and through).	*Individual* Place the ball in sand and grass; attempt to get the ball (1) a short distance from the hole in one stroke or (2) a long distance from the poor lie in one stroke. *Partners* Place the ball in grass and sand; see who can get the ball to a target area in the least number of strokes.
Play balls on a slope. Play a downhill lie.	Use open stance perpendicular to the slope; play ball near right foot with right knee flexed. Backswing first pickup with striking action down the slope. Use well-lofted clubs. Aim to the left of the target.	*Group* Use three balls for each of four positions (downhill lie, uphill lie, ball higher than feet, and ball lower than feet); use same target area for each group of players and each condition; record number of strokes it takes players to get all twelve balls into the target.
Play an uphill lie.	Swing parallel to the slope. Aim to the right of the target. Use more club to increase height.	
Play a ball higher than the feet.	Use erect address. Use flatter swing. Aim to the right of the target. Use shorter club. Open stance slightly.	

Continued.

This analysis forms the basis for establishing a progression of experiences that moves from less complex to more complex conditions (extension).

Doing a developmental analysis of open skills is more difficult than doing a developmental analysis of closed skills, since the learner must be prepared to adapt the skill to rapidly changing conditions. Students who can perform the skill under

---

The Golf Swing in Different Environments (Right-handed Performer)—cont'd

Extension	Refinement	Application
Play a ball lower than the feet.	Bend over to address ball.	
	Stand closer to ball.	
	Swing in an upright plane.	
	Use longer club.	
	Aim to the left of the target.	

Discussion: The teacher has anticipated the different environments the students will have to adjust to. The teacher has provided experience in those different environments and cues that change the way the basic stroke is performed in those environments.

Cues used for this analysis were taken from Seidel BL et al: *Sports skills: a conceptual approach to meaningful movement* ed 2, Dubuque, Iowa, 1975, 1980, Wm C Brown. NOTE: A major assumption in this progression is that the students have developed some degree of consistency with wood and iron shots under ideal conditions.

---

one set of conditions may not be able to perform appropriately under other conditions unless prepared to do so.

Many of the same concerns that guide the development of closed skills are concerns in the development of open skills. Decisions regarding modifying conditions, choosing between whole and part progressions, changing practice conditions, and encouraging force production before accuracy are based on criteria similar to those discussed for closed skills. However, some decisions are unique to the development of open skills.

Teaching open skills initially as closed skills

- *Practice of open skills in closed environments should be limited.*

A critical controversy among physical educators is whether an open skill should be taught first as a closed skill. A typical example of teaching an open skill first as a closed skill is to have the student bat off a tee before swinging at a moving ball. Batting off a tee is a closed skill because the batter does not have to adjust the skill to the speed, level, or direction of an oncoming ball. Most theorists and practicing teachers agree that there is merit in

reducing the complexity of the open skill for the beginning learner to the extent that the skill becomes more closed in its characteristics. Teaching open skills in closed conditions, however, does pose problems.

If teachers think in terms of two separate abilities involved in the development of open skills, decisions about progressions become easier. The first is the ability to respond with the proper movement pattern. In batting, this first ability is to swing the bat with the proper form (efficiency). The second is the ability to adapt the skill to the situation. In batting, the batter has to time the swing properly and at a level appropriate to the oncoming ball, an element of the situation over which the batter has no control. A skill cannot be performed effectively unless the student has acquired skill in both the *response* and the *use of the response* (adjustment).

Initially, it may be desirable to practice a response (particularly complex patterns) without the environmental cues that govern the use of the skill. There is, however, a danger in practicing open skills in closed environments for too long a time. If the skill becomes highly developed as a closed skill, the performer may not be able to adapt the skill to the appropriate environmental cues. The environment of the closed skill is predictable, whereas the environment of the open skill is not. Preparation for unpredictable environments requires variability of practice and practice in changing environments.

Practicing the execution (response) and use of response

- *Progressions for open skills should include opportunities both to practice the execution of a response and to practice responding appropriately.*

There are two aspects to skill development in open skills. The first aspect develops the ability to execute a response by moving in a particular way. The second aspect prepares the learner for selecting the proper response. Both are necessary for the complete development of skillfulness.

In the game of basketball, the basketball dribbler must be able to do the following:

- Dribble at different speeds
- Dribble the ball at different levels
- Use different locomotor patterns with the dribble
- Change direction while dribbling
- Dribble and pass
- Dribble and shoot a basket
- Dribble and stop while maintaining possession

All of the abilities just listed are responses that the basketball dribbler must have available to be successful at dribbling the ball in a game situation. These are abilities to execute a response. The basketball dribbler must also be able to choose the appropriate response to any given situation. The skilled dribbler chooses the appropriate time to dribble fast, slow, or at different levels; to change direction; to pass or shoot from the dribble; or to stop. The ability is related to the use of the response. The appropriate response depends on the conditions of the game at any particular point.

In progressions for open skills, practicing not only the execution of the movement but also the use of the response must be considered and planned for in any developmental analysis of content. Practicing the use of the response adds *perceptual complexity* to the environment and helps the learner decide how to respond. It is easier to develop progressions for

responses alone than it is to develop progressions that help the learner respond correctly to the perceptual cues of the environment.

An example of practicing the use of the response in basketball dribbling is teaching students how to respond to a defensive player who is trying to get the ball away. In this situation the cues for using the response become the following:

- Defend the ball by placing the body between the ball and the defense
- Keep the dribble low
- Change direction quickly
- Keep an eye on the defense

The student should be able to dribble close and at a low level and protect the ball with the body. In volleyball the concern in a progression for teaching the overhead set is not how to do the overhead set, but when to select it and where to direct it. In a badminton progression of the drop shot the concern no longer is how to do a drop shot, but when to choose a drop shot. It is obvious that the development of "use of a skill" follows the development of a reasonable amount of skill in the response itself. When students reach the point of choosing responses in a complex environment, the responses should be already developed to a reasonable level of consistency.

SUMMARY

1. Content development is the progression of tasks teachers use to take the learner from one level of learning to another.
2. Different kinds of content (closed skills, open skills, closed skills in different conditions, movement concepts) require an emphasis on different aspects of skilled performance and therefore an emphasis on different kinds of development.
3. In a lesson the teacher develops the content through a process using extending tasks, refining tasks, and application tasks:
   - Extension tasks change the complexity or difficulty of the prior task.
   - Refining tasks focus the learner on a qualitative aspect of performance.

- Application tasks ask the learner to use the prior task in a competitive, performance, or self-testing way.
4. The teacher can plan for different aspects of development by doing a developmental analysis of the content.
5. Open skills must ultimately be developed to the level of complexity that is part of the way the skill will be used. This means that complex conditions must be gradually added to practice.
6. Closed skills and closed skills in different environments may be initially practiced by reducing the complexity and difficulty, but should be practiced primarily in the conditions the skill will be used.

CHECKING YOUR UNDERSTANDING

1. Identify and describe the three different content moves that establish progression and represent the way the teacher develops lesson content.
2. What are six aspects of a movement task that can be manipulated by the teacher to increase or decrease the complexity or difficulties of practicing a motor skill?
3. How should the progression established for an open skill differ from that of a closed skill?
4. What purpose does the refinement column of a developmental analysis serve in helping the teacher in actual instruction?
5. Develop the extension column for a closed skill and open skill, attending to the unique aspects of progression established in the chapter.
6. For the progressions established in the previous question, fill in the refining aspects and possibilities for application.
7. Why are application tasks such a powerful focus for student work? What guidelines should the teacher follow in deciding to move to an application task?
8. When the teacher does a developmental analysis and uses it as a guide to plan a lesson, how does the teacher know when to give a refining task or when to extend the task further?

9. What is the difference between practicing the response and practicing the use of the response in an open skill?

REFERENCES

Rink J et al: The differential effects of three teachers over a unit of instruction, *Research Quarterly for Exercise and Sport* 57(2):132-138, 1985.

Shulman L: Knowledge and teaching: foundations of the new reform, *Harvard Education Review* 57(1):1-22, 1987.

SUGGESTED READINGS

Barrette K: Games teaching: adaptable skills, versatile players, *J Phys Ed Recr* 48(8), 1978.

French K et al: The effects of practice progressions on learning two volleyball skills, *J Teaching Phys Ed* 10(3):261-275, 1991.

French K, Rink J, Werner P: Effects of contextual interference on retention of three volleyabll skills, *Perceptual and Motor Skills* 71: 179-186, 1990.

Masser L: The effect of refinement on student achievement in a fundamental motor skill in grades K-6, *J Teaching Phys Ed* 6(2):174-182, 1985.

Rink J: *Development of a system for the observation of content development in physical education*, Unpublished doctoral dissertation, The Ohio State University, 1979.

Rink J et al: The influence of content development on the effectiveness of instruction, *J Teaching Phys Ed* 11:139, 1992.

Developing and Maintaining a Learning Environment

❖ ❖ ❖ ❖ ❖ ❖ ❖ ❖ ❖ ❖

OVERVIEW

One of the most difficult functions of teaching for beginning teachers is management. Teachers must elicit the cooperation of students to engage in learning and must develop and maintain a learning environment that supports learning. This chapter is meant to help you design and maintain a learning environment and to help you move students from teacher control to student self-control. The chapter presents the interrelationships between a management system and the teaching of content. Ideas for establishing and maintaining rules, as well as routines and strategies for developing self-control and handling student discipline problems, are presented.

❖ ❖ ❖ ❖ ❖ ❖ ❖ ❖ ❖ ❖

CONCEPTS

- **The ecology of the gymnasium**
- **Establishing and maintaining a management system**
  Establishing routines
    Teaching routines
    Degree of structure
    Reinforcing routines
  Establishing class rules
  Developing self-management skills

- **Strategies for developing student control**
  Behavioral modification
  Authoritative orientations to management
  Group process strategies for developing self-direction
- **Discipline—what to do if it does not work**
  Deterring problems before they become problems
  Continued inappropriate behavior

◆ THE ECOLOGY OF THE GYMNASIUM

Physical education classes should be characterized by an environment that is conducive to learning. Gymnasiums should be places where all students can have positive experiences. Teachers and students should enjoy being there. Gymnasiums should be places where teachers want to work and have something to teach students and where students want to learn. Teachers have a responsibility to (1) provide students with content to learn that is appropriate and challenging; (2) develop and maintain an environment that is conducive to learning that content; and (3) cultivate increasing levels of student self-discipline. When teachers fail to use their authority, knowledge, and skills to develop these abilities, they are abdicating their responsibility.

We usually think about teaching in terms of both management functions of teaching and content functions of teaching:

- **Management:** Arranging the environment for learning and maintaining and developing student-appropriate behavior and engagement in the content
- **Content:** The substance of a curriculum area—what is to be learned

Good management skills of the teacher are essential for effective teaching. They alone are not sufficient to make you an effective teacher, but you cannot be an effective teacher without them. Even though it is helpful to talk about teaching in terms of management functions and content functions of teaching, it is important to recognize that these two functions are in reality very connected. They interact with each other in the context of a class that has unique characteristics. As was described, the teacher may have designed a suitable learning experience but may not be able to obtain or maintain student cooperation to engage in that learning experience. Likewise, a teacher may have good basic management skills but may have nothing valuable to teach students; therefore student cooperation is lost, regardless of good management techniques.

The teaching/learning process is often referred to as an ecological system, because the idea of an ecological system implies an interdependence of many systems working at the same time. The content and management systems that you establish with your class are two such interdependent systems. Because management and content are interdependent systems of instruction, they should share the same curriculum objectives. It is incongruent to expect learners to work with content at advanced levels and be independent learners within a management system that aspires to student obedience (McCaslin and Good, 1992). An example from physical education illustrates the strong relationship between content and management.

EXAMPLE: Kevin is a high school teacher who is taking a course in teaching strategies for his master's degree . The faculty at Kevin's high school has been working on ways to help students to be more motivated and to be engaged in learning experiences at a higher level. Kevin has begun to think about the potential of physical education to contribute to student independence, interdependence, and higher-order thinking skills. Kevin's teaching is very direct. Kevin believes that he needs to keep students in control at all times and that the student's role should be primarily one of obedience. Kevin rejects every strategy mentioned in his graduate class because his perspective of using that strategy is that students will be out of his control and not engaged in the content without his direct involvement in everything they do. Because Kevin has not worked on helping students to be more self-directed in their learning, Kevin's options for how to teach the content are very limited. Kevin has limited not only *how* students will learn, but *what* students will learn.

Educators have come to think about management as a problem of obtaining and maintaining order (Doyle, 1986). *Order in an educational setting means high levels of engagement in what the student is supposed to be doing and low levels of inappropriate and disruptive behavior.* It is useful to remember that a student who is technically "on task" may not be engaged in the content in a meaningful way—that is, a level of engagement that has the potential to effect learning. It is useful to remember also that students who are interacting with each other may be engaged in the content in an appropriate way. It does not necessarily follow that because students are being "good," they are learning, or because classes appear to be disorganized or students appear to be off task, they are.

Students can be taught to manage their own behavior. (Courtesy SIUE Photo.)

Student compliance alone is a very limited goal for an educational program. Student compliance suggests that the students are able to do what the teacher says—they are willing to cooperate with the teacher. In most settings, teachers should have higher expectations for student behavior. A better measure of effective teaching is the degree to which the teacher has been able to develop high levels of student engagement in the content. Engagement in the content is a necessary condition for learning and is a minimum expectation for effective teaching.

To achieve high levels of student engagement in the content, the teacher should be able to use a variety of teaching strategies with the assurance that the students will be able to function within these strategies. From a managerial perspective, this means that students must be able to act responsibly without much teacher direction or monitoring and must be able to interact with each other in positive and supportive ways. In some gymnasiums, students work quite independently of the teacher on a variety of tasks. In other gymnasiums, students can work in groups very productively and very supportively of each other. The teachers have established expectations for much more than just control with their classes. In other gymnasiums, there seems to be a constant battle between the teacher and students for control. Even minimal levels of compliance have not been established.

This chapter is designed to help you establish and develop a management system with your classes. We will consider strategies for both obtaining and maintaining control, as well as teaching, for more advanced levels of student engagement with the content and self-directed behavior. It is important to remember that you cannot get to the higher levels of student self-directed behavior without first establishing minimal levels of control in your classes. Also, the manner in which you establish this control will affect your ability to move students to more advanced levels of self-direction.

◆ ESTABLISHING A MANAGEMENT SYSTEM

As you move through this chapter and begin to think about the management system you will establish for your classes, several ideas should be remembered relative to establishing a management system.

Positive is more effective than negative. Positive approaches to engaging students and maintaining their cooperation are more effective than negative ones. Teachers should not be in adversarial roles with students and spend class time primarily as policemen trying to catch students misbehaving. Positive environments are more easily established and maintained when teachers teach expectations and the reasons for rules and expectations in advance and address problems constructively and cooperatively with students. Maintaining a positive approach to behavior and management is easier if teachers view inappropriate behavior as they would an incorrect answer to an academic question or incorrect form in a motor skill.

Teachers should not see inappropriate behavior as a personally threatening student response. Teachers should be willing to understand and work with students who have special problems and, in general, have a respect for the individuality of each of their students. Teachers can be caring and concerned and still have high expectations for student behavior and respond in a firm manner. Effective managers rely on instruction and persuasion rather than power and assertion (Brophy, 1983).

Know what you expect. Before you can institute a management system, you must decide what constitutes order and engagement and what constitutes inappropriate behavior for both man-

agement and content tasks.

This is often the most important part of establishing control in a class and the most often neglected. Because beginning teachers find it difficult to deal in advance with expectations for student behavior, they often are very inconsistent in terms of what they expect from students and have to regain control after losing it. Observing good teachers and the expectations they have for student behavior can help you make decisions about what you want in your classes. After you have decided what you expect, you can decide how to get there.

You must also decide what your ultimate goal is for student behavior. Students may not be ready for many of the ideas you may have, but you should have a long-term goal. Where would you like your students to be at the end of the year? At the end of 2 years? Are you willing to take the time to teach students these behaviors? Do you think the goals for students (self-direction and control) are important enough?

Two distinct management roles. The management role of the teacher consists of two distinct roles. The first is teaching students what is expected, and the second is maintaining what is expected.

Students should not learn what is expected by doing it "wrong." Unfortunately, because teachers have not made their expectations clear to students in advance, students often learn what the teacher really expects only by engaging in inappropriate behavior. This chapter considers the ideas of *establishing* a management system and *maintaining* it.

Students at different ages need different emphases in management. Brophy and Evertson (1978) developed four stages of development that can help teachers direct their efforts in establishing and maintaining a learning environment in the gymnasium (Box 7-1, p. 130).

Although this developmental perspective is helpful, it must be remembered that a new teacher in a new situation must establish his or her own management system; that system may be different from what the students are accustomed to and therefore must be taught.

BOX 7-1

Stages of Development Relative to Learning Environment in Gymnasium

Stage One: kindergarten through grades 2,3

Students are compliant and want mostly to please adults. They need to be socialized into "going to school" roles. They require a great deal of formal instruction in rules, procedures, and expectations in the gymnasium.

Stage Two: grades 2,3 through grades 5,6

Most students still want to obey and cooperate with the teacher. Less time needs to be spent in management.

Stage Three: grades 5,6, through grades 9,10

Peer group relationships become extremely important. Students tend to question authority and seek ways to get attention through humorous, disruptive remarks and horseplay. The management task becomes one of motivating and controlling students to do what they know they should be doing. Working with individual students becomes more important.

Stage Four: after grades 9,10

A return to an academic orientation toward school usually develops. Student social development and emotional development are more stable. Management generally takes less time.

From Brophy J, Evertson C: Context variables in teaching, *J Educ Psychol* 12:310-316, 1978.

Student management behavior is learned. Many beginning teachers talk about "good" students and "bad" students as though students are born with these characteristics. As a teacher you will need to think about teaching student behavior in your classes in much the same way as you will consider teaching your students a new motor skill. Students are starting at different points, and taking a student from one level to another requires that you plan experiences at an appropriate level. It would be foolish to expect students who have difficulty working independently in learning tasks without a great deal of supervision to work independ-

dently with a small group in an unstructured learning activity. It is not that the goal is not worthwhile; it is that the teacher must first teach students to become more independent of teacher supervision if they do not already have those skills. The teacher needs a **progression** to teach independent working skills and productive group skills.

Students will internalize appropriate behavior more if they are helped to understand why particular responses are appropriate. Teachers want students to choose to behave in appropriate ways—not because there will be negative consequences if they do not, but because the students value appropriate behavior. Students can be helped to value appropriate behavior and internalize expectations if they are given reasons why particular behaviors are appropriate and others are not.

EXAMPLES:
- "If everyone calls out at one time, no one will be able to here anyone."
- "How can we have everyone working at one time without worrying about getting hit with a ball?"
- "Why do you think I am concerned with what I see?"

Expectations for appropriate engagement in learning experiences must also be established. Most often teachers have taken the time to teach students rules and procedures for organizational tasks, such as taking out equipment, dressing for activity, lining up, and taking attendance, but have failed to teach students what is expected in terms of participation in learning tasks. Teaching rules for social participation and expectations for participation in learning experiences reduces inappropriate behavior in the content of your lesson. What is expected when practicing by yourself? How should you work with a partner or small group? What should you do if your ball moves into another person's practice area? What does it really mean to practice a skill to try and get better at it? What do you do if you need help? All of these ideas are critical to the quality of the learning experience and must be considered by teachers and taught and reinforced to students.

Management is never achieved. Many teachers tell students at the beginning of the school year what their expectations are for behavior, and then the teachers gradually lose control. Management goals are really never achieved. It is an ongoing process. Once the teacher has established a learning environment that is characterized by control, he or she must maintain it. Once the teacher establishes a learning environment with minimal levels of student control, he or she should be working toward helping students to greater and greater levels of self-control.

Establishing Routines

An essential ingredient of good management in the gymnasium and one of the first steps a teacher must consider when establishing a management system is the use of established routines. Many events occur over and over again. Teachers should establish routines with students for frequently occurring events in the gymnasium so that more time can be devoted to substantive parts of a lesson. Routines are a customary way of handling a situation. Many teachers in physical education have established customary ways of handling the following events:

Locker room routines
  When to enter
  Where to put clothes
  Permitted social behavior
  Amount of time for dressing before and after class
  Leaving the locker room, where to wait, when to leave
  Permission to enter locker room during class
Before-class routines
  What to do when leaving the locker room before class actually starts
  For elementary, how to enter gymnasium and where to go first
  Attendance procedures
Lesson-related routines
  What areas of the gymnasium are "out of bounds"
  How to obtain and put away different kinds of equipment
  What signal you will use to stop and start activity
  When you want to talk to students, should they stay where they are or gather in an area of the gymnasium; should they stop work on command or finish their movement; should they put their equipment down; should they sit off the mats
  How students will get a partner; small group; large group
  What to do when your equipment invades the working space of others
  How to distribute space for practice among individuals or groups
  How students should get your attention for help
End-of-lesson routines
  How a lesson should be ended
  If students take less time to dress, can they continue to practice
Other considerations
  How to handle late arrivals
  How to deal with students who are not dressed out
  How to handle water breaks
  How to handle going to the bathroom
  How to handle fire alarms
  What to do in case of an injured student

Routines should be designed to make events run more smoothly and to maximize the opportunity to engage in the content. Routines should be taught to students, practiced, and reinforced. Guidelines for each of the routines just mentioned are described in Box 7-2 (pp. 132-133). Some basic principles regarding establishing and maintaining routines follow.

Teaching routines. Routines can be taught to students in different ways. Usually teachers will spend time at the beginning of the year explaining and in some cases practicing routines. Young learners will need practice of many routines and constant reinforcement. The teacher may have to practice routines for several weeks before a routine becomes well established in a class. Older learners usually have established routines that the teacher may want to modify. In either case, the teacher must share expectations with students for a routine and the appropriate behavior that is expected in carrying out a routine. Students will learn what is expected if both positive and negative examples of appropriate behavior are used and if students understand the need for appropriate behavior.

BOX 7-2

Guidelines for Establishing Routines

Locker room routines

The objective in establishing locker room routines is to make changing clothes a safe, sensitive, and efficient process. Locker rooms must be monitored by the teacher initially and in some cases every time a group of students is in the locker room. Students should have sufficient time and space to dress and should have a safe place to hang their clothes so that coming to physical education is not a hassle.

Many secondary programs allow 5 to 7 minutes before and after class for dressing. If students need showers, more time must be allotted. Absolutely no horseplay should be permitted in the locker room, and all students should come into the locker room and leave at the same time to prevent any problems with theft. If locker rooms are crowded, students should be allowed to wait for the next class elsewhere after dressing. Most schools request that students not be allowed into the hall to go to their next class until the bell ending a class has rung.

Before-class routines
Elementary

Elementary students usually enter the gymnasium as a class. Generally it is helpful for the teacher to greet the students at the door and then move them right into the beginning of class. If this is not possible because of back-to-back classes, which is often the case in the elementary school, a routine should be established to have the students quietly come into the gymnasium to a designated location (center circle or line on the side of the gymnasium) to sit and wait for the teacher.

Secondary

After students finish dressing, they will come into the gymnasium. If possible, equipment and a supervising teacher should be in the gymnasium so that students will have an opportunity for more practice while waiting for others. Generally students will dress more quickly if they know there is something for them to do when they get into the gymnasium.

Attendance

It is not necessary to check attendance in most elementary school settings in self-contained units. Who is absent for the day is information easily obtained from students or the teacher as students come into the gymnasium. In secondary school, the objective should be to check attendance in the most efficient way. There are many good ways to check attendance that do not waste time having the teacher call out the names of every student.

Each student has a spot to go to; the teacher scans for empty spots.

Each student has a squad; the squad leader (this position should rotate) checks attendance for a squad and hands an attendance card back to the teacher.

Lesson-related routines
Distributing equipment

Teachers should have several access points for distributing and putting away equipment. In the elementary school this prevents a "rush" to get the equipment. At all levels this saves time.

Out-of-bounds

Early on, teachers should designate where it is appropriate for students to find a "working space" and where it is not. For elementary children, having a working area several feet from the wall eliminates "wall huggers." In the secondary school, often large equipment is placed in some areas of the gymnasium, which presents a safety problem.

Signals

The use of signals is very context specific. Signals are essential to stop and start work in the elementary school, because as soon as an activity is mentioned, young children want to do it before the teacher finishes giving all the instructions. Teachers often must use the phrase, "When I say 'go,' I want you to....." If this is not a problem in the secondary school, teachers can be more informal about the communication to "go."

Guidelines for Establishing Routines —cont'd

In large spaces or outside, most teachers must use a whistle or a drum to get student attention to stop what they are doing and listen to further directions. In smaller spaces, usually a voice command is sufficient. If you do not need to use a whistle, it is more desirable not to use one.

Instead of demanding an immediate halt to activity, the "stop" signal should mean to "bring to a close what you are doing." This helps avoid the risk of students endangering themselves if they are in the middle of a movement.

If you do not have to bring students "in" to change the activity or change the task, it is better not to do so. However, if attention, hearing, or seeing is a problem, teachers should gather students closer to them for transitions.

Grouping

Alternatives for grouping are described in Chapter 4. Generally students should be taught to group themselves unless the teacher wants to use other criteria for putting students into groups.

End-of lesson routines
Closure

Before students leave the gymnasium to go back to their class or to the locker room, it is usually recommended that they gather for a summary of the lesson and preparation by the teacher for the next lesson.

Dismissal

Elementary children need a procedure for lining up to go back to their class. It is helpful for teachers to establish a consistent location for students to line up that does not interfere with the class coming in. Students should know that when they are dismissed, they will go to this location to line up. Secondary students can go into the locker room after being dismissed.

Other needed routines
Late Arrivals

Late students usually come into a class when the teacher is occupied giving directions to students. The teacher should not stop the whole class to deal with a late arrival but should establish a procedure to have that student wait until a more opportune time to become involved with the class.

Water and bathroom breaks

If a water fountain and bathroom are available in the gymnasium, the teacher should allow students to get a drink of water and go to the bathroom at any time. Sometimes elementary students make a "game" of going to the water fountain. This is one of those areas in which the teacher may have to have specific rules that become more flexible as students demonstrate that they can handle the responsibility. When an entire class lines up for water, a great deal of time is taken out of class. In many secondary schools, water and bathrooms are located in the locker room and locker rooms have to be locked.

Injured students

If a student is not badly injured, generally the teacher can allow other students to continue with what they are doing while the teacher attends the injured student. Usually a teacher can send the injured student to the nurse's office with another student. If the student needs a great deal of help, the teacher should have the class stop and sit while the teacher sends for help.

Degree of structure. Different groups of learners need different degrees of structure in routines. Young learners and groups of learners who cannot handle less formal ways of doing things need more structure. For instance, some young children can get a piece of equipment, move to their own spot on the gymnasium floor, and begin working immediately as a total group. Other learners may need to have the teacher send students a few at a time and ask them to sit in their own space before they begin. Some secondary students can come into a gymnasium and work productively practicing with equipment before the rest of the class is ready to begin the lesson. Other groups of secondary students may need to come into the gymnasium and wait for other students and the official beginning of a lesson before they can practice. Highly structured situations are characterized by step-by-step teacher directions and student responses. The more structure, the smaller the steps. In less structured situations, the learner is asked to respond to more than a simple direction without being cued by the teacher. The ultimate goal should be for the teacher to work toward less structure as students can manage and be responsible for their own behavior. Less structured routines that are not "command" performances encourage student responsibility and decision making about appropriate behavior. Less structure does not mean less appropriate behavior—it means more appropriate behavior that permits more time to be spent on the lesson content. Effective teachers add structure when needed and begin removing it as students are ready to become more independent.

EXAMPLE: "Let's see if you and your partner can find a place to work and begin working without me having to give you a signal to begin. What am I going to be looking for as you try to do this without a signal?"

Reinforcing routines. Once a routine has been taught, it must be reinforced. Many teachers think because they have taught students how to do something, they will not ever have to deal with that idea again. However, even after routines are taught, student behavior can begin to drift without reminders, class discussions, and occasional reteaching. This is particularly true as the school year progresses, after

vacations, and toward the end of the year.

EXAMPLE: "I called you back here today because I saw as I asked you to begin working on the task that several people were not able to handle this yet. What is it that we should be doing when you move to your area of work?"

EXAMPLE: "Your team is supposed to be working on a defense for your game today. Some of the teams are working very hard and getting a lot done. A few of the teams are having trouble focusing their efforts. How can I help you get started?"

Establishing Class Rules

Whereas procedures should be established for customary ways to perform regularly occurring activities in classes, rules should be established that make clear expectations for appropriate conduct in class. Rules are general expectations for behavior in a setting. Children who have been in school for a number of years already have been exposed to many "going-to-school rules." When you work with very young children, you will find that ideas such as raising the hand, lining up, calling out, and following directions that have not been targeted specifically to the child may not be demonstrated by the child. Physical education classes share many of the rules established by the faculty and administration for a particular school. In addition, the unique setting of physical education requires additional rules to make the time spent in the gymnasium both a positive and safe learning experience (Box 7-3).

Rules are basically concepts. As concepts they are not specific to any one situation and can be applied to many situations. Because rules are concepts, their

---

BOX 7-3

Basic Rules in Physical Education

The following rules are generally accepted as those basic to a positive and safe learning environment in physical education:

- When others are talking, we try not to talk.
- We are supportive of our classmates' efforts.
- We respect the rights of others.
- We take care of equipment.
- We try our best.

meaning is often implicit rather than explicit in a situation. Teachers will have to teach what rules mean in a variety of situations using both positive and negative examples of appropriate behavior. For instance, teachers may find students work independently without interfering with each other in a manipulative skill lesson, but when they are in a gymnastics lesson, they tend to socialize and create dangerous situations by trying to help each other through a movement. The rule of not interfering with others who are practicing may need to be taught for a particular situation. Teaching may imply sharing expectations or the problem and students and teacher cooperatively deciding on solutions to the problem. Rules, like other concepts, are learned through continuous examples of what is an appropriate response to a rule and what is not appropriate. The younger the child, the more examples of appropriate and inappropriate behavior are necessary to develop and communicate a rule. Generally, rules should be:

- Developed cooperatively with students when possible
- Stated positively
- Made explicit to learners (posted if necessary)
- Reinforced consistently and fairly
- Few in number

Teachers may consider more specific rules for particular lessons or content areas. For instance, a teacher may make a rule, "no resting on the gymnastics equipment" or "no resting on a mat" to eliminate attention problems that can occur when students are in contact with equipment.

Developing Self-Management Skills

Most of this chapter to this point has addressed minimal expectations for control in the physical education class. Establishing basic routines and rules will help classes run smoother and will help make the physical education class a positive and productive learning experience. Students cannot learn unless teachers have been able to elicit the cooperation of students to this minimal level. The role of the teacher in this context is to teach and persuade students to comply with procedures and class rules that have been developed cooperatively or established solely by the teacher. The need for control and com-

Students may need help initially in handling routines like water breaks. (Photo by Michael Gelfand-Grant.)

pliance should in no way be underestimated. It is a first step to creating an environment where more important kinds of learning can take place.

Physical education settings have a great deal of potential to contribute to student attitudes about themselves, others, and the interdependent world in which they live. The very nature of what we teach and how we teach it is a laboratory of important life skills. The active, social nature of the physical education environment offers the educator a powerful setting for teaching human values and relationships and for helping young people find a place and meaning in their world.

The idea of going beyond mere compliance in our classes necessitates an understanding of what is minimal and what is the desired direction. Minimal levels of control that permit instruction to take place in the gymnasium require primarily that students do what the teacher says. This critical idea is essential for student learning to take place but provides the students little they can take with them to real life settings and limits the nature of the types of learning experiences the teacher can provide.

Children today, as well as adults, have an unprecedented amount of freedom and choice in their lives. They will need to learn how to choose what they do and what is important to them based on a set of developing values that will help them lead happy, productive, and meaningful lives. Students will eventually leave the control of the teacher and other people who control their lives. Making the transition from external to internal control of behavior must begin in school. Unfortunately, many kindergarten students have more opportunity to practice and exercise self-control than many high school students (McCaslin and Good, 1992).

Hellison (1985) described five developmental levels en route to acquiring values and a life-style that would help students make wise choices and lead them to a personally satisfying life-style. These developmental stages are described in Box 7-4. The manner in which Hellison described each stage is not as important as the implications of what is happening from the zero level of control to the more advanced stages. The first four stages described by Hellison trace development from behavior that shows no control to behavior that accepts a more self-directed sense of responsibility for behavior and decisions. The last stage takes the student beyond the self to feeling some sense of responsibility for others.

Many physical education teachers assume that their classes are going well if students are operating at Hellison's level I. To aspire to level I is to disregard the great potential of our field to move students to much higher levels of functioning. To move students to higher levels of functioning, teachers must be willing to aspire to more than control. They must be willing to take time to teach students how to function at higher levels and to share their power and control. You may encounter students who are operating with no control. What is important is that you do not leave them there.

BOX 7-4

Hellison's Developmental Levels

Level 0: Irresponsibility

Characteristics: Unmotivated; undisciplined; denies personal responsibility; verbally or physically abusive of others; interrupts; off task on a continuous basis; needs constant supervision

Level I: Self-Control

Characteristics: Not highly engaged in the lesson, but not disruptive; does not need constant supervision; goes through the motions of compliance

Level II: Involvement

Characteristics: Demonstrates self-control and an enthusiasm for the subject matter

Level III: Self-Responsibility

Characteristics: Ability to work without direct supervision; can identify own needs and interests and is independent in his or her pursuit of them

Level IV: Caring

Characteristics: Cooperative, supportive, and caring about others; willing to help others

From Hellison D: *Goals and strategies for teaching physical education,* Champaign, Il, 1985, Human Kinetics Publishers.

◆ STRATEGIES FOR DEVELOPING STUDENT CONTROL

There are many approaches for developing values and higher level behaviors with students. The effective teacher will use different strategies for different purposes and different contexts. Helping students to become more self-directed, responsible, and caring people takes time and will initially cut down on content time in your classes. In the long run, however, a learning environment will be established that will support learning the objectives you have for motor skill learning and fitness and will make a valuable contribution to the educative goals of your program.

When your students become more self-directed in your classes, you not only will save time, but will open up many opportunities to work with students in ways not possible without self-management skills. Each of the strategies described in the following discussion is based on certain assumptions about human behavior and what controls it.

Behavior Modification

Strategies related to behavior modification have their roots in behavioral psychology. Behaviorists believe that human behavior is primarily the result of conditions and that if the conditions can be changed, the behavior can be changed. Although it is impossible to be aware of the specific behavior of all their students, teachers can look primarily for reasons students are responding the way they are that possibly can be changed in the instructional environment. The key to a behavioral approach to changing behavior is the idea of **reinforcement.** A major assumption of behaviorism is that people respond in certain ways because they are reinforced by those responses. The job of the teacher is essentially to reward students for responding in positive ways and to not reward students for responding in ways that are not positive behaviors.

Teachers who use behaviorism are specific about what is appropriate behavior and take time to help students clearly understand the meaning of what that behavior might be. Lower level expectations usually take the form of rules or stated teacher objectives for student behavior that are taught, posted, and shared. Objectives for more complex and higher order behaviors are shared explicitly and taught to students as the students are ready.

Suggestions for using behavioral techniques
Define the behavior explicitly. Before you attempt to teach students to behave in any particular way, make a list of what you consider appropriate behavior and inappropriate behavior. The more important the behavior, the more complex it is likely to be and the more important it is that you can give enough examples to get the message across. Do not make your expectations trivial, but make the exam-

ples of those expectations specific. Know why the behavior is important and share this with students. The example that follows was selected to demonstrate how a complex behavior can be taught using behavioral principles.

EXAMPLE: You want students to be supportive of others in the class. You make a list of appropriate and inappropriate responses. Some of the behaviors you list are as follows:

Appropriate	Inappropriate
Willing to work with all students in the class	Complains when has to work with a girl, a boy, a student who is unskilled, or any student who might be considered by others as "undesirable"
When another student tries very hard but still makes a mistake or has difficulty, encourages that person for his or her efforts, even if that student is an opponent in a game situation	Ridicules, laughs at, or otherwise makes another feel inferior about his or her effort
Catches another person's ball when it comes into own space and hands it to that person	Kicks another person's ball when it comes into own space

Take time to teach and communicate the behavior. Although rules and procedures can be easily communicated by the teacher or designed by a class without much effort, important and complex behaviors are probably best shared in an interactive discussion with students. The teacher can help students to know the concept of the behavior by the following:

- Developing consensus for the importance of the behavior
- Describing situations where students have choices of how to respond and are helped to understand what the significance of the choices might be

- Developing enough examples of both appropriate examples of the behavior and inappropriate responses

In some cases it may be necessary to emphasize what you are trying to teach by having students practice the behavior or role play situations where the choice of response is most likely to occur.

EXAMPLES:

- "Johnny, I want you to help me out here. Sally's ball has rolled into your space. Show me what you think you might do that is a supportive response to the situation."
- "Freddie is on your team and has just served the ball into the net. In fact, every time Freddie serves the ball, it goes into the net. How do you think players on Freddie's team should react to Freddie? Who would like to pretend to be Freddie? Who would like to react to Freddie?"

Reinforce positive responses. When teachers are working on a behavior, they can reinforce that behavior by calling attention to the behavior either publicly or privately. Because young primary children are still at a stage in which adult approval is important, public praise is often helpful. However, it may not be reinforcing to have the teacher praise older students. Initially immediate and frequent praise helps to define the behavior and make clear the expectations. Gradually the teacher should withdraw both the immediacy and frequency of praise.

You can also reinforce positive responses immediately when they are very low-frequency behaviors by stopping the class and sharing with the class that you have seen an appropriate response (like the kind of behavior we have been talking about). You can also privately reinforce a behavior with a student. Or you can talk about what you have seen at the end of class.

In cases where teachers are working with students who are operating at low levels of control, many teachers resort to more tangible rewards as reinforcers other than teacher praise. For example, placing student names on a board who were observed behaving appropriately, setting up a system of points or rewards, or using free time or some other special arrangement as a reinforcer does work to initially create compliance and a heightened awareness of appropriate behavior. The teacher's goal is to help students internalize appropriate behavior and gain a sense of self-control. The teacher must adopt a long-term plan for removing the external reinforcers he or she uses to create compliance. Continued and extensive use of external rewards makes the transition to self-control more difficult. External rewards should be used when necessary, but they should be gradually withdrawn.

Ignore inappropriate behavior in some cases if it is not disruptive to others. Some children behave inappropriately so that they can get the attention of the teacher or other students. If you determine that students are doing this, it is appropriate to ignore their inappropriate behavior and reward their appropriate behavior as long as the inappropriate behavior is not disruptive to others.

Other important ideas in behavioral techniques. Model appropriate behavior yourself. Students cannot be expected to behave in particular ways unless the teacher also behaves in those ways. Students learn a great deal more from what you do rather than from what you say.

Develop reflective skills on the part of learners. Ask students to evaluate their own behavior and responses either in writing or verbally at the end of a class or week.

EXAMPLE: "Write down in your journal today one thing you did that showed support for another person in the class and one task you worked on with a great effort today."

One of the problems with behavioral orientations to management and student discipline is that although behavioral methods are effective in producing student compliance and obedience, they are often used in a way that does not help the student to internalize appropriate behavior, develop self-discipline, or learn to be a risk taker. Student compliance is not a sufficient goal for educational programs that seek to develop self-discipline and risk taking in students. Part of the problem is the manner in which behavioral approaches have been used, and part of the problem is the goal to which teachers aspire.

It has been difficult for behavioral orientations to management to help students make the transition from teacher control to student control. The overuse of external rewards and failure to withdraw them; a lack of flexibility in rules, regulations, and expected behavior for changes in context; and a complacency on the part of teachers to be content with what is called in physical education "the busy-happy-good" syndrome (Placek, 1983) have all contributed to ineffective management systems.

Authoritative Orientations to Management

In response to the poor management of the schools, McCaslin and Good (1992) suggest that teachers should think in terms of an authoritative management system, the goal of which is self-discipline. Authoritarian management is discussed in the next section, not as a total management system but as a perspective on making management appropriate for the situation and changing needs of students toward self-discipline.

Teachers should take firm but flexible perspective on management. Authoritative managers have very clear expectations for students, but these expectations remain flexible. This means that the rules, procedures, and expectations are considered flexible and context specific. Expectations change from one group of students to another, one content area to another, one learning experience to another, and one student to another.

Teachers should take time to teach students self-directed behavior. Authoritative managers discuss with students why particular behaviors are important and how students might meet the expectations teachers have for them. Internal control and self-discipline are valued, and it is made clear that it is valued.

Teacher control is released as students are ready to accept more responsibility for own behavior. One of the problems with the manner in which behavioral systems have been implemented is that rules, procedures, and expectations for behavior do not change. Teachers tend to maintain the same level of expectations for students, and for the most part, in physical education this level of expectation has been very low in terms of students' responsibility

for their own behavior. Sixth graders should be capable of more independent behavior than first graders, and tenth graders should be capable of more independent behavior than sixth graders. The focus of authoritative discipline is on transferring the responsibility for behavior to students as students are ready. As students are ready to handle more of the responsibility for their own behavior and are ready to be put in situations that demand more self-responsibility, the teacher's management system should change with the emerging capabilities of students. Rigid, highly specific gymnasium rules are not flexible enough to encourage students with different abilities to be more responsible.

Group Process Strategies for Developing Self-Direction

In most classes, teachers find that group process strategies are effective ways of working with groups of learners to establish higher expectations for behavior and to solve problems that occur in relation to behavior. Group process strategies stress the group and social context of the school environment. Some of the basic strategies used in this approach follow.

Involve students in decision making. Using this strategy means that many rules and procedures, as well as more content-oriented decisions, can be made with student input. The teacher poses a problem (even if it is only a problem for the teacher) that needs a rule or procedure, and the students help establish the rules or procedures. Using this strategy well means that the teacher must be willing to take the time to work through solutions with students. It means that you may want to let students try solutions you feel may not work and then let them evaluate and reformulate their solutions.

Students are more likely to behave in ways consistent with rules, procedures, and goals if they have had a part in designing them. However, the teacher must be willing to take the time to bring problems back to the students when compliance is not acceptable.

Resolve conflicts through discussion. When conflicts arise, teachers stop what they are doing and make students aware that there is a problem. They then lead a discussion with students on how to resolve the conflict. The goals of the discussion are to help students gain a sense of responsibility for their own behavior and to help them recognize their responsibility toward others.

Role playing. Role playing was previously discussed as a strategy in behavioral modification. It is used here in a similar way—to help students come to know a desired behavior in a meaningful way. Role playing involves allowing students to put themselves in the position of another person and actually act out that role in a situation. The goal of role playing is to help students see other perspectives of a problem. Usually the teacher structures the role-playing situation by framing the problem or conflict and describing how people representing each of the parts feel about the problem. Potential learning in role playing is increased if the teacher makes explicit what is happening in the acting out and summarizes the lesson to be learned.

◆ DISCIPLINE: WHAT TO DO IF IT DOES NOT WORK

Discipline is what you do when, in spite of your best efforts, students do not cooperate and choose to behave in inappropriate ways. Teachers will have fewer discipline problems if they follow the guidelines presented in Box 7-5.

Not all students will choose to cooperate when you have been very positive about establishing the learning environment you desire. You will have to

---

BOX 7-5

Guidelines to Prevent Discipline Problems

- Establish an effective management system
- Have a positive attitude toward all students
- Share your expectations clearly and in advance
- Involve students in rules and procedures
- Have an appropriate and challenging curriculum
- Display enthusiasm toward what you are teaching

---

discipline students in spite of the your best efforts. Effective discipline matches the consequence of misbehavior to the behavior; for example, you do not call the principal because a child did not listen to directions one time.

Deterring Problems Before They Become Problems

If the teacher has made expectations clear to students and has provided enough structure and reasonable expectations for behavior, most infractions of rules or behavior expectations will be short term and easily handled with some simple techniques.

Maintaining eye contact. Generally if the teacher catches a student behaving inappropriately and briefly maintains eye contact with that student, the student will eventually stop the behavior. Sometimes it is necessary for the teacher to stop what he or she is doing and saying to emphasize the point.

Proximity control. When teachers use proximity control, they move physically closer to the student to make known that they are aware that inappropriate behavior is taking place. They do not have to say anything, and usually students will stop the inappropriate behavior.

Asking students to stop what they are doing. This is the most fundamental and sometimes forgotten technique a teacher has to eliminate inappropriate behavior. It is called a **desist.** Desists work only if they are not overused. If a teacher has to continually remind the same student or if a class of students is behaving inappropriately, desists are *not working* and it is time to move on to other techniques that address the issue more seriously. When possible, desists should be private communications with the student, although it is not always possible to do this.

Clarifying appropriate behavior. Instead of just asking students to stop misbehaving, sometimes it is helpful to clarify for students what they should be doing. This focuses the student on appropriate rather than inappropriate responses. Two examples of teacher clarification of appropriate behavior follow:

- "How are we supposed to get the equipment out?"
- "Yelling at your partner is not appropriate behavior."

Removing the student physically from the problem. If a student is having difficulty behaving appropriately because of the equipment or working close to an area that presents problems (e.g., water fountains, baskets, other equipment) or if he or she is close to other students who encourage misbehavior, the teacher can ask the student to work in another location or assign him or her to a different partner or group.

Continued Inappropriate Behavior

If the techniques just discussed do not eliminate inappropriate behavior for more than a very short time, the teacher must increase the level of response. The following ideas are useful.

Widespread class misbehavior. If you find that more than one or two students are engaging in inappropriate behavior, working with individual children may not be appropriate. You will need to stop the class and address the problem specifically. Consider the following teacher/student interaction.

> "Would everyone come in here for a minute. I don't know what the problem is today, but for some reason we are having trouble attending to what we are supposed to be doing. There must be some kind of a crazy bug going around or something. Who can tell me why you think I am having trouble with what is going on?"
>
> "What is it that we are supposed to be doing?"
>
> "Let's go back to work and see if we can try this again."

In the conversation just described, the teacher is calling attention to the problem, making it clear that what has occurred is inappropriate, and focusing the students on what they should be doing. The impor-

tant issue is that at this level the approach is still very positive. It is more like a class desist and will normally eliminate most problems. If the problems continue, the teacher may need to continue with the following remarks:

> "Some of you are obviously not ready to work today. Let's just sit here for a minute. When you think you are ready to continue and work appropriately, stand up and begin. If you are not, you may sit here until you are ready. If you go out to work and you are still having problems, I may need to sit you over on the side to think about what you should be doing."

Time out. Time out is a useful technique to handle disruptive and inappropriate behavior for young children and for students who actually want to participate in class. It is not appropriate for students who would rather not be participating, since it actually reinforces inappropriate behavior for these students.

The teacher who uses time out asks a student to sit out of activity in a designated area. Sometimes teachers ask students to sit out for a designated time, for example, 5 minutes. Sometimes teachers will say, "When you think you are ready to participate again, come tell me." Sometimes the teacher will leave students in time out until the teacher comes and tells them they can rejoin the activity. Time out works best if students are not left the entire period.

Negotiation/Confrontation. When teachers use negotiation/confrontation to solve problems either between themselves and students or between students, they are attempting to get students to accept responsibility for their behavior and to design a plan of action to improve their behavior. It is important when using this strategy to help the students recognize and own the behavior and then to work through a plan of action to improve the behavior. A description of a simple interaction of this type follows:

> Teacher: "What do you think is the problem here?"
> Student: "We were hitting balls over the fence."
> Teacher: "Why do you think we don't want balls over the fence?"
> Student: "Because we waste time going to get them."

Teacher: "How are we going to change what you are doing?"

Student: "We are not going to hit the balls over the fence any more."

Teacher: "What do you think I should do if it happens again?"

Student: "Not let us use the balls."

Handling students who continually misbehave. Individual students who continually misbehave in class are not easily handled without one-on-one attention of the teacher. Initially you should focus on this student and get a real sense of what exactly the student is doing during class and under what conditions. You should single this student out for extra positive attention to show him or her that you care, but do not reinforce misbehavior. If misbehavior continues, you will have to begin to plan on spending time with this student individually. Doing this during class time is sometimes difficult because the rest of the class is then left on their own. Individual conferences are best held when the teacher has time either before or after class or before or after school.

Several ideas should be considered when dealing with individual behavior problems.

- *What you do with the group must not affect the child negatively, and consequently, what you do for the child must not affect the group negatively.* This means that you cannot allow the individual student to disrupt the learning experiences of the rest of the students in your class. You must act. Second, you should not for the sake of the rest of the class respond to individual students in a way that can harm them (e.g., using students for a negative example).

- *Try to understand the cause of the behavior.* Students usually misbehave because of either personal or social adjustment problems they are having. Sometimes they misbehave because they are seeking attention, control, or power or because they simply have low self-esteem. There may be ways that you can help the student meet his or her needs in this area in positive, constructive ways. These kinds of solutions are usually long term and may not solve the immediate need for behavior change. Examples are (1) giving students the attention they need for positive behavior and (2) putting them in charge of something for the class or something they can do outside of class.

- *Check with other teachers and personnel in the school to find out if the problems the student is having are unique to your class or are a general pattern of behavior.* If you are having a major problem with a student, you will usually find that this same student is having problems with other teachers in the school and other areas of school life. Get some input from other teachers so you can understand the problem and cooperate with other teachers to come up with a consistent plan in handling the problem.

- *Respond negatively to the behavior—not the person.* One of the most useful ideas that teachers should maintain when dealing with inappropriate behavior is to separate their response to the misbehavior from their response to the person who is misbehaving. Teachers should maintain a concerned, caring attitude toward students and approach misbehavior positively. This does not mean that teachers should not be firm about the expectations for changing behavior.

- *Focus interactions with students on a resolution of the problem.* For emotionallly charged problems with students, the teacher should initially be an active listener. You should allow the student to vent anger if necessary, help him or her to understand where the anger may be coming from, and then begin to focus the student on defining the problem and coming up with solutions to the problem. You should explore possible solutions and come to some agreement on implementation of those solutions. Follow up on whether those solutions are working, and revise the plan if necessary.

- *If less formal methods of changing behavior do not work, explore the idea of contingency contracts with students.* If you have talked with students and set goals for changing behavior, only to learn that students are not complying with expectations for behavior change, you may have to begin more formal procedures for changing behavior. Contingency contracts are one such technique. Contingency contracts set goals for student behavior that are achievable (one step at a time) and reward students extrinsically for demonstrating that they have reached their goals. Rewards can be something as simple as a star, a small token, candy, time to do special things in class, and, in general, anything that is positively reinforcing for a particular individual. The teacher establishes a contract with the student and specifies what the student must do to meet the goals set for a particular period of time. At the conclusion of the time period, the student is rewarded for meeting the goal and a new goal is established that leads the student closer and closer to the desired behavior. Usually rewards will be sufficient to change behavior. If not, the teacher may want to build into the contract negative consequences for not meeting the goals, such as having to spend time after school or being denied a privilege. Monitoring of the contract should be done for each class and can be done by the student through self-evaluation or done initially by the teacher and later by the student. The long-term goal of contingency contracting should be to bring the student to self-directed behavior. To do this, the time periods for rewards and the expectations for rewards will increase until the student is responding appropriately without the rewards. Box 7-6 presents some guidelines for discipline.

BOX 7-6

Some Do's and Don't's of Discipline

Do	Don't
Use student names	Publicly reprimand
Expect students to behave	Downgrade students
Ask youself why	Engage in confrontation
Be firm and consistent	Give threats

Involving others in your efforts with problem students. If you have done all that you can with many of the ideas just expressed, it may necessary to enlist the help of others.

Involving parents. Schools usually have policies for calling parents about behavior problems in class. You will need to know what these policies are before enlisting the help of parents. Most parents are really concerned about their child's progress and behavior in your class. If you call them, you should clearly explain what the problem is and what you are doing about it. What you do not want is for the parents to overreact to the child's problem; you want merely to have them support you in your efforts by communicating their concern to the student and maintaining communication with the parents. Communicate not only setbacks, but positive attempts on the part of students to correct behavior problems.

Involving the principal. Most schools have policies regarding teachers sending students to the office or a designated place when they present behavior problems the teacher cannot handle within the class. Teachers should use the threat of the principal or detention center as a last resort, only when they cannot handle the problems themselves. School administrators are then primarily responsible for making decisions about what to do with these students. Punishment, detention, suspension, and involvement of school counselors are alternatives.

SUMMARY

1. Good management skills are essential for good teaching.
2. Content and management are interdependent systems of instruction.
3. The objective of a good management system is a high level of engagement in what the student is supposed to be doing.
4. Teachers must teach students what is expected and then maintain the environment they establish.
5. Routines are events that occur frequently in the teaching/learning environment that are handled in a similar manner.

6. Class rules should be few in number, taught as concepts, and reinforced consistently.

7. Behavior modification primarily uses clear expectations and reinforcement to establish student control.

8. Authoritative discipline establishes student understanding of appropriate behavior and remains firm but flexible to teach students self-direction.

9. Group process strategies stress the group and social context of the school environment and focus on involving students as a group in decision making.

10. The best approach to discipline is a preventive one.

11. Teachers should attempt to solve minor discipline problems before they become major ones.

12. If in spite of the teacher's best efforts, a student does not choose to cooperate, the teacher should solicit the help of others within the school.

CHECKING YOUR UNDERSTANDING

1. What is meant by the idea that instruction and management are part of an interdependent ecological system?

2. What is the major purpose of a management system?

3. List five key ideas important to establishing a management system.

4. Describe how you would establish a routine for taking attendance with high school students?

5. How are self-management skills developed? How would you begin to develop self-management skills for the attendance-taking routine you established in the above question?

6. Describe the similarities and differences between behavioral modification, authoritative discipline, and group process orientations to developing student control.

7. List five things you can do to prevent small incidences of misbehavior from becoming large ones.

8. What should you do with a student who, in spite of your best efforts, is disruptive on a continuous basis and chooses not to cooperate?

REFERENCES

Brophy J, Evertson C: Context variables in teaching, *J Educ Psychol* 12: 310-316, 1978.

Brophy JE: Classroom organization and management, *Elementary School Journal* 83(4):265-286, 1983.

Doyle W: Classroom organization and management. In Wittrock M, editor: *Handbook of research on teaching,* ed 3, New York, 1986, MacMillan Publishing.

Hellison D: *Goals and strategies for teaching physical education,* Champaign, IL, 1985, Human Kinetics Publishers.

McCaslin M, Good T: Compliant cognition: the misalliance of management and instructional goals in current school reform, *Educ Researcher* 21: 3, 1992.

Placek J: Conceptions of success in teaching: busy, happy, and good? In Templin T, Olson J, editors: *Teaching in physical education,* Champaign, IL, 1983, Human Kinetics Publishers.

Teacher Functions During Activity

❖❖❖❖❖❖❖❖❖❖
OVERVIEW

Teachers can perform many functions while students are engaged in a movement task. Some of these functions contribute directly to lesson objectives, some make only an indirect contribution to lesson objectives, and others make no contribution to lesson objectives. Effective teachers are active teachers who are actively engaged in promoting learning. Active teachers minimize the time they spend on activities that cannot contribute to lesson objectives and maximize the time they spend on those activities that can contribute to lesson objectives.

The purpose of this chapter is to describe and help the teacher arrange in order of priority the many different instructional functions that teachers engage in during the time students are working on the task.

❖❖❖❖❖❖❖❖❖❖
CONCEPTS

- **I've sent the students off to practice—Now what?**

- **Maintaining a safe learning environment**

- **Clarifying and reinforcing tasks for learners**

- **Maintaining a productive learning environment**

- **Observing and analyzing student responses**

- **Providing feedback to learners**

- **Changing and modifying tasks for individuals and small groups**

- **Indirectly contributing behaviors**
  Attending to injured students
  Engaging in off-topic discussions
  Dealing with the personal needs of students
  Participating with students and officiating

- **Noncontributing behaviors**

M ANY beginning teachers quickly acquire the skills of task presentation because that is the role of the teacher most common to our perspective of what it means to teach: teaching means telling people what to do. Few beginning teachers give much thought to what happens after they ask learners to engage in a movement task or learning experience. This is an uncomfortable period in the instructional process for beginning teachers because, actually, what they do as teachers depends greatly on what the students do in relation to what the teachers asked them to do.

In reality, teachers are just as active during this time as they are at all other lesson times. This is the time, more than all other times, that teachers must function in many different ways. Teachers must be able to handle the many different things that are going on in the gymnasium while maintaining an awareness of exactly what every student is doing. Kounin (1970) called this **withitness**: the ability to be aware at all times of what is going on regardless of what you are doing. He also coined a term **over-lappingness**, which is the ability of the teacher to do many things at one time and do them well. Effective teachers demonstrate both withitness and overlappingness. The following examples of real lessons illustrate the point.

EXAMPLE: Ms. S. meets the class of 27 first-graders at the door of the all-purpose room and asks them to move into the room and quietly take off their shoes and socks. Tommy cannot get the knots out of his laces, so the teacher helps Tommy. Sally comes up to say that she got new tennis shoes last night and they really run fast. The class gradually gathers in the center of the room, and the teacher explains that they will be working with tossing and throwing bean bags. During the explanation of the day's activities, the classroom teacher comes into the room with two additional students, who had arrived late for school. Ms. S. asks them to take off their shoes and join the class.

Ms. S. asks the students to pick up a bean bag from those scattered on the floor, to find a space in the room, and to start tossing and catching the bean bag without letting it hit the floor or going outside their own space. Ms. S. picks up the extra bean bags as the students begin their work and puts them into a basket. She comments to the whole class that their work is quiet and very controlled because she has heard no voices and has heard no bean bags touch the floor. She helps Mary direct her bean bag to

remain in front of her and asks Kevin to reduce the level of his toss so that he can maintain better control.

Ms. S. asks the class to begin tossing the bean bag to different levels while still maintaining control and to try catching the bean bag so that it makes no noise in their hands. She moves over to Brian, who has lost his bean bag on a light fixture on the ceiling, and asks him to get another one from the basket. Sheila comes up to the teacher to say that she has to go to the bathroom. Ms. S. gives her permission and resumes her observation of the class.

Now compare the actions of the first grade teacher with those of a ninth grade teacher during the following episode:

EXAMPLE: A coed ninth grade class is working on covering space in fielding in a modified softball game. Three fields are set up, with 10 students at each field. One student is "up at bat" and throws the ball into the field, trying to advance as far as possible without being put out. Players rotate into the nine fielding positions and keep personal scores.

Mr. T. is moving from one field to another, providing assistance to individuals and feedback to the whole group. Jeff, a rather heavy boy, has let a simple catch pass him without making any attempt to receive it. Other students in Jeff's group are yelling at him. Mr. T. moves out to Jeff and asks another player to cover Jeff's position. He pulls Jeff aside to ask what the problem is. Jeff relates to Mr. T. that if he tried he would miss it anyway, so he doesn't want to try. Mr. T. asks Kevin to come over to the side and asks him to work with Jeff until Jeff feels secure with fielding balls. Mr. T. explains to Kevin that Jeff should start with slow balls coming right to him and then should try balls coming faster that force him to move. Darlene comes over to tell Mr. T. that her glove is broken. Mr. T. motions to Darlene to take another.

Mr. T. moves to another group and asks how many have scored beyond first base. Nobody raises a hand, and Mr. T. comments that their fielding must be getting better. He blows his whistle and calls all the groups to one spot. He explains to the group that they are now going to try to prevent any runner from getting to first base. Any fielder who touches a ball that results in an out before first base will get one point. Any runner who scores will double his or her own points.

Refer to Box 8-1 for some common teacher functions that can be identified from the examples just presented, as well as other lesson observations. The functions in group 1 are those related to working directly with the lesson content. These functions con-

---

┌─ **BOX 8-1** ─────────────────────────

Common Teacher Functions During Activity

Group 1: Directly contributing behaviors

- Maintaining a safe learning environment
- Clarifying and reinforcing tasks for learners
- Observing and analyzing student responses
- Providing feedback to learners
- Changing or modifying tasks for individuals and small groups
- Maintaining a productive learning environment

Group 2: Indirectly contributing behaviors

- Participating with students and officiating
- Dealing with the personal needs of students
- Engaging in off-topic discussions
- Attending to injured students

└──────────────────────────────────────

tribute the most to lesson objectives and student learning. The functions in group 2 are an important part of teaching but can contribute only indirectly to lesson objectives. It is important for teachers to know how to handle all of these.

This chapter discusses the teaching functions that contribute the most to student learning. These functions are referred to as **directly contributing behaviors** because they have the potential to directly contribute to the content of the lesson. Teachers also must deal with the situations listed in group 2 in Box 8-1, which are a part of every lesson. These behaviors of the teacher will be referred to as **indirectly contributing behaviors.** They are a necessary and important part of teaching but are not actually lesson related and only *indirectly* contribute to the lesson content. The chapter ends with a discussion of behaviors teachers should avoid that make *no contribution* to the lesson.

◆ I'VE SENT THE STUDENTS OFF TO PRACTICE—NOW WHAT?

Our work with experienced and successful teachers identified the idea that teachers really do have a strategy for dealing with what their role is during the time students are active. What these teachers did was to identify some priorities for what to do first. Whereas beginning teachers are likely to move into the group when they first start to practice to offer individual students help, the first efforts of experienced teachers are toward standing back in a position to observe the whole group and then ensuring that the learning environment is a safe one and a productive one. The teacher then focuses on student responses to make a determination of how the class as a whole is handling the task. What follows is a chronological list that describes what experienced teachers are likely to do first as they send students off to practice a task. Each of these ideas will then be discussed separately in terms of suggestions for how to do it.

1. Make sure the environment is a safe one.
2. Make sure students understand the task and are engaged in the task as it was designed.
3. Observe to determine the specific responses of the class as a whole to the task in terms of the learning objective. Adjust the task as needed.
4. Recheck continuously that student work is productive.
5. Observe individual performance and assist as possible.
6. Maintain awareness of the whole group. Be alert for task pacing needs and task engagement.

Several ideas should be obvious from the activites just listed. First, successfully performing all of these functions depends on the teacher's ability to observe and analyze what the students are doing. Second, all of these functions are interrelated. They affect each other. When task environments are safe and when tasks are clear to learners and appropriate for both the group and individuals, learners are likely to be engaged in the task. A teacher actively engaged in giving feedback to learners potentially maintains a productive and usually safe learning environment. Teachers who modify tasks for individuals or small groups within a class also make the environment safer and more productive. All behaviors that have the potential to contribute directly to student content learning communicate to the student the teacher's interest in the student learning. Communicating the intent that learning should occur is essential to effective teaching.

During this scenario the teacher is always alert to the needs of both the group and individuals within the group. However, unlike many beginning teachers, experienced teachers are likely to recognize the importanc e of maintaining contact with the group and meeting the needs of the group. Only when the group is engaged appropriately and productively can the teacher attend to individuals. The teacher does not neglect individuals but must put them on "hold" until group needs are met.

The priorities just discussed are those that directly contribute to lesson content. It is likely that during this time the teacher must also effectively handle many indirectly contributing episodes and perhaps some that make no contribution at all to the lesson.

◆ MAINTAINING A SAFE LEARNING ENVIRONMENT

Safe learning environments can almost always be prepared for in advance. Experienced teachers learn to anticipate safety problems and to arrange equipment, space, and people so that the environment both is safe and facilitates learning. Experienced teachers also learn to build safety into the tasks they give learners (e.g., coming down on the feet softly from a handstand; making sure no one is around before swinging a racket, stick, or club). Experienced teachers teach for safety and student responsibility for safety.

In situations where advance preparation has not been adequate, the teacher's first priority during activity is to make the environment safe. The first thing a teacher always needs to determine is whether the learning environment is a safe one. Safety takes precedence over all other concerns. Regardless of the cause, unsafe conditions must be changed either by stopping the activity of the entire class or of the individuals involved or by removing the unsafe conditions in a less obtrusive way.

◆ CLARIFYING AND REINFORCING TASKS FOR LEARNERS

Many teachers find it necessary to clarify or restate the task for learners shortly after students begin work on a task. Sometimes this is necessary because the teacher observes that students are not responding to the task in the way intended and sometimes a teacher restates the task to reinforce on-task behavior and hold students accountable for the task as it was presented.

Teachers who are working with students who are not accustomed to working within the limits of a task or with a more narrow focus on tasks may need to clarify tasks on a more continuous basis until students recognize that they must attend to task directions because they will be held accountable for them in their work.

EXAMPLE: The teacher has asked students to focus on stepping into a tennis swing. Although the students are working on their swing, the teacher sees no evidence that students are attending to stepping into their swing.

The ideal situation is to avoid the need for clarifying or restating a task by presenting the task with clarity the first time around. However, if the teacher observes that students are not responding quickly or correctly to the task presented, clarification and reinforcement are necessary. Teachers who continuously find it necessary to reinforce or clarify the task should reexamine their original presentations. Inexperienced teachers tend to blame off-task behavior on "bad" students when the fault actually lies in how the teacher prepared the students for the task.

Teachers can clarify or reinforce the task without stopping the class by restating the task while students are preparing for or engaged in activity. If confusion is not widespread, a few individuals who are not on task can be redirected. This can be accomplished by positively reinforcing those students who are on task. For example, during a tennis lesson the teacher might say, "Tommy has his racket and is practicing sending the ball to the wall with one bounce in between."

Nevertheless, there are times when, after realizing that students are not responding to the task as the teacher originally intended, the entire class must be stopped and directions explained. Teachers should not be afraid to do this. If the teacher selected the original task because it was appropriate, it is important that students work with this task. If students do not respond to a task in the way teachers intended them to respond, it usually is because the students do not know what they are supposed to be doing. Sometimes this is because the teacher is not clear to begin with, and sometimes it is because students are not listening or are accustomed to not attending to the specifics of what a teacher has said. No matter what the cause, teachers should not hesitate to stop and get what they want in student responses. Inexperienced teachers have a tendency to accept any response of students rather than reinforcing only the desired response.

◆ MAINTAINING A PRODUCTIVE LEARNING ENVIRONMENT

The idea of clarifying and reinforcing the task for the learners during an activity is closely related to the idea of maintaining a productive learning environment. Choosing to clarify and reinforce the task usually indicates that the teacher has decided that off-task responses are occurring because the students did not understand or were not attending to the directives involved in a task. This is usually the case when off-task behavior occurs shortly after the task has begun. However, when teachers find a productive learning environment slipping away from them as the activity progresses, they should look for other causes for the off-task behavior and respond differently. For example, a sudden increase in noise directly outside the classroom may be preventing students from properly concentrating on the task.

Off-task behavior is difficult to deal with because of the many different causes. A more complete discussion of how to handle off-task behavior is presented in Chapter 7 and will not be duplicated here. A primary cause of off-task behavior with students is that the task is inappropriate for either the group or individuals, either because of the content of the task or the manner in which the task is organized.

EXAMPLES:

- The teacher has asked students to work on a backward roll. Students who cannot do a backward roll are likely to find something else to do. Students lose interest quickly when the task is not appropriate because it is too difficult or too easy. Again, the teacher should strive for an error rate that is challenging but not frustrating for the student.

- The teacher has lined up students to wait for a turn to practice a skill. Students waiting for a turn are likely to find something else to do.
- The teacher has grouped students and has put students together who cannot work productively together. The teacher has not focused students on working together before sending them off to practice.
- The teacher has sent students off without much structure to practice a skill for which they have little experience. The teacher may need to initially add structure to the practice before students are sent off on their own.

Sometimes the task needs more structure to maintain interest. Structure, as previously discussed, can be added by (1) giving the students a certain time period in which to accomplish specific goals, (2) having students perform on signal, (3) putting students in an organizational arrangement that is easier for the teacher to directly monitor, or (4) narrowing the focus of the task.

To make a judgment about what to do, a teacher must first decide why students are off task. The examples just given describe situations that are the result of the task and the arrangements the teacher has made for organizing students to work on the task. If students begin to work on the task but gradually lose interest in the task, the problem is most likely related to *task pacing*. Task pacing has to do with the amount of time teachers give students to work on a task before changing the focus of the task, providing some kind of a break from the task, or changing to a new task. Task pacing is a significant concept in motor skill learning because to learn motor skills, students will need much practice and teachers must acquire strategies to help students maintain interest in that practice. The following ideas will help maintain student interest and on-task behavior for longer periods of time.

- *Provide feedback to students on performance.* When teachers are actively engaged in providing both individual and group feedback during instruction, student interest in the task is maintained for longer periods of time.
- *Provide a break from practice.* Often students need a break from practice. The teacher can call students in and have some students demonstrate what they have done. The teacher can keep the

same focus when practice is resumed or can change the focus to an aspect of practice that needs work.

- *Reorganize the practice.* Teachers can work on the same task in different ways, can change the manner in which students are grouped (different partners), or can change the equipment or space students will use. Because each of these ideas provides a change, it is likely to increase productive practice for longer periods of time.

When individual students are having difficulty attending to the lesson and the teacher has decided that the task is appropriate for these students, the teacher must act to stop or change off-task behavior before it becomes a problem. A complete discussion of management and discipline is provided in Chapter 7. What follows are some actions that teachers can take during the time students are working on a task that will usually solve most problems.

EXAMPLE: The student knows what is expected but has made the decision not to respond appropriately. The teacher has the following alternatives:

- Move the student to another location.
- Redirect the student to the task.
- Inform the student that the conditions of participation are that the student respond with appropriate behavior.
- Remove the student from the situation on the condition that the student may return when ready to accept responsibility for proper behavior.

Sometimes, in spite of all efforts to keep students productive, teachers have a few students who make the decision not to respond appropriately. If this type of behavior involves more than a few students, the cause of this lack of appropriate response should be looked for in teacher behavior.

◆ OBSERVING AND ANALYZING STUDENT RESPONSES

Observation of student responses is an essential skill for teachers. You cannot provide students with feedback, assess their performance, or make decision about what to do unless you can observe and accurately determine what it is students are doing. In recent years physical educators have begun to look at the processes of observation and analysis as separate learned skills that do not come naturally to most teachers.

Your skill in observing depends on many factors, including your personal knowledge of what you are teaching, who you are teaching, and the context of the specific class you are teaching, as well as the complexity of the environment and the content you are observing. Teachers who have many students, who are observing unfamiliar skills, or who are not comfortable in the teaching role will not be as good at observation of movement responses as teachers who have smaller classes, who are dealing with familiar content, and who are comfortable in a teaching role. Problems with some skills are also more difficult to see. Skills like the overhand throw pattern or the standing broad jump occur so quickly that it is difficult to do an accurate analysis of problems without being able to slow down the skill.

The following key points from the work of Barrett (1979; 1983), Biscan (1976), and Craft (1977) provide some guidelines for teachers who want to improve their observation of student responses:

- The position that the teacher observes from is critical.
- Teachers do better if they know in advance specifically what they will be looking for.
- Observation of large groups of learners seems to be enhanced if teachers have a strategy for observing a large group.

The following section considers the implications of each of these statements for the teacher during activity time.

Positioning of the Teacher

The position of the teacher during activity time is critical from three perspectives. First, teachers who are responsible for a whole group of learners should never remove themselves entirely from a position that allows them to constantly view the whole group. Second, teachers may need to change positions to get a new observation perspective when looking for different aspects of performance. Third, where teachers stand affects the performance of students.

Teachers of large groups learn early that moving throughout the group and getting to all parts of the available space increase on-task behavior and tend to keep students more productive. Teachers should try not to get caught in the center for any length of time. The center does not allow the teacher to remain visually in contact with the whole group. Furthermore, students will not use the space a teacher has reserved for the teaching position. Teachers who do not make any place in the work area a home base avoid this problems.

Where teachers position themselves is critical to their ability to judge particular aspects of performance. Different motor skills and different parts of a motor skill require different views of performance. For example, teachers cannot discriminate lateral movement in the run if they are observing from the side. Similarly, teachers are probably in a better position to judge some aspects of the overhand throw pattern from the front and others from the side. Inexperienced teachers need to consciously select an observation position based on the specific aspect of the skill they are trying to observe.

Determining a Plan for Observing Large Groups

In studying observation skills, Barrett (1979; 1983) found that if teachers of large groups have a plan for observing individuals, they are more likely to use their observation time effectively. The observation plan may be (1) to scan the whole group for one particular movement aspect, (2) to select a few individuals known to be of different skill levels, or (3) to observe only a few students at one time, selecting different students at another time. A plan for observation helps the teacher avoid the problem of looking but not really seeing. This problem can occur easily when the teacher is confronted with a sea of performers.

Closely related to the idea of who to observe and what to look for is the decision of how long to stay with one student. The length of time a teacher observes one student depends largely on what the teacher is looking for. Although some judgments about performance can be made quickly, many can-

not, thus requiring the teacher to see more than one trial of the same skill. The teacher must determine how many students to observe and what is most important to observe. In observing a skill such as the tennis forehand, critical aspects such as arm extension can probably be observed rather quickly with a scanning strategy. If the important cues are determined before instruction using a developmental analysis of the content, the teacher's selection is easier. However, the teacher still must order sequentially what the initial focuses of observation will be and what can be delayed.

Knowing What to Look For

If a teacher presents the following tennis task to a group of learners, what should be looked for?

EXAMPLE: The student and a partner should send the ball back and forth to each other with forehand strokes, concentrating on getting the arm extended.

The first observation cue in this task is an obvious one: the teacher should be looking for arm extension. Where should the teacher stand to observe arm extension? What levels of feedback statements would be congruent with this task? Arm extension can probably be observed best from the front. To be congruent, teacher feedback should be related to arm extension. What is most important to remember in this example is that the teacher has to make a decision about what to look for.

Deciding what to look for is complicated by tasks that ask students to focus on many aspects of performance at the same time and by tasks that have no specific focus. If students are asked to focus on so many specifics that the teacher cannot determine an observation focus, it can probably be assumed that students are being overloaded with cues on which to focus their work.

There are times when a task has no specific stated focus that provides the teacher with a clear cue of what to focus on. An example of this situation is when students, primarily beginners, are simply given the idea of a movement and then asked to try it. As previously stated, the teacher in this case should first observe to make sure students are trying to perform in a way consistent with how the skill is grossly performed. For example, if the teacher has asked students (1) to support their weight on their hands by raising their feet in the air and (2) to bring their feet down softly and close to their hands, the teacher probably should be assessing their intent to come down softly and close to their hands. Knowing that students who do not initiate their movement by raising their hips will have difficulty bringing their feet down close to their hands helps the teacher to assess causes of feet not landing close to the hands. Next, the teacher probably should assess the gross aspects of performance and note them mentally to provide further cues after students have had an opportunity to practice.

In the case of the handstand task, the gross aspects might be the position of the head and hips and the push off the floor with the foot. As Barrett (1979) suggested, there probably are critical features of movements that are more important to observe than others. It is not enough just to be able to analyze a movement. Teachers must be able to select cues according to their own objectives and the stage of the learner.

If the tennis forehand is being presented for the first time, what gross observation cues are most important for the teacher to observe? There is, of course, no set answer to this question, but rather a range of correct answers that experienced and successful teachers have discovered through trial and error and much educated guessing. When presenting tasks to beginning learners, teachers should select a limited number of critical features of the task to communicate. The cues the teacher gives to the learner should also serve as the observation cues for the teacher. For the tennis forehand, a teacher of beginners would probably want to observe first whether the student's side is toward the net and then the path of the racket head through space.

Perhaps there will be a time when the study of teaching physical education will involve learning critical observation cues for teaching different skills at different levels. Until such time, teachers will need to do much skill analysis and put much effort into consciously and deliberately selecting observation cues

for the tasks they give. Many of these decisions should be made in planning and should be identified specifically on the lesson plan for beginning teachers.

◆ **PROVIDING FEEDBACK TO LEARNERS**

All of the teacher functions and behaviors that have been discussed so far are necessary to maintain an on-task, safe, and productive learning environment. However, none of the behaviors communicates the actual content of the task to students. Instead, the behaviors establish and maintain the conditions for learning.

Feedback is information learners receive about their performance. The teacher of motor skills does not have permanent products of student work, such as examinations or written assignments, that can be taken home and carefully evaluated. A large percentage of feedback students get on motor performance occurs during or immediately after performance. Although the specific relationship between teacher feedback and student learning in physical education classes has not been demonstrated, teacher feedback plays many other roles in group instruction, other than just providing individual students with information on their performance.

Teacher feedback maintains student focus on the learning task and serves to motivate and monitor student responses. When the teacher gives attention to the student, that student (and others as well) is likely to be more motivated and also to remain on task. Feedback that is specifically content related communicates the teacher's intent to help students improve the quality of their responses and therefore is likely to contribute to a task-oriented and productive learning environment.

The need to react immediately to student responses places a heavy burden on the observation and analysis skills of the teacher. Providing feedback that is appropriate is perhaps the behavior that most taxes a teacher's knowledge and observational skills.

Types of feedback can be classified in many ways. Each type of feedback serves a different purpose in the instructional setting and therefore should be used with a very specific intent. Table 8-1 illustrates the classifications of feedback discussed in this chapter.

Evaluative and Corrective Feedback

Evaluative feedback occurs when a value judgment concerning how well or poorly a task was performed is directly communicated to the learner. Evaluative feedback is a judgement made about the past performance of the student. Corrective feedback gives the learner information on what to do or on what not to do in future performances. Teachers will often couple evaluative and corrective feedback together, such as, "You really got your feet into position that time; now let's try and follow through on your stroke."

Evaluative and corrective feedback can be (1) congruent with the focus of the task or incongruent with the focus of the task; (2) positive or negative; (3) directed to the class, a group within the class, or an individual; and (4) general or specific.

Congruency of Feedback

Congruency refers to the relationships between the content of feedback, the focus of the task, and the cues that teachers give for the task. Congruent feedback gives information on performance or results that is directly related to what the learners have been asked to focus on. Some examples of congruent feedback for the task of dribbling a soccer ball while concentrating on using the inside of the foot are the following:

- "You're still using the outside of your foot occasionally."
- "Not the front of your toes, John."
- "That's it, Betty, the inside of the foot each time."
- "Stay with the inside of your foot, Susan."

Each of these feedback statements refers directly to the inside characteristic of the foot dribble.

Incongruent feedback gives information to the learner that may be important to the skill but is not

TABLE 8-1	Evaluative and corrrective examples of the different classifications of feedback	
Classification	**Evaluative**	**Corrective**
General	"Good job."	"Don't do it that way."
Specific	"You really got your legs extended that time."	"Point your toes."
Negative	"First-graders play better than you."	"Try not to bend your knees."
Positive	"Tommy has got his ball in the target every time."	"Keep your knees locked."
Class	"This class has improved 100%."	"Don't forget to get back to home base position after you hit the ball."
Group	"This group is not working as well as I know you can."	"Play your own position."
Individual	"You're not stepping into the ball."	"Step into the ball."
Congruent*	"Your pass made the receiver stop."	"Lead the receiver a little more."
Incongruent*	"Don't dribble the ball until you look to see if someone is open."	"You are not passing to everyone in your group."

*Assuming the task is to work on getting the pass ahead of the receiver so that the receiver does not have to stop to receive it.

specifically related to the task focus. Some examples of incongruent feedback for the task just described are the following:

- "Keep the ball closer to you."
- "Watch where you're going."
- "Get those feet around when you're changing direction."

When teachers give a high percentage of congruent feedback, their teaching becomes more narrow and more focused. Student effort can also become more narrow and more focused. The usual approach to feedback is to use what is called the *shotgun approach*. The shotgun approach involves asking the learner to focus on a task and then giving feedback on everything the teacher knows or observes that is related to that skill. Physical education would be more effective if teachers narrowed the number of cues they give students related to a movement task and tried to keep their feedback related to those cues. Students can focus on only a limited number of cues. These cues should be carefully selected by the teacher, and the feedback the teacher gives should reinforce the cues given. Student focuses are hard to maintain when the teacher continuously uses feedback to switch focuses within short time periods. This is particularly true in situations using an interactive strategy, where all students are working on the same task.

Teacher feedback is a powerful agent in focusing student responses. It is a great help when it reinforces the desired intent of the task, but it can be just as powerful in changing the intent of students' work. Consider the situation where a teacher asks students to balance on a variety of body parts. The teacher observes a student doing a headstand and cries out, "Johnny is doing a headstand." Within seconds the entire class is doing headstands. The headstand, however, was not the intent of the task—a variety of ways of balancing on three parts was. The teacher in this instance has changed the intent through the feedback provided. A better approach would be either to positively praise the idea of the headstand and challenge students to seek other responses as well or to make sure that a variety of student responses is praised.

The teacher who asks students to focus on the quality of performance and then does nothing but reinforce winning, losing, or scoring in games probably will not see quality. A competitive situation is a student focus that is difficult to orient in another direction. The more that competition becomes part of the feedback structure of the teacher, the more intense the focus becomes in the minds and work of the students. It is obvious that all feedback cannot always be congruent. Students need individual help, and sometimes this means asking for higher or lower levels of refinement from individuals within a class. The first observation cue the teacher should use, however, is to look at performance in relation to the focus of the task. The teacher should then provide appropriate congruent feedback.

General Versus Specific Feedback

The use of general versus specific feedback has been the subject of much research in motor learning and in teaching. Theoretically, specific information should be more valuable to the learner. Specific feedback has the potential to contribute to student learning a great deal more than general feedback. Specific feedback also serves a major role in maintaining student attention to the task and in developing accountability for tasks. Most teachers are trained to be specific in their feedback.

For specific feedback to be helpful to the learner, it must be related to an aspect or a result of performance that is fairly consistent. At the very beginning stages, learners who do not make the same response consistently probably cannot use feedback related to inconsistent errors. Young children and beginners probably should be given general information that clarifies the *intent* of the performance rather than the details of the performance. Experienced teachers who work with students with low self-concepts probably will agree also that sometimes more general positive feedback that provides high motivation is more critical than specific feedback on incorrect performance. In any case, the concepts used in verbal feedback should be those that are understood by the learner.

There are many levels of general and specific feedback. Consider the following statements:

- "Good."
- "Good hit."
- "Good follow-through on the hit."

Obviously the word "good" is the most general of the three statements. Teachers use general feedback statements like "good" primarily to motivate students. What is being evaluated with the word "good" is sometimes difficult to determine. Teachers may use "good" to mean "good effort," "good, you're on task," or "good hit" in the content of a hitting task. The learner will probably be confused. The word "good" should be used to reinforce good performance by helping students understand *what* was good about performance.

The ability to give accurate and appropriate specific feedback depends on clear skill goals, knowledge of how skills are performed, and good observation and analysis skills. When teachers realize that they are giving mostly general feedback on performance, they should train themselves to follow up the feedback by questioning *what* was good about the performance.

There appears to be some real differences in the frequency with which teachers give feedback on skill and other student behaviors at different age levels (Rink, 1979). Elementary teachers give more feedback, college teachers rank second, and secondary teachers provide the least feedback to their students. A great percentage of that feedback is general, however, which seems to indicate that the teachers are using the feedback more as a motivating and monitoring tool rather than as specific information to learners on their performance.

Negative Versus Positive Feedback

Descriptive studies in physical education have shown that feedback in gymnasiums tends to be more negative than positive (Anderson, 1980). This is unfortunate but probably attributable to the notion that the physical educator's job is to correct errors. Actually, students can be helped to correct errors in positive ways. Information about what is good in a performance is just as valuable as infor-

mation about what is wrong. Consider the following statements:

- "You're putting too much force on the ball."
- "Use less force on the ball."

The difference between these two statements is a subtle one. The first is a perspective on past performance and the second a perspective on future performance. Teachers often assume that students know what to do when told what not to do. This may be a false assumption.

Clarity of feedback can be enhanced by helping students to understand the difference between their performance and the desired performance. For example, this can be achieved if both of the statements just given are used in conjunction with each other when the teacher feels the need to provide corrective feedback. The student then benefits from examples of both what to do and what not to do. This type of feedback becomes even more effective if the teacher can spend time with the student (or group) until the student has had an opportunity to use the information provided. The student's understanding of the feedback then can be checked. Teachers who are not needed by the whole class can afford to do this.

Some recent interpretations of research have overemphasized the idea of positive versus negative feedback and implied that teachers should not even tell students when the students are doing something wrong. This research has been misinterpreted. What is implied in the research is that negative criticism is to be avoided, particularly criticism that is attached to the person rather than the behavior. Information on performance that tells the students the response is not correct is valuable and does not need to be harsh or critical in its delivery. Teachers can correct errors without appraising the individual and should make the distinction between the *behavior* of the person and the *person* when providing feedback (e.g., the teacher should say "Get the snap in the wrist quicker" rather than "You're not doing it right, John"). Teachers who are sensitive to the student's need to be successful, particularly in the eyes of the teacher, will sensitively communicate error to students.

For individual feedback to be effective, teachers must have time to work with students. (Courtesy SIUE Photo.)

Target of Feedback

Teachers will want to direct their responses to different units of learners at different times during a lesson. The following categories describe the targets of teachers' feedback:

- *Class*: Feedback is directed to all the learners in the class.
- *Group*: Feedback is directed to a part of the learners in a class.
- *Individual (Class)*: Feedback is directed to one individual so that the whole class benefits from the comment.

A typical model of instruction in physical education describes the teacher giving a task and then frantically running from student to student to correct errors. If students can work independently and productively for long periods of time, individual private communications may allow the teacher opportunities to be more specific and to individualize. However, one problem with this model is that there usually is

not time to get to every student. Teachers who try earnestly to get to every student at least once during the class period frequently fail. There are better ways to provide more information on performance to more learners.

Many times in physical education classes, particularly with beginners, the majority of learners can profit from the same feedback. In these instances teachers should consider directing their comments to the whole class. Comments directed to an individual so that the whole class can hear or comments directed to the class as a whole also serve a strong monitoring function in group instruction. Where active monitoring is necessary, such as in elementary schools, feedback directed in this way can be especially helpful. However, singling out a secondary school student for public feedback may have strong social consequences for this age student and should be avoided.

The following examples of feedback directed to the class and feedback directed to an individual so that the whole class can hear illustrate the use of these types of feedback:

- **Feedback directed to the class**
  Situation: The teacher has given high school tennis students the task of tossing the ball in the air continuously until it consistently falls in front of the toe. The teacher observes that many of the students are gripping the ball incorrectly for the toss.
  Feedback: The teacher stops the whole class and says, "Many of you are tossing the ball from the palm of your hand. Toss the ball from the pads of your fingers." The teacher then demonstrates the proper toss.
- **Feedback directed to a student so that the whole class can hear**
  Situation: The teacher has asked a class of second grade students to jump off benches softly so that their landing cannot be heard. The teacher notices that a few students continue to land hard from these jumps.
  Feedback: The teacher selects a student who is landing very quietly and says to him so that the whole class can hear, "Johnny's landings are so soft that I can't even hear them."

Timing of Feedback

The sooner feedback is given after performance, the more potential it has to help the learner. Feedback can immediately follow performance, or it can be delayed. A teacher moving from student to student most often provides feedback immediately after performance, as does a teacher who stops a group of students who have similar problems.

Teachers who give students time to practice and then provide evaluative and corrective feedback as a task focus delay feedback but provide a future focus that is valuable. Delayed feedback with a new task focused on improvement may increase the quality of performance in large instructional groups, particularly beginners. Delayed feedback with no opportunity to improve performance does little to help students improve performance.

Use of Feedback to Promote Student Understanding

Teacher feedback is a useful tool to help students understand cognitively what they are doing, what they should be doing, and why adjustments should be made. If teachers have time to spend with individuals, they can promote cognitive understanding of movement information on why it is important to perform in particular ways. Consider the following episode:

EXAMPLE: Teacher A. observes a student not transferring weight to the forward foot on a tennis backhand. Teacher A. goes up to the student and says, "Where is your weight when you finish your stroke?" The student replies, "I don't know." Teacher A. tells the student, "Do it again and tell me." The student follows the teacher's instructions and replies, "On my back foot." Teacher A. asks, "Where should it be?" and the student replies, "On my forward foot." Asked "why," the student says, "Because I can hit harder." Teacher A. confirms the student's discovery and says, "Yes, because you are then using your body weight to help you get more power, you're able to hit the ball harder."

The problem of weight transfer could have been handled easily with a simple "Step forward into your swing as you come through." The teacher might have been successful in correcting student error in

this case. The teacher chose to take a less efficient route to change, hoping more understanding would develop on the part of the student.

Understanding is largely a cognitive goal. Its influence on skill development is not clear. Like movement concepts, the intent is not only immediate change in the single skill, but also transfer to other skills.

◆ CHANGING AND MODIFYING TASKS FOR INDIVIDUALS AND SMALL GROUPS

No matter how much effort a teacher has put into individualizing tasks, there always seems to be a need to make tasks more appropriate for individuals or small groups within a class. Increased opportunities for participation outside the school setting have increased, not decreased, the range of abilities within physical education classes. Teachers can modify tasks to make them more appropriate for individual learners in much the same way that they develop tasks for an entire class. They can do the following:

- Change the content of the task entirely by asking individual students to work on something the whole class is not working on.
- Extend the task for individuals by reducing the complexity, expanding the complexity, or seeking a variety of responses from the same individual or group.
- Move students into or out of competitive situations.
- Prescribe levels of refinement or correct errors on an individual basis.

For example, if the task is for partners to strike a ball back and forth across the net continuously without losing control, there are numerous ways the task can be modified for individuals or small groups of learners. (It is assumed that each student has a paddle or racket and that each set of partners has a whiffle ball or tennis ball and a net or some other barrier to send the ball over.) Using the example, the following discussion explores the possibilities for making the task appropriate for different individuals within the class. These possibilities are described in terms of the constructs of extending, refining, and applying that are used for the analysis and development of content.

Extending

The first modification considered here are ways in which the teacher may have to change the conditions of the task. Based on individual needs, the teacher in this example may need to do the following:

- Move students who are having difficulty controlling the ball closer to each other.
- Move students back who are not getting a powerful enough hit on the ball and are just tapping it.
- Create boundaries for students who are not controlling the direction of the hit.
- Ask students to start placing the ball away from their partners when the students have achieved a high level of control and continuous hits with the task the way it is.
- Move some students back to hitting the ball against the wall by themselves.
- Change the tennis or whiffle ball to an object that is easier to control.

These are all adjustments the teacher can make in the conditions of the task based on the observed needs of individuals within a group. There are few lessons in which tasks do not need some modification for individual students, either because the students are working above their level of ability and are not successful at the task or because they are successful every time and are not being challenged.

The concept of error rate is again a very useful concept for many of the tasks teachers give in physical education. If students are successful with a task almost every time, the teachers should consider challenging the students above the conditions of the task. If students fail more often than they succeed, the teacher probably should assume that the conditions of the task are too difficult. Even in situations that allow students to choose a level of response, the teacher should help them work at the appropriate level of response.

Applying

A second way the teacher can modify tasks for individuals is to move them into or out of a competitive setting. Unfortunately, it is the applying task that

is most often inappropriate for individuals and groups within a class. This is also a task that teachers are reluctant to modify for students.

The teacher in the sample task can move students into a competitive situation by asking students who are ready for the challenge to keep track of the number of times they can send the ball back and forth to their partner without missing. The teacher can also ask some students to design a game using the skills they have been practicing. Students who have both competence and confidence in these skills will be highly motivated by the opportunity to test them under more gamelike conditions.

When a large portion of the class is not ready for a competitive experience, the teacher may have to meet the needs of students who are ready by changing the task to an applied task on an individual basis. In situations where a large portion of the class is ready for a competitive experience and a small portion is not, the teacher may have to remove individual students from the competitive task.

Changing the Task Completely

A third alternative for making the task appropriate for individuals or small groups is to change the task completely. To completely change rather than modify the sample task, the teacher must change it from a striking task to a nonstriking task. In classes involving mainstreamed handicapped students, changing the task becomes a critical need. In the sample task this can be done by having students throw and catch a ball rather than strike it at each other.

Complete changes of tasks for individuals or small groups are most appropriate in situations where teachers have chosen to introduce specialized skills. Asking students who cannot place any weight on their own hands to do a cartwheel is not only a waste of time but inexcusable from the standpoint of both safety and the students' motivation. Asking students to serve a volleyball overhead when they cannot contact the ball with an underhand serve is equally unacceptable. The teacher who has chosen to give highly specialized tasks that offer little room for varied responses must be willing to change the task appropriately for students who are not ready for these skills and to move advanced students beyond the skill given.

Refining

An alternative to modifying tasks on an individual or small group basis is to provide a focus with a greater or lesser degree of quality. The refining task asks students to perform some aspect of the original task with better quality but also enables teachers to reduce overall expectations. In the tennis example, typical refining tasks might be the following:

- "Get your side to the net."
- "Contact the ball further from your body."
- "Control the ball within your own space."
- "Follow through with your weight on the forward foot."

Refining tasks that ask students to improve some aspect of their response are the most common attempts to individualize tasks for different learners, as discussed in the previous section on feedback.

◆ INDIRECTLY CONTRIBUTING BEHAVIORS

Indirectly contributing behaviors focus the teacher's attention on the students and the learning environment but do not make a direct contribution to the content of the lesson. Some examples of behaviors that do not serve a content function are attending to an ill or injured student, engaging in off-topic discussions with students, or repairing equipment that breaks during a lesson. As is the case with noncontributing behaviors, teachers do not always have a choice in performing these functions. The following discussion of some of the most common events in this category, however, focuses on those situations where teachers do have a choice of actions.

Attending to Injured Students

Injured students must be attended to. Once again, the goal is to handle the problem in the least disruptive way. Most schools have standard procedures for handling the problem of injured students, and teachers are obliged to follow this policy. The teacher must decide whether to allow the rest of the class to continue or, in the case of a serious injury, to stop class activity. Minor injuries can be handled by older students with direction from the teacher. Almost all schools have someone designated for first aid. The

teacher should quickly dispatch students with minor injuries to this person and resume work with the rest of the class. Under *no* conditions should the class be left unattended.

Engaging in Off-Topic Discussions

Discussions with students about intramurals, favorite professional sports teams, new tennis shoes, or baby brothers may enhance relationships between the teacher and the students but contribute little to the content of a lesson. Physical education lessons are almost always structured by time and have a clear beginning and end. Off-topic conversations thus are probably best left for times before the official beginning of the lesson content or immediately after. This is particularly true if the conversation involves more than one interaction with a student. Saying "Let's talk about it after class" and then following up after class usually helps to keep students on task, allows teachers to resume their obligation to the rest of the class, and meets the need for personal interaction between teachers and students.

There are also critical times during a lesson when the teacher is needed by the whole group, such as at the beginning of a task. At these times a personal conversation with one student can have a disastrous effect on the productive work of the group.

This stance may seem like a harsh, unfeeling, and antiaffective approach to student-teacher personal interaction. In fact, teachers should not ignore or turn off a student who wants to talk. However, off-topic discussions should be handled graciously but quickly and then picked up again by the teacher at a more opportune time.

Dealing with the Personal Needs of Students

During activity is the time when teachers are most often forced to deal with the essential and often nonessential bathroom needs of students. Inexperienced teachers often are frustrated by the intrusion of such earthy requests into their well-planned lesson. These intrusions are, however, facts of life in the gymnasium, and teachers should be prepared in advance to deal with their occurrence.

The ideal situation, of course, is to have students leave and take care of these needs without having to request permission of the teacher. All teachers should work toward this goal, even though it may still be necessary to know when a student is leaving the room.

The beginning teacher should be aware of potential problems with these situations. In the elementary school and middle school environments, getting a drink and leaving the gymnasium can become a contagious game with as much importance to the elementary school child as being first or last in line. Many teachers handle this situation effectively by discriminating between real needs and requests that are part of a game. When the request is part of a game, the teacher does not grant the request. Some teachers also challenge students to make the decision involved in this situation and help them to choose wisely. Teachers who have resorted to "water at the end of class" procedures have decided that the time needed to help students make. wise decisions in this area is not worth the time needed for other objectives.

Although most secondary students are capable of taking care of such needs before class, the teacher must be prepared for emergency requests. The problems connected with these requests are different from those identified at the elementary and middle school levels. Increased vandalism, drug problems, and theft prevent teachers from allowing students unsupervised freedom. Many locker rooms, where toilet facilities are usually located, must be locked during class to protect the personal items of students and to assure teacher supervision of the facilities. Again, it should be stated that this is not a desirable situation and teachers should carefully consider ways in which more responsible student behavior can be supported and encouraged.

Participating with Students and Officiating

In most instances, teachers who participate in an activity with students, officiate student play, or merely supervise student activity remove themselves from teaching behaviors that might have a more direct effect on student performance. A teacher might participate for short periods of time to illustrate a point or motivate student performance. When the teacher participates with only a small part of the

class, however, the remaining members of the class do not have a teacher.

Teachers who put themselves solely in the role of an official make it difficult to play more of a direct role with students. The rationale the teacher has when doing this is usually that the students need uninterrupted play and "no coaching." This rationale is difficult to accept, since even most professional players are continuously coached during game play.

Teachers who see themselves primarily as supervisors of activity usually give as their rationale the need of students for more unstructured free play. Whether the instructional period is the proper place to meet this need is arguable. When time is limited, as in a classroom situation, the need for guidance in the learning process would seem to be greater. Quality instruction increases student learning.

Many teachers successfully combine officiating, supervising, and participating with more active roles, such as providing feedback to learners.

Indirectly contributing teacher behaviors are often necessary to maintain a productive learning environment. The teacher must, however, guard against becoming so engrossed in participating, officiating, and supervising that no time is left for the directly contributing behaviors discussed in the previous section.

◆ NONCONTRIBUTING BEHAVIORS

Noncontributing behaviors add nothing to lesson content. Fire drills, announcements over a public address system, and conversations with principals who enter the classroom and immediately want to talk to the teacher are all events that occur during real instructional situations. Teachers have little control over these situations, but there are two ways the teacher can minimize disruption in these and similar situations. First, the teacher should prepare students to respond to events like announcements and fire drills with behaviors that are structured ahead of time. Second, the teacher must respond in a consistent manner to these events. For example, the disruptive effect of visitors can be minimized by asking students to continue to work independently when possible. Even principals and supervising teachers can be asked to talk with the teacher later and should respect the teacher's desire to attend to the class. As a routine procedure, students should be asked to stop work and remain still during public address announcements without direction from the teacher. They should be asked to stop work and await teacher directions for a fire drill.

Unfortunately, some teachers remove themselves from an instructional situation by choice. Teachers who line the field for another class, physically leave the room, or attend to any activity that is not related to the students and the lesson are not functioning as teachers and make a very unwise choice.

In summary, noncontributing behaviors have a negative effect on instruction. They are to be avoided when possible and handled in the least disruptive way when unavoidable.

SUMMARY

1. Teachers perform many functions during the time students are engaged in a movement task.
2. Six major teacher functions have the potential to directly contribute to lesson content:
     Maintaining a safe learning environment
     Clarifying and reinforcing tasks for learners
     Maintaining a productive learning environment
     Observing and analyzing student responses
     Providing feedback to learners
     Changing and modifying tasks for individuals and small groups
3. Active teachers are continuously engaged in directly contributing behaviors.
4. Each of the directly contributing teacher functions during activity are interrelated.
5. Indirectly contributing behaviors focus the teacher's attention on the students and the learning environment but do not make a direct contribution to lesson content. Injured students, off-topic discussions, and equipment breakdowns are some examples of indirectly contributing behaviors. These events must be dealt with in ways that do not unnecessarily remove teachers from more directly contributing behaviors.

6. Noncontributing teacher behaviors have no potential to contribute to lesson content. These behaviors include events such as fire drills, public address announcements, teacher conversations with those outside the class, and the removal of the teacher, either physically or psychologically, from the students. Noncontributing behaviors should be avoided when possible and their disruptive influence minimized when avoidance is not possible.

CHECKING YOUR UNDERSTANDING

1. How can a teacher best handle a visit by a parent or principal that occurs during class time?
2. What is the best way to respond to a student who wants to engage the teacher in an off-topic discussion during a critical part of the lesson?
3. Why is the role of the participant or official not usually a wise choice for the teacher during activity?
4. List six behaviors teachers can engage in during activity that have the potential to directly contribute to lesson objectives.
5. Why should the teacher not hesitate to clarify a task when student responses are not what is expected?
6. How can a teacher get off-task students on task?
7. Write an example for each of the following types of feedback: (1) general, positive, directed to the class, and evaluative; (2) specific, negative, directed to a group, incongruent, and corrective; and (3) specific, positive, directed to the individual, corrective, and congruent.
8. Listen to an audio tape of teaching and categorize the feedback of the teacher as being (1) general or specific; (2) negative or positive; (3) congruent or incongruent; and (4) addressed to an individual, group, or class. Evaluate the teacher's responses for each of these categories.

9. Design two movement tasks and show how they might be modified during activity (either up or down) for students by extending, applying, refining, or completely changing the task.

10. Watch a video of a physical education lesson and identify from the tape students who should have the task modified for them.

11. List three different tasks from different motor skills and indicate where the teacher should be located to best observe performance.

12. For the tasks chosen for the preceding question, determine what the focus of teacher observation should be.

REFERENCES

Anderson W: *Analysis of teaching physical education*, St Louis, 1980, Mosby–Year Book.

Barrett K: Observation of movement for teachers: a synthesis and implications, *Motor Skills: Theory Into Practice* 3(2):67-76, 1979.

Barrett K: Observing as a teaching skill, *J Teaching Phys Ed* 3(1):22-31, 1983.

Biscan D, Hoffman S: Movement analysis as a generic ability of physical education teachers and students, *Res Q Exercise Sport* 47(1):161-163, 1976.

Craft A: The teaching of skills for the observation of movement: inquiry into a model, doctoral dissertation, 1977, University of North Carolina at Greensboro, *Dissertation Abstracts International* 38(4): 1977, University Microfilms No. 77-21,735, 1975-A.

Kounin JS: *Discipline and group management in classrooms,* New York, 1970, Holt, Rinehart & Winston.

Rink J: *Development of an observation system for content development in physical education*, unpublished doctoral dissertation, 1979, Ohio State University.

Teaching Strategies

❖❖❖❖❖❖❖❖❖❖❖

OVERVIEW

Teaching functions are usually performed within an instructional framework—a delivery system for getting the content to the learner. This instructional framework is called a teaching strategy, and in group instruction it organizes both student and teacher roles. Teachers select an instructional strategy based on the nature of the content, the objectives of the teacher, and the characteristics of the learner.

This chapter compares and contrasts direct instruction and indirect instruction and then describes seven major teaching strategies and how they provide for specific instructional functions. Their advantages and disadvantages for use in a group instructional setting are explored.

❖❖❖❖❖❖❖❖❖❖❖

CONCEPTS

- **Direct and indirect instruction**
- **The teaching strategy as a delivery system**
  Selection of content
  Communication of tasks
  Progression of content
  Provision for feedback and
    evaluation

- **Interactive teaching**
- **Station teaching**
- **Peer teaching**
- **Cooperative learning**
- **Self-instructional strategies**
- **Cognitive strategies**
- **Team teaching**
- **Selecting a teaching strategy**

HAPTER 4 discusses different ways in which the teacher can design learning experiences and movement tasks to achieve different learning outcomes. In a large group instructional setting, teachers can organize these experiences in different ways: (1) by varying the level of responsibility and engagement of the learner with the content and (2) by organizing the experiences so that both the student and teacher function in different ways in the instructional setting.

In 1966 Mosston made a monumental contribution to methodology in teaching physical education with the first edition of his book *Teaching Physical Education.* He described several styles of teaching, which range from command to discovery teaching. The spectrum of teaching styles is based largely on the amount of decision making given the learner in each style, with command teaching giving the learner few options (other than to do exactly what the teacher says to do when the teacher says to do it) and problem solving involving the students in the process of seeking answers to problems independently. With the spectrum of teaching styles came the perspective that physical education should involve the learner more holistically in the learning process. The role of the learner should not be just to do what the teacher says in a very narrow sense.

Mosston's work was revised in 1986 (Mosston and Ashworthy) to reflect a perspective on teaching as a chain of decision making and a continuum of teaching strategies. At one end of the continuum the teacher makes all the decisions. At the other end of the continuum a majority of the decisions are shared with the student. Box 9-1 lists and describes Mosston's expanded styles

Since the introduction of Mosston's work, teachers have a better understanding of the complexity of the teaching process. It has been learned that teachers rarely stay with one style for any length of time in the single lesson. Although specific strategies have varied potential for different learner outcomes, each teaching act itself brings to the fore the same set of decisions, which can be handled in different ways at different times. For instance, a teacher can decide to give individuals feedback by telling them how to correct their errors, by asking them to problem solve

the errors, or by asking another student to help them. It has also been realized that deciding what teaching method to employ does not only include questions

---

BOX 9-1

Mosston's Styles of Teaching

Style A	*Command* All decisions are controlled by the teacher.
Style B	*Practice* Teacher gives students several tasks. Student selects where, when, how, and which task to work on first. Teacher provides feedback.
Style C	*Reciprocal* One student practices; another provides feedback.
Style D	*Self-check* Students evaluate their own work.
Style E	*Inclusion* Teacher provides levels of a task. Students decide what level of the task they want to work with to achieve success.
Style F	*Guided discovery* Teacher guides students to a correct answer through a sequence of tasks.
Style G	*Divergent* Teacher provides a task to which there are multiple correct responses.
Styles H, I, J	*Learner designed program/ learner initiated/self-teaching* Students begin to take responsibility for what is to be learned and how it is to be learned.

Modified from Mosston M, Ashworth S: *Teaching physical education* ed 3, Columbus, OH, 1986, Merrill Publishing.

about the involvement of the learner in the learning process. Teachers can choose specialized approaches for cognitive processes to encourage positive social interaction among students or to use space and equipment more efficiently. They can choose to design lessons with different organizational formats (e.g., individual, group, partners, whole class). They can also choose different ways of communicating tasks to learners and providing for content progression, student feedback, and evaluation.

No one schema for or description of method can address all of these issues in the gymnasium. The type of cognitive learner involvement, the organizational format for instruction, and the degree of student decision making can be combined in many different ways, as is evident in Chapter 7. The approach used in this book is to look specifically at strategies for teaching as delivery systems of the content to the learner. A strategy used in this context is a framework for instruction around which teaching functions (selecting content, communicating tasks, and providing for progression, feedback, and evaluation) are performed in a lesson. *How something is delivered, not what is delivered, is the major concern of the teaching strategy.* Teaching strategies are selected because they deliver content to learners in a way that best meets objectives for a particular content and context. They are not the objective or the content of a lesson.

◆ DIRECT AND INDIRECT INSTRUCTION

The teacher effectiveness research of the 1970s led educators to the realization that students are more likely to learn specific content when teachers teach that content directly (see Chapter 3). Direct teaching involves:

- A task-oriented but relaxed environment with a clear focus on academic goals
- The selection of clear instructional goals and materials and highly active monitoring of student progress toward these goals
- Structured learning activities
- Immediate academically oriented feedback

Highly active teaching, focused learning, and student accountability are inherent in the idea of direct

instruction. In physical education, direct instruction usually implies that the teacher is in total control of what the students are learning and how they are learning it. Physical educators who use direct instruction do the following:

- Break down skills into manageable, success-oriented parts.
- Clearly describe and demonstrate exactly what the learner is supposed to do.
- Design structured tasks for students to practice what is to be learned.
- Hold students accountable for the tasks they present through active teaching and specific feedback.
- Evaluate students and their own teaching on what the student has learned.

As instruction moves to more indirect methods of teaching, teacher control of the learning process becomes shared with the learner. Indirect instruction is not as easily described as direct instruction but usually involves one or more of the following descriptors:

- Content is presented more holistically. Instead of breaking down what is to be learned into many subskills, chunks of content more meaningful to the learner are used.
- The student's role in the process of learning is usually expanded so that student thinking, feeling, or interaction skills are built into learning experiences designed by the teacher.
- The individual nature of student abilities, interests, and needs receive more consideration.

A basketball lesson presented using direct instruction and indirect instruction is described in Box 9-2 (p. 166).

Direct instruction is the best way to teach when content has a hierarchical structure and is primarily basic-skill–oriented and when efficiency of learning is a concern. When teacher objectives and goals require more complex learning and when teachers have lesson objectives that involve other learning domains (cognitive, affective), direct instruction may not be the best choice in spite of its efficiency. In physical education the decision of whether to teach material with direct or indirect instruction is complicated by the idea that motor skills are learned primarily through practice, not through complex cognitive processes. Maximum practice in limited program time is often attained through direct instruction.

BOX 9-2

Basketball Lesson: Direct and Indirect Instruction

Direct Instruction Basketball Chest Pass

1. Teacher demonstrates a chest pass with clear cues and organizes students in groups of two to practice the chest pass from a stationary position.
2. After observing the students, the teacher refines the chest pass with the following tasks:
   Demonstrates the step into the throw and asks students to "Do five more chest passes and step in to your throw this time."
3. Teacher extends the task with "When I give you and your partner the signal, take two steps back and see if you can maintain a good crisp pass."
4. "Now let's try sending the chest pass to a moving receiver."

Indirect Instruction Basketball Chest Pass

1. "Today we are going to work on getting the ball to a receiver a short distance away as quickly as possible. Let's look at this tape of professional players and see if we can identify the really good short and quick passes and how the players seem to do it."
2. "You and your partner find a place to practice, and see if you can identify at least three things that are important to doing this skill well from a stationary position."
3. Students come back in and share their responses. Teacher summarizes what a good short, quick chest pass should look like.
4. Students attempt to use the cues defined by the group to practice the chest pass from a stationary position. Teacher refines individually and through tasks as necessary.
5. The teacher moves around the room and asks students who are ready to move back and try the skill from an increased distance.
6. "When you feel that you are ready, try the pass with the receiver moving into a space to the left or right of you."

Advocates of indirect instruction are very concerned with the relevance and meaningfulness of what is to be learned. Too often direct instruction results in learning out of context with little meaning to the learner and little attention to engaging the learner at a more holistic and higher level. The decision of whether to use direct or indirect instruction should be based on teacher goals and objectives and the nature of what is to be learned in the context of a specific situation. Effective teachers do not make a decision to operate at one end of this continuum or another based on beliefs about which method is better. Effective teachers choose direct instruction when it is important for learners to master basic skills. They choose more indirect methods appropriately for other objectives and goals. Effective teachers should have available to them a broad spectrum of teaching strategies that they can use effectively.

The teacher must remember also that the selection of a teaching strategy also depends on the level of self-direction teachers have developed with their students. Although many teaching strategies can be designed to use more direct or indirect methods of teaching, others require that students be able to function more independent of a high degree of teacher monitoring. Teachers who do not develop these skills with students are limited in the teaching strategies they can use effectively.

Direct instruction and indirect instruction are holistic concepts representing two poles of a continuum primarily representing an approach to organizing content. Therefore many instructional factors can be varied by the teacher that can either support direct or indirect instruction. In other words, you can use a variety of teaching strategies to deliver either direct or indirect instruction. Many of the teaching strategies described in this chapter can be used to present content either directly or indirectly.

◆ THE TEACHING STRATEGY AS A DELIVERY SYSTEM

Teaching strategies are designed to arrange an instructional environment for group instruction. A key point here is that groups do not learn—individuals do. This means that group instructional environments must be arranged to facilitate the learning of individuals. Individual learners in physical education must still be provided with appropriate content that is clearly communicated. They must be provided with the opportunity to practice accurately and to progress appropriately, and they must be provided with feedback on their performance.

Teaching strategies organize group instruction so that teaching functions are performed in different ways in the instructional process. The major teacher functions important to discriminating teaching strategies are the following:

- Selection of content
- Communication of tasks
- Progression of content
- Provision for feedback and evaluation

The decisions teachers make in regard to these functions significantly affect the potential of instruction to accomplish intended objectives. The nature of these decisions is described in the following section.

Selection of Content

A major problem in group instruction is that students function at different levels of ability in most tasks. The content that is selected must meet the needs of individuals within a group setting. In large group instruction this involves decisions such as the following:

- How can content be made appropriate for many learners with different content needs?
- Should each student be doing the same thing at the same time?
- Should content be different for different students?
- Who makes decisions relative to content—the teacher or the student?
- What level of student engagement should the contact seek to develop?

Communication of Tasks

In a learning experience, students must be told what they are expected to do. This instructional function describes the way tasks are communicated to groups of learners. It involves decisions on how to communicate the learning task to students. Possibilities include verbal communication of the teacher or student, demonstration, written handouts, posters, and audiovisual materials.

Progression of Content

In an instructional setting, arrangements must be made for students to progress from skill to skill and from one level of performance of a skill to another. Progression from one skill to another is called *intertask development* and progression from one level of performance of a skill to another is called *intratask development* (see Chapter 6).

Progression of content focuses on the arrangements for both skill-to-skill progression (intertask development) and within-skill progression (intratask development) in a learning experience. A teaching strategy must build in the extension, refinement, and, where appropriate, application aspects of the development of content. Progression of content involves answering questions such as the following:

- Who decides when a student advances in difficulty or to another skill?
- Should criteria be established for perforamance?
- Should those criteria be established ahead of time?
- Should the criteria be communicated to students? If so, how should they be communicated?

Provision for Feedback and Evaluation

Providing feedback to learners and evaluating student responses is a critical teaching function in instruction. Group instructional settings make giving individual feedback and evaluating performance difficult. To give individual feedback and evaluate performance, the teacher can consider some of the following alternatives:

- Teacher observation
- Peer feedback
- Environmental design
- Formal testing
- Videotaping

The Teaching Strategies Described

Seven basic teaching strategies for the design of learning experiences in physical education have been identified:

- Interactive teaching
- Station teaching
- Peer teaching
- Cooperative learning
- Self-instructional strategies
- Cognitive strategies
- Team teaching

The strategies described here are by no means inclusive, nor do they always appear in a pure form as a strategy for an entire lesson in a real situation. Many of these strategies can be and are used in combination with each other for different learning experiences throughout a lesson.

Each of these strategies will be discussed relative to the way it arranges the instructional environment. You will find as you read about each of the strategies that each focuses and highlights one aspect of instruction but says little about others. Although the arrangement of conditions for one instructional function affects possibilities for arranging other functions, it is also possible to use several teaching strategies simultaneously.

◆ INTERACTIVE TEACHING

By far the most common strategy for the design of learning experiences in physical education is a strategy that is interactive in nature. Most people will have no trouble conceptualizing the interactive strategy. The word *teaching* often implies a teacher telling, showing, or directing a group of students on what to do; students doing it; and a teacher evaluating how well it is done and developing the content further. This is a type of interactive strategy. In interactive teaching the instructional process is teacher controlled. Like an orchestra without a conductor, instruction cannot continue without the teacher.

In interactive teaching, a teacher move is based on the response of students to a previous teacher

BOX 9-3

Interactive Teaching of Tennis Forehand (Middle School)

The teacher is in the first days of a tennis unit with eighth grade students. A few of the students play tennis outside of school, but most students have no tennis experience.

Before class begins, the teacher asks to speak with the students who are experienced. He tells them that during the first part of the period they are to go baseline to baseline, alternating forehand and backhand strokes, and see if they can begin placing the ball closer to the corners as they are successful.

The teacher then reviews the cues of the forehand with the rest of the class by walking the students through the skill without the ball. He paces the practice the first few times and then asks the students to practice the action faster on their own. The teacher breaks down the group into partners (their choice) and explains that each set of partners will have six balls. One partner tosses the ball from a few feet away so that it bounces to the forehand side of the hitter. The hitter then strikes the ball with a forehand stroke. The teacher demonstrates by tossing the ball to a class member, emphasizing where the toss should be placed. He asks the students to put two hitters on each side of each court, and practice begins.

During practice, the teacher reminds several tossers to try to place the ball so that it bounces to the hitter about waist high. He gives specific feedback to several hitters on "swinging through the ball." The teacher stops the class and asks students how far away from the ball they should be when hitting it. Several students give different answers. Students are again asked to swing their rackets without the ball and to freeze the action when they think contact occurs. Students respond, and the teacher asks them to go back to what they were doing and try to make sure they are extended at the contact point by judging the distance from the ball. The teacher moves to the advanced group to give feedback and to change the task to practicing serving.

move. Teacher planning facilitates the process, but teachers' next moves are based on student responses. The teacher is dominant in this strategy and is most often responsible for all four components of a learning experience. Usually an entire class of students works on the same task or within the same task framework.

An interactive teaching strategy can be used to teach any content. Examples of teachers using interactive teaching to teach the open skill of the tennis forehand and a movement concept related to balance are given in Boxes 9-3 and 9-4. The discussion now focuses on how each instructional component is arranged when an interactive teaching strategy is used.

Selection of Content—Interactive Teaching

Interactive teaching uses the movement task directed to an entire group. Content can be individualized or not individualized, depending on the design of the task itself. The following examples of alternative tasks for a lesson in basketball shooting illustrates the flexibility of the movement task for selecting appropriate content for individuals within a group:

- "Everyone do 10 lay-ups from each direction and 10 foul shots."
- "Decide whether you need to work on lay-ups or foul shots, and do 10 of what you need the most work on."
- "We will be working on foul shots today. Choose a distance from the basket where you can be successful. As you become more consistent in getting the ball into the basket, move back toward the foul line."

Each of these tasks gives students a greater or lesser degree of freedom to choose appropriate content. The tasks involve open and closed skills of a specialized sport. When concepts are the content, the same degrees of freedom are present also, as illustrated by the following tasks within the concept of balance:

- "Balance on your head and two hands."
- "Balance on three parts of your body."
- "Find a balance you can hold for 6 seconds."

BOX 9-4

Interactive Teaching of Balance (Upper Elementary School)

The students are met at the door by the teacher. They are asked to warm up on the mats scattered throughout the all-purpose room by taking their weight on different parts of their body and getting good extension. The teacher moves throughout the group while the students are warming up. She asks individuals to get more extension and clarity in the body shape they are assuming and positively reinforces those students who have clarity of shape and extension.

The teacher begins the lesson by asking students to select an inverted balance that they can hold for at least 6 seconds. She then asks students to find at least three ways they can get out of this balanced position to a new base of support. While the students are working, the teacher moves through the group, helping individual with the balances they have chosen. She stops the group and asks several students to demonstrate the way that they have chosen to move out of their balances. The teacher comments that she has seen rolls, twists, steplike actions, and slides. She asks students to go back and continue to explore possibilities for moving out of their balances and tells them that they may choose a new balance if they want to.

While the students are working, the teacher asks some of them to try some specific way of moving out of their balances, such as a transfer of weight onto another body part, a roll, or a twist. As students work, the teacher reminds them that they can try moving forward, backward, or sideways out of their balances.

The teacher stops the whole class. She asks them to put together a sequence that includes a balance, a transfer of weight out of their balance, and a new balance. She tells them that they may include traveling if they wish. Students are reminded that the balances must be still for at least 6 seconds and have a clear shape and that weight must be transferred in a logical and controlled way.

The first task offers students little freedom of choice, whereas the second task offers more choice. The third offers even more choice and allows the content to be most individualized.

When teachers use an interactive teaching strategy, the appropriateness of the movement task itself determines the ability of the strategy to meet the needs of individuals within the group. Students should be given different amounts of freedom to respond, depending on the learning objectives and the variance in ability levels within the group. A task that allows little freedom of response can be given only when it can be assumed that the task is appropriate for all students. When it cannot be assumed that one single response is appropriate for all, the task must be structured to permit the potential for success for all students.

When the teacher gives students little freedom in what to do or how to do it, interactive teaching becomes Mosston's **command teaching** (Mosston and Ashworth, 1986), such as when a teacher is leading exercises or karate drills and students are asked to respond to a signal on command. When students have an opportunity to self-pace their own practice of a teacher-presented task, the amount of teacher control is decreased (Mosston's **practice style).**

At the other end of the continuum is much of what has been called **movement education.** In movement education the teacher is likely to give students a task (usually related to a concept) that has potentially more than one correct response (e.g., "Balance on four parts of your body."). Both command teaching and movement education tend to be interactive teaching strategies in that the teacher is primarily responsible for the selection of task, the communication of the task, the progression, and feedback and evaluation. Although small group and other organizational patterns can be used, largely the teacher directs his or her efforts to the whole class.

Communication of Tasks—Interactive Teaching

When an interactive strategy is used to teach a specific skill, the teacher usually takes complete responsibility for communicating tasks. This does not mean the teacher cannot be assisted by students

or materials. It simply means that the teacher is always responsible for the communication of the task and never entirely gives up the role of task communication to other sources. The selection of cues and the clarity of presentation become critical components of task communication.

In interactive teaching, the teacher plays the dominant role in task communication because tasks are largely the result of an interactive process. Tasks are based on previous student responses, and content cannot be locked into a predesigned progression. Teachers do not know exactly what the next task will be until they see students respond to a previous task. Sometimes the next task will ask for quality (refinement), sometimes it will expand or reduce complexity or difficulty (extension), and sometimes it will test the effectiveness of student responses in an applied setting (application).

Progression of Content—Interactive Teaching

In interactive teaching, the teacher usually takes complete responsibility for progression but may share this responsibility with students. One of the advantages of interactive teaching is that progression can be appropriately selected and paced based on teacher observation of the performance of students. Astute observers know when to ask for quality and know what kind of quality to expect (refinement). They also know when to increase the level of difficulty of a task and when to lessen the level of difficulty (extension). When the next task is based on the observed performance of a previous task rather than the passage of time, the interactive teaching strategy is being used effectively. Without this interactive process between student responses and the teacher's next move, an interactive strategy loses its advantage over more managerial and predetermined strategies.

Provision for Feedback and Evaluation— Interactive Teaching

In a purely interactive strategy, the teacher takes primary responsibility for feedback and evaluation. In interactive teaching the teacher should be free during activity to provide students with feedback; thus the teacher should give serious thought before doing anything other than attending to this role (e.g., being a partner to an odd student, participating, arranging equipment for the next task).

Feedback can be given to individuals or to the group as a whole while the students are active or after activity has stopped. By pacing performance to the extent that students must rely on teacher cues to start, continue, and stop performance (command teaching), the teacher limits the amount of feedback, particularly individual help, that can be provided to students. A teacher who sends students off to practice on their own is in a better position to provide feedback but assumes students know what to do and can work independent of specific cues.

Strengths and Weaknesses of Strategy— Interactive Teaching

The strength of interactive teaching as a strategy for the design of learning experiences is that it *is* interactive. Teachers can establish progression and provide for the individualization of content through the movement task itself by delivering it at an appropriate time. Because the teacher usually addresses the whole group when communicating the content, student understanding can be determined and communication immediately adjusted. Feedback and evaluation are more difficult in interactive teaching with large groups because the teacher is actively involved in task selection, communication, and progression.

One weakness of interactive teaching arises because some teachers find it difficult to use an interactive strategy. They have trouble designing movement tasks that actually do individualize the selection of content and progression or have not developed independent working skills with students that would make working on different tasks or different levels of tasks productive. In this case interactive teaching may turn into a situation where the content is not appropriate for all learners.

◆ STATION TEACHING

Station teaching arranges the environment so that two or more tasks are going on in a class simultaneously. Usually, each separate task is assigned an area or a station in the gymnasium, and students rotate from one station to another. Sometimes station teaching is called *task teaching*.

Station teaching has become a very popular teaching strategy in physical education. When used effectively, it can provide a framework for learning experiences that satisfies all instructional functions. However, there are times when station teaching, like all other strategies, is not a wise selection. These situations will be pointed out as station teaching is explained. An example of a station-teaching lesson is provided in Box 9-5.

Selection of Content—Interactive Teaching

In station teaching, the teacher decides on the tasks ahead of time. There are many reasons teachers may want different tasks going on at the same time. When there is not enough equipment, the teacher may feel it is important for all students to use this equipment. It may be advantageous to mix tasks that require much space with those that do not require much space. A learning experience might be individualized by assigning students to stations based on their ability or interests and by not having students

---

BOX 9-5

Station Teaching of Volleyball (High School)

The teacher begins the lesson by explaining that from now on the first 15 minutes of each class in the unit will be devoted to the stations arranged in the gymnasium. He describes the following stations:
- Set against the wall
- Serve against the wall
- Bump with a partner
- Spike against the wall from a set
- Dive

The teacher reviews each task and tells the students to do each task 10 times. Students work with partners and record their progress each day on an individual progress sheet. Each group of two has one ball that is taken with them from station to station. Partners move to another station when they finish.

rotate to all of the stations. Teachers may also want to keep students motivated by practicing many similar tasks for short periods of time in different ways at different stations.

Communication of Tasks—Station Teaching

One of the most difficult aspects of station teaching is arranging for the communication of tasks. Usually, several tasks must be presented at the same time. The problem is to get everyone going quickly without losing students in a sea of directions for tasks that do not immediately concern them.

Teachers using station teaching have tried to solve the problem of task presentation in many ways. Large posters or task cards can be used to communicate tasks. Older students or peers can be assigned task communication at a station. Each individual student can also have written directions for a station before going to that station. More often, the teacher attempts to give directions for each station at the beginning of the learning experience.

To be effective, tasks must be simple and clearly stated. With younger students a demonstration at each station is almost a necessity. It is difficult to use station teaching to introduce new skills to students because of the limited task presentation time available. It is also critical that the tasks selected take about the same amount of time and are self-motivating. When one task is over quickly and others take more time, students are left waiting at one station until everyone finishes or if they are permitted to move on, a disproportionate number of students are at one station.

Sometimes station teaching can be used to work with advanced students or students needing more help with a task. By getting the majority of students productively engaged in a self-motivating task, the teacher becomes free to establish another station for more individualized help or to introduce a skill that needs close teacher involvement. This strategy is often effective in a gymnastics lesson. Students can practice skills previously introduced without the teacher while the teacher establishes another group to introduce new tasks or to give individual help.

Progression of Content—Station Teaching

Task progression in station teaching may be difficult to design because of the need to establish easily understood criteria to move from one level of a skill to another or from one skill to another. It is difficult to put criteria into words or pictures that communicate form or qualitative cues. It is easier to establish criteria that are quantitative, such as "When you can do this two times in a row without losing control, move on to the next task."

Teachers must also take care to design stations with equivalent tasks in terms of time for completion. When one station is a prerequisite to another, often too many students are stalled at one of the stations.

Teachers often make no attempt to establish progression but instead use station teaching to practice unrelated skills, tasks at the same level, or skills that have already been introduced to the students by the teacher.

Provision for Feedback and Evaluation—Station Teaching

In station teaching, many different tasks are going on at the same time. The teacher in this situation most often plays the role of a manager, maintaining productive work and pacing the work from one station to another. Provision for feedback and evaluation should be a teaching function that station teaching handles well, simply because the teacher is freed from other teaching functions once the assignment at a station is made. The teacher has more freedom to (1) move from one station to another to provide feedback or (2) remain at one station to present a new task to students or provide specific help. Students must be able to maintain a productive level of engagement for the teacher to be freed to perform these functions.

Many beginning teachers who have not established independent working skills with students find that they will be needed as managers and must therefore make other arrangements for feedback and evaluation. Tasks in most content areas can be designed so that students receive information on their performance from the task itself (e.g., throwing at a target). Self-testing activities are usually successful and can be made even more so if students are required to record their scores and later their progress when tasks are repeated. Tasks structured with minimal numbers of repetitions for a skill, such as 10 overhead passes or 10 smashes over the net, also provide feedback and the potential to help students remain productive. Students have more difficulty with qualitative tasks that focus on form without some accountability for form.

Strengths and Weaknesses of Strategy— Station Teaching

Many teachers chose station teaching as a teaching strategy because it offers flexibility in content selection. All students can be active doing different things. The exact nature of the content and the arrangements for time at each station can be decided by the teacher or the student.

Independent working skills must be taught and established before station teaching can be used effectively. When students can work independently without close teacher monitoring, the teacher is free to provide feedback, evaluate student progress, or work with a small group at a single station.

Some kinds of content work better than others in station teaching. In most school situations, limited provisions for task communication make new or complex skills difficult to work with in a station-teaching format. New process-oriented tasks, such as those emphasizing form, are difficult to communicate and to establish accountability systems for. Individual self-testing, product-oriented tasks, and practice of skills already learned that do not need a great deal of teacher refinement or development are usually the most successful.

The most difficult part of station teaching is maintaining quality of performance in student responses. It is not uncommon to see students racing through gymnastic skills or exercises or manipulating tasks with no attention to how they are completing a skill. If quality of performance is important to the task, teachers must find ways to hold students accountable for quality. Writing process criteria on the task card usually is not an adequate way to communicate qualitative concerns or to hold students accountable for quality. Teachers must clearly communicate the qualitative goal orientation of the task in their task

presentation and stop the work of students when the quality of the work is not being attended to.

◆ PEER TEACHING

Peer teaching is an instructional strategy that transfers the teacher's responsibility for instructional functions to the student. It generally is used in conjunction with other strategies but is worth exploring separately. Actually, a peer-teaching strategy can be used with any teaching function defined in this chapter. Examples of the use of peer teaching, both in a complete lesson and in parts of a lesson, are provided in Boxes 9-6 and 9-7.

BOX 9-6

Peer Teaching (Whole Lesson)

Gymnastics (high school)

The teacher divides students in a gymnastics class into ability groups of four socially compatible students each. The students had been working on apparatus and floor exercise routines. Each student in the group now teaches her or his routine to the other members of the group.

The teacher explains that the student who is teaching the routines (the peer teacher) is responsible for the quality of performance of the learners and that groups will not be evaluated on the level of difficulty but on the following criteria:

- Clarity of body shape throughout the routine
- Smoothness of transition from one move to another
- Control of movement
- Dynamic quality of execution

The peer teacher is encouraged to first demonstrate and explain how each part of the routine is done and then to give students practice on parts. When students can do each part with quality, the peer teacher moves to put the parts together. Groups move at their own pace but are encouraged to practice one routine until it is done well before moving on to another routine.

The experience takes three class periods. On the last day each group demonstrates what it has done.

BOX 9-7

Peer Teaching (Part of a Lesson)

Dance (high school)

The teacher teaches a complex dance step to a large group of students. All but a few students are ready to move on to a more advanced use of the step. The teacher appoints several students who have mastered the step to work with those who have not. He encourages the peer teacher to use the proper cue words and to slow down the step pattern until it is attained by the learners.

Dance (elementary school)

A third grade class is divided into groups of four learners. Each group choreographs its own dance to simple folk dance music. The teacher selects two of the group to teach their dances to the whole class. Each group demonstrates its dance to the whole class. The teacher then asks each member of the group to teach a part of the dance to the whole class by explaining how it is done and then helping the rest of the class perform.

Volleyball (middle school)

The teacher works with the whole class on the volleyball underhand serve. She then divides the class into groups of four. One student serves the ball on one side of the net, and one student serves the ball on the other side of the net. One student on each side coaches the server. The coach's job is to check for the following teaching cues that have been given for underhand serve:

- Using up and back stance with body lean
- Hitting ball out of hand with no toss
- Finishing with weight on forward foot

Each group has a skill card with the cues listed. Coaches are told to look for only one cue each time the ball is served and to tell the server whether that cue has been observed

Selection of Content—Peer Teaching

The teacher usually selects the content in a peer-teaching strategy, but sometimes a movement idea or concept is presented by the teacher and students teach their response to another student. For example, elementary school students might design sequences of locomotor patterns and then teach these patterns to other students, thus choosing the task within a framework set by the teacher. Secondary school students might participate in the same type of experience by sharing strategies for game play or dance experiences.

Communication of Tasks—Peer Teaching

In peer teaching, one student is often used to show or, more literally, teach a skill to another. Skilled or experienced students can be matched with students who are having difficulty or who are inexperienced. Students can be asked to communicate a task to the whole class or to part of a class (in conjunction with station teaching). When a student is used as an auxiliary teacher at a separate station from the teacher, it must be remembered that students acting as teachers also have needs—not only personal skill needs, but also needs for support and guidance in their teaching efforts. Peer teaching is most successful in classroom work when older students help younger students. Peers many times have a communication advantage that the teacher does not. Thus even if peers serve no other function within an instructional experience, they often communicate tasks well.

Progression of Content—Peer Teaching

Progression of content is almost always a teacher function even when peer teaching is used. Skill-to-skill or within-task progression should be clearly communicated when the peer teacher has responsibility for progression. This progression can be verbally communicated to the whole group and is usually planned ahead of time with the peer teacher. The qualitative criteria must also be clear to the peer teacher.

Provision for Feedback and Evaluation—Peer Teaching

Of all the instructional functions most appropriately assigned to peer teaching, the function of feedback and evaluation is one of the most appropriate. Teachers of large groups have difficulty performing this necessary function because of large classes and limited time. Students who are trained to be good observers and who are given guidance on what to look for in providing feed-

Students can be taught to provide feedback to each other. (Courtesy SIUE Photo.)

back can help each other a great deal.

Partner work is often used effectively to establish a peer relationship for feedback and evaluation. When peer feedback does not work, it is often because the teacher has not given the observer *clear and limited criteria for observation* and because a clear expectation for improved performance has not been communicated.

Peers are often used successfully to evaluate performance (1) when the product of performance is easily measured, such as the number of trials out of 10 throws that hit a target or (2) when students are given one aspect of performance to look at, such as "Tell your partner whether he stepped into his swing." Students are capable of helping each other in more sophisticated ways if the teacher is willing to teach peers how to help each other. Productive

peer relationships, however, take time to develop, and teachers should not expect students to function well in these situations without clear guidance or expectations.

Strengths and Weaknesses of Strategy—Peer Teaching

As a teaching strategy, peer teaching can be used for all instructional functions or only one. Like all teaching strategies, it can be used for part of a lesson or for a whole lesson. The key to peer teaching is the peer relationship. The teacher must be sure that students will work together in a productive way. A productive relationship between peers will not occur unless the expectations of the relationship are clear and students are held accountable for specific criteria and responsibilities. In other words, the peer relationship and responsibilities must be structured. Teachers who put students together to teach or observe each other with no guidance will be disappointed by the results.

When peer-teaching experiences are used well for one or more instructional functions, more individualized work can be done. The teacher's attention in peer teaching should shift from the performance of the learner to guiding the peer relationship.

Peer-teaching experiences have the potential to develop in the peer teacher important skills of observation and analysis and a more thorough understanding of both motor and social skills. Both the learner and the peer teacher can profit from such experiences.

◆ COOPERATIVE LEARNING

Cooperative learning is a teaching strategy that has become popular in recent times (Kagen, 1990; Slavin, 1988, 1990; Smith, 1987) and was initially developed by Johnson and Johnson (1975). Cooperative learning has grown out of a recognition that adults in today's society need to be able to appreciate diversity and work with others in a very diverse society to lead productive and happy lives. Cooperative learning has the potential to increase student learning, as well as to contribute to social and affective development.

In cooperative learning, groups of learners are assigned a learning task or project to complete as a team. Students are grouped heterogeneously according to different factors such as race, ability, or social needs. Groups, as well as individuals, are evaluated according to how well they complete the task or project, in addition to the manner in which they worked together to complete the tasks. Like all strategies, these gains are not automatic. Students must be well prepared for the expectations involved in working together for a common goal. Positive results are attained only if the goals students are given are meaningful, students are taught how to cooperate, and accountability for both the process and the product of the learning experience are evident to the student.

Selection of Content—Cooperative Learning

Usually the teacher selects the task or project to be completed by the students in cooperative learning, although students may have a choice or role in defining the goal to be achieved. To produce meaningful interaction with both the content and each other, tasks must be selected that have the potential for teaching something meaningful and at the same time requiring the cooperation and skills of the group. If a task can be solved immediately by one member of the group, the task was not a good choice for cooperative learning. The goal in task selection should be to design an experience that develops the interdependency of all the members of the group.

Although cooperative learning is not widely used at this time in physical education, the very nature of our content has great potential for its use as a teaching strategy. It is possible to design cooperative student experiences that are fun and do achieve some social and affective goals in physical education without actually contributing to student learning in the content of physical education. Many cooperative games of this nature have been designed, such as working as a team to get through a pretend swamp. The skills needed in activities such as this are cooperative but contribute little to the unique content goals of our field. Cooperative learning experiences should be designed to contribute in some way to the psychomotor goals of physical education, as well as the social and emotional development of students.

Four different cooperative learning formats have been used extensively in the classroom. Brief descriptions of these follow:

Jigsaw (Aronson et al, 1978). In the jigsaw approach to cooperative learning, a project is designed that has the potential to be divided into components. The project is divided into component parts essential for its completion. Each student in the group is given a part of a project. All the students who are responsible for a particular component form an initial group and are given resources to learn their part. In a modification of Jigsaw I, Jigsaw II does not require that each student be given separate materials on a subject, but all students are exposed to the same materials and one member assumes responsibility for a part of the materials. Each student then has an essential part of the project, which he or she must share with the group. The jigsaw creates interdependency because each student has a unique part of the project.

Potential PE Jigsaw. Every member of a team or group is responsible for a different component of fitness in building a warm-up routine.

Each member of a group is responsible for a different skill in a sport in a sport unit or a different folk dance in a folk dance unit.

■   ■   ■

Teams-Games Tournament (TGT) (Slavin, 1983). In TGT, heterogeneously grouped teams work together to master content for competition against other teams. For the actual tournament and competition, students are grouped homogeneously according to ability. Both individual scores and cooperative team scores are kept.

Potential PE TGT. TGT has great potential for physical education, particularly in individual sports. Teams are formed heterogeneously for practice and homogeneously for competition. Practice groups must be taught how to facilitate the improvement of all members.

■   ■   ■

Pairs-Check. In the pairs-check, two groups of two students work together. Each pair is set up as a peer-teaching group, as described in the previous section. In pairs-check, two groups of pairs come back together as a group of four to check, evaluate, and revise what they have done.

Potential PE Pairs-Check. Peer-teaching groups are established to learn a skill. The pairs then form a group of four with another two students to help each other.

Peers are used to develop a "double stunt" in tumbling or a movement sequence; pairs-check is used to teach what one group has developed to another group.

■   ■   ■

Co-op. In co-op, a project is designed that has many components. The group decides which components members will be responsible for. Individual students are evaluated on the extent to which they fulfill their specific responsibility to the group.

Potential PE Co-Op. Teams balanced in ability are developed for a sport. Each team is responsible for equipment, warm-up, officials, a 10-minute practice schedule each day, scoring, and coaching during play. Students are assigned roles, which may change each

week (similar to sport education model developed by Siedentop, 1992).

Groups are responsible for designing an aerobic dance routine that balances the components of fitness.

You will notice that the experiences just described are broader than most tasks used in other strategies. More effective cooperative learning experiences have the potential for students to have *different* interdependent roles.

Communication of Tasks—Cooperative Learning

Teachers will want to communicate a cooperative learning task after groups have been selected to work on the task. Group selection is one of the most important aspects of cooperative learning. Groups should be selected that are heterogeneous in relation to gender, skill ability, ethnic orientation, or race. The social interaction skills of all of the learners are a strong consideration in group membership.

Teachers have several options for communicating cooperative learning tasks. Usually teachers will communicate the task to all the groups at the same time. Task communication must involve both the expectation the teacher has for the goal of the learning experience and expectations for how the goal should be reached as a group. The more independent the groups of learners, the more open the teacher can be about the process to be used. Students who are just beginning to work cooperatively will need more structure by the teacher as to how the task is to be solved. They may need to have the teacher give the directions for getting organized, give students some time to complete the organizational responsibilities, and then have the students report what they intend to do before they move on with a project.

Clarity of expectations is critical to a well-designed cooperative learning task, both for the group and the individual. Written materials are often used to summarize the task for students. These materials can describe the following:

- Finished product
- Steps to be completed en route to the finished product

- Project components
- Resources available to students
- Time frame for completing the project
- "Rules" for how the project is to be completed
- Evaluation procedures for the group and individuals in the group

Progression of Content—Cooperative Learning

Progression of content in cooperative learning experiences is either built into the task itself or left to the learners. When teachers are just beginning to work with students in cooperative learning experiences, they may want to structure the task to include a progression such as the following:

1. Elect a leader.
2. Divide your group into three teams of two people.
3. Formulate three different possible defenses.
4. Try all three defenses, and evaluate them according to the criteria listed.
5. Choose one defense you think is the best.
6. Work on the defense until everyone can do it well.
7. Prepare to present your defense to the class as a whole.

Each step of the progression can initially be checked by the teacher. Students who are more experienced with working in groups may not need as much structure in process and should be allowed to design their own strategies for arriving at solutions to the task and work at their own pace. The teacher should intervene with groups that are having trouble getting started and should suggest an approach.

Provision for Feedback and Evaluation—Cooperative Learning

Once a task has been presented, the teacher should be free to provide feedback to groups on how they are working and how well they are completing the assigned task. One of the advantages of cooperative learning is that the teacher is free to stay with a group for as long as needed, under the assumption that other students are productively engaged in their own work. The teacher should be an astute observer of group process to be effective in this role. Teachers can suggest alternative strategies for completing the task and resources. Students should be allowed to work out their own problems and false starts without a great deal of teacher interference. However, groups should not be permitted to flounder for long periods of time without teacher help. If some groups need direction and structure, it should be provided.

Because it is likely that different groups not only will arrive at a different solution to the problem, but will use a different process, all groups can usually benefit from "sharing" sessions, in which groups have the opportunity to present to other groups what they developed and how they developed it. The teacher can use these opportunities to emphasize group process skills and to make students aware of the advantages of diverse talents and abilities. The teacher can also use these opportunities to talk about strengths and weaknesses of the products produced by the groups, such as "What did you like about the solution this group developed?" or "How do you think this group could improve what they did?"

More formal evaluation sessions that provide feedback to individual groups on the "product" and the process are helpful. Feedback and evaluation are easier if the teacher establishes *clear criteria* in advance when communicating expectations to students. One of the primary goals in using cooperative learning is to help students understand (1) how to work with others so that everyone benefits and (2) the advantages in working with others to accomplish a task in a cooperative way. Because group process is so important to this strategy, feedback and evaluation must be concerned with not only the product of the group, but the process that was used. If the teacher is going to do an evaluation of group process and not share this evaluation with the students, much is lost.

Strengths and Weaknesses of Strategy—Cooperative Learning

Cooperative learning is an investment in time. Teachers use cooperative learning because they think the time spent in helping students to learn how to work together and to deal with content at a higher level is a good investment. Not all group work or partner work is cooperative learning. Cooperative learning experiences are structured very specifically to accomplish cooperative learning goals and improve the interaction among students. If the teacher is not willing to take the time to help students interact in positive ways with each other, cooperative learning often falls short of its goals.

◆ **SELF-INSTRUCTIONAL STRATEGIES**

In the simplest sense, self-instructional strategies involve a preestablished program for learning that may involve the teacher in a tutorial or managerial role but basically eliminates the teacher from more traditional instructional functions during the instructional process itself. Self-instructional strategies rely heavily on preestablished written materials, media, and evaluative procedures. They may be used to fulfill one or more, and sometimes all, of the functions of instruction.

In addition to being used for single lessons or parts of lessons, self-instructional models can be designed for an entire course. Students can work either within the confines of a class or independent of a structured class period. Materials that include progressions of tasks, instructions for task performance, practice recommendations, and evaluative tools are provided. The students and/or the teacher decide where the student enters the progression and where the student ends the progression. *Mastery learning* usually involves a preconceived exit point. The amount of time a student takes to reach this point is flexible. *Contract teaching* and most other forms of individualized program instruction evaluate the student with agreed-on exit criteria. The important aspect of self-instructional strategies is that all the necessary ingredients for student learning must be included in the materials.

It should be clear that students who are to profit from self-instructional strategies must be highly motivated, self-directed, and, to some extent, knowledgeable in how to make the best use of time and the materials provided. Motivation, self-direction, and skill in using instructional materials take time to develop. A teacher would be unwise to move completely to a self-instructional model until these skills are developed. An example of a secondary lesson using a self-instructional strategy is presented in Box 9-8, and an example of self-instructional materials

---

BOX 9-8

Self-instructional Strategies for Gymnastics (High School)

A teacher is using a partial self-instructional model to teach high school gymnastics skills. Each student is pretested on basic gymnastics skills and selects an area of concentration, either floor exercise or a piece of apparatus. The teacher develops an individual program for each student, which tests basic skills on several pieces of equipment, and a more extensive list of objectives for the student's area of specialization, which indicates a self-designed routine.

The teacher sets up several kinds of media at each station that explain how each skill is performed and the criteria for performance. Sometimes the task is communicated with a large visual poster depicting difficult phases of the skill. Sometimes a loop film or a videotape is set up at a station. In previous years the teacher taught students how to use media materials on a less extensive basis.

The class is organized for 3 days per week. Students are free to move to any piece of equipment they would like to at any time. The teacher spends a half day at each piece of equipment to provide help at that piece or to evaluate student performance. Students may be evaluated only twice on each skill.

Lists are posted of students who have successfully completed skills at a high level and who are willing to help others.

---

that might be used in an elementary school setting is presented in Box 9-9 (p. 180).

Selection of Content—Self-Instructional Strategies

The content in self-instructional strategies is usually established beforehand through a list of progressive tasks that are criterion referenced (i.e., they have attached evaluative criteria). Sometimes skills for entire sports are sequenced from beginning to advanced levels with small gradations in between. Students (or teachers) thus can decide to enter the progression at any point. Students are permitted to

Self-instructional Strategies for Gymnastics (Elementary School)

Learning center

Make sequences on a piece of equipment.

Objective

When you have completed these activities, you will be able to perform a sequence of movements on the equipment provided.

Equipment

This learning center can be used on any of the equipment in the activity area, such as a box or a balance beam.

Tasks

1. Find a piece of equipment where there is room for you to work.
2. Try several different ways of *getting on* the equipment safely. If you always use your hands and feet, try to get on the equipment backward or sideways.
3. When you have chosen the way you like best to get on the equipment, balance two body parts in a twisted shape. Practice the getting on and balancing in the twisted shape until it is easy. Hold the balance while you say your name twice.
4. Change your shape to a wide, stretched shape, balancing on body parts different from before.
5. Now find a way to get off the equipment safely. If you use a jump to get off, land as softly as you can.
6. Practice the whole sequence: getting on, balancing in a twisted shape, and changing to a stretched shape and getting off. Keep doing the sequence until it is easy and then go on to the checklist.

Checklist (check off each thing after it is accomplished)

—Is your sequence difficult enough for you, or have you chosen movements that are very easy for you to do? If it is too easy, make one part of it more difficult for yourself.

—Are your balance shapes really held still, or do they wobble around? Practice the balance until you can hold very still.

—Is your sequence smooth when you do it, or are there some jerky parts in it that do not seem to go well? You might want to change some of the movements if there are.

Other possibilities

Try changing the speed of the sequence. Start very quickly and end slowly, or start slowly and end quickly.

Change the place to get on the equipment. Approach it from the other side or one end.

Add another balanced shape to the two on the apparatus.

Finish your sequence with a roll and balance *after* you have landed from the equipment.

Change the speed as you move in the sequence. Begin very slowly and then speed up.

Begin with a quick movement and end very slowly.

Put a turning movement in between two of the shapes.

Start the sequence very high and finish it very low to the ground.

Find a vocal sound that you can make as you do your sequence. If you cannot think of one, try saying "sh-h-h-h-h" in different ways as you move.

Find a partner and see how you can put your sequences together so that you have a duet.

Remember that you *do not* have to do the *same thing* as your partner.

Watch a dance program on television and draw some of the *shapes* the dancers make when they balance in different positions.

Make up a chant that you can say as you do your sequence. Post your chant on the bulletin board.

Write a letter to some aliens on Mars telling them why we dance on earth.

From Hoffman H, Young J, Klesius S: *Meaningful movement for children: a developmental theme approach to physical education,* Boston, 1981, Allyn Bacon.

advance quickly from one level to another through competency testing.

Communication of Tasks—Self-Instructional Strategies

Tasks are usually defined and communicated in written form through charts, printed materials, or task cards. For complex tasks, other media are needed (e.g., loop films, charts, 16 mm movies). When students are ready to do a task, they seek direction or descriptions on how to do it.

Obviously, students must know how to use materials effectively to learn a skill. In addition, enough materials must be available and convenient for the chosen method of task communication to be effective.

It is possible for teachers to perform task communication in an otherwise self-instructional strategy. In this case students are told that a certain task will be presented at a particular time for those students who are ready to learn it. The rest of the students in the class can remain with their own practice programs. Variations of station teaching can be used also, with different tasks presented at different stations.

Progression of Content—Self-Instructional Strategies

One of the advantages of a self-instructional model is that each student can start, progress, and end work in content at an appropriate level. A disadvantage is that the progression is preestablished and may not be appropriate for all students. The example in Box 9-9 individualizes the content by using a movement concept from which the student may choose an appropriate response. Some preestablished programs allow for remedial loops and horizontal development of materials. In these instances practice materials are provided that permit practice of the same level of an experience in different ways. More sophisticated materials can be designed so that students can work on specific problems in different ways, as the example in Box 9-9 illustrates.

Criteria for the quality of performance must be built into the instructional and evaluation materials. The two examples provided here do this in different ways.

Provision for Feedback and Evaluation—Self-Instructional Strategies

Feedback is essential for learning to occur. Knowledge of results can be built into instructional materials, but knowledge of performance is more difficult to obtain through self-instructional means.

Some self-instructional models in psychomotor skills depend heavily on videotape or peer feedback. Ideally, the teacher in a class instructional situation should be available to provide feedback. The teacher's role in a self-instructional strategy, however, is complicated by the teacher's role as a manager. Because of the need to evaluate students and help students use the materials, the teacher may find it difficult to provide adequate feedback.

Self-instructional strategies depend heavily on evaluation. In computer-assisted instructional models used in the classroom for cognitive learning, the computer provides the necessary feedback and evaluation to the learner as part of a program. In physical education, motor skills cannot be evaluated with paper and pencil tests or computer responses. Students are most often expected to meet criteria before going on to a new skill or a new level of the same skill. Often the teacher must judge proficiency and thus spends much time evaluating. Teachers who designate particular times during a class or particular days for checking students' progress are usually more successful in fulfilling other roles.

Strengths and Weaknesses of Strategy—Self-Instructional Strategies

Self-instructional strategies should probably be the goal of well-developed physical education programs. When students leave school programs, it is a great advantage for them to have the ability (1) to use available materials, equipment, and facilities to facilitate their own learning; (2) to use readily available self-instructional books; and (3) to direct their own instruction. Students do not start at this point, however, and teachers should decide whether they want to use program time to teach students how to function in this environment. This is curricular decision.

Self-instructional models involve predicted progressions. The more specific the progression, the more appropriately a student may be placed in that progression. Progressions may be designed with alternative loops that anticipate a less-than-linear advancement of skill. Such a design aids individualization.

A disadvantage of self-instructional models is the time required to prepare materials. Good progressions, media materials, and evaluative materials require much time to prepare. Commercially developed materials are available but expensive. In addition, teachers usually spend most of their time teaching students how to use the materials and evaluating progress.

◆ COGNITIVE STRATEGIES

Cognitive strategies is a label given to a group of teaching strategies designed to engage the learner cognitively in the content through the presentation of tasks. The terms *problem solving, guided discovery, divergent style* (Mosston, 1986), *teaching through questions* (Siedentop, 1991), *inquiry learning* (Harrison and Blakemore, 1992), and other terms have been used to describe approaches to the content itself that engage the learner in formulating responses rather than duplicating the response they have been shown by the teacher. Teachers use a cognitive strategy because they support one or more of the following ideas:

- The process of learning is as important as what is to be learned.
- Students are more likely to be engaged at a higher level with the content when their role in the learning process is more extensive.
- Cognitive strategies allow the content to be individualized.
- Cognitive strategies are a good way to teach concepts to students, and concepts have the potential to transfer to other similar content.

The teacher has several alternatives if the objective is to involve the learner cognitively. Cognitive strategies usually involve some type of problem-solving process on the part of the learner or groups of learners initiated through the presentation of a task. Problems can be as simple as "Is it better to bend your knees when landing or keep your knees straight" or as complicated as "Design a sequence of exercises that can be used for a warm-up in volley-

ball." The level of involvement of the learner varies with the level of cognitive response. When the teacher is looking for a single correct response, problem solving is usually called **guided discovery** (Mosston, 1986). When the problem is open and there is not one best response but many good responses, problem solving is usually called a **divergent style.** In the examples just given, the task related to bending the knees on landing is termed *guided discovery* and the task related to designing a warm-up routine is called *divergent style*. Examples of both guided discovery and divergent style are presented in Box 9-10.

Cognitive strategies focus on the nature of the task presented to the learner and not the organization of instruction. Therefore cognitive strategies can be used with any of the strategies previously discussed in this chapter that organizes instruction. Interactive teaching, peer teaching, cooperative learning strategies, and self-instruction strategies can all be used as a framework for involving the learner cognitively in the process of instruction. Movement education, which is used extensively in many elementary physical education programs, uses an interactive strategy of teaching that presents to learners both divergent movement tasks and guided discovery tasks, often with a direct instruction approach. Teaching balance as an interactive teaching strategy (presented in Box 9-4) is an example of such an approach.

◆ TEAM TEACHING

Team teaching is a teaching strategy in which more than one teacher is responsible for delivering instruction to a group of learners. When physical education classes became co-educational, many educators looked toward team teaching as a way to meet the needs of both boys and girls heterogeneously grouped by having both a male teacher and a female teacher responsible for a larger group of learners. Team teaching as strategy has a great potential to meet this need, as well as to deliver very effective instruction. Unfortunately, team teaching in practice has not lived up to its potential. Teachers were not trained in how to use team teaching or were not able to develop the interactive relationship needed between teachers to make team teaching work. In

---

BOX 9-10

Guided Discovery and Divergent Tasks

Guided discovery: lead the learner to a correct solution

Task one: When you are practicing your tennis forehand, try it a few times with your weight staying on your trailing foot and then with your weight on your lead foot. See if you can come to some conclusion as to which is more helpful to you. *(The teacher presents the task, either to individuals or to partners; has students work on it; and then brings the group back to make a decision.)*

Task two: You have several tasks on your task card related to the production of force. One of these tasks asks you to throw, another to jump, and another to strike a ball with a bat. All of these tasks require that you produce force. Each of your three-member group is responsible for leading the group through one of these skills—first with little force so that you don't throw hard, jump high, or hit far. Then I want you to do just the opposite—I want you to do it as hard as you can. What you are trying to do is to see if you can tell me what you do differently in these skills when you want to produce force. Then see if you can come up with a rule that might be used for all of these skills.

Divergent tasks: ask the learner to provide a solution where many are possible

Task one: Design a sequence of movements that incorporates traveling and balancing. You must start in a clear and still position and end in a clear and still position. Your transitions must be smooth and your balance held stretched and still for at least 6 seconds.

Task two: Your team must decide which is the skill you need the most work on and must develop a practice drill that practices that skill the way you think it should be used.

---

most situations team teaching is nothing more than turn teaching. Instead of 40 students having 2 teachers, in many cases, 40 students now have 1 teacher.

Team teaching is included in this chapter because, in spite of its abuse, team teaching presents some unique opportunities to solve instructional problems in gymnasiums that are shared by several groups of learners and several teachers. When used appropriately, team teaching has the potential to be a "best" solution to many situations that prohibit or make difficult self-contained classes. Even when self-contained classes are a possibility, teachers should seriously consider the following advantages of team teaching:

- **Flexible grouping** A primary advantage of team teaching is flexible grouping. Team teaching can use any of the previous instructional strategies. The advantage of team teaching is that students can be divided differently each class period or part of a class period to individualize instruction, based on skill level, interest, social needs, or whatever criteria the teachers feel are important. Group size can remain flexible so that sometime the support teacher may have only a small group that may need extra help or may need to move faster than the rest of the class. Teacher roles can change so that the same teacher is not always the support teacher or the primary teacher for instruction. Many effective teachers who use team teaching change roles at the unit level, based on expertise and interest in a content area.

- **Individual help** The support teacher can be used in instruction to identify students who need help and give help to these students without having the responsibility for the whole class. Feedback and evaluation is difficult in group instruction with only one teacher. Meeting the needs of individuals is a primary potential strength of team teaching.

Strengths and Weaknesses of Strategy— Team Teaching

If team teaching is to be used effectively, teachers must establish a relationship with each other that allows them to feel comfortable teaching "in front of" another professional. For teachers who are not comfortable working in front of their peers , this initially can be threatening but well worth the risk. Teachers must also be willing to plan together and evaluate what they have done together. In some situations this much togetherness is difficult because of personality difficulties or differences in professional goals. As in all relationships, there must be some compromise. Teachers who can establish a real team-teaching relationship tend to learn a great deal from each other. A productive interactive relationship with another professional tends to be growth producing and highly motivating.

◆ SELECTING A TEACHING STRATEGY

As discussed early in the chapter, teachers do not select a teaching strategy and then decide what to teach. The selection of a teaching strategy is based on

what teachers hope to accomplish in terms of their goals and objectives. Teachers should be able to appropriately use all of the instructional strategies described in this chapter for different lessons and even for different parts of a lesson.

Many factors influence the choice of a teaching strategy, including the content itself, the characteristics of the learner, and the objectives and preferences of the teacher. It is the blend of these factors that ultimately causes a teacher to choose one strategy over the other. Table 9-1 summarizes the use of the seven different strategies discussed.

TABLE 9-1   **Summary of the strengths and weaknesses of seven teaching strategies**

Teaching strategy	Teacher function	Strengths	Weaknesses
Interactive teaching	Selection of content	Teaching can be individualized by giving learners alternative responses. New content can be presented.	Strategy is often abused by selecting one task that is inappropriate for all learners.
	Communication of tasks	Communication can be adjusted in midstream if students do not understand.	Teacher plays a dominant role in task communication, thereby minimizing the role of the learner.
	Progression of content	Progression is based on previous responses of students and can therefore be appropriate.*	Strategy requires highly developed teacher analysis and observation skills to adjust progression while teaching.
	Provision for feedback and evaluation	Teacher is free to give feedback during activity.	Teacher cannot get to all students.
Station teaching	Selection of content	Many tasks can be given at one time to individualize content or better use space or equipment.*	Strategy requires that students have independent working skills and some familiarity with the tasks.
	Communication of tasks	Materials can be preplanned and established.	Media to communicate tasks are often not used well by students, and teachers cannot take the time needed to explain many different tasks at one time.
	Progression of content	Progression appropriate for students can be built into materials.	Quality of response is difficult to attain, thus limiting tasks to those that do not have a *form* focus.
	Provision for feedback and evaluation	Feedback must be built into task materials; teacher can spend time providing feedback if not needed as a manager or task presenter.	Feedback is hard to provide on a group basis because of the variety of different tasks being performed and management concerns.

* Indicates major strength of the teaching strategy.

TABLE 9-1	Summary of the strengths and weaknesses of seven teaching strategies—cont'd		
Teaching strategy	**Teacher function**	**Strengths**	**Weaknesses**
Peer teaching	Selection of content	When content is selected by peer teacher, then peer teacher profits from the process.	Peer teachers are not qualified to select appropriate content for their peers.
		Many different tasks and levels of tasks can be presented because of the number of "teachers."	Peer-teaching role requires a lot of teacher structuring.
	Communication of tasks	Peer teachers often use simpler language to communicate tasks.	Peer teachers do not have the experience to select appropriate teaching cues.
	Progression of content	—	Progression is usually determined by the teacher or must be guided by the teacher.
	Provision for feedback and evaluation	Immediate feedback can be given to many students at one time; many students can be evaluated in a short period of time.*	Feedback must be guided by the teacher.
Cooperative learning	Selection of content	Content can be selected to be meaningful to learners. Content is more holistic in nature.	It is difficult to select content appropriate for heterogeneous groups. More time is required to prepare task and materials ahead of time. More student independent learning skills are required.
	Communication of tasks	Content can be communicated using a variety of methods ranging from totally teacher directed to student directed.	Most cooperative learning tasks are broader in scope and therefore require more time to present to learners.
	Progression of content	Teacher can build progression into tasks and materials. Teacher is freed once activity on the task begins to individualize.	Students left to their own progression may not always select an appropriate one.
	Provision for feedback and evaluation	Teachers can provide feedback during independent work of students. Project usually has a culmination that can be evaluated.	It is not always easy to separate individual contributions from the group effort.
Self-instruction	Selection of content	Content can be made completely appropriate for the individual.*	The amount of time it takes to prepare materials necessitates self-motivated learners who are able to use materials.
	Communication of tasks	Learner can refer back to materials when there is a question.	It is difficult to communicate what is important in movement through written materials, which makes media important.

* Indicates major strength of the teaching strategy.

Continued.

TABLE 9-1		Summary of the strengths and weaknesses of seven teaching strategies—cont'd	
Teaching strategy	**Teacher function**	**Strengths**	**Weaknesses**
Self-instruction-cont'd	Progression of content	Progression can be built into materials in very gradual steps.	Because progression is preestablished, it may not be appropriate for all individuals.
	Provision for feedback and evaluation	—	Feedback must be built into materials; teachers usually spend most of their time evaluating.
Cognitive strategies	Selection of content	Content can involve the learner more holistically and at any level of student responsibility.	Time spent in the cognitive is time spent away from psychomotor practice.
	Communication of tasks	Tasks can be presented using any organizational strategy (e.g., media, task cards).	Tasks requiring more student involvement usually take longer to prepare and present.
	Progression of content	Full range of teacher directed to student directed can be used by this strategy.	It depends on how the teacher decides to develop and communicate the progression.
	Provision for feedback and evaluation	If used with more indirect teaching styles, the teacher is freed to provide feedback during the time students are working on the task.	If used with direct instruction, feedback is limited as in interactive teaching.
Team teaching	Selection of content	The expertise of two teachers making the decision as to appropriate content is usually better than a teacher working in isolation. Any teaching strategy can be used. The second teacher is free to individualize content or to take students in a special group for whom the task is not appropriate.	It requires more planning time and for the teachers working together to have a good working relationship
	Communication of tasks	Task can be presented using any method or strategy by one or both teachers. Teacher not responsible for task presentation can assist or play different role during task presentation.	It is difficult to establish a relationship between two teachers that permits responsibility for the communication of the task to shift appropriately during instruction. A lead teacher usually has to be established who takes the responsibility for task presentation.
	Progression of content	The second teacher is free to individualize progressions.	It is always more difficult when several different progressions are occurring within the same class.
	Provision for feedback and evaluation	Feedback and evaluation can be assigned to the free teacher.	When one teacher is doing feedback and evaluation, the lead teacher has to cope with a large group.

SUMMARY

1. Teaching strategies provide an instructional framework for the delivery of instruction.
2. As instruction moves from direct teaching to more indirect teaching, teacher control of the learning process becomes shared with the learner.
3. Most teaching strategies can be used for either direct or indirect instruction.
4. Each of the seven teaching strategies discussed arranges the instructional environment differently for the selection of content, the communication of tasks, the progression of content, and the provision for feedback and evaluation.
5. Each strategy has its advantages and disadvantages. The selection of a strategy depends on the objectives of the teacher for instruction, the content to be learned, and the characteristics of the learners.

CHECKING YOUR UNDERSTANDING

1. Describe the differences between direct and indirect instruction.
2. Describe the advantages and disadvantages of each teaching strategy.
3. Give an example of a lesson best taught with each of the teaching strategies.
4. Produce a developmental analysis of content for the example of a self-instructional strategy for teaching gymnastics presented in Box 9-9. (The extension and refinement is very clear in this example.)

REFERENCES

Aronson E et al: *The jigsaw classroom,* Beverly Hills, CA, 1978, Sage Publications.

Harrison J, Blakemore C: *Instructional strategies for secondary school physical education,* Dubuque, IA, 1992.

Hoffman H, Young J, Klesius S: *Meaningful movement for children: a developmental approach to physical education,* Boston, 1981, Allyn & Bacon.

Johnson D, Johnson R: *Learning together and alone,* Englewood Cliffs, NJ, 1975, Prentice-Hall.

Kagen S: The structural approach to cooperative learning, *Educ Leadership* 47(4):12-15, 1990.

Mosston M: *Teaching physical education,* Columbus, OH, 1966, Merrill Publishing.

Mosston M, Ashworth S: *Teaching physical education,* ed 3, Columbus, OH, 1986, Merrill Publishing.

Siedentop D: *Developing teaching skills in physical education,* Mountain View, CA, 1991, Mayfield Publishing.

Slavin R: *Cooperative learning,* New York, 1983, Longman.

Slavin R: Cooperative learning and student achievement, *Educ Leadership* 45(2):31-33, 1988.

Slavin R: Research on cooperative learning: consensus and controversy, *Educ Leadership* 47(4):52-55, 1990.

Smith RA: A teacher's views on cooperative learning, *Phi Delta Kappan* 68(9):663-666, 1987.

SUGGESTED READING

Zakrajsek D, Carnes L: *Individualizing physical education,* ed 2, Champaign, IL, 1986, Human Kinetics Publishers.

chapter 10

Motivation and Personal Growth

❖ ❖ ❖ ❖ ❖ ❖ ❖ ❖ ❖ ❖

OVERVIEW

Motivation and concerns for student personal growth are critical and integral parts of teaching. Students who are not motivated to learn most likely will not learn. When personal needs for growth are not met, students have difficulty learning and growing as contributing members of society. The purpose of this chapter is to discuss the role of student motivation and teacher concerns for student personal growth in teaching and to describe how teachers can attend to these needs through their teaching.

❖ ❖ ❖ ❖ ❖ ❖ ❖ ❖ ❖ ❖

CONCEPTS

- **Motivation in learning**
  Theories of motivation
    Need theory
    Intrinsic motivation
    Cognitive theories
  Implications of theories of
    motivation
- **Promoting personal growth through personal interaction**
- **Motivation and personal growth through instructional decision making**
  Planning
  Selection of tasks and design of
    learning experiences
  Presentation of units and tasks

  Organizational arrangements
  Teacher functions during activity
  Pacing of lessons
  Evaluation of units and lessons
- **Teaching affective goals as a lesson focus**
  The unique and shared goals of phys-
    ical education
  Instructional strategies for teaching
    affect
- **Discussion of affective goals of physical education**

AFFECT is described in Chapter 1 as that aspect of development that relates to student feelings, attitudes, and values. Student affect always plays a role in teaching, whether the teacher chooses to focus on student affect in interactions with students or instructional decisions and whether the teacher chooses to work with affective concerns explicitly as part of the curriculum. Student feelings, perceptions, attitudes, and values influence how students respond to themselves, the teacher, each other, and the learning experiences teachers plan.

Educators have focused on the role of affect in learning primarily in terms of issues related to motivating students to learn that which has been decided to be important to learn. Motivation to learn is an essential ingredient of learning. Teachers need methods to motivate students extrinsically, as well as methods to develop students' intrinsic motivation toward what the teachers are teaching.

Educators have also focused on student affect as it relates to the personal growth of students. Student personal growth has always been an expectation of the schools to some degree. Changes in societal expectations of the role of the school and differences in school and teacher philosophy usually affect the balance between the emphasis on subject matter mastery and the emphasis given to student personal growth. Personal growth is usually associated with the development of positive feelings of self, the acquisition of a value system internally driven, and a tolerance and respect for others. Some educators say that personal growth involves a responsibility for the needs and welfare of others as well.

As a teacher, you must learn how to motivate students and you should know how best to contribute to the personal growth of each child. Many of you have chosen teaching as a career because you want to play a major role in the personal growth of young people and you want to use the skills and knowledges associated with physical education to facilitate this growth. In many respects it is the successes teachers have in the development of student motivation and student affect that provide the greatest rewards in teaching.

What makes concerns for the development of student motivation and personal growth so difficult to apply is the uniqueness of the needs of individuals. What motivates one student may not necessarily motivate another. What one student needs in terms of personal growth is not necessarily what another student needs. The art of teaching will always involve the ability to reach individuals while meeting the needs of the group.

The chapter begins with a discussion of student motivation and is followed by sections on teacher-student interaction, building affect into instruction, and teaching values and affect directly and explicitly.

◆ MOTIVATION IN LEARNING

Although it is possible for students to learn who are not highly motivated to learn, it is certainly easier for a teacher to facilitate learning if students are motivated. In the simplest sense, motivation is a construct developed to explain the degree of attraction the learner has to a particular behavior or learning task. We say that students who persist at a task, spend a long time on a task, or choose to do a task are motivated. Likewise, students who show little persistence, intensity, or initiative toward a particular task are unmotivated. Student motivation is continuously cited by teachers as a major problem in teaching, particularly in secondary physical education.

Theories of Motivation

Although many theories are designed to explain motivation, most theories fit into one of two basic explanations for motivated behavior—*need theory* and *achievement theory*. Like most attempts to explain human behavior, each seems to have a part of the answer, but neither fully explains motivation or the lack of it in students.

Need theory. Need theory assumes that people act to fill needs. A need is a tension that exists that creates a void that people seek to resolve. The work of both Maslow (1962) and Murray (1978) are briefly summarized.

Maslow. One of the most useful classifications of needs was developed by Abraham Maslow, who described the following basic human needs:

- **Physiological:** What the body needs to survive (e.g., food, sleep, exercise, water)
- **Safety/Security:** Order and protection (both physical and psychological)
- **Love and belonging:** Friends, group identification, family
- **Esteem:** Self-respect and the confidence and admiration of others
- **Self-actualization:** Need to develop one's potential

Several principles associated with Maslow's need theory are important to education. First, Maslow's list of needs are said to be **hierarchical.** This means that basic needs, such as physiological and safety needs, must be met before the individual seeks to satisfy higher-order needs, such as self-actualization and self-esteem. People who have satisfied more basic needs can begin to work on self-actualization, which is not as much a function of what a person achieves as it is how secure a person feels about himself or herself as an individual. In this sense, Maslow's need theory combines both the notion of acting to satisfy deficiencies with the notion of moving toward personal growth after basic needs have been satisfied.

Maslow helps us to learn to understand why students might not be motivated. Hungry children or children deprived of self-esteem or love find it difficult to be motivated to learn or to grow toward being a fully functioning individual.

Murray. Murray suggested that behavior is a function of the need to avoid unpleasant tensions and the need to achieve, affiliate with others, and have some sense of power. In Murray's perspective, students will find a way to meet these needs either through positive and constructive behaviors or negative and destructive behaviors. He attributed much negative behavior by students to their dealing with tensions negatively because they have not been successful dealing with them positively.

Intrinsic motivation. According to Piaget (1970) and other theorists who view human behavior as being essentially instrinsically motivated, defi-

ciency theories of motivation are not sufficient to explain human behavior. Human beings are intrinsically motivated to seek and to fulfill their potential. They will engage in particular activities because they find them rewarding; that is, they feel competent and self-determining when they engage in them. According to Deci (Deci and Ryan, 1985), two types of situations motivate people intrinsically. The first situation is when a person is bored and acts for stimulation. The second situation involves the desire to be challenged and reduce dissonance (ideas that do not go together). Appropriate experiences are both interesting and difficult enough to be challenging yet achievable.

Cognitive theories. Cognitive theories of motivation focus on the subjective experience of the individual. What people think about what is happening to them and what might happen to them as a result of a behavior is an important determinant of behavior. Several important theories from this perspective are presented.

Achievement theory. According to Atkinson (1964), a person's motivation toward a particular goal is a function of the relative strength of both the desire to reach the goal and the tendency to avoid failure. Obviously some students approach learning with little or no anxiety about the potential for failure, and others approach the task severely limited by their fear of failure. Students who have a strong need to achieve will usually select goals of an intermediate level of difficulty, whereas students who have a great deal of anxiety about failure will usually choose goals that they are sure they can accomplish or that are very difficult. Choosing very difficult goals and failing is of little consequence because the individual can rationalize that the task was too difficult. The motivation to play it safe may be ultimately unproductive, although students who are motivated by a fear of failure may need to start with tasks that ensure success.

Attribution theory. Attribution theorists have focused on understanding achievement-related behavior and have shown that what individuals attribute their success or failure to in a task is critical

Teachers need to be sensitive and encouraging.

to explaining their approach to achievement-related tasks (Ames, 1978; Friese et al, 1983; Nicholls, 1976; Rotter, 1966; Weiner, 1984). Typically we attribute our success or failure in achievement situations to *our ability, our effort, luck, or the difficulty of the task.* If you consider these four attributions (causes), you will notice that ability and effort are *internal* characteristics of the individual and luck and task difficulty are *externally* controlled. Attribution theorists refer to these ideas as **characteristics of locus of control.**

Success always brings a greater positive emotion than failure, regardless of the way in which the student perceives the cause. Students who attribute success to internal causes, such as their ability, effort, or native traits, also are more likely to experience feelings of competence and satisfaction. Students who attribute failure to internal causes are likely to experience hopelessness and low self-esteem,

whereas failure attributed to lack of effort always holds out the possibility that if you try harder, you will succeed. Generally, students who are success oriented tend to believe that they are capable of handling tasks and therefore attribute lack of success to their own effort. Failure for these students tends to be motivating. Students who are not success oriented tend to blame their own ability for their failures but do not take credit (they attribute their successes to external factors) for their own success. These students tend to be motivated to avoid failure by not engaging in the task and putting themselves at risk. To put forth great effort and to fail is the worst situation of all.

Cognitive theorists all agree that motivation is increased when (1) students perceive tasks as being of moderate difficulty, (2) tasks can be accomplished with reasonable effort, (3) students engage in the task for their own reasons (internal) rather than external control, and (4) students do not have to be concerned with how what they do will be perceived by others.

Implications of Theories of Motivation

Several basic principles are common to all of the theories just discussed that are useful to keep in mind when creating a climate for learning for all students.

Students cannot address higher needs unless they have achieved lower needs. Needs for confidence and security precede those of esteem and self-actualization. Students who are hungry, have difficult home lives, or find school threatening to their psychological security need to have these deficiencies corrected before meaningful autonomy in learning can be expected. At the same time, students need to be allowed to grow and work toward higher-order needs as they are ready. Students should not be restrained by a system set up to control motivation externally and therefore limit the potential for personal growth.

Meeting the needs of every child in a class is difficult simply because every child is likely to have different needs and because in some cases meeting some student needs is out of the control of the teacher. Teacher sensitivity and efforts to provide the needed security for a child who cannot find this security outside of the school often can be enough to help that child continue to grow to higher levels of personal growth.

EXAMPLES:

- "John, you handled that very well today. Would you like to help me put out the equipment today?"
- "Sally, I would like for you to be Joanna's partner today. She needs some extra support and encouragement, and I think you can give that to her."

Teachers must find ways for students to meet their needs in positive ways. Often misbehavior can be attributed to the need for attention and power. If students can meet this need in more positive ways, they will not have to resort to negative behaviors.

EXAMPLES:

- "Karen, you are really good at taking weight on your hands. Would you like to demonstrate how you do it?"
- "Frank, as we begin class today, I would like to hear you say two nice things to somebody in your class before the end of the class."

Students must perceive what is to be learned as meaningful. Teachers must find ways to help students see the importance of what they are doing. Teachers also must take care to assure that what they are doing has meaning. Pointless and repetitious drill for skills that are never used in a game is usually perceived by students as meaningless. If students know they will get to use the skills or if skills are applied in game situations as the skills are developed, students are likely to be more motivated. If students have some say in determining their need for practice, they are likely to be even more motivated.

EXAMPLES:

- "Let's look at this video tape of the Olympics, and see if we can identify what it is that these people are doing when they run. What do you think we should work on first?"
- (*Teacher begins a unit with the game rather than skills. After the first day of games, the teacher has an evaluation session.*) "After your games today, what can you identify as what you need to work on? We will try and work on an area of game play and skills and then put it back in the game. After each game we will evaluate what we are doing and choose another area of work."

Use a variety of teaching strategies. Even the best strategies used on a continuous basis are likely to lose their motivating effect. Teachers must continuously search for new ways to do things. Student interest and motivation are increased also through the use of fantasy, imagination (even older students), and group activities.

EXAMPLES:

- The teacher plans the unit in detail ahead of time by building in the use of as many different teaching strategies as possible and matching the strategy to the appropriate unit objective.
- "Let's pretend we are going on a safari today through the jungles. The stations are set up to be different challenges. For example, there will be trees to climb, mountains to get over, and chases with wild animals."
- "We're going to set up our tournament as the real Olympics."
- "Today we are going to conduct class as a society that has no tensions among people. In our society everyone is supportive and polite and sensitive to each other's needs. Today is going to be an 'other-centered day.'"

Tasks should be designed to permit each student to function at an optimal level of challenge. For most students this means that the student should be able to be successful with a reasonable effort. Tasks that are too simple or too difficult are likely to result in decreased motivation. Continued failure is likely to result in poor achievement motivation and poor self-esteem.

EXAMPLE: The teacher sits down with her lesson plan and for each task designed, redesigns that task to permit different students to operate at different levels within the task. (*See p. 198 for specific ways to do this.*)

Tasks should be designed to allow the student to function with autonomy. Although it is not always possible to have each student intrinsically motivated to do every task the teacher has planned, teachers should attempt to work toward providing all students with tasks that are meaningful and permit choice and autonomy. Tasks should be presented to create personal interest, dissonance (conflicts that need to be resolved), and curiosity. External control of all learning tasks leads to decreased motivation and a decreased sense of competency. Rewards should be made personal.

EXAMPLES:

- "Today we are going to be working on building a personal warm-up routine for our volleyball unit. The components of the routine are listed on the sheet that you have. You may work to design exercises in one of these components. Each group will be responsible for a different component and for teaching the exercises they have selected to the rest of the class."
- "I have decided that we need to work on combining dribbling and passing on the move in our games. Why is dribbling and passing important? What is it that gives some of you trouble when you are doing this?"

When teachers use external methods of motivation, the student is motivated by the value of the consequence and not the value of the activity. There are times when teachers must use external motivators to increase student effort. External motivators can be used more effectively if the following occur:

1. Rewards are used primarily for mastery of basic tasks rather than learning experiences involving the student at a higher level.

EXAMPLE: "Yesterday I asked you to keep your score at each station of practice. You got one point for each of ten successful trials at each station. We will do this at the end of each week of classes. At the end of the unit there will be prizes for those students who make the most progress from the beginning to the end. Why do you think I have decided that prizes would be awarded for improvement rather than for the highest score?"

2. Teachers use rewards to link behavior to the internal rewards of being successful at the activity.

EXAMPLE : "The following students will get their names on the list of students who were good sports this week in physical education. I would like each of these students to come up and tell you what they did that they think showed that they were a good sport and to tell you how it made them feel when they were supportive of another person."

3. Competition should ensure that all students have an equal chance of being successful and that winning and losing are depersonalized (not attributed to internal causes). Competition is an ego-involved activity, and therefore students tend to have more at risk in participating.

EXAMPLES:

- "We will play a round robin tournament at three levels. Each level will have different rules and will involve a different level of competition. You may choose the level of competition you feel is appropriate for you."
- "The winners of today's games really worked hard and showed us good performance. How many of you really enjoyed today's games? I could tell all of you were having a good time. We'll see who gets to be the winner tomorrow."

4. Teachers work toward removing external motivators and replace them with methods to increase internal motivation.

EXAMPLE: "I would like to point out something I saw today that really pleased me. I didn't say that any kind of points would be given for people who really worked hard today, and what I noticed was that many of you worked really hard at the lesson even though today was not a point day. How many of you think you could work really hard tomorrow even if we do not give awards?"

5. Use self-testing activities with a focus on personal improvement rather than comparison with others.

EXAMPLES:

- "See if you can do one more this time than you did last time."
- "How many of you feel like you were able to pass quicker in that first game?"

Variety in learning activities and novel and interesting tasks tend to increase motivation. Teachers should strive to provide a variety of tasks. Teachers need not change an objective but need to find different ways to accomplish the same objective to sustain interest (horizontal development).

EXAMPLES:

- The volleyball set can be practiced (1) against a wall, (2) with a partner toss, or (3) over the net to a target.
- Instead of spending a full day or days developing one skill, distribute the practice of skills over a unit and spend less time on each skill per day (distributed practice).

Help students to see the purpose for what you are doing and attach a personal meaning to what you are doing from the student's perspective. Most students identify with sport-related and health-related fitness. Personalizing means to find ways to attach the importance of what you are doing to a particular student or group of students.

EXAMPLES:

- "Who are your favorite basketball players? What do you like about the way they are playing?"
- "How many of you see joggers on the streets when you are coming to school? Why do you think they are doing this?"

Use culminating activities that permit students to demonstrate efforts of extended and motivated practice. Motivation is increased if students are working toward something that is in the more immediate future than a life skill. Most physical education units can have culminating activities. Although tournaments are used frequently, the nature of culminating activities and how they are conducted can be changed and modified to add variety and interest.

EXAMPLES:

- "At the end of this unit we are going to have each of you present a routine that is your best effort. It does not make any difference how hard the skills are. What we are interested in is if you put your routine together smoothly and with good form. We will invite the other class to come see what you have done."
- "The tournament for this unit will also have a value focus. Each team will select one value that they think is an important characteristic to have in life that is often a part of doing well in sports as well. The

names of your teams will reflect these values. During game play we expect your team to really demonstrate those values. At the end of the tournament there will be a tournament winner for the group that most demonstrated their value, as well as a winner for competition."

Help students to understand that all of us are beginners at some point and to understand what it means to be a beginner. Many students (and many teachers) attribute success in motor skills to ability; they downplay the role of effort. Motor skill acquisition takes time and effort. Teachers must help students to appreciate the idea that we are all beginners at some time and beginners make mistakes and cannot perform as well as people who have had experience. Teachers can discuss with students what it means to be a beginner at motor skills and help them feel secure that it is alright to be a beginner. When individuals stop wanting to do things because they are beginners, they stop learning and growing.

EXAMPLE: "We are going to begin a tennis unit today. How many of you have never played tennis before? Some of you have played a lot of tennis, and some of you have not had any experience playing tennis. Those of you who have not played before will not be as good to start with as those of you who have. Why not? What do beginners look like? What would happen if we never wanted to try anything because we were afraid of looking like a beginner? How can those of you who have played before help those who are beginners?"

Help students to set goals for physical education that are those of the participant, not the professional. Television and other forms of communication have given us immediate access to the very best performances, not only in sports but in all of the performing arts. One of the negative results of this kind of access is that many of us no longer can appreciate an amateur performance and choose not to be participants ourselves because we cannot be world class performers. The goal of physical education should be to develop participants. Students need to be helped to understand the value of participation, not just the value of superior performance.

EXAMPLE: "Why do people play sports? How many of

you enjoy playing basketball? Why do you enjoy playing basketball? Do you have to be a Michael Jordon to enjoy playing? What can sports do for you?"

Use humor. Teachers should be able to laugh at events and to create humorous situations to develop interest and motivation.

EXAMPLES:
- The teacher makes a point about lack of control in movement by playing the clown.
- The teacher makes a point about being supportive of others' efforts by role playing an exaggerated unsupportive student.

Help students to attribute their success and failure to a cause that is controllable by the student. Students are likely to protect themself from failure by not trying if they do not perceive themselves as able to master a task or perceive control of success outside themselves. The teacher can help students to attribute success to effort and therefore to increase the likelihood that students will risk failure by (1) giving students criteria on which to judge their own success and (2) helping them to set reasonable goals for themselves. For low-achievement students, teachers can focus their efforts on the students' efforts and the level at which the students are engaged in the task. Teachers should help all students understand that learning in physical education, particularly motor skills, is an investment in time.

EXAMPLES:
- "Tommie, I am really excited about what you have done today. Yesterday you were having trouble bringing those feet down softly from your weight on hands. Today I could hardly hear them. You must be really concentrating on what you are doing."
  "If you can do one more today than you did yesterday, you are really making good progress."

◆ PROMOTING PERSONAL GROWTH THROUGH PERSONAL INTERACTION

One of the most difficult aspects of teaching for a beginning teacher is to find the best way to interact with students. Some beginning teachers err in the direction of trying to make students like them. The role of the teacher is *not* that of a "friend." Teachers should act in a student's best interest from the perspective of an adult. At the other extreme, some beginning teachers are so concerned with losing control in their classes, they are often reluctant to communicate their humanness to students. Students want a relationship with an adult that is supportive and guiding. They want to know that the teacher cares about them and about what they do.

Teaching is largely about affect: adults who are caring and concerned professionals who have a responsibility to (1) help students learn and (2) promote students' personal growth as individuals and as responsible, self-directed members of society.

Through the manner in which they interact with students, teachers can communicate a professional and supportive relationship with students that says, "I care." Although each of you as a unique individual will find your own way of sharing yourself with young people to promote their own growth, the following ideas should be considered:

1. *Learn students' names and use them.*

Physical education teachers often have many students in each class. Nonetheless, an essential and minimal form of recognition for students is that you know and are able to use their names. Use your role book after each class to identify students you have yet to make some kind of personal contact with. Make learning names at the beginning of school a number one priority.

2. *Be enthusiastic and positive about what you are doing.*

Enthusiasm is catching. Many people assume that enthusiasm is a personality trait of very outgoing and "bubbly" people. Enthusiasm does not necessarily always have to be such high-energy behavior. Students will know by the tone of the teachers' voices and the manner in which they approach a lesson how enthusiastic they are about what they are doing.

3. *Project a caring attitude toward all students.*

Caring is projected by the teacher primarily through a genuine interest and recognition of each child. If you go through your student list and you cannot identify in a positive and meaningful way a particular child's needs for growth, it is probably a good indication that you have yet to tune into that child as a growing person. Caring is projected by the teacher through a sensitivity to the feelings of students and the meaning and significance students attach to events and their interactions with you. Caring teachers tune in to the child as a feeling human being—no matter what behavior the student is demonstrating. Caring teachers do not condone misbehavior, but in dealing with misbehavior they do not undermine the integrity of the individual child as a person.

4. *Reinforce basic and shared beliefs of honesty, tolerance, respect, risk taking, and effort by modeling these behaviors, as well as reinforcing them when they occur in the class.*

Recent societal problems have emphasized the need for not only student personal growth (a return to values that make a democratic and interdependent society and world work), but a responsibility for developing prosocial behaviors of students (Good and Brophy, 1990). Prosocial behaviors are those behaviors exhibited by students that demonstrate a responsibility for helping other people without being prompted by external rewards.

Many of the messages students receive from their families and the society outside of school teach them to fear and to interact in destructive ways with those who are different, whether these differences are race, culture, socioeconomic, gender, or physical conditions. Schools and teachers have a responsibility not only to make students aware of the destructiveness of these attitudes and behaviors, but to act positively to change them.

5. *Do not reinforce behavior destructive to self or others by doing nothing about it.*

Students learn acceptable ways of interacting with each other not only by what you do, but also by what you do not do. Values, tolerance, and respect for others are learned. Teachers must find ways of communicating what is acceptable and what is not acceptable. Develop an awareness for the effects of your unintended behavior. When you permit students to act in inappropriate ways (name calling, fighting), you give your approval to these behaviors by not doing anything about them.

6. *Do not allow yourself to become personally threatened by student misbehavior.*

Many beginning teachers consider misbehavior of students a personal threat, and they respond to student misbehavior emotionally. This negative emotional behavior can take the form of anger, threats, personal criticism of students, and sometimes even physical abuse. As soon as teachers put themselves in this position, they lose the ability to positively affect student behavior, and in the case of physical abuse, leave themself open to being dismissed for inappropriate conduct. Teachers can avoid putting themselves in this position by not allowing themselves to be personally threatened by student misbehavior. Professional teachers treat misbehavior as they would an incorrect answer or response in a lesson. They accept that as where the student is at the time and take steps to move the student forward. They do not allow themselves to be personally threatened by a student.

7. *Make it a practice to intentionally treat all students equitably. Develop an awareness of your own personal patterns of communication to different students.*

It is easy for teachers to gravitate to the more skilled students or the students who the teacher believes will threaten their class control. Many students get lost in the everyday interaction of classes unless the teacher makes a conscious effort to recognize and interact with all the students equally. This is difficult for physical education teachers, who see students infrequently, but attention to all students can be facilitated if teachers will periodically review class lists, consider each student, and make it a point to give attention to students they have been slighting.

8. *Learn to be a good listener and observer of student responses.*

You can become attuned to your students by listening to and observing the subtle meanings of their messages communicated by the manner in which they interact with you, each other, and learning tasks. Listen for motivation and feeling. Give students an opportunity to voice opinions and approach problems constructively with a shared responsibility for solving them.

9. *Chart your own life for personal growth.*

Teachers who have the most to contribute to young people are those who have met their own basic needs and are working on their own higher-order needs for esteem and self-actualization. Set your own goals to actualize your own potential, both as a teacher and as a multidimensional individual.

◆ MOTIVATION AND PERSONAL GROWTH THROUGH INSTRUCTIONAL DECISION MAKING

There was a time when planning for student motivation and concerns about student personal growth was not considered necessary. These ideas were inherent in what it meant to *teach*. More recent emphases on subject matter competence and the difficulties in motivating some students make it necessary for teachers to think through and make explicit how they are going to incorporate both motivation and student personal growth into their teaching. Each function the teacher performs has the capability to be designed for different purposes. Moreover, it

Competence and success are great motivators. (Courtesy SIUE Photo.)

is possible to integrate into every decision concerns for subject matter competency, motivation, and personal growth. What follows is a discussion of considerations for motivating and developing the personal growth of students through different instructional functions. The unique objectives of physical education are not neglected, but made richer in their development.

Planning

Integrating concerns for student motivation and student personal growth into your teaching requires planning. Although affective goals are cited most often by physical education teachers as primary goals of their program, they receive the least attention as explicit objectives and even less attention in their planning. Integrating concerns for affect and motivation means that these objectives should be an explicit part of the lesson. It is not sufficient to say that you want students to work cooperatively as partners. Unless you have discussed with students what it means to work cooperatively as partners, it is unlikely that much will be learned about cooperation. Physical education by its very nature offers many opportunities to develop personal growth skills of students, but it is not sufficient to put students into situations that have the potential for personal growth. A primary example of this is the use of team sports by teachers to develop sportsmanship. Team sports have the potential to develop sportsmanship, but they have the potential to develop just the opposite as well. Unless teachers make clear their expectations for what sportsmanship is and unless they reinforce sportsmanship in their classes, it is unlikely that merely playing a team sport will result in sportsmanship. In your planning you should do the following:

- Consider not only content, but student motivation—how you can build in student motivation to each phase of the lesson and unit.
- Do more long-term planning. Teachers who plan only lessons miss opportunities to build in variety, long-term goals, and motivation.
- Make goals for student conduct and values explicit in your yearly, unit, and lesson plans as progressive content. Identify what you want to

work on, and integrate it with your units and lesson plans.

- If you have to motivate using external motivation, build in progressive efforts to remove external motivation and replace it with internal motivation.

Selection of Tasks and Design of Learning Experiences

The learning experiences and tasks teachers design are the primary mechanism for not only subject matter competence, but motivation and work on student personal growth. It is not enough to just be able to identify that students need to work on a two-on-two offense or defensive strategy. How that task is designed in group instruction is critical to its potential to motivate or contribute to student growth. The following ideas should be considered in the design of learning experiences and tasks:

- Tasks should be selected that are at an appropriate level of difficulty for all students. It is reasonable to assume that all students are not at the same level of ability in our classes. To make tasks appropriate for all students, teachers must do one of the following:

  Provide alternative tasks, such as: "If you can get the underhand serve over the net from half court 8 of 10 times, move back to the end line."

  Design tasks that inherently allow each student to operate within his or her own ability, such as: "Find a comfortable distance for you and your partner to practice fielding ground balls" or "Choose an inverted balance you can hold for at least 6 seconds."

  Give students a choice in the level they wish to play, such as: "You can choose to be on a team of two on two or five on five" or "Each group gets to decide what the rules are for their games."

  Manipulate the conditions of tasks that the whole class is working on, for example, by changing distances, equipment, rules, targets, or force levels required.

  Use self-testing activities that permit students to test their ability within a framework of

self-improvement, such as: "How many times in a row can you toss and catch without the ball leaving the ground" or "How many times can your group keep the ball up in the air using either a forearm or overhead pass?" Tasks should be designed to create student interest and maintain student motivation.

- Tasks that involve competition should be used appropriately. Consider the following:

  Design experiences where all students have an equal chance of winning. If the same students always win and the same students always lose, competition loses its value for both groups and can be detrimental to personal growth.

  Focus students on external and controllable aspects of competition and not internal factors, such as ability. Eliminate as much ego involvement as is possible. Attribute winning to effort.

  In groups with mixed ability there is some merit for practice to be in heterogeneous groups, but competition should be with students of the same ability.

  Use self-testing activities that focus on personal improvement where possible.

  Give students a choice of competing and a choice of the level of competition. Competition can enhance performance for skilled students and may decrease performance for unskilled students and beginners.

  Use group self-testing tasks, such as: "See how long your group (or you and your partner) can keep the ball going."

- Find different ways to practice the same thing.

  When you have identified a learning experience that students need to progress in their ability, see if you can identify several ways to practice the same thing.

  Distribute practice of the same task over days in a unit.

  Design the curriculum so that the use of some pieces of equipment are reserved for older students.

- Involve students in projects and more long-term goals. Link lessons. Students are more likely to work on parts of a whole they feel is meaningful.

- Use a variety of teaching strategies throughout the unit of work.

Presentation of Units and Tasks

How students perceive a content area before you begin a lesson or a unit in that content area plays a major role in the motivation they are likely to have for fully engaging in that content. An enthusiastic teacher who is well-prepared to motivate a group of students in a lesson can sometimes change the mind of even the student most determined not to like what is coming. The following techniques should be considered:

- Use advance organizers for units and lessons. Advance organizers share with students what is to come in the lesson and the unit. It is also important when possible to share with students why you have decided to do something a certain way and why what you have decided to do is important.

  EXAMPLE: "Today we are going to start a unit in soccer. You have a check sheet of skills and abilities in soccer in front of you. I know you have played soccer before, and I would like for you to check those skills you do very well with a *check plus;* those skills you do fairly well with a *check;* and those skills you think you really do not do well at all with a *check minus.* That will help me in my planning to make the experiences meaningful to you. We will start off today with three-on-three games and spend some time at the end of the period talking about what we have done. By the end of the unit we should get to play at least seven-on-seven games with a class tournament."

- Use motivating introductions to lessons and units that will stimulate interest and curiosity.

  EXAMPLE: One teacher wrote a poem about how much fun the unit was going to be. One male teacher began a hockey unit dressed in a kilt. Other teachers have brought in high school or community athletes.

- When beginning a unit in an activity that is relatively unfamiliar to students, find a way to give them a sense of the whole (what they are working toward). Many students are learning volleyball for the first time who actually have never seen volleyball played as a team sport. Many elementary chil-

dren have never actually focused in on what many sports really look like played well.

  EXAMPLE: Short segments of videotape and film of sports and activities are available and will help give students some idea of what they are working toward.

- Personalize introductions to units and lessons. Use your own experiences or those of members of the class to help students understand that what you are teaching may be relevant to them.

  EXAMPLE: "When I leave school a few afternoons a week, I play on a softball team. How many of you have parents or know someone who plays on a softball team as an adult?"

Organizational Arrangements

The manner in which teachers organize equipment, students, and space for instruction is just as important as the content they select to teach. Organizational arrangements for instruction should be intentionally designed to accomplish specific purposes and not be so routinized by the teacher that the potential for contributing to motivation and the personal growth of students is lost.

Use individual, group, and other organizations to make the practice of a skill interesting. Individual practice, partner practice, and group practice of the same skill add variety and interest to a lesson. Consider the following:

- Group students with a purpose. Assignment to work with others or partners depends on the task and the needs of a particular group.
- There are times when students need to work with others of their own ability. When given a choice, students will generally choose someone with whom they are compatible and who is of their own ability. Unless some students are always "left out" of the selection process, this system is efficient and normally works well.
- Heterogeneous groups should be chosen by the teacher to encourage the development of tolerance and understanding among students or to improve the skill ability of students who can profit from working with another of higher ability. Heterogeneous groups should never be used

without attention to assigning different roles to students and ensuring that each student can contribute.

- At times there is value in maintaining group membership through a longer period so that students have the opportunity to work through problems. In yearly planning, vary group membership and the time spent with a particular group.
- Give students within a group different responsibilities and be explicit about what those responsibilities might be.
- Learn to distinguish productive group interaction from nonproductive group interaction that deteriorates the task orientation of the group.
- Use novel types of equipment or novel types of arrangements of equipment to add variety and interest to lessons.

Teacher Functions During Activity

Depending on the nature of the task and the nature of the self-management skills of the student, the teacher in physical education should be free to observe and offer individualized help to students during the time the students are engaged in the learning task. This time, when used wisely, can significantly impact the appropriateness of the learning experience for individuals within the class and the effectiveness of the learning experience. Consider the following:

- When students are sent off to work on a task and you are assured that work is safe and focused, use this time to begin to zero in on individual children, particularly those who tend to get lost in the group because they may not necessarily do anything to draw your attention to them. Be alert to subtle hidden messages in student behavior regarding participation and social interactions taking place within the group.
- Use instructional time freed of presenting information and directing students to individualize both the affective goals that you have, as well as the content objectives of a lesson.
- Attend to the guidelines presented for feedback in Chapter 8, paying particular attention to providing more support for insecure students.

Begin to withdraw adult support for achievement-oriented students. Encourage effort, and attempt to attribute the success of students to their effort.

- Use this time when needed for "off task" interactions with students you need to communicate with when no other time seems to be available.

Pacing of a Lesson

One of the arts of teaching is knowing when to let students continue to practice a particular task and when to call them in to refocus their efforts or to change the task on which they are working. Student motivation can be affected by teachers who do not allow enough time to practice before calling students in, as well as teachers who let a practice deteriorate because student motivation has waned. Consider the following:

- When students are involved in game play, they often resent having their games stopped on a continuous basis. Alert students to the idea that some games will be scrimmages that you will stop when you see the need to. If games are focused on working on a particular aspect of skill or strategy, make clear your expectations ahead of time and make clear that you will stop them when there is a problem on this particular aspect. Try not to stop the play in a shotgun array of "coaching tips."
- Often it is the teacher who is bored with a particular task and not the students. Learn to distinguish between students who just need a physical reprieve and students who are unmotivated and off task.

Evaluation of Units and Lessons

Evaluation of learning is probably the most neglected function in teaching physical education. Generally this is because teachers believe that they do not have the time to do any kind of evaluation. However, evaluation is a critical aspect of learning and an important dimension of motivation to learn. Consider the following:

- Take time for evaluation, even if it means reducing the amount of material that is taught.

- Evaluation begins with setting clear expectations for students and providing feedback to students on performance throughout their work.
- Provide opportunities for students to establish criteria for their own work and opportunities for self-evaluation through a unit of work, as well as culminating a unit of work. Hold students to the criteria they establish, either as a group or as individuals.
- Take a few minutes after every lesson to review what students have done on an individual basis.

◆ TEACHING AFFECTIVE GOALS AS A LESSON FOCUS

Affective goals have always been a part of the explicit, as well as the implicit, goals of teaching. Affective goals have not been an explicit part of most educational curricula and therefore have not always received the attention that subject matter competence and other areas of development have received. This is probably for several reasons, including (1) the difficulty of measuring change and growth in affective objectives, (2) the idea that because affective objectives are an implicit aspect of the idea of teaching, it is often assumed that they will be automatic in the teaching/learning environment, and (3) a concern that values are cultural and not shared in a pluralistic society. Previous sections of this chapter have identified ways in which teachers can implement a concern for affect in their instruction. In these discussions affect is built into a primarily content-oriented instructional perspective. Affect can also be taught as a primary objective of a lesson and the central focus around which all other concerns are built. Goals and objectives for affective outcomes in physical education come from many sources but primarily from the affective dimensions of the content of physical education and the identified goals of education in general or schooling.

The Unique and Shared Affective Goals of Physical Education

The National Association for Sport and Physical Education outcomes project (1992) identified several dimensions of affect that are uniquely the responsibility of physical education. Several examples of benchmarks for different grade levels are described below:

- Values the role of regular physical activity in the maintenance of a healthy life-style.
- Values relationships with others that result from participation in physical activity.
- Understands the role that regular physical activity plays in the pursuit of health and well-being.
- Values the feelings that result from regular participation in physical activity.
- Recognizes that personal health involves more than being physically fit.

The benchmarks for different age groups are replete with affective goals, using terms such as feeling, value, enjoy, appreciate, accept, respect, and desire. These goals were meant to be unique to physical education. Physical education is also uniquely concerned with expression through movement. Movement is used to both express feeling and elicit feeling. Anger, sadness, shame, joy, and almost every emotion are expressed in the manner in which we carry ourselves and the manner in which we move. Dance, and creative dance in particular, is designed to develop skills to use movement to express feeling.

In addition to the unique affective goals that are part of physical education are those that physical education shares with all of education. These goals are related to concerns for the development of values such as honesty, a concern for excellence, a concern and respect for others, hard work to achieve the benefits of effort, self-discipline, group interaction skills, integrity, aesthetics, and emotional control. The social nature of physical education activities and the public nature of movement responses make physical education a laboratory of affect. Students are continuously engaged in demonstrating their attitudes, values, and feelings by their responses and interactions with the content, the teacher, and each other.

Physical educators have always assumed that participation in sport and physical education was "character building." This is because participation in sport has the potential to provide real experiences in such areas as social skills, honesty, integrity, working hard to achieve goals, and handling winning and losing. The mistake that physical educators make is to assume that merely participating in sport will teach these values. In reality, sport participation can teach all of these ideas, but sport can also teach students just the opposite of all of these values.

It is also possible to make affective goals the framework on which physical education curriculum is designed. An example of an approach to physical education focusing on affective goals is the work of Hellison (1985) discussed in Chapter 7. In Hellison's work, a student moves developmentally through five levels of affect, from no control to caring. Lessons are designed to facilitate student growth toward higher levels.

Instructional Strategies for Teaching Affect

Attitudes and values can be taught. A variety of theories describe how values are learned. Likewise, a variety of programs are designed and packaged specifically to teach values. Most of these ideas work because they focus the learner on developing an awareness of value positions, the importance of different value positions, and the implications of values for behavior. Values are like other important learning—they usually develop slowly. Ownership of values, the point where you act on a value consistently, takes time. Students who do not share a value and indeed may even act in contradiction to it can be helped to own that value but may not immediately incorporate it into their actions.

Incorporating values into self-initiated action is the goal and not necessarily en route behavior. Because changes in values and attitudes take a long time to develop, building affective objectives into instruction and reinforcing affective objectives on a daily basis are the most effective ways to teach affect.

You can build affective objectives into your teaching in many ways, including the following:

1. Modeling the affective objectives you wish students to acquire.

   EXAMPLE: "I'm sorry, Selena, that I interrupted you. I should not have done that."

2. Making clear your expectations for personal and social behavior by the following:
   - Designing learning experiences that have multiple objectives including affective objectives (rich experiences).

     EXAMPLE: "We will be working on trying to get our feet in the air in a handstandlike position. Some of you will be able to get off the floor only a little bit and then bring your feet back down safely. This is okay, because I know that if you go a little bit higher each time, in a few weeks you will be getting your feet up all the way. What you have to do is learn to be patient with yourself and still work safely and in control. That's what I am really looking for. Can you work hard, be patient with yourself, and be in control?"

   - Helping students to see the value of the behavior through discussion, role playing, and examples.

     EXAMPLE: "When we choose partners, all of you have different reasons for choosing a partner. Can you tell me why you choose a partner? Can you tell me what kinds of things 'good partners' do?"

     EXAMPLE: Bring in a videotape of early morning joggers in different parts of the community, the corporate facilities for exercise in neighboring work places, and community facilities for recreation. Discuss why these adults are doing what they are doing.

   - Putting the application of that value into concrete examples and behaviors specific to the learning experience of the day.

     EXAMPLE: "What we are going to learn to do today takes a lot of practice to be good. We will practice today for a while, and we may practice this skill a little bit each day. To really learn from practice, you have to really pay attention to what you are doing. I am going to look for hard workers today—people who want to get better and therefore are really thinking about what they are doing as they practice."

   - Positively reinforcing the affective objectives and goals of your program.

     EXAMPLE: "I would like to share something I observed today as you were practicing. When Elaine first started today, she couldn't do this skill very well. I would like for Elaine to share with you how much she has learned. Is there someone else that you observed that you think worked very hard today and really got better?"

3. Making learning experiences positive experiences for all students. The potential for positive experiences in physical education largely depends on the appropriateness of the content for the class and for individuals and a supportive environment for all the students. Teacher support is not sufficient—the social environment created by other students is as critical as the interactions teacher have with classes and individual students. Teachers can teach positive social environment in situations where individuals feel threatened.

4. Helping students to be receptive to new ideas and different perspectives.

   EXAMPLE: "George has a very different way of accomplishing this task. George, can you show us your idea?"

   EXAMPLE: "I know that some of you may have felt uncomfortable with the dance we did today. Can you put into words how you felt? Why do you think we did the dance? Who got some really good feelings about what we did? Can you tell me what you were feeling? You are going to have to be a little patient with yourself if you had some problems today. I think if you give it a real try, you will learn to enjoy what we are doing."

5. Helping students to appreciate and celebrate diversity.

   EXAMPLE: "All of you will not be as good at everything we do or may not like everything we do to the same degree as others. That's okay. Isn't it wonderful that we are not all the same!"

6. Helping students to begin to take responsibility for their actions and to become independent.

   EXAMPLE: "When you watch sports on TV, sometimes players are not always honest about the fouls they commit. When we play, I am going to ask you to take responsibility for your fouls by raising your hands. I am doing this for two reasons: first, because I cannot officiate all of your games; and second, because I think that learning how to do the 'right' thing, even when we may not get caught doing something wrong, is important. How do you feel about it?"

7. Focusing your evaluation of students on affective as well as other objectives.

   EXAMPLE: Use a videotape of your class or reflect back on the class as soon after it is over as possible to determine the extent to which students are behaving in ways consistent with your affective objectives.

◆ DISCUSSION OF AFFECTIVE GOALS FOR PHYSICAL EDUCATION

Many of the guidelines discussed in this chapter attend to motivation and personal growth of students by transferring instructional decision making from the teacher to the student. Many teachers make the mistake of assuming that student freedom and student choice always result in positive experiences for students and that teacher control is to be avoided if positive affect is to be developed. As is discussed in Chapter 7, self-direction and students who respond from an internal sense of control are the goals. The amount of freedom, the amount of choice, and the degree to which motivation efforts focus on internal rather than external control depend on where students are in their development of internal control. It is appropriate for the teacher to act where students are at the time. It is inappropriate to leave them there.

SUMMARY

1. Motivation is an essential part of learning.
2. Students cannot work on fulfilling higher needs until more basic needs are satisfied.
3. The motivation of people toward a particular goal is both a function of their desire to reach the goal and their tendency to want to avoid failure.
4. We tend to attribute success and failure to our ability, our effort, luck, or the difficulty of the task.
5. High-achievement students attribute success to effort and are more motivated by failure. Low-achievement students tend to attribute success to external factors and failure to internal factors. They are therefore not motivated by failure.
6. Teachers can motivate students by attending to principles of motivation in their teaching.

7. The manner in which a teacher interacts with students in a class, as well as on a personal level, impacts the manner in which students are motivated to learn and achieve personal growth.
8. Teachers can build into all aspects of their lessons specific strategies for promoting motivation and the personal growth of students.
9. Affective goals are a specific part of the content of physical education, as well as a shared concern with all education programs.
10. Effective teachers balance students needs for structure with those for more student control of learning experiences.

CHECKING YOUR UNDERSTANDING

1. Describe why students may not be motivated to learn from the perspective of need theory, intrinsic motivation, and cognitive theory.
2. State at least five general principles that are implications for teaching from motivation theory.
3. Describe nine ways teachers can promote the personal growth of students through personal interaction.
4. Describe how teachers can integrate motivation and personal growth into their teaching through the following functions:
   - Planning
   - Selection and design of learning experiences
   - Presentation of units and tasks
   - Organizational arrangements
   - Teacher functions during activity
   - Lesson pacing
   - Evaluation
5. What are the unique affective goals of physical education? What goals does education share with other educational programs?
6. How can the teacher teach values and affect?
7. Are needs for student choice and more responsibility in the educational process at odds with student needs for structure and teacher control? Why?

REFERENCES

Ames C: Children's achievement attributions and self-reinforcement: effects of self-concept and competitive reward structure, *J Educ Psychol* 70:345-355, 1978.

Atkinson J: *An introduction to motivation,* Princeton, NJ, 1964, Von Nostrand.

Deci E, Ryan R: *Intrinsic motivation and self-determination in human behavior,* New York, 1985, Plenum Publishing.

Frieze I, Francis W, Hanusa B: Defining success in classroom settings. In Levine J, Wang M, editors: *Teacher and student perceptions: implications for learning,* Hillsdale, NJ, 1983, Earlbaum.

Good T, Brophy J: *Educational psychology: a realistic approach,* New York, 1990, Longman.

Hellison D: *Goals and strategies for teaching physical education,* Champaign, IL, 1985, Human Kinetics Publishers.

Maslow A: *Toward a psychology of being,* Princeton, NJ, 1962, Von Nostrand.

Murray E: *Motivation and emotion,* New York, 1978, Prentice Hall.

National Association for Sport and Physical Education: *Physical education outcomes,* Reston, VA, 1992.

Nicholls J: Effort is virtuous, but it's better to have ability, *J Res Personality* 10:306-315, 1976.

Piaget J: *Science of education and the psychology of the child,* New York, 1970, Orion.

Rotter J: Generalized expectancies for internal versus external control of reinforcement, *Psychological Monographs* 80:1-28, 1966.

Weiner B: Principles for a theory of student motivation and their applications within an attributional framework. In Ames R, Ames C, editors: *Research on motivation in education,* vol 1, Orlando, FL, 1984, Academic Press.

SUGGESTED READING

National Association for Sport and Physical Education: *Basic Stuff Series I and II,* Reston, VA, 1987.

Planning and Evaluating Instruction

CHAPTER

11

❖ ❖ ❖ ❖ ❖ ❖ ❖ ❖ ❖ ❖

OVERVIEW

Instruction is a process involving preactive, active, and postactive decision making. Preactive decisions *are those involved in planning curriculum, units, and lessons;* active decisions *are those made during the conduct of the actual lesson; and* postactive decisions *are those made as a result of evaluating the processes and products of instruction.*

The purpose of this chapter is to focus on planning and evaluation procedures used in the instructional process. Because many programs have established course work in curriculum and evaluation in physical education, a comprehensive discussion of these areas is not attempted in a single chapter. They are described only in terms of their importance to planning and evaluating the instructional process.

The emphasis of the chapter is on lesson and unit planning and evaluation.

❖ ❖ ❖ ❖ ❖ ❖ ❖ ❖ ❖ ❖

CONCEPTS

- **Establishing goals and objectives for learning**
  Writing objectives in terms of what students will learn
  Levels of specificity in educational objectives
  Objectives in the three learning domains

- **Planning physical education experiences**
  Planning the lesson
  Planning the curriculum
  Planning for units of instruction

- **Evaluating instruction**
  Formative and summative evaluations
  Evaluating in the three domains
  Collecting information: formal and informal evaluation
  Practical approaches to assessment
  Grading students

THE major focus of this text has been the instructional process itself—the time students and teachers spend together in the physical education class. To make the instructional process effective in accomplishing program goals, teachers must both plan for and evaluate the process itself. Planning takes place before instruction; evaluation takes place during and after instruction.

Educators plan and evaluate educational experiences at many levels of specificity. National task force groups plan for and evaluate schooling in the country as a whole. States, to whom the Constitution has delegated responsibility for education, establish statewide goals and evaluative procedures for their own programs. Local school districts choose curriculums and monitor student performance in those curricular areas to which they attach greatest importance. Teachers themselves plan, implement, and evaluate curriculums on a long-term basis and units of instruction and lessons on a short-term basis.

Physical educators, unlike classroom teachers, rarely operate under national, state, or local guidelines for curriculum. Most physical educators have complete autonomy regarding curriculum. This is both a professional advantage and disadvantage. Because the curriculum can reflect local student needs, the creative teacher is not limited. However, the lack of accountability for program goals more often than not leads to programs without goals or programs without any chance of meeting those goals that have been established.

One of the reasons many physical education programs are not effective is that little long-term or short-term planning takes place. The recent publication of *Physical Education Outcomes* by the National Association for Sport and Physical Education (NASPE) (1992) should help states, districts, and individual teachers more carefully plan appropriate experiences for students in physical education.

The processes of planning and evaluation are integrally related. Planning establishes goals and specific procedures for reaching those goals. Evaluation discovers the extent to which those goals have been reached and whether those procedures have been effective. *Beginning teachers will not really begin to think as educators until they can establish goals for what they want to do, select what they do in light of those goals, and evaluate what they do based on those goals.* Although more experienced teachers can probably reduce some of the detail with which they write short-term lesson plans and still be effective, more extensive planning has a positive effect on the quality of programs. Long-term planning of curriculum and units of instruction is essential for all teachers at any level of experience. Planning is not easy for the teacher to do—the process can be a painful and frustrating one. Although this essential function in teaching requires less effort with experience, it is never easy.

This chapter is divided into three major sections: the first section is designed to help teachers establish goals and objectives for learning; the second section treats planning at the lesson, unit, and curriculum level; the third section discusses the evaluation process.

◆ ESTABLISHING GOALS AND OBJECTIVES FOR LEARNING

Learning outcomes are usually written in terms of educational objectives for students at different levels of specificity and for different areas of human development. Inherent in this idea are the following important points:

- Objectives are written in terms of what students learn, not what teachers or students do, during instruction.
- Objectives can be written broadly (e.g., "Students will learn how to do a foul shot") or specifically (e.g., "Students will be able to get 8 of 10 foul shots in the basket").
- Objectives are written for psychomotor, affective, and cognitive learning outcomes.

Each of these points is critical to planning and evaluating instruction. They will be considered separately in the following discussion.

Writing Objectives in Terms of What Students Will Learn

Learning outcomes should be specified for educational programs at all levels of planning in terms of what students will learn from the educational experience. In contrast to this, objectives are sometimes written in terms of what the teacher or the student will do. The following examples illustrate the difference between specifying objectives as a teacher activity, a student activity, and a student outcome.

Teacher activity. Demonstrate for students how to do a volleyball set.

Student activity. Practice the overhead set.

Student outcome. Set the volleyball effectively to a front line player from a toss.

The teacher will want to write objectives in terms of *student outcomes*. Student objectives are usually prefaced with the phrase *"students will be able to."* This helps the planner focus on a learning product rather than on a learning process. The following objectives are written appropriately in terms of what the learner will be able to do as a result of instruction:

- Pass a ball to a team mate on the move ahead of the receiver without having to stop.
- Demonstrate support for a partner by using an appropriate force level on passes and verbally supporting a partner's effort.

Objectives are written in terms of three component parts:

- *Behavior* expected of the student (e.g., strike, hit, show support, pass)
- *Condition* or *situation* under which the behavior is to be exhibited (e.g., work with a partner from 10 feet)
- *Criterion* to be met or *performance level* expected   (e.g., use accurate form; be 90% accurate)

In the following examples the three parts of an objective are specified:

- The student will be able to travel in general space, using the feet in at least three different ways, without touching anyone else.
  Behavior: Travel
  Condition: In general space on the feet
  Criterion: Use three different ways of traveling without touching anyone else
- The student will be able to pass the volleyball effectively to a front line player from the back line using a legal forearm pass from a ball tossed over the net (the receiver should not have to take more than one step).

Behavior: Use a forearm pass
Condition: Pass a ball, which is tossed over the net, from the back line to a front line player
Criterion: Use a legal, effective pass

- The student will be able to shift positions in a basketball game in relation to the location of the ball using the 2-1-2 zone defense.
  Behavior: Shift defensive position
  Condition: Use the 2-1-2 zone defense in game play
  Criterion: Shift appropriately in relation to the position of the ball
- The student will be able to demonstrate responsibility for the partner relationship by passing the ball at a level of difficulty appropriate to challenge the student's partner.
  Behavior: Pass the ball
  Condition: Pass the ball to a partner
  Criterion: Use an appropriate level to challenge partner

The **behavior** component of an instructional objective is written as a verb that describes what the student is to do. It is almost always an action verb and should be written in terms that specify the same thing to anyone who might refer to the term. The following examples illustrate verbs from the three domains that communicate a behavior:

Psychomotor	Affective	Cognitive
Put the shot	Value	Describe
Kick	Enjoy	List
Defend	Express	Identify

The **condition** component of an instructional objective describes the situation under which the action will be performed. The specification of conditions in physical education objectives is critical. Reviewing the discussion on conditions in Chapter 2 will help you understand the implications of conditions for designing appropriate objectives for a particular group of students. For example, a student successful at returning a tennis ball across a net with a forehand drive from an easy toss might not be as successful when the ball is hit to the student, especially if the student has to move to get it. A student who can demonstrate good form in a forearm pass in volleyball from a partner toss may not be able to even contact a ball served over the net. A student who can control a basketball dribble moving forward at a slow speed may not be able to change direction or control the dribble at a faster speed. Conditions, therefore, are crucial.

The **criterion** component of an objective describes minimal levels of performance for the action specified. The criteria are really evaluative criteria that indicate when success has been achieved. Criteria are usually specified in two ways: (1) as quantitative criteria, which usually deal with the effectiveness of the movement response or other behavior, such as how many, how long, how high, how far; or (2) as qualitative criteria, which deal with the process characteristics of the movement, such as the form of the movement. Process characteristics describe the extent to which the student is doing the movement correctly, such as stepping into the swing, getting into position, or showing the characteristics of mature form.

It should be obvious at this point that writing objectives is not simple. Writing good instructional objectives takes practice.

Levels of Specificity in Educational Objectives

In writing an objective, teachers are forced to consider the level of specificity of the objective. Teachers must determine to what extent it is necessary to spell out exactly the terms of the behavior they want to describe. The degree of specificity of an objective is based initially on the level of planning. However, degree of specificity of educational objectives is an issue widely debated in education circles.

Box 11-1 describes several levels of specificity in educational objectives that might be used in a physical education program at three different levels of planning. At a **curricular level**, objectives are broad enough to include the total curricular program; that is, they describe what students should be able to do when they leave the program (in this case, an elementary and secondary school program). At the **unit level**, objectives are exit criteria for the completion of a unit; that is, they describe what students should

be able to do after completing a unit of instruction. At the **lesson level**, objectives are statements reflecting what students should be able to do at the end of a single lesson. Sometimes the terms **aims** or **goals** distinguish broad curricular objectives from more specific learning outcomes used in lesson planning (instructional or educational objectives). Outcomes can be described differently at all levels of learning.

The question "How specific is specific?" will continue to be a source of educational debate for a long time. Proponents of specific objectives would have educators spell out precise behaviors for all learning outcomes. Precise in this sense means describing the behavior and the exact way in which the behavior is measured. An explicit (or precise) behavioral outcome for a physical education class in softball might be the following:

> Each student should be able to field a batted medium-speed infield grounder that falls within the student's space responsibilities and then throw the ball to the appropriate infielder in time to put the runner out 8 of 10 times.

It is obvious in this example that all conditions and criteria must be spelled out to leave no question about what the learner should be able to do on the completion of the lesson. Learning outcomes speci-

---

BOX 11-1

Objectives at Different Levels of Planning

Curricular

The student will be able to play one individual sport at an intermediate level of difficulty.

Unit

The student will be able to use the tennis backhand stroke to get the ball over the net in a game situation on balls coming within a few steps of the student's position.

Lesson

Taking just one step, the student will be able to hit a backhand stroke with good form into the opponent's court from a tossed ball.

fied in this way help the teacher plan appropriate instruction and also help the teacher evaluate what students have learned. What would a lesson for the stated objective look like? How would the teacher evaluate the degree to which students had accomplished the objective? Compare the responses to these questions with the lesson the teacher would have to design for the following objective:

- *The student will be able to field balls.*

It is obvious which learning objective provides more help to the teacher in both conducting and evaluating a lesson.

The assumption underlying the use of precise and explicit educational objectives is that all learning outcomes can be explicitly described and are measurable at all levels of planning. It is also assumed that learning is enhanced when teachers do this. Obviously, not all educators value the use of precise educational objectives. Some teachers assert that not all learning outcomes are measurable or even should be measured.

Much of the criticism surrounding the use of precise educational objectives centers on the idea that much more is involved in a learning experience than a single measurable objective or a group of measurable objectives. Obviously, different students will gain different skills or knowledge from the same experience, and teachers have more than a single measurable experience in mind when they think about learning outcomes. This is particularly true in physical education at the instructional level of planning content. Learning motor skills is a slow process, and describing what students should be able to do in a measurable form after a single lesson is difficult. Measurable outcomes often address what can be quantified (e.g., how much, how many) and leave out those elements more difficult to measure (e.g., game play, student form in skills, strategies, affective concerns). Teachers who use precise educational objectives to guide planning, particularly at the instructional level, may tend to restrict and narrow learning experiences only to the measurable. Learning experiences thus become flattened and in some cases trivialized in their focus. Skilled teachers have learned to describe learning outcomes at useful levels of specificity.

At the other end of the spectrum are teachers who have not thought through learning outcomes or who deal with them so broadly that the objective provides no direction for the design or evaluation of educational experiences. The following objective for a lesson in soccer will serve as a case in point:

- *The student will be able to dribble the soccer ball.*

No conditions that describe the level of the experience and no criteria for performance are specified at any level in this example. The objective is basically useless for anything beyond saying that the lesson will have something to do with soccer dribbling.

A more common position in education regarding educational objectives is to say that educational objectives should be specified to the degree that they provide direction for the design and evaluation of educational experiences without narrowing those experiences to what is most easily measured. Objectives still include the components of behavior, conditions, and criteria, but in cases where explicit statements describing the criteria are not appropriate, these components are written in such a way that learning outcomes are more implicit than explicit. Following are examples of implicit objectives:

- *The student will be able to use accurately the appropriate fielding strategy for grounders, line drives, and fly balls in a game situation.*
- *The student will be able to demonstrate independence in working on a movement task.*

Implicit in the first objective is the idea that the student will be taught fielding strategies for grounders, line drives, and fly balls and will be given an opportunity to practice these strategies. The terms *appropriate* and *accurate* are criteria that are not explicitly defined but are assumed to be part of instruction. Teachers who do not clearly understand what the terms *accurate* and *appropriate* mean are ill served by implicit objectives. Teachers who have done a developmental analysis of the content they are teaching (in this case, softball fielding) will have specified in their planning what these criteria mean. Learning how to be a teacher is facilitated by making intended learning outcomes clear and explicit. In the second example the assumption is that the teacher has talked with students and taught students what independent work looks like.

Objectives in the Three Learning Domains

The primary and unique contribution physical education makes to the development of students is the development of physical skills and abilities. As an educational program, physical education also has responsibilities to the cognitive (intellect) and affective (attitude, values, and interests) development of students. There is a tendency in physical education to assume that cognitive and affective concerns will be developed automatically as a result of participating in physical education programs. Yet little that is not purposely designed occurs as a specific learning outcome. Students do not learn the rules of games unless the rules are taught; they do not learn to identify concepts unless they are taught to do so; and they will not learn how to interact positively with each other in cooperative or competitive activities unless they are helped to interact appropriately.

Learning outcomes in the affective and cognitive domains can be specified in much the same way as psychomotor outcomes are specified. The two volumes of *A Taxonomy of Educational Objectives* (Bloom et al., 1956; Krathwohl, Bloom, and Masia, 1964) were written to establish a hierarchy of learning levels within these two domains. The cognitive domain establishes skills with cognitive material that require increasingly difficult intellectual ability. The affective hierarchy progresses from the point at which students become aware of their attitudes toward affective concepts to the point at which their values have a direct influence on what they choose to do. These levels are described in Box 11-2.

These cognitive and affective hierarchies are important because they remind the lesson planner that a decision about where students are regarding cognitive or affective material must be made *before* determining expectations for performance in these areas. Just as students cannot be expected to use a basketball dribble in a game before they have developed skills under less complex conditions, students cannot be expected to use cognitive information in complex ways until they have been able to use it at less complicated levels. Students cannot be expected to respond affectively on an internalized level unless they have had opportunities to develop value positions at lower levels of expectation.

Examples of cognitive and affective objectives

Affective

- The student will be able to choose a level of practice that is challenging and appropriate for his or her own level of ability.
- The student will demonstrate honest behavior by indicating when he or she has committed a rules' violation.
- The student will demonstrate self-direction by using available practice time productively before and during class.

Cognitive

- The student will be able to identify the appropriate cues for the overhand serve.
- The student will be able to describe why it is important to warm up before strenuous activity.
- The student will be able to distinguish between aerobic an anaerobic activities

◆ PLANNING PHYSICAL EDUCATION EXPERIENCES

Planning for physical education experiences occurs on three levels. At the broadest level, teachers plan curriculums (programs of study) for a single year or perhaps several years of educational experience. At the next level, teachers divide curriculums into units of instruction, major topics or themes of study within the curriculum itself. The lesson is the most narrowly focused unit and the smallest time period for which teachers plan.

It should be noted that all levels of planning are interrelated. The teacher uses the curriculum guide to plan units and uses the unit plan as a guide to plan lessons. Much of this text is devoted to decision making at the learning experience and task levels under the assumption that it is at these levels that the student actually experiences the curriculum. However, there must be consistency between all lev-

BOX 11-2

Categories in Cognitive and Affective Domains

Cognitive Domain

Knowledge. Student has the ability to recall information.

> EXAMPLE: The student will be able to state the infield fly rule.
>
> BEHAVIORAL TERMS: Student states, describes, lists, identifies.

Comprehension. Student has the ability to grasp the meaning of information.

> EXAMPLE: The student will be able to describe correct form from an observation of performance.
>
> BEHAVIORAL TERMS: Student explains, summarizes, distinguishes, gives examples.

Application. Student has the ability to use information in new and concrete situations.

> EXAMPLE: The student will be able to apply the principle of wide base of support to a new balance.
>
> BEHAVIORAL TERMS: Student uses, demonstrates, discovers, modifies.

Analysis. Student has the ability to break down material into its component parts.

> EXAMPLE: The student will be able to describe how force is produced in the overarm throw pattern.
>
> BEHAVIORAL TERMS: Student distinguishes, identifies, selects.

Synthesis. Student has the ability to put parts together into a whole.

> EXAMPLE: The student will be able to describe what all striking skills have in common.
>
> BEHAVIORAL TERMS: Student creates, designs, explains, modifies.

Evaluation. Student has the ability to judge the value of material.

> EXAMPLE: The student will be able to evaluate the performance of classmates based on task criteria.
>
> BEHAVIORAL TERMS: Student appraises, contrasts, discriminates, supports.

Affective Domain

Reception. Student is willing to attend to an idea, phenomenon, or stimulus.

> EXAMPLE: The student will be able to attend to teacher directions while holding equipment in the hand.
>
> BEHAVIORAL TERMS: Student follows directions, replies, uses, names.

Response. Student chooses to act in some way to an idea, phenomenon, or stimulus.

> EXAMPLE: The student will stop work on a task and follow directions at the teacher's signal.
>
> BEHAVIORAL TERMS: Student assists, complies, conforms, helps, practices.

Valuation. Student accepts or assumes responsibility for a value.

> EXAMPLE: The student will demonstrate responsibility for a safe and productive class environment by working quietly, independently, and with concern for controlled movement.
>
> BEHAVIORAL TERMS: Student differentiates, initiates, joins.

Organization. Student synthesizes and resolves conflicts between value positions.

> EXAMPLE: The student will be able to describe what a supportive team member is expected to do in a game situation.
>
> BEHAVIORAL TERMS: Student integrates, defends, explains, identifies, alters.

Internalization. Student uses a value to control behavior in a consistent way.

> EXAMPLE: The student will be able to work on a task, independent of teacher monitoring, in a productive way.
>
> BEHAVIORAL TERMS: Student acts, discriminates, solves, displays.

els of planning. Goals identified in curriculums must be reflected in lessons and what students actually experience.

Affective and cognitive objectives receive much attention from curriculum and unit planners, but few lesson plans show evidence of affective or cognitive planning. If asked what students should learn from a good program in physical education, most people would respond with a long list of affective concerns. If next asked what could be done in a lesson to achieve those goals, most people would have difficulty coming up with specific ideas. If goals are regarded as important on a curricular level, they should be reflected on the unit and lesson level as well. Although practicing teachers will begin the planning process at the curriculum and unit level, preservice teachers often are called on to begin their experiences with planning at the lesson level. Therefore lesson planning begins our discussion.

Planning the Lesson

The lesson plan is a guide for the process of instruction for a single lesson and is based on unit objectives. The lesson plan must translate broader aims and goals into specific learning experiences for the student. Good lesson plans are difficult to write, because the more specific teachers are asked to be in describing their intentions, the more difficult planning becomes. For example, few would question a goal such as "Students should understand how force is produced in the throw pattern." But what does this goal look like as an actual learning experience? What does teamwork look like, or positive social interaction, or good defense? The lesson plan must translate broad goals and objectives into actual experiences for particular learners.

The lesson plan is in one sense a teacher's best guess at how to produce student learning for particular objectives and particular students (Good and Brophy, 1990). In the lesson plan the teacher describes the learning that is expected and the learning experiences he or she will use to produce that learning. The lesson plan is a tentative hypothesis. Good teachers will reflect on the effectiveness of what they have done during the lesson and after

teaching and make some judgment about how successful they were so that they may learn from each teaching experience.

Each lesson, however, is more than just a piece of a bigger objective, unit, or curriculum. Each lesson must by itself have integrity and represent a holistic experience that is more than merely the continuation of the lesson before. Lessons have beginnings, middles, and ends that give structure and meaning to learning experiences. A description of these aspects of the lesson follows.

Beginning the lesson. The beginning of a lesson is one of the most important aspects of the lesson. Often teachers are so eager to get students into the activity of the day, they fail to spend a few minutes to help induct students into the lesson. The following ideas are part of beginning lessons. They do not have to be present in all lessons but should be considered in planning all lessons.

Set induction. Set induction is a fancy term for orienting the learners with whom you are working to what they will be doing, how they will be doing it, and why it is important. A teacher's set induction acclimates students to what they can expect in the lesson and should motivate learners to full engagement in what is to come. Adults, as well as children, are more secure if they know what is going to happen before it happens. They find more meaning in what they are asked to do if they are helped to understand why it is important.

EXAMPLE: "Yesterday when I was observing what you were doing in the two-on-two games at the end of class, I noticed that the persons who were on the offense without the ball didn't really have a clear idea of where they were supposed to go or what they were supposed to do. Today we are going to work on what to do when you don't have the ball. We will start off with a passing warm-up and then try to come up with some ideas on what to do when you don't have the ball. Then we will see if you can put these ideas into your games."

All-class activity. Lessons are usually helped to get off to a good start if the teacher has planned an all-class vigorous activity at the beginning of the class. This is particularly true for young children but just as applicable for older students. An all-class activity tends to focus the students and get them involved vigorously. Vigorous warm-ups can be related to fitness objectives or the content of the day's lesson. The warm-up can precede or follow the set induction for the lesson.

EXAMPLE (ELEMENTARY): The teacher asks the students to find a space in the general work area and to begin traveling in general space in different directions. Students are then asked to add jumps and turns to their traveling and to stop at the signal and freeze. Each time they freeze, they must stop for about 6 seconds and then take weight on their hands in a handstand action two times. This is repeated several times.

EXAMPLE (SECONDARY): The class is in the middle of a basketball unit. Each student is given a ball and asked to begin to dribble in general space. Two students do not have a ball and are "IT". "IT" tries to tag the balls of other players as they are dribbling. Anyone whose ball is tagged puts his or her ball down and becomes "IT" as well. The game continues until no one has a ball. This is repeated several times.

Developing the lesson. Each lesson is unique, and therefore specific guidelines for how to develop each particular lesson cannot be given. However, some aspects of lessons should be considered regardless of the content.

Use a variety of teaching strategies. As is explained in Chapter 10, motivation is increased when teachers use a variety of teaching strategies. These do not necessarily occur in the same lesson but should be reflected over several lessons.

Change the practice conditions for variety. Individual work, partner work, group work; refinement tasks, extension tasks, application tasks; and different equipment and different arrangements and use of equipment can all be used to change the task and still work on the same objectives (intratask development). The use of variety does not have to change the objective. There are many ways teachers can practice the same objective to add interest to a lesson.

Use common sense about the physical demands of a lesson. Seldom should a teacher spend an entire lesson on one skill, particularly in the same conditions. It is difficult to turn upside down and practice rolling for an entire class period. It is also difficult to do just about any single skill (especially when the conditions cannot be changed) for an entire period. Teachers should use common sense when determining lesson objectives for an entire class period. It is better to practice two skills for two days than one skill each of two days. Combine vigorous work with less vigorous practice in a single lesson.

Ending the lesson. Although it is not always possible because of time constraints and the manner in which a lesson proceeds, there should be a culmination to a lesson. Too often lessons just stop in the middle of a task because time is up. Secondary students are sent quickly to the locker room, and the classroom teacher is at the door waiting for the elementary class. The class just ends with no real ending. A lesson closing completes a lesson. Often this culmination should take the form of a review of what was learned and an opportunity for teachers to check for understanding and orient the students to what may come in the next lesson. Sometimes teachers use this culmination time for students to reflect on what they have done in terms of the objectives for the lesson and to write down important points in journals. This closing does not have to take a great deal of time. Verbalizing what was learned often helps give meaning to what was done and prepares the learner for what is to come.

EXAMPLES:
- "Today we worked on trying to keep the ball away from a defensive player. Who can tell me several things you can do to accomplish this? I'm going to write these ideas on the board, and you write them in your journal as we list them."
- "I have put five different ideas on this chart that represent the amount of effort different students put into the class today. I didn't see anyone in this lowest category. I would like for you to think for a minute about where you would be on this chart. The next time you come into the gym, I will ask each one of you to write down where you would like to be on this chart and we're going to see if we can accomplish getting everyone to where they should be in the next lesson."

Format for lesson planning. As a preservice teacher you will spend more time planning for and evaluating teaching than you will spend teaching. The written lesson plan is designed to help you think through every step of the teaching process. The more detail you can supply about your lesson, the more prepared you will be to teach that lesson.

Many different formats for lesson plans have been proposed. The plan that you are requested to use at your school may differ from the format suggested here, but most plans have similar requirements. The lesson plan format suggested here is an extensive one. Beginning teachers and teachers teaching content new to them will have to plan in greater detail than teachers experienced with particular content. Planning is difficult and tedious, but it is essential if appropriate instruction with clear goals is to be provided to students. An example of a lesson plan is presented in Tables 11-1, 11-2, and 11-3. You may want to refer to this plan as different aspects of the lesson plan form are discussed.

Heading material. The heading material example in Table 11-1 helps identify the purpose of the lesson. The unit to which the lesson is a part and the specific focus of the lesson within that unit are described. The specific class for which the lesson is designed and the equipment needed for the lesson are also provided in the heading for quick reference.

As a beginning teacher you will probably be tempted to decide what you want to teach and then to write an objective for what you want to teach. You will not really begin to think as a teacher until you can begin planning by writing down what you expect students to be able to do. The advantage of planning by writing an objective first is that the objective forces you to begin to think about different ways to accomplish the same goal. The objective of a lesson is very rarely the task or the activity. Many different tasks and activities can accomplish the same objective. To check your understanding of the use of objectives, it will be helpful for you to consider an objective and see if you can design several different lesson plans to accomplish the same objective.

Two types of objectives are presented in the lesson material example in Table 11-1. **Student objectives** describe what students should be able to do as a result of the lesson. **Teacher objectives** describe specifically what the teacher is working to achieve in the lesson. Listing teaching objectives helps the teacher focus more specifically on instructional behavior that the teacher wants to improve. The same rules regarding specifying behavior, conditions, and criteria that apply to the design of student objectives apply to teacher objectives.

EXAMPLES:
- The teacher will be able to call students by name.
- The teacher will be able to keep the tone voice positive when reacting to off-task students.

Developmental analysis of content. The developmental analysis of the lesson content (Table 11-2, p. 216) describes the *major tasks* of the lesson and explains how these tasks can be extended and how each extension can be refined or applied. Teachers experienced with content may not have to complete this section of the lesson plan. Inexperienced teachers should make sure that they have thought through the content.

Specific procedures for doing a developmental analysis are described in Chapter 6. Developmental analyses of content can be done at the unit level. Teachers who have done a developmental analysis as part of their unit plan will not have to prepare one for each lesson. Good developmental analyses of content should be modified and saved for future use. The developmental analysis of the content will assure that the teacher is secure with the content.

Instructional plan. After the teacher has decided on the objectives for the lesson and has thought through the content by doing a developmental analysis, the teacher must put together a plan for instruction (Table 11-3, pp. 217-218). Again, beginning teachers should think through each step and plan in great detail exactly what they will do, how they will do it, and the purpose for which they are designing each task. The specificity of planning for more experienced teachers does not have to be as great. The sample instructional plan is written at a medium level of specificity. Task design, presentation, and arrangements are the specific focus of other

TABLE 11-1	Sample lesson plan: heading material and objectives

High school folk dance

Class: Ninth grade
Unit: Folk dance

Lesson focus: The schottische step
Equipment: Variable speed record player and record (such as *Happy Folk Dances*, RCA LPM 1620).

Student objectives

Each student should be able to do the following:
Accurately perform the schottische step alone and with a partner to the rhythm of the music (psychomotor domain).
Identify the cues to the schottische step (cognitive domain).
Work productively with a partner to perform the buggy schottische and later to create a new dance (affective domain).
Use a variety of different spatial dynamics and step variations to design a dance with a partner (psychomotor domain), using the schottische step.

Teacher objectives

The teacher should be able to do the following:
Give appropriate and specific comments to students on their performance of the schottische step and their self-designed dances.
Design learning experiences with different amounts of structures that are appropriate for different lesson objectives within the lesson.

chapters in this text. The parts of the instructional plan are described in the following discussion.

Anticipated progression of tasks. In the first column of the plan teachers should describe the specific tasks that will be assigned the students. Inexperienced teachers should specify *exactly* what they will say to students to present the task (in almost a script form).

EXAMPLES:
- "Find a partner, go to a space, and begin passing the soccer ball to your partner as quickly as you can."
- "If you can pass five times in a row without losing control of the ball at a high speed, take two steps back from your partner."

You should also make sure that you have built into your plan learning experiences for not only the psychomotor objective, but the affective and cognitive objectives. It cannot be assumed that these objectives will be learned unless the teacher attends to them explicitly in the lesson. As a beginning teacher you should identify specifically where you are going to attend to these objectives.
EXAMPLE: "Demonstrate cooperative work with your

partner by sending the ball to him or her at a challenging but achievable speed and force level."

How task will be communicated. In the second column the teacher should describe how the task will be communicated for each task specified. Simpler tasks can be communicated verbally, but more complex tasks will need more complicated task presentation (e.g., demonstrations, specific cues, films, handouts).

EXAMPLES:
- Walk-through cues with students
- Teacher explanation/demonstration
- Film with teacher describing cues

Organizational arrangements. In the plan's third column, specific organizational arrangements for people, time, equipment, and space should be described for each task, including how the teacher will get students into these arrangements. Remember that the organizational arrangements that you make for a task are critical decisions and ones that should not be taken lightly. You should organize for safety and maximum activity and with appropriate task conditions for the objective and group of learners with whom you are working.

TABLE 11-2	Sample lesson plan: the developmental analysis of content	
Major task	**Extension**	**Refinement**
The basic schottische step	Move in forward direction alone with no music.	Take small steps.
	Do part one of step (step, step—step, hop—step, step—step, hop).	Have slight elevation.
	Do part two of step (step, hop—step, hop—step, hop).	
	Combine parts one and two.	
	Add music to above.	Keep rhythm with music.
	Play music at reduced speed.	
	Play music at normal speed.	
	Add turns and changes in direction.	Maintain order of steps.
	Add partner.	Adjust steps to need.
	Hold two hands facing.	Decide where to make turn in the pattern.
	Move in forward and backward direction.	Adjust to partner.
	Move in sideways direction and turn.	Establish lead.
	Combine all of the above.	Adjust to partner.
	Experiment all different partner relationships.	Use minimum of three different relationships.
The buggy schottische	Do part one of buggy schottische (sets of two couples with hands joined face line of direction and follow one lead couple).	Accurately reproduce pattern while synchronized with group.
	Do two schottische steps (no music and teacher paced).	
	Take four step hops forward.	
	Do part two of buggy schottische.	
	Do two schottische steps (no music and teacher paced).	
	Take four step hops with lead couple dropping hands and casting off (no music and teacher paced).	Drop hands and cast off in line of direction.
	Join hands and repeat dance (student paced).	
	Combine parts one and two with the music.	Combine parts one and two with no break.
		Dance accurately with the music.
Self-designed dances	Using music just worked with, create a dance using the schottische step in groups of four that shows (1) a change in pathway (2) a change in direction, and (3) at least two different relationships with others.	Be consistent with task criteria.
		Use phrases and measures.
		Involve entire group in planning.
	Observe half of the class and select one dance that is choreographed and performed well.	Make smooth transitions between parts of the dance.
		Identify what makes good choreography and what makes good performance.

TABLE 11-3	Sample lesson plan: instructional plan		
Anticipated progression of tasks	**How task will be communicated**	**Organizational arrangements**	**Goal orientation**
Introduce schottische step.	Demonstration with music		
Do part one of schottische step. Step is teacher paced. Step is self-paced.	Demonstration with cue words (step, step—step, hop—step, step—step, hop)	Individual students are scattered, facing teacher; dance is teacher paced with cues. Dance is self-paced; students move forward within own area.	Perform part one with proper rhythm.
Do part two of schottische step. Practice repeatedly. Step is teacher paced. Step is self-paced.	Demonstration with cue words (step, hop—step, hop—step, hop—step, hop)	Individual students are scattered, facing teacher; dance is teacher paced with cues. Dance is self-paced; students move forward in own area.	Perform accurate step pattern.
Combine parts one and two. Practice repeatedly.	Walk-through with teacher cueing	Same as above.	Make smooth transition from part one to part two. Have ability to repeat pattern.
Do schottische step with music. Listen to music first. Perform to music at slow speed. Perform to music at regular speed.	Teacher explanation only	Individual students are scattered, facing teacher; students move anywhere within the group; dance is paced by music.	Adjust to music.
Use direction changes. Alternate forward and backward movement. Add turns, sideways movement, and music when ready. Design a pattern using directional turns.	Teacher explanation and demonstration	Individual students are scattered.	Make changes without interrupting the flow of the pattern. Decide on what step to make the turn.

Continued.

TABLE 11-3	Sample Lesson Plan: Instructional Plan—cont'd		
Anticipated progression of tasks	**How task will be communicated**	**Organizational arrangements**	**Goal orientation**
Do the step with a partner (step is initially teacher paced and then self-paced). Go forward. Go backward. Combine forward and backward. Add sideways movement and turns. Add different partner relationships.	Teacher explanation and demonstration	Partners are scattered.	Start fast and lead partner. Develop versatility to perform step in a variety of ways.
Do the buggy schottische. Do part one (no music). Do part two (no music). Combine parts one and two (no music).	Listen to music demonstration	Partners are scattered.	Accurately reproduce dance.
	Teacher explanation only	Sets of two partners are scattered; students have choice of partners.	
Do self-designed dances. Create a dance sequence in sets of two partners using the schottische criteria (change in pathway; change in direction; at least two different relationships with others).	Teacher explanation and demonstration of an example	Sets of two partners are scattered.	Develop versatility in use of schottische. Understand phrasing and dynamics of choreography.

EXAMPLES:

- Student-selected partners in general space
- Students in two lines facing each other (teacher divides class to stand on each line)

Goal orientation.   Each task should be oriented toward a clear goal, which is described in the last column. Goal orientation should describe specifically what the teacher is working for in each task. Goal orientation is not the objective for the lesson, but what the teacher hopes to accomplish with the specific task described. Teachers should plan to share the goal orientation of a task with the students.

EXAMPLES:

- "Work to get the whole idea of the skill."
- "Practice until toss is accurate."
- "Just contact the ball with no concern for accuracy."
- "Think about and demonstrate concern for the needs of your partner."

Planning the Curriculum

A curriculum guide is a plan for a program of study. Curriculum guides specify what students should be able to do after the program of study is completed. Sometimes this means after 12 years of physical education and sometimes this means after elementary school or middle school or high school. Long-term planning of curriculum can help teachers and school districts set priorities, make learning more meaningful, and integrate the work of different schools and years of instruction. Curriculum guides are value positions because they help educators set priorities for what is most worth learning. Because programs of preparation in physical education include complete courses in curriculum planning, no attempt is made in this chapter to prepare you for curriculum planning, but rather to help you to understand the relationship between curriculum planning and unit and lesson planning.

In addition to determining long-term goals for programs, curriculum guides also determine the *scope* of the content to be offered and the *sequence* in which the content will be presented. Most curriculum guides in physical education establish a framework for content that conceptually structures the program's activities.

Most readers probably have come from programs at the secondary level that were organized using a movement form framework. With this format the curriculum and its units are organized by sport forms and units (e.g., volleyball, weight lifting, dance). This is the most common conceptual scheme for secondary school physical education program, and it is unlikely that major change will occur in this design. However, at the elementary level, the movement form curriculum has been replaced to a significant degree with a movement concept framework. With movement concepts or movement themes, curriculums are organized around such ideas as striking, throwing, traveling, and balancing.

Curriculum guides may assign specific skills or levels of skills to different years of instruction, such as development of mature skipping patterns for the second grade or seven-on-seven soccer play for the seventh grade. When curriculums are written in this way, they guide the teacher in what to teach and the level students are expected to achieve. There is a danger in assuming that all students should be at the same level at a particular grade, and teachers should use these guides as they were meant to be—as minimal standards for most students of a particular age given good instruction. Wide ranges of student abili-

ties within any age group make this level of specificity difficult. However, somewhere between the extremes of *no direction* and *specification of minimal competencies for each age* is probably a level of specificity that teachers will find helpful but not restrictive.

The most desirable curriculum plan is that which encompasses an elementary through secondary school program. The reasons should be obvious: experiences can be sequenced, and continuity can be established among schools and teachers for any particular student. Knowing the curriculum framework that is used for a program and the priorities set by that curriculum is essential for planning units within that curriculum.

Planning for Units of Instruction

The unit plan is a plan for a group of lessons related to a theme. Units are usually taken from a planned curriculum, which means that the type of unit taught depends on the ideas that are used to organize the curriculum. If a curriculum is organized by movement form (the names of the sport or the activities), usually each movement form will become a unit of instruction (e.g., tennis, volleyball, badminton, basketball). If a curriculum is organized with a motor development scheme or movement themes, units of instruction could be striking, throwing, locomotor patterns, or ideas such as jumping or landing. If a curriculum is organized around affective themes, units of instruction are designed with those themes in mind (e.g., "becoming independent" or "working cooperatively with a diverse group"). Generally, each movement form, theme, or idea becomes a unit of instruction in the curriculum.

Many times, curriculums are combinations of those just discussed, and the selection of units thus reflects the eclectic organization of the curriculum.

Example units

- Volleyball
- Tossing and catching
- Force production—softball
- Feeling good about myself and others—basketball

In the last two examples, the unit name indicates that basketball will be used in conjunction with the theme of "feeling good about myself and others." This unit on basketball would thus be taught with an affective, as well as a psychomotor, emphasis, and the learning experiences in the unit would have to be designed specifically to address both the psychomotor and affective focus.

Units are not always taught on successive days. The unit plan defines the scope and sequence of a theme but does not identify how lessons will be arranged within a program. Units can be taught in sequential class periods, on alternate class days, or in any arrangement the teacher finds desirable. Many programs run several units at one time. Some programs space a particular unit of instruction throughout a school year or teach a unit on rainy days only. Teachers can begin a unit, drop it for awhile, and then continue the unit.

Deciding what should be taught in a year or several years of a program is a curriculum decision. Sample block plans for a year's instruction are provided in Box 11-3 as an example of what might result after curriculum planning. The elementary example uses a developmental organizing framework, movement form, and a movement concept or theme format. Units tend to be shorter in the elementary school and rotate throughout the year. Elementary units are often cycled and returned to in slightly different forms. It would be foolish, for instance, to run a 3-week unit on throwing and catching in the primary grades and then not return to it until the following year. It might make more sense to run a throwing unit over 12 weeks for the first 10 minutes of each class period. Elementary children are involved primarily in learning basic skills, which need a great deal of repetition and practice.

The secondary example uses primarily the movement form as the organizing ideas of the curriculum but adds some work on movement concepts. Students in this curriculum have choices within blocked time periods. You will also notice that the units are long enough for meaningful learning to occur. Secondary programs usually begin and complete units at one time and do not return to them in the same year.

There is a great deal of flexibility in deciding when and how units are taught throughout a program. Most programs have not exploited this potential flexibility to enhance student learning and interest. Potential alternative ways to block units are provided in Box 11-4 (p. 222).

Considerations in planning units. Once the teacher has decided on the units to be taught in a year's program, individual units should be planned. Consideration must be given to how to achieve the goals and objectives of that unit, how to organize the time spent in that unit, and how to evaluate student learning. Just as a lesson has an integrity of its own, so does the unit.

Amount of time. Blocking time for units is actually a curriculum decision, but one that has a crucial effect on instruction. The amount of time devoted to a unit is a critical decision, particularly because when more time is spent in one area of the program, there is less time for other areas of the program. The amount of time spent depends on the age of the students, whether that content area is going to be taught again in the same year or different years, and the amount of time required to help students to be able to meaningfully use the information and skills taught.

Physical education programs in the United States have traditionally opted for teaching more activities and sports for less time each year. Currently physical educators are rethinking this practice as they come to grips with research on how long it actually takes to learn motor skills and the notion that competence is a primary motivator for participation. Many physical educators suspect that rather than students being exposed to many activities they can learn later, students are actually being exposed to what they cannot do and therefore may not want to try. Many students are participating in the same units with the same beginning point, the same progressions, and the same ending point year after year in their physical education programs because they did not have enough time in any single unit to really learn the skills. High school students should not be spending a significant part of their last soccer unit learning how to dribble a ball straight down a field.

Longer units give the teacher the opportunity to actually teach for learning and, more important, get the students to a level in an activity where participation can be meaningful. Sport was meaningful to most people who go into physical education as a profession, because they could participate meaningfully in an activity. Volleyball games in which the ball is served and usually just bounces on the other side,

soccer games in which half the players get out of the way of more aggressive players, and tennis games in which the ball is never kept in play more than twice in a row are simply not meaningful for the participants. Longer units also have the advantage of giving the teacher time in a unit not only to help students to be skillful, but to work with affective and cognitive concerns and curricular objectives. Giving students

---

BOX 11-3

Block Plan for a Year of Instruction

Week	Elementary	Week	Secondary
1	Traveling (feet only)	1	Students have a choice of soccer,
2	Traveling (other body parts)	2	beginning tennis, aerobic activities,
3	Weight bearing	3	or outdoor pursuits
4	Throwing and catching	4	
5	Throwing and catching	5	
6	Jumping	6	
7	Fitness	7	
8	Creative dance (body awareness)	8	
9	Creative dance (body awareness)	9	
10	Throwing and catching	10	
11	Throwing and catching	11	
12	Kicking	12	
13	Balancing	13	
14	Traveling and balancing	14	Comprehensive fitness unit required
15	Striking (body parts)	15	
16	Striking (body parts)	16	Activity choice of two of the follow-
17	Creative dance (spatial awareness)	17	ing: aerobic dance, weight lifting,
18	Creative dance (spaitial awareness)	18	jogging, interval training, aerobic
19	Traveling and rolling	19	volleyball
20	Traveling and balancing	20	
21	Fitness	21	Students have a choice of team hand-
22	Throwing and catching	22	ball, track and field, dance, or out-
23	Throwing and catching	23	door pursuits
24	Folk dance and rhythmics	24	
25	Folk dance and rhythmics	25	
26	Self-testing events	26	
27	Self-testing events	27	
28	Traveling and balancing	28	
29	Traveling and balancing	29	Miniunits in archery, golf, table
30	Creative dance (temporal awareness)	30	tennis, Frisbee
31	Creative dance (temporal awareness)	31	
32	Throwing and catching	32	

BOX 11-4

Possible Organization of Secondary Units

5-Day-a-week program—fitness/sport skill split

M/W/F Students have choice of sport skill units run in six 9-week blocks.
Examples: (Fall) Soccer, tennis, golf, volleyball
Fitness activities and concepts
T/Th Fitness activities and concepts.
Examples: Aerobic dance, weight lifting, interval training, jogging

Affective integration with sport skill units

Each unit is paired with an affective concept that will receive emphasis.
Examples:
    Soccer—interaction for inclusion
    Tennis—independent goal setting and follow through
    Fitness-valuing my body

Cognitive integration with sport skill units

Each unit is paired with a cognitive concept that will receive emphasis.
Examples:
    Volleyball—force production and reduction
    Basketball—open and closed skills
    Aerobic dance—principles of cardiorespiratory endurance.

---

choices of units at the secondary level helps ensure that the students are not "stuck" in an activity that they have no interest in or may not be well suited for. Reducing elementary programs to essential skills and devoting more time to those skills help ensure that the fundamental skills that should be part of the elementary program are indeed learned.

Beginning a unit. How a teacher begins a unit of work in physical education can determine the extent to which students are motivated and the extent to which what they learn is meaningful to them.

Orientation to a unit. Units should have their own set induction in which the teacher shares with students what they will be doing, how they will be doing it, and why it is important. If students have not had a great deal of experience with an activity, teachers should consider showing students what the final product will look like so that they will have some idea of what they are working toward. Often teachers assume every student knows what a volleyball or soccer game looks like, and in actuality most of the class have never seen one. The use of video tape, even tapes of previous students at the end of a unit, can help orient the learners to what it is they are working toward. Consider the following examples of an elementary and secondary unit orientation.

EXAMPLE: (ELEMENTARY) The teacher is beginning an educational gymnastics unit with the fourth grade. The focus of the unit will be on combining traveling, rolling, and balancing actions into smooth sequences. The teacher has videotaped Olympic performers in free exercise and also sixth graders from the same school and uses these tapes to focus the students on what is common to both (extended and held balances, clear beginning and ending, and smooth transitions). The teacher comments that each student may not be able to perform all of these skills but that the teacher will be looking for the manner in which the students put together and execute the skills they do select. The teacher then communicates how they will go about learning to do this over the unit.

EXAMPLE: (SECONDARY) The teacher is beginning a unit on team handball, which is relatively unfamiliar to most of the students. The teacher has videotaped some material from the Olympics to begin a discussion of the idea of the game and an analysis of the skills that are needed for the game. The teacher then divides the students into teams and lets them play team handball. After the games, each team makes a list of those skills they will need to practice and the rules they do not know that they feel they will need for their games. The teacher suggests that the students will practice a little every day and play a little every day.

Where to begin. Although units usually begin with a simple to complex development of skills and abilities, as was just described in the secondary example, the beginning of a unit does not always have to start with basic skills. Sometimes students will better understand the importance of practicing skills if the teacher begins with game play, works backward, and then uses this experience to help the students see the importance of what they are doing. Chapter 12 describes an approach to teaching games that does not emphasize the teaching of fundamental skills, but rather the fundamental strategies, as a beginning point.

Pretesting. If teachers do not have a clear idea of where students are at the beginning of a unit, it is often helpful to pretest students on the objectives to be attained in the unit. The teacher might do this informally through an observation check sheet, but more formal testing allows the teacher to share information with individual students so that they may participate in goal setting. Pretesting has the advantage of helping students to set goals and to evaluate their progress through a unit. It also has the advantage of helping the teacher to plan more appropriate experiences for both the class and individual students. For teachers to evaluate students on their progress, pretesting is critical. Otherwise there is no real basis on which to measure progress. In situations where students have had a previous unit in an area and posttesting has been done, pretesting is not necessary.

Developing the unit. Although much of the development for units takes place when the teacher plans individual lessons, certain ideas should receive the teacher's attention as the unit is planned.

Integrate game play with practice in sport units. Even if the unit objective is that students do not play more than two-on-two in a game situation, it is important to integrate game play through a unit. The practice of teaching all skills the first days of a unit and all game play the last days of a unit cannot be justified. Practice is more meaningful when it is related to game play. Game play does not necessarily mean to play the full game. It means that students should have an opportunity to use the skills they have in a gamelike situation. Likewise, game play is more meaningful if an opportunity to practice between games is provided.

Plan for repetition. Skills are learned through practice. Spaced practice throughout a unit is better

than all practice of one skill on 1 or 2 days, never to be returned to again. Teachers should also consider that once students have learned a game, a dance, or another activity, opportunities should be provided throughout the year for students to use these skills and to enjoy participating.

Vary the individual lessons. Try not to spend the entire day on one skill. After skills have been introduced, include short practices of more than one skill each day. Find alternative ways to practice the same skill at the same level if necessary and continuously add complexity toward gamelike conditions as student skill increases.

Vary the type of learning experiences. Build in opportunities for cognitive, affective, group, individual, and self-testing focuses throughout the unit, as well as the use of different teaching strategies to maintain interest and motivation.

Give students a role in the progress of the unit. Student interest and motivation is maintained in units if students are given choices and decisions about the experiences they have.

Ending the unit. Units should have a meaningful end. The culmination of a unit should provide an opportunity for students to use what they have learned and an opportunity for students, as well as teachers, to evaluate student progress.

Because a large part of physical education is concerned with performance that is directly observable, students should be asked at culminations of units to demonstrate through performance what they have learned. Sport units typically end with some kind of tournament. Dance and gymnastic units typically end with some kind of demonstration of what has been practiced over a period of time. When conducted as learning opportunities, these opportunities provide the student a meaningful experience with the content.

Evaluation. Evaluation of units can be either formal or informal but should provide both the teacher and the student the opportunity to determine to what extent unit objectives were met. As is discussed in the last section of this chapter, too often evaluation is used for grading purposes only. Grading is only one use for evaluation. Evaluation also helps the student and teacher determine how much was learned over a unit.

The Unit Plan

Written unit plans are often neglected in planning in physical education. Often teachers plan lessons one at a time, missing opportunities to do long-term planning that could have a significant effect on the meaningfulness, motivation, and learning involved in a unit of instruction. Doing a written unit plan helps the teacher think through what the unit hopes to accomplish and helps the teacher view the organization of learning experiences more holistically.

There is no best way to format a written unit plan. Generally a unit plan includes the following components:

- Clearly stated objectives for the unit
- An identification of the scope and sequence of content
- A block time plan for the unit
- Evaluation procedures

Although different teacher preparation programs require different formats for unit plans, the basic elements are usually similar.

Unit plan objectives. At the unit level, teachers should be able to write meaningful objectives with a high level of specificity. Unlike the lesson plan, which has time constraints for measurable skill objectives, the unit of instruction should permit skill and behavior changes that are measurable in all three domains. Examples of measurable unit objectives are described in Box 11-5.

Scope and sequence of content. It is at the unit level of planning that a teacher can fully use the developmental analysis of content. As described in Chapter 6, the developmental analysis of content is concerned with the scope and sequence of instructional content in the psychomotor domain. Chapter 6 describes a developmental analysis for single skills or small groups of skills. Inherent in any large unit of instruction are both progressions within skills and progressions from skill to skill that must be considered. Complex games and activities are more than the use of separate, isolated skills. Teachers will need to plan for the development of combined skills, as well

---

> **BOX 11-5**
>
> ### Example Unit Objectives
>
> **Elementary: locomotion**
>
> *Psychomotor*: Students will be able to combine locomotor patterns into short sequences with smooth transitions.
> *Cognitive*: Students will be able to describe what makes a good sequence and good transitions between movements.
> *Affective*: Students will be able to work to refine their responses independently.
>
> **Secondary: flag football**
>
> *Psychomotor*: Students will be able to pass a ball accurately from at least 15 yards to a moving player in a game situation.
> *Cognitive*: Students will be able to develop a defense for several basic offensive plays.
> *Affective*: Students will be able to work with a team in an inclusive and supportive way for all team members.

as transitions into game play. A good developmental analysis of the content will help the teacher sequence material in ways congruent with learning. Strategies for teaching sport and games, as well as other content areas, are described in detail in Chapter 12.

Block time plan for a unit. After the teacher has done a developmental analysis of the content to be taught, he or she should begin to lay out the content in the time frame of the unit. Boxes 11-6 and 11-7 illustrate blocked time frames for a secondary and an elementary school unit. Some teachers use flexible unit times. Thus they can vary the time rather than the content as the unit progresses and adjustments have to be made. What is to be avoided in using a time-frame format is the stubborn insistence on finishing a unit or moving to later stages of the progression regardless of how the students are learning.

Time frames are flexible. If the teacher has assigned several lessons to the development of a particular skill and students have not learned that skill to a consistent level, it makes no sense to move on.

BOX 11-6

Blocked Time Frame for a Middle School Volleyball Unit

1. Show volleyball film
   Introduce set
     Individual practice
     Wall practice
     Partner toss

2. Practice set
     Individual practice
     Wall practice (self-
       test)
     Moving partner toss
     Consecutive sets
       with partner
     Direction change
     Introduce forearm pass
     Stationary partner
       toss

3. Practice set
     Wall practice
       (timed)
     Consecutive sets
       with partner (10
       sets in a row)
     Practice forearm pass
       Moving partner toss
       Direction change
       Wall practice

4. Practice set
     Consecutive sets
       with partner (self-
       test)
     Consecutive sets
       with groups of
       four players (self-
       test)
     Practice forearm pass
     Consecutive sets
       with partner

5. Combine set and pass
     Toss-pass-set and
       catch with partner
     Pass-set-catch with
       parner
     Consecutive passes
       and sets with part-
       ner

6. Practice set and pass
     Individual practice
       of pass and alter-
       nate set
     Self-test
     Passes and alternate
       sets with partner
     Keep-it-up game
       with small group

7. Play one-on-one game
     (start with toss; make
     partner miss to score;
     use limited bound-
     aries; emphasize
     maintaining same
     position)
   Play two-on-two game
     (play side by side;
     emphasize coopera-
     tion, sharing space,
     passing to partner,
     and returning to
     cover space)

8. Warm up
     Individual practice
       of 20 sets
     Wall practice of 20
       sets
     20 sets with partner
     Wall practice of 20
       passes
   Play two-on-two game
     (play side by side;
     place competitive
     emphasis on offen-
     sive strategy and
     opening up)

9. Warm up
     Individual practice
       of 20 sets
     Wall practice of 20
       sets
     Wall practice of 20
       passes
   Play two-on-two game
     (play side by side)
   Cooperative game
     (self-test)
   Competitive game
     (10-minute game)

10. Warm up
      Same as previous
        block
    Play two-on-two game
      (play up and back;
      emphasize adjust-
      ments to up-and-
      back position)

11. Warm up
      Same as previous
        block
    Introduce serve (use
      modified distance;
      emphasize consis-
      tency over net)

12. Warm up
      20 sets with partner
      20 passes with part-
        ner
      10 serves with part-
        ner
    Play four-on-four
      game (use no serve;
      allow unlimited hits;
      require three passes
      on a side; emphasize
      spatial relationships
      and rotation)

13. Warm up
      Same as previous
        block
    Play four-on-four game
      (serve from any point
      or toss; give extra
      point for three hits on a
      side; emphasize offen-
      sive relationships)

14. Warm up
      Choice of warm-up
        activities
    Have class tournament
      of four-on-four
      games
    Use team evaluation of
      game play as focus
      of next lesson

15. Same as previous
      block

16. Same as previous
      block

BOX 11-7

Blocked Time Frame for an Elementary School Educational Gymnastics Unit (Third Grade)

---

1. Review traveling on the feet
   Practice of floor work
   Practice on small apparatus
   Practice of sequences
   Review traveling on the
   hands and feet (emphasize
   clear placement, floor
   work, and work on small
   apparatus)

2. Practice traveling on the hands
   and feet on large apparatus
   Practice of arriving
   Practice of traveling along
   Practice of moving off and
   on

3. Practice traveling on the hands
   and feet on large apparatus
   Practice of sequences
   Partner work

4. Review traveling on the
   hands only or feet only
   Practice of floor work
   Practice on small apparatus
   Combine traveling on the
   hands and feet with hands
   only and feet only
   Practice on small app-
   aratus

5. Combine traveling on the
   hands and feet with rolling
   actions
   Practice of floor work
   Practice on large apparatus

6. Practice traveling on the hands
   and feet with rolling actions
   Practice of sequences
   Partner work

Unit plans are flexible guides. The job of the teacher is to see that the students learn, not simply to cover content at all costs.

The more specificity a teacher can include in a blocked time frame for each day of the unit, the more valuable blocked time frames become. It is not useful just to list the name of the skill for each day without giving any indication of the level or type of learning experiences to be included on that day. The examples given in Boxes 11-6 and 11-7 provide a useful level of specificity without losing the ability to see the total picture of the progression of the unit.

Not useful	Useful
Basketball dribble	Dribbling changing speeds and directions in control in general space and against a defender
Locomotor skills	Combining locomotor patterns in a sequence using small equipment

Evaluation procedures for unit. If the teacher has specified unit objectives with an appropriate level of specificity, evaluating the unit of instruction will be easier. The unit plan should describe the tools and procedures used to evaluate a unit.

EXAMPLE: VOLLEYBALL UNIT EVALUATION
- AAHPERD tests for overhead set, serve, and bump
- Game play check sheet (attached)
- Knowledge test on the rules
- Student self-evaluation of skill/game play
- Students' evaluation of what they liked and disliked about the unit

Evaluation procedures should determine the extent to which unit objectives have been achieved for each student and should be described before the unit is taught. Evaluation procedures should include all objectives in all domains of development and should be specified in the unit plan. Evaluation procedures are described in the next section of this chapter.

◆ EVALUATING INSTRUCTION

Evaluation is the process of gathering information to make a judgment about products and processes in the instructional situation. The type of evaluation used depends on the purpose for which the information is being gathered and the type of information desired. Evaluation in physical education is legitimately used for the following purposes:

- To provide students with information on their progress and status
- To make a judgment about the effectiveness of teaching
- To provide the teacher with information on the current status of students in relation to objectives so that instruction can be adjusted
- To evaluate the curriculum or program
- To place students in an appropriate instructional group
- To provide the teacher with objective information on students' status for grading proposes

Evaluation is important because it provides both students and teachers with objective evidence with which to make decisions. Although evaluation is considered a critical part of the teaching/learning process, it is perhaps the most neglected aspect of what we do. Teachers often cite lack of time and lack of appropriate measuring instruments to effectively evaluate students, teachers, and program and therefore do little to assess what they do or what students do. This is unfortunate because there are ways to evaluate all aspects of the teaching/learning process that will provide important information. Teachers who have clear objectives and evaluate what they do in terms of those objectives teach differently. Their work becomes focused and accountable.

Formative and Summative Evaluation

Evaluation usually takes place either (1) to provide feedback to students and the teacher about progress during a lesson, unit, or curriculum or (2) to determine at the end of a unit or program whether objectives have been achieved. When evaluation occurs during the unit or program, the evaluation is said to be **formative evaluation**. When the evalua-

tion takes place at the end of a program or unit, the evaluation is said to be **summative evaluation**.

Formative evaluation is evaluation that attempts to assess progress toward a goal. Formative evaluation procedures are used to make adjustments in the learning process. Summative evaluation measures the degree to which objectives have been achieved and is conducted at the conclusion of a lesson or unit of instruction. Summative evaluation information is used primarily to measure achievement and to compare students with others or with a defined standard established by the teacher.

Formative evaluation is an ongoing process in instruction. Teachers should continuously assess student progress toward program and unit objectives. Continuous assessment has the advantage of providing guidance to the teacher about where students are so that teaching and objectives can be modified. Information obtained from continuous assessment is also useful to share with students for motivation purposes so that students are clear on learning objectives and can participate in personal goal setting.

The emphasis in this text is on a clearly defined teacher intent and the use of observation and analysis procedures to determine the teacher's "next move"—this process is one type of formative evaluation. It is successful only to the extent that (1) teachers clearly define their objectives for lessons, (2) the tasks are goal oriented, and (3) the teacher is capable of both observing and analyzing the student responses in respect to the established goals and objectives. Information collected through observation and analysis is used to make a decision about how to adjust the instructional process for both the whole class and the individual learner.

Summative evaluation usually takes place at the end of instruction. Most summative evaluation in physical education occurs at the end of a unit of instruction or school year. Evaluative information collected at the end of instruction generally is used to determine the relationship between (1) what a student can do and (2) what other students in the class can do or what the teacher has established as an objective. When students are evaluated in terms of what other students can do, it is called **norm-refer-**

enced evaluation. Most physical fitness tests are norm referenced for particular age levels and gender. When students are evaluated in terms of what the teacher has decided is the objective, it is called **criterion-referenced** evaluation. Students in this case are assessed according to the extent to which they have achieved the objective the teacher has established for that class. The difference between criterion-referenced and norm-referenced evaluation is the standard you want to use to make a comparison. If you compare students with other students (either national or school-based norms), you are using norm-referenced evaluation. If you compare students with a criterion you have set for a class, you are using criterion-referenced evaluation.

If teachers have support for establishing a standard criterion on which to evaluate students, criterion-referenced evaluation has some advantages. If the teacher has selected the criterion arbitrarily and has done little to help students achieve the criterion, program goals are not well served by criterion-referenced evaluation. Most teachers are familiar with fitness norm-referenced tests. Although there are tests for other areas of the program, such as sport skills, that do provide normative information, teachers will be involved primarily in establishing criterion-referenced evaluative materials that are directly applicable to their own situation. The National Association for Sport and Physical Education is developing evaluation and assessment materials for the Physical Education Benchmarks described in Chapter 1.

Summative evaluation information is used for giving student grades, for classifying future instruction of students, and for evaluating the effectiveness of the instructional process itself. Evaluative information collected but not used to help with future instruction or shared with students does not represent a wise use of instructional time.

Evaluating in the Three Domains

Teachers are encouraged to plan goals and objectives in the three domains of learning: cognitive, affective, and psychomotor. Evaluation of instruction, both summative and formative, should include evaluation in these three domains. Written tests and testing techniques are available for many content areas and for students of all ages. Teachers also have available a wide variety of techniques for gathering information on affective concerns. It is beyond the scope of this text to describe these evaluation tools and techniques. The reader is encouraged to consult the Suggested Readings at the end of this chapter for specific help.

Collecting Information: Formal and Informal Evaluation

Evaluative information on instructional products and processes can be collected using both formal and informal means of collecting data. Teachers who give a volleyball serve test to their students are using a formal means to collect data on student serving ability. Teachers who observe students serving a volleyball and mentally note their ability are using informal means of evaluation. Teachers who use a checklist to evaluate a student's serve every time that student serves during a game are making an informal means of evaluation more objective. Following are examples of formal and informal means of evaluation:

Formal	Informal
Skill tests	Rating scale
Written tests	Description of student performance based on observation
Records of performance (e.g., in archery, bowling, tennis, fitness scores, golf)	Checklist of skills completed
Videotaped formal analysis using an observation system	Observation system for student use of time
Win/loss record of a student	Student interviews

Formal evaluation techniques are used primarily when more complete and accurate information is required on each student. Designing valid and reliable tests takes a great deal of time and effort, particularly if normative data are to be supplied with the test. Generally teachers do not take advantage of the tests that are available to evaluate students in all areas of the physical education program. The References and Suggested Readings listed at the end of the chapter can help the teacher access many already developed instruments.

Informal evaluation techniques are much more common in physical education; they are also more commonly abused. Information teachers collect for evaluative purposes should accurately reflect what they are measuring. Teachers who list observation as their only form of evaluation do not often approach the collection of information in a systematic or a specific way. Momentary, casual glances at a class to assess generally how the students are progressing will not produce helpful data. Observation and analysis are skills that need to be guided by a plan for observation and by specific criteria that allow the teacher to seek out and evaluate what is seen (see the discussion on observation in Chapter 13).

Practical Approaches to Assessment

One of the reasons teachers most commonly give for not doing an assessment is the time it takes to do it. Because many measurement issues are involved in collecting reliable and valid data when these data are going to be used for research purposes or for important decisions affecting individuals, educators are cautioned against more informal means of evaluation. However, the practicing teacher must balance the need for reliable and valid information against the practical issues involved in limited program time and too many students. Too much concern for the validity and reliability of tools for assessment has actually had the effect of eliminating any attempts at assessment. What follows are some practical ideas that the teacher can use to collect information on the instructional process. The intent is to be practical and to provide the teacher with better information than can be gathered from just "eyeballing" a class.

Use self-testing tasks frequently.   Instruction can be designed to include self-testing or other application tasks to assess student progress, such as asking, "How many times can you keep the ball going across the net to a partner?" When the content lends itself to application tasks, such tasks should be spaced frequently throughout the instructional process to provide feedback to both the teacher and the student. Sometimes it is useful to have students actually record their scores on self-testing activities so that both students and teacher can check student progress.

Use simple check sheets and rating scales. Many important objectives in physical education are too complex to be assessed with simple self-testing activities, and the teacher may not want to use more formal tests that take a great deal of time out of the program itself. Rating scales basically assign point values to different levels of ability of a skill, component of a skill, or behavioral characteristic. For instance, you might decide to look at the form with which students execute an overhand serve in tennis. At the very simplest level you would assign a "1" to students who cannot make contact, a "2" to students who can make contact from a high toss, and a "3" to those students who are showing good beginning form based on their ability to toss and hit the ball in one continuous overhead motion. In a more complex scale you would divide up the serve into its component parts. The teacher would observe a student during practice and rate each student in the class or do a sample of students of different abilities to make a determination of what needed to be done in the next class period.

Simple rating scales can be used to assess more complex types of behavior as well, such as the ability to work independently, stay focused, or game play. Rating scales are difficult to use reliably without very clear definitions of what each category represents, so they have limited value for research or for summative evaluation. They are very useful, however, for the practicing teacher who needs quick and practical ways to collect information that is more than "eyeballing" student progress. Rating scales force the teacher to look at and assess individual students, which is a key to the value of rating scales in instruction.

Use peer teaching to have students assess each other.   Peer teaching is a useful way to collect much information on student progress in a brief time. Students can be given a rating sheet or asked to score a more formal test. With clear directions from the teacher, good information can be collected on student performance.

Ask students to assess themselves.
Students can be given descriptions of different levels or components of skills and asked to determine which best describes where they are. Students can also be expected to keep track of their own scores on a more formal test of ability. Student self-assessment provides a valuable learning experience for students, as well as useful information to the teacher on student status.

Use 30-second wonders. Teachers can take a few minutes out of a class to have students answer questions, such as the following:
- How hard did I work today?
- What do I need to work on in this skill?
- What did I like and dislike about class today?
- What did I do today to help someone else?
- What does my team need help with?

Teachers should have pencil and paper available, because students will need more orientation to what they are doing and why. The more teachers use this technique, the less time it should take.

Use videotape. Videotape should be used widely by physical education teachers to assess performance. The advantage is that the teacher does not have to take time out of class to do the actual assessment. Videotape can record performance or behavior in a lesson to be evaluated later by the teacher, such as the following:
- Formal tests of students
- Game play to be assessed by the teacher
- Skill practice to be spot checked by the teacher to determine where students are
- Management or affective concerns and objectives evaluation
- Teacher instructional skills (see Chapters 13 and 14)

Make use of the student interview.
Teachers can collect a great deal of information on student perceptions of their program by using the student interview. A few minutes spent with a sample of students, individually if possible, before or after school or on a lunch break can help the teacher gather valuable information on what students are

learning, what students are feeling, and how students perceive what is happening in their classes. This information can serve to guide the teacher in planning future experiences by helping them to understand what is actually happening in their classes from the student perspective.

Sample student behavior. Most teachers think that every student has to be evaluated on every objective. If evaluation is going to result in student grades, this is true. If, however, the teacher is using evaluation to collect information on program objectives or teaching, this is not true. Teachers can sample classes or students, perhaps assessing different things with different students.

EXAMPLE: You have three volleyball classes, and you want to assess the extent to which students have acquired game skills, as well as other skills. The teacher can videotape only one representative class and assess the extent to which students are able to use skills and strategies in a game situation. The teacher might also assess a different skill in each class more formally.

The teacher would use this information to determine the percentage of students who have actually accomplished the intended objectives for a program or unit and to what degree.

Develop student portfolios. With *many* students it is difficult for teachers to do a more holistic assessment of *each* student, but by keeping all student assessment material in a single folder for a year, the teacher can get a good idea of where students are in their abilities, attitudes, and knowledges. Portfolios might include all fitness scores, skill tests, written tests, 30-second wonders, or interviews.

Student Grading

The reality is that teachers need to give students grades in most teaching situations in spite of the number of students and the limited program time usually assigned to physical education. Grades are used by different people for different purposes. They are sent home to inform parents about the progress of their child; they are used by the administration and others who see the grades to determine whether a student is successful in an educational experience; and they are used often by the teacher to both inform the students of their progress and create accountability for students' effort and achievement.

Debates regarding grading usually center around the question, "What criteria shall be used for grading students?" Usually the following criteria are considered:

- Student performance
- Student improvement
- Student effort
- Behavioral characteristics of student participation

Student performance includes an objective assessment of where the student is relative to either a standard the teacher has established or normative data, such as scores on a fitness test, skill test, written tests, evaluation of game play, or what the student can do with fundamental or developmental skills. Grading on student performance has the advantage of communicating more accurately where the student is relative to the objectives of the program. Parents, for instance, know that their child is good in physical education if the student receives an "A". College admissions personnel know how good a person is in physical education by the grade received. Almost all school subjects use student performance as the primary criteria on which to base grades.

Grades based on **student improvement** are determined by assessing where students begin in an area to be evaluated and then assessing where they are at the completion of a grading period. Students who make the most progress receive the best grades. Using student improvement in physical education classes does, however, have problems. More skilled students and sometimes less skilled students will not make as much progress as students who have the prerequisites for learning but have not had much experience with skills. For this reason teachers who do consider student improvement will often grade on a combination of both student performance and improvement.

Student effort is usually a subjective judgment by the teacher relative to how hard students try to improve. The assumption is that you cannot expect

any more from students than to have them work at their capacity and that if they are working at their capacity, they will learn. Unfortunately, many teachers set their expectations at such low levels in their classes that maximum effort means that the student does not give the teacher any trouble—what Placek calls "busy, happy, good" (1984). In this sense, effort is actually more a behavioral characteristic than it is real effort to get better at the content of physical education.

Behavioral characteristics usually include such factors as dressing out, coming on time, listening to instruction, and the affective behavioral concerns of the program and school (e.g., honesty, courtesy, respect for others). Judgments regarding behavioral characteristics are made with student attendance and dress records, as well as subjective judgments regarding the conduct of the student in class.

Whereas most practitioners in the field tend to grade primarily on student effort and student behavioral characteristics, most leaders in physical education advocate basing student grades on student performance, improvement, or a combination of the two. Teachers cite as reasons for lack of adequate assessment (1) large numbers of students and (2) inadequate amount of program time. Leaders in the field recognize that respect for physical education programs is hindered by a lack of meaningful assessment. Dressing and participation should be an expectation, not a criterion for getting an "A".

The best situation in grading is to be able to report all of the criteria or at least some of the criteria separately. In this way, effort is not confused with ability or behavioral characteristics. If this is not possible, teachers should try to report student improvement and performance apart from effort and behavioral characteristics.

EXAMPLE: "B-1" in which "B" represents a combination of performance and improvement and "1" represents effort and behavioral characteristics.

In the elementary school, grades are used primarily to report to the parents on the progress of their child. The most important information for parents to have is some kind of assessment of where their child is in relation to other children developmentally in basic skills. This is difficult to do in a single grade, and most teachers have developed letters that are sent home to parents with report cards with an assessment of where their child is in basic skills part of the program, fitness data when available, and an assessment of behavioral characteristics, as well as suggestions for parents on how to work with their children in the motor skill area.

Whatever criteria the teacher uses, particularly at the secondary level, these criteria should be shared with students ahead of time. Students should know at all times where they stand in a class. The grades that they receive should not be a surprise.

SUMMARY

1. Learning objectives at all levels of planning should be written as student learning outcomes.
2. Criterion-referenced objectives specify the behavior expected of the student, the condition or situation under which the behavior is to be exhibited, and the criterion or performance level expected.
3. Objectives in the three learning domains should take into consideration the level of the student before instruction and be written in terms of an expected level after instruction.
4. The lesson plan is a guide for the process of instruction for a single lesson and is based on unit objectives. The lesson plan includes heading material, student and teacher objectives, the developmental analysis of content, the instructional plan, and evaluative procedures.
5. A curriculum guide is a plan for a program of study and is usually organized conceptually using an organizing element. The organizing element used to structure a curriculum determines the units of instruction.
6. The unit plan consists of clearly stated terminal objectives, an identification of the scope and sequence of content material, a block time plan for the unit, and evaluation procedures.

7. Evaluation is the process of gathering information to make a judgment about products and processes in the instructional situation. Evaluation can be formal or informal, formative or summative, and norm referenced or criterion referenced.

CHECKING YOUR UNDERSTANDING

1. What is the relationship between planning and evaluating instruction?
2. What are the advantages and disadvantages of writing objectives at a high level of specificity?
3. Write an instructional objective for a beginning learner in softball. Check to ensure that all three components are included.
4. Write two instructional objectives for each of the three learning domains and underline the behavior, the conditions, and the criteria in each.
5. Write a lesson plan for an age level and content area of your choice that conforms to the guidelines established in the chapter.
6. Write a curriculum goal that is affectively oriented. Write an affective instructional objective that is consistent with that goal.
7. Write a unit plan for an age level and content area of your choice that involves a sequence of 15 lessons and conforms to the guidelines established in the chapter.
8. Discriminate between formal and informal evaluation, and give two examples of each appropriate to physical education.
9. Discriminate between formative and summative evaluation, and give two examples of each appropriate to physical education.

REFERENCES

Bloom B et al, editors: *A taxonomy of educational objectives: handbook 10—cognitive domain*, New York, 1956, David McKay.

Good T, Brophy J: *Educational psychology: a realistic approach*, New York, 1990, Longman.

Krathwohl D, Bloom B, Masia B: *Taxonomy of educational objectives: handbook 2—affective domain*, New York, 1964, David McKay.

NASPE: *Physical education outcomes*, Reston, VA, 1992, National Association for Sport and Physical Education.

SUGGESTED READINGS

Barrow H, McGee R: *A practical approach to measurement in physical education*, ed 2, Philadelphia, 1971, Lea & Febiger.

Baumgartner T: *Measurement for evaluation in physical education*, Dubuque, IA, 1982, Wm C Brown.

Boyce B: Grading practices: how do they influence student skill performance? *J Phys Ed Recr and Dance* 61(6):46-48, 1990.

McGee R: Evaluation of processes and products. In Logsdon BJ et al: *Physical education for children: a focus on the teaching process*, Philadelphia, 1984, Lea & Febiger.

McGee R, Farrow A: *Test questions for physical education activities*, Champaign, IL, 1987, Human Kinetics Publishers.

Placek J: Conceptions of success in teaching: busy, happy and good? In Templin T, Olson J, editors: *Teaching in physical education,* Champaign, Il, 1983, Human Kinetics Publishers.

Tyler RW: *Basic principles of curriculum and instruction*, Chicago, 1949, University of Chicago Press.

Context-Specific Pedagogy

❖❖❖❖❖❖❖❖❖❖
OVERVIEW

Most methods of teaching texts, as this one, provide descriptions of generic teaching skills—those that can be used across contexts that are likely to be encountered. In reality, these skills become principles that, when applied appropriately to different situations, will help you be effective as a teacher. Skilled teachers are effective at knowing which principles to apply in different situations and how to modify principles for different contexts. The more you know about a situation, the more appropriate your decision can be about what you do. The purpose of this chapter is to help you consider what is appropriate for some very specific contexts.

The first section considers equity issues relative to physical education. The chapter is not designed to be a course in multicultural education, equity in education, or adapted physical education; the purpose is to help you deal with issues of "differentness" more holistically—to teach physical education for inclusion *, not* exclusion.

The second section presents a conceptual model for thinking about the way we teach games and sports. The intent again is to help you think about games more holistically and to help you do long-term planning in this area.

The third section identifies typical concepts included in physical education and presents a framework for thinking about how to teach concepts for transfer of learning.

The fourth section presents some basic ideas for thinking about how to teach fitness, dance, gymnastics, and outdoor pursuits as content-specific pedagogy.

❖❖❖❖❖❖❖❖❖❖
CONCEPTS

- **Physical education for inclusion**
  Becoming aware
  Developing a climate for inclusion
  Building equity

- **The games stages**
  Stage one
  Stage two
  Stage three
  Stage four
  Considerations using the games
    stages

- **Movement concepts**
  Action words
  Movement qualities
  Movement principles
  Movement strategies
  Movement effects
  Movement affects

- **Content-specific pedagogy**
  Fitness
  Dance
  Gymnastics
  Outdoor pursuits

◆ PHYSICAL EDUCATION FOR INCLUSION

In the United States in recent times struggles for power have emerged between special interest and minority groups. Many of these groups of people and the individuals who constitute these groups have suffered in silence for years as their differentness has created conditions that have made it difficult for them to fully develop their potential. Students who are different because of their socioeconomic status, gender, class, race, or physical and mental impairments have struggled to be treated equitably. Equitable treatment of all students is not only a moral imperative, it is an investment in the future.

Many people in society tend to be threatened by people different from themselves. It is the role of the teacher to help all students to see diversity in society as strength. The moral foundation of this country is based on the idea that this diversity contributes to, not diminishes, who we are and what we are. Unfortunately, placing the battle for equity on power issues, rather than larger moral issues, has created disconnected struggles for power by separate groups. In many cases, the result has created confrontation and defensiveness. Establishing equity as a moral issue has the potential to create understanding, personal growth, and tolerance.

Tolerance is the ability to respect the integrity of others who are different. The development of tolerance as a characteristic of an educated individual should be a major goal of all teachers—not because people are part of a different culture, or gender, or race or because they have particular physical characteristics, but because they are people who have the same rights, dreams, needs, and aspirations as all other people. Just as hate, bigotry, injustice, and intolerance are learned, so are tolerance and sensitivity to the feelings of others. These characteristics are learned in physical education and are taught by physical education teachers.

As a teacher you are part of society. You have developed many of the beliefs, attitudes, and values of your own culture. You communicate the values you have through what you say, what you do, and how you do it. We know from research that most teachers tend to sort students into good and bad cate-gories and that usually these categories are highly influenced by student gender, culture, and physical characteristics. Most teachers are unaware that they are making these judgments, but the results are the same. Students tend to be prejudged or avoided or to receive disparate amounts of attention. The student receives these messages loud and clear and responds accordingly, generally with behaviors characteristic of students with low esteem and low achievement orientation, described in Chapter 10. Equally important, other students in the class pick up the messages you send and respond to these students in a similar fashion.

This section is divided into several important parts. In the first part you are encouraged to become aware of your own values, attitudes, and behaviors—you cannot teach others to be tolerant and to be sensitive to others if you are not. The second part deals with ways in which you can teach tolerance, sensitivity, and inclusion to others. The third part deals with specific needs of students in our classes who are different.

Becoming Aware

Teachers are models. Because physical education is the social laboratory that it is, physical education teachers tend to have a great influence on the formation of values and attitudes students develop toward others. One of the most critical incidences quoted nationally by speakers in both professional and nonprofessional circles is the negative effect on students who are selected last for a team in their physical education classes. Such practices have had a devastating influence on these students and have ensured that the very goal of our programs—participation in activity—will be avoided at all costs. Consider the messages teachers of physical education send with the following practices:

- The handicapped student is left to sit on the side because the teacher has not found a way to include him or her in the day's lesson.
- When students choose partners, they consistently choose those of their own race, culture, or gender. The teacher says and does nothing.
- Students within the class use ethnic and racial degrading comments and remarks to each other.

The teacher does nothing.

- The teacher organizes students by gender (for practice, to line up, to go back to their class room) or chooses teams by gender.
- The teacher acts on the assumption that all Asian students are good academically, but poor in physical skills; all black students are good in physical skills, but poor academically; and girls cannot throw.
- The teacher assumes that a black student who will not look at her when being disciplined is being disrespectful.

All of these incidences are examples of teachers who have not developed the skills and attitudes needed for a physical education program of inclusion.

A first step toward teaching physical education for inclusion is to develop an awareness of your own values and attitudes toward students who represent different cultures, races, genders, socioeconomic classes, and so on. The following are suggestions for becoming aware of your own values and attitudes and developing a sensitivity for the needs of those students who may be different from you. Some of these suggestions appeared in a University of South Carolina publication (1992).

- Watch for stereotyping in language, roles, media, and practices in your own school and own community. Make a list of the things you do, as well as the school and community you serve. Become sensitized to issues of social justice.
- Recognize that equal does not always mean fair. Some students need to be treated differently and in a manner that is more supportive.
- Avoid the tendency to lump all people into a single group. See people as individuals, not as members of a group.
- Become familiar with the world views of different cultures. Try not to put a value judgment on these ideas. Recognize them as different, not wrong. Provide a forum for discussing differences when there is conflict.

Physical education is a laboratory for social development.

- Take some risks. Attend events and activities sponsored by individuals and groups outside your own.
- Participate in workshops, conferences, and classes that deal with race and culture.
- Involve representatives from different cultures in the planning of your program.
- Videotape or audiotape your own teaching. Do an analysis of who you are interacting with and how you are interacting with them in terms of gender, culture, race, physical ability, and so on. Observe the responses of your students to each other. Note how are they treating each other.

Developing a Climate for Inclusion

In spite of any moral imperative they may feel toward inclusionary practices, many teachers are in environments where they must cope with not only their own values and attitudes toward differentness, but also the values and attitudes of other students in their classes. The lack of social acceptance by peers influences all aspects of students' lives and perceptions of themselves. In these cases, doing nothing is not an option. Ideas relative to socially integrating students who are different can provide some help.

Model attitudes toward differentness. Teachers can make a major contribution to the development of positive attitudes toward self and others by the manner in which they treat students and respond to them. It is easy to like those students who fit in, who are skilled, and who relate positively to both the teacher and other students. By responding to all students in a more positive, supportive manner, even when disciplining a child, the teacher sends very powerful messages about what is appropriate and what is not appropriate interaction between people. Teachers who abuse their power by the manner in which they threaten students send the wrong messages.

EXAMPLE: "Tommy, I asked you not to shoot baskets when you were supposed to be working on dribbling the basketball. You will have to take time out for a few minutes. When you think you can come back and join the group and follow directions, let me know and we will discuss it."

Teach students to respect the person and property of others. Let students know that it is not appropriate to hurt others or to make them feel bad. Help students build a sensitivity to the feelings of others.

EXAMPLE: The teacher has observed that a small group of students has excluded a black child from participation by not ever giving the student a turn. The teacher asks the black child to join another group temporarily and then sits down with the group and talks about how that child must feel in their group. The teacher tries to help them understand how they would feel if they were being excluded because they were different. The teacher makes it clear that such behavior is unacceptable and asks them to try again. After observing the students, the teacher asks those students to stay a minute at the end of the class and positively reinforces their appropriate behavior.

When students demonstrate disrespectful behavior toward you, do not respond in kind. Teach students to ignore the disrespectful behavior of others and to rise above it.

EXAMPLES:
- A minority student uses a racial slur when addressing the teacher. The teacher comments, "I know that you are feeling angry at me at this time, but it hurts me when you feel the need to degrade me in this way. I want you to think about what you just did. Let's talk about it after the class is over."
- The teacher hears comments in the class that represent racial or cultural tension. The teacher stops the class and takes time to talk about that type of behavior: why it is unproductive and how to respond to it.

Positively reinforce appropriate behavior.

EXAMPLE: A team of students includes a mainstreamed student. Some of the students are adjusting what they do based on the ability of this mainstreamed student, and some of the students are not. The teacher comments, "I saw some of you making a decision in what to do with the ball based on the ability of your teammates. I want to really thank and support those of you who were reacting sensitively to the needs of others you were working with."

Facilitate but do not force interaction between students who demonstrate unfriendly behavior toward each other.

EXAMPLE: When you select a partner or small group to work with, I have noticed that somehow we get all the black students on one team and all the white students on another team. This concerns me because from my perspective you are making the decision of who to work with on the basis of skin color—which to me is the wrong reason to be chosen for anything. I can choose the groups myself, but I would rather you begin to think about what you are doing. When we come in tomorrow, I would like to see if all of you can be sensitive to this issue. I would like to see groups that do not represent two races in my classes. For some of you this will be difficult. I am asking that you try.

Use cooperative learning strategies. Cooperative learning as a teaching strategy has the advantage of making students within a group interdependent for achievement of the learning task. Cooperative learning as a teaching strategy is described in Chapter 9.

Build into your program opportunities to teach students about different cultures.

EXAMPLES:

- The student population of a class consists of a large number of Mexican Americans and those of Latino descent. The teacher has selected activities common to these cultures for a unit in rhythms and dance.
- The student population of a class consists of several students of Asian decent. The teacher has decided that she would take several minutes out of the beginning of each class to help students understand the cultural differences of these students in terms of social interaction, world beliefs, and popular leisure time activities.

Building Equity

Gender. Gender is an issue in physical education classes because of some major assumptions our society makes about participation in sport and activity. Primarily boys are supposed to be skilled and interested in aggressive sport activities, and girls are not. Girls are supposed to be interested in gymnastics and dance activities, and boys are not. Fortunately, many of the social stigmas attached to participation or lack of participation are changing. Teachers can facilitate this change and help all students actualize their potential and interests in physical activity by attending to the stereotypes inherent in the sport cul-

ture and common practice in physical education.

Teachers can help students feel good about themselves as participants in an active life-style by becoming aware of the powerful culture attached to gender-related sport participation and by trying not to attach interest in or successful participation in sport or physical activity to gender. Consider the following teacher comments and their effect on stereotyping participation by gender:

- "You throw like a girl."
- "Get in there and get the ball—be a man."
- "The girls may not want to do this."
- "The boys will do touch football, and the girls dance."
- "You don't want to lose to a girl."

Consider the effect of gender identification of the following practices:

- Lining students up by girls and boys
- Using men professional sport models on a continuous basis
- Having a gymnasium filled with pictures of male sport figures and no female sport figures
- Excluding dance from the boys' curriculum
- Always asking a boy to demonstrate
- Continuously using gender-specific language

Not all boys like football—not all girls do not. Not all boys are aggressive or highly skilled—not all girls are unskilled or nonaggressive. If physical education is to meet the needs of all students, sport and gender must begin to be disassociated.

Ethnic and cultural differences. Recent work in classrooms has begun to explore the problems of communication inherent in classrooms, including students and teachers from different races (Casanova, 1987). Students from different ethnic and cultural origins (1) may attach different meanings to language, (2) may hold differing perspectives on events, and (3) are taught to value different behaviors and interrelate socially in different ways. What may be perceived by the teacher as a social or learning problem may in fact be a cultural difference. Unfortunately, it is sometimes only in schools where children actually get to interact with others from a different culture. For students who are a minority, the problems of going to school are increased because of cultural conflicts encountered between the home and the school. The typical classroom values are such things as being on time and turn taking, but some students from different cultures do not share these values. Teachers who work in multicultural environments must resolve these differences in positive ways.

The issue of cultural differences and what should be done in the schools to accommodate these differences is largely a political one. For the student the problem is an immediate one and it is real. Many of the ideas on developing a climate for inclusion in the previous section are appropriate general guidelines for working in positive ways in multicultural environments. In addition, the following thoughts are provided.

- **Do not stereotype students into a cultural group. Treat students as individuals.** For example, do not assume that all Mexican Americans are late because they do not value time.

- **Learn about the culture of the students with whom you are working.** If you are employed in a school district that serves a large multicultural student body, you will need to do all you can to learn about their cultures by attending community events, reading, and just being a good observer of behavior.

- **Find out why a student is behaving in a particular way—do not assume it is always a cultural difference.** If you observe a particular behavior on the part of the student that you do not value, try and find out from the student why he or she is behaving in that way. Sometimes the reason may have little to do with cultural differences, but more with another matter that needs attention.

- **Treat conflicts in culture as independent decisions.** If the conflict is over an idea you deem critical for the child's learning, explain why you are asking the students to conform even though it may be inconsistent with their way of doing things or seeing things. If at all possible, try to teach the child within his or her own cultural practices.

Disadvantaged students.   Students who come from families in low socioeconomic brackets of society are often disadvantaged in school settings. They are disadvantaged not because they do not have material things, but because often their parents are unable to give them the life skills, cognitive development, and social skills necessary to function effectively in the schools. Teachers who work with disadvantaged students and teachers who have disadvantaged students in their classes must make some adjustments for these students.

Actually, recommendations for teaching disadvantaged students are no different from those for all students. The difference is that disadvantaged students are not likely to learn unless the teacher accommodates their needs, and advantaged students often will learn in spite of what the teacher does. The following ideas are helpful.

- **Establish a positive personal relationship with the disadvantaged student.** Unless teachers can break down communication barriers with students, they are unlikely to be effective in teaching disadvantaged students. However, a warm personal level of communication and support is not used to excuse students' inappropriate behavior or lack of learning. Effective teachers of disadvantaged students have very high expectations for students and hold them accountable for learning and behavior. Teachers should not allow students to negotiate lack of learning and performance for behavioral compliance.

- **Teach social and academic skills necessary for learning.** Many disadvantaged students do not have the tools for learning or the social skills needed to function in school settings. These must be taught before real learning can take place. Skills such as listening and paying attention to the teacher, working with a partner, and practicing independent of a high amount of teacher supervision should be taught.

- **Work on ways to positively increase motivation and self-esteem.** All of the ideas in Chapter 10 relative to increasing motivation and self-esteem are relevant for disadvantaged students. Many disadvantaged students are from minority cultures, may not have high self-esteem, and may not be highly motivated to learn. Tasks should be designed to be challenging but should ensure success. These students will need much positive reinforcement from the teacher, as well as their peers.

Use positive models from their culture. In the case of sport figures, select not only those figures who have achieved in professional sports, but those who are good role models in their personal life and academic life.

- **Work with other teachers and support personnel in the school, community, and home to meet the needs of the disadvantaged student.** Often the physical education teacher operates in the gymnasium as a "Lone Ranger" with students who need consistent and integrated help throughout the school. The physical education teacher should join planning teams to focus on the needs of individual students and to develop comprehensive approaches to disadvantaged students within the school. Teachers should not be afraid to elicit the help of parents and other school personnel in working with students with problems. Do not allow problems to build. Act to correct problems when you can identify them.
- **Be alert to the idea that many of the disadvantaged students may not share your life experiences and so the examples you may use in your language and explanations may not be understood.** In these cases you must explain and give examples. Continuously check for student understanding. Observe insightfully for how a student might be interpreting what you say.
- **Be alert for the possibility that disadvantaged students may have improper diets and healthcare problems that may need attention of school and community services.**
- **Direct instruction and teacher-directed learning seem to be the most effective teaching strategies with the disadvantaged students.** Although direct instruction is found to be the most effective teaching strategy with disadvantaged students, it is again a question of

weaning the students from such high dependency on teacher control (see Chapter 9).

Students with disabilities. Because many students with disabilities are mainstreamed into regular classes, it is likely that physical education teachers will have to find ways to meet the needs of these students within regular physical education classes. There is always a danger in classifying students and suggesting teaching techniques appropriate for students with particular characteristics. Although disabled students may share a disabling condition, it is possible that they share little else with those with the same condition (Schloss, 1992). It is critical that teachers maintain an individual perspective with these students that focuses primarily on what they can do and not what they cannot do. Because most professional preparation programs have a specific course that addresses the needs of specific disability conditions in physical education, this material is not duplicated in this text. The following general guidelines reinforce the needs of these students.

- **Prepare the rest of the class.** Teachers who successfully integrate students with disabling conditions into their classes prepare the rest of the class for their coming. All of us tend to be afraid of those things we do not understand. Teachers should first help other students in their classes understand the disabling condition and how they can help.
- **Use peer tutors.** The use of peer tutors has been one of the most effective ways to meet the needs of students with disabling conditions. The peer tutor should be selected very carefully so that the experience is a positive one for both the disabled student and the peer tutor. The peer tutor must be skilled at the lesson material, dependable, and sensitive to the needs of others. It is helpful to meet with students who are going to be tutors and teach them how to be tutors. In individual lessons the peer tutor should be given specific directions on how to help and adapt what is going on for the disabled student.
- **Facilitate—do not force—interaction.** It may take some time for the disabled student to be integrated into your class. Do not force students

who are uncomfortable working with a disabled student to work with this student—give it time. If you need to meet with the whole class not in the presence of the disabled student after the disabled student has been introduced into your class, arrange to do this. Do not let negative experiences for either the individual student or the rest of the class continue without intervention.

- **Help the student to socially integrate with peers.** Teach the disabled student the skills he or she will need to make integration into the regular class work. There are many "going to physical education class" skills that your students have learned over time. A disabled student who has not been part of regular physical education has not had the opportunity to learn these skills. When you see this child is perplexed and not responding, ask yourself if there are any skills that are needed that this child has not had the opportunity to learn.

If the disabled student has a problem socially with the other students, it may be because he or she does not know how to socialize with peers in positive ways. Do not be afraid to help this student directly with these problems. The other students must make allowances, but the disabled student needs these skills to be fully integrated into the class.

- **Focus on what the students can do.** It is unfortunate for the child with a disabling condition that most of the attention the child receives is for what he or she cannot do. Teachers need to help these students discover the limits of what they *can* do, not what they *cannot* do. One of the most exciting experiences I observed was to watch a student with full leg braces take a full run and "ditch" his crutches before going over a vaulting box and lowering himself into a roll. When teachers put the emphasis on what students can do and encourage students to extend their abilities in a supportive environment, student motivation, effort, and success increase.

- **Participate in multidisciplinary planning.** Physical education teachers need to have input into and be part of the planning meetings for students with disabling conditions. This is sometimes difficult when so many students are involved, but it is necessary if the child's physical education experiences are to be positive ones. If you cannot meet with each committee, make it a point to find out what was discussed.

◆ THE GAMES STAGES

Most of the discussion throughout this text has been on the development of individual motor skills and singular concepts. For many closed skills, the action of one skill is all that must be considered. For complex team sports that use many open skills, such as basketball, tennis, and volleyball, the game itself is more than the sum of the individual skills of the game.

Preparation for complex games play requires that the individual be able to combine skills, use skills in more complex ways, and relate to others in both offensive and defensive relationships. This section presents a way to look at developing games players from a more "macro" perspective that considers both the development of skills and strategies in games from a developmental framework. The important aspects of the games stages have emerged from studying how skills are acutally used in games rather than how individual skills are executed. Any progression of teaching must involve moving from gradually increasing the level of complexity of practice to gamelike conditions.

The development of games players can be conceived as consisting of four stages, which are described in Box 12-1 and illustrated in Table 12-1 (pp. 246-249) for the game of basketball. The stages are described individually in the following discussion.

Stage One

In stage one the teacher is concerned with the ability to *control* the object or body. Beginning learners are faced with the problem of not knowing what an object will do when they strike, hit, catch, or collect it. Minimal levels of control are established in this stage of learning to play games. Control means rather specific things for different skills. Generally, control means the following:

- **Sending actions** (e.g., striking, kicking, throwing). The individual can direct the object to a place with the intended force qualities consistently.
- **Receiving actions** (e.g., catching, collecting) The individual can obtain possession of an object that is coming to the student from any level, direction, or speed.
- **Carrying and propelling actions** (e.g., carrying a football, dribbling) The individual can maintain possession of the object moving in different ways and at different speeds.

The development of skill in stage one involves providing experiences in obtaining control. These experiences are first given in the easiest of conditions, and gradually the attainment of control is made more difficult by manipulating the level, direction, and force of the object being sent or received. The development in stage one also includes the changes from stationary to moving objects and from stationary to moving receivers. Consider the sequence a young child might follow learning how to catch a ball, and contrast that with the sequence you might use to develop the forearm pass in volleyball.

Catching a ball	Forearm pass
Light toss out of hand	Pass from light toss
Increase height of toss	Increase height of toss
Increase distance of toss	Increase distance of tosser
Toss to left and right	Receive toss from left and right
Receive toss from another	Move into toss and pass
Increase force and distance	Increase force and distance
Vary levels of throw	Vary levels of throw
Increase force and distance	Pass served ball coming from different directions
Catch on the move	

In each of these examples a gradual progression is established that will lead the student to increasing levels of mastery and control over the object by changing the conditions. The idea of establishing a gradual level of progression is also illustrated in the basketball example on pp. 246-247. All manipulative

---

BOX 12-1

The Games Stages

Stage one

- Concern with individual skills
- Ability to control an object

Sending actions—direct the object to a place with the intended force qualities, level, and direction in a consistent manner, stationary and on the move.

Examples:

> Simple—forearm pass from a light toss directly back to the tosser.
>
> Complex—forearm pass from a served ball to players on the left and right who catch it.

Receiving actions—can obtain possession of the object that is coming toward them from any level, direction, or speed, stationary and on the move.

Examples:

> Simple—fielding a ball rolled from a short distance directly to the player.
>
> Complex—fielding a ball thrown hard to the left or right of a player.

Stage two

- Using skills in combination with each other
- Relating movement to others in cooperative ways

Examples:

> Simple—dribbling and doing a set shot in basketball.
>
> Complex—keeping the ball going across a net in tennis with a variety of strokes/keep it up in volleyball.

Stage three

- Basic offensive and defensive strategy

Examples:

> Simple—one-on-one basketball; no shooting.
>
> Complex—five-on-five soccer with two goalies.

Stage four

- Modified games with changes in the rules, boundaries, number of players, etc.—specialized positions
- The full game

Examples:

> Simple—introduction of specialized basketball positions.
>
> Complex—the full game with all the rules.

Text continued on p. 250.

TABLE 12-1	The four stages of games skills development: basketball	
Extension	**Refinement**	**Application**
STAGE ONE *Skill: dribbling* ■ *Major task: dribbling in self-space*		
Change levels. Dribble around the body. Step forward, backward, and sideways.	Use pads of fingers on the ball (giving). Work on body position (bend knees and have action at elbow). Use a slide step.	Go as long as possible without losing control of the ball. Change direction as quickly as possible without losing control of the ball.
■ *Major task: dribbling in general space*		
Change direction. Move from slow to increased speeds. Change levels. Take eye contact off the ball occasionally. Increase complexity of environment (more people, smaller space, obstacles).	Be aware of others and appropriately change speed and direction for encounters. Place ball out from body for increased speed. Contact ball behind line of direction for change in direction.	Go as fast as possible and still maintain control of the ball.
Skill: passing and receiving ■ *Major task: stationary passing to a stationary receiver*		
Stand at different levels. Receive at different levels. Pass the ball from different levels. Receive a ball at full extension from personal space. Pass a ball from the level at which it was received. Use a bounce.	Use body flexion to generate force and step in to the pass. Use two hands to guide the ball. Give with the ball to receive it. Use one continuous action for receiving and passing. Find the point at which the ball will rebound to desired place for a particular force level.	Make as many passes as possible without losing control. Make as many passes as possible in 30 seconds.
■ *Major task: stationary passing to a moving receiver*		
Vary the distances. Vary the levels of the pass. Move away from, toward, and to the side of the passer.	Place the ball ahead of the receiver to where the receiver will be. Use the pivot. Use the pivot to face the line of direction. Choose the appropriate level of the pass for the direction of the receiver.	Make as many passes in a row as possible without losing control. Make as many passes as possible in 1 minute without traveling as a receiver.

NOTE: No attempt has been made to be inclusive in this analysis. For example, the skill of shooting has been left out of early stages to save space.

TABLE 12-1	The four stages of games skills development: basketball—cont'd		
Extension	**Refinement**	**Application**

■ *Major task: moving passes to a moving receiver*

Extension	Refinement	Application
Pass to stationary receiver. Pass to moving receiver. Use different levels of pass. Vary distances. Pass to force partner to receive the ball at full extension.	Send the ball so that the receiver does no have to stop (lead pass). Find the point the receiver can catch the ball at full extension. Use appropriate levels of pass for distance from partner. Get rid of the ball before steps are taken.	Make as many passes in a row from as far away as possible without losing control. Make as many passes as is possible, using all the space available, in 1 minute.

STAGE TWO
Skill: combining dribbling and passing
■ *Major task: individual dribbling and passing to a wall on the move*

Extension	Refinement	Application
Change speed. Increase complexity of the environment. Change direction. Change pathway.	Be aware of others. Receive the ball from the dribble to make the pass a continuous action. Place the ball on the wall so that it returns (angles) ahead of the receiver.	Get to as many different walls as possible in 1 minute.

■ *Major task: dribbling and passing to a partner*

Extension	Refinement	Application
Dribble and pass moving in the same direction. Dribble and pass moving in different directions. Increase distance between partners.	Make smooth transition from the dribble to the pass (one action). Use minimal number of dribbles before pass. Maintain awareness of location of receiver. Use appropriate pass for relationship to partner (direction and distance).	Make as many continuous passes as possible without losing control of the ball. Make as many passes as possible in 30 seconds without losing control of the ball.

■ *Major task: passing in groups of three or four*

Extension	Refinement	Application
Have no directional goal. Have directional goal. Use unlimited space. Use limited space. Add the dribble.	Cut into an open space to receive ball. Move behind receiver. Maintain awareness of passes and potential receivers. Use the dribble only to await a potential receiver.	Go as long as possible without losing control of the ball.

Continued.

TABLE 12-1	The four stages of games skills development: basketball—cont'd	
Extension	**Refinement**	**Application**

STAGE THREE
Skill: offensive and defensive strategies against the dribble
- *Major task: seat tag (two students, using no ball, face each other and try to tag each other's seat)*

Use unlimited space. Use limited space.	Use quick changes in direction to "fake". Maintain facing relationship in offensive moves. Use quick slide steps with the feet.	Go as long as possible without having the seat tagged.

- *Major task: individual dribbling with defender trying to touch the ball*

Use unlimited space.
Use limited space.
Add rule infractions.
Add line of direction.
	Offense
	  Use body to protect ball.
	  Change hands.
	  Use quick actions to fake defense.
	  Keep body position and level of dribble low.
	Defense
	  Stay close to dribble.
	  Use fakes to get possession.
	  Maintain eye contact with trunk and upper body of dribbler.
	  Stay between defensive player and desired direction.
		Maintain possession of the ball for as long as possible.
		Try to get by the defense.

Skill: offensive and defensive strategies using the pass, dribbling and shooting
- *Major task: two offensive against one defense (traveling violation liberally enforced)*

Use unlimited space.
Use limited space.
Enforce traveling violation.
Have no directional goal.
Have directional goal.
Combine dribbling and passing.
	Offense
	  Use quick passes.
	  Use appropriate pass for position of defensive player (high for player in middle, bounce for passes closely guarded, chest for open receiver and passes).
	  Move into an open space to receive a pass (cut).
	  Time cut.
	  Use the dribble only when receiver is not free.
	Defense
	  Choose to stay with one player.
	  Remain between ball and receiver.
	  Make body shape wide and low to receive quickly.
		Play keep-away game (change middle player when play is touched by defense).

TABLE 12-1	The four stages of games skills development: basketball—cont'd	
Extension	**Refinement**	**Application**

■ *Major task: two offense against two defense (no dribbling)*

Use unlimited space. Use limited space. Have no directional goal. Have directional goal. Combine dribbling and passing. Combine dribbling and passing with shooting to a target.	Same as above with more emphasis on quick passes and on defense remaining between ball and intended direction of offense. Make quick changes from offensive to defensive role.	Same as above.

■ *Major task: three offense against two (or three) defense (no dribbling)*

Use unlimited space.
Use limited space.
Have no directional goal.
Have directional goal.
Combine dribbling and passing.
Combine dribbling and passing with shooting to a target.
Add offensive and defensive fouls.
Add out-of-bounds rules.
	Offense
	    Emphasize third offensive player setting up a future play using spatial relationships of offense and defense.
	Defense
	    Practice zone defense possibilities once scoring is added.
	    Make quick changes from offensive to defensive role.
		Play half-court ball.
		Play full-court ball.

STAGE FOUR

Skill: modified basketball game

■ *Major tasks: four offense against four defense using all skills and major rules*

Require minimum of three passes before scoring. Use no dribbling. Use no foul shooting. Start game with a throw in. Use zone defense only. Determine set plays to get into the key. Use half court.	Use advanced strategies (plays) for offense and defense. Discuss specific game situations and establish strategies for specific conditions. Modify games to encourage particular aspects of play that the teacher finds are weaknesses.	Play half court ball. Play full-court ball.

■ *Major task: regulation basketball*

tasks can be reduced or increased in complexity by manipulating the force (speed), direction, and level of the object, as well as the idea of stationary or moving players. Catching or throwing on the move is more difficult than catching or throwing from a stationary position.

Stage Two

Stage two is also concerned with the individual's control of the object, but the practice of the skills becomes more complex. In stage two skills are **combined** (such as dribbling and passing); **rules** are emphasized that limit the way an action can be performed (such as traveling in basketball); and skills are practiced in cooperative **relationships** with others (e.g., volleyball keep-it-up).

Practicing skills in combination is a critical and often neglected aspect of learning how to play games. A student who can dribble a ball and pass or shoot a ball may not easily dribble and shoot or dribble and pass. This is because the preparation for the second skill actually takes place during the first skill (transition). Many beginning learners in basketball will dribble—stop—and then shoot. The focus on teaching students in stage two activities is on the transition movements between skills. Although many students with practice will come to a smooth transition, many students will not without help from the teacher. In the soccer dribble and shoot, for example, players must actually place the ball at the end of the dribble in a position where they can shoot or pass the ball—not stop and then move the ball into position to shoot or pass. The following example from the complex game of soccer illustrates some of the possible combinations necessary for full development of stage two.

Soccer stage two combinations
- Receive a pass and dribble
- Dribble and pass
- Dribble and shoot
- Receive a pass, dribble, and shoot
- Head a ball and dribble
- Head a ball and pass
- Head a ball and shoot

Even in game situations that involve discrete skills, practicing skills in combination is important.

In stage two in volleyball, for example, one student may bump the ball to another, who will set it for a spike or set it to another player, who will set it for a spike. To determine what skills to practice in combination, teachers must analyze a game to determine what skills will be used in combination in a game. Skills should ultimately be practiced the way in which they will be used in a game, even to the point of serving a volleyball and then moving into position.

Stage two also engages students in cooperative practice activities with others, such as the game of keep-it-up in volleyball or keeping the shuttlecock going across the net in badminton. At this stage the object of the game is still mastery and control of the object, not competition against those with whom you are working. Activities are in one sense group cooperative activities in which the focus of the activity is mastery of control of the object.

Stage Three

In stage three the focus is removed from the execution of the skill to simple offensive and defensive roles with the use of the skill. When stage three experiences are introduced, the assumption is that students do not have to devote all of their attention to controlling the object and can focus on the use of the skill in offensive and defensive relationships.

Stage three considers the very basic strategies involved in sport activities and begins to build these strategies—first in very uncomplex conditions and then in increasingly more complex conditions.

Basically two forms of popular sports have complex strategies. The first is an invasion game (sometimes called *keep-away*). Basketball, soccer, speedball, lacrosse, hockey, and to some extent football fall into this category. In invasion games players share the same court or field offensively and defensively and roles change according to who has the ball. In this type of game the object is to maintain possession of the object and score offensively. The defensive object is to get possession of the object. Stage three in these types of sport activities is concerned with establishing ways to obtain and maintain possession of objects in order to score. The following examples of beginning strategies from invasion games illustrate the skills and abilities that need to be taught at this stage.

Invasion game strategies

How to maintain possession one-on-one
How to obtain possession one-on-one

How to maintain possession two-on-one
How to obtain possession two-on-one

How to maintain possession two-on-two
How to obtain possession two-on-two

How to maintain possession three-on-two
How to obtain possession three-on-two

How to maintain possession three-on-three
How to obtain possession three-on-three

Each of the ideas just listed has a set of critical cues related to the strategy that is part of each game. Each offensive player (the player with the ball and the player(s) without the ball) all have separate roles. Each defensive player (the player with the ball and the player(s) without the ball) likewise have separate roles to play. When these roles are taught before the game gets too complex, students have the foundation for playing the game in more complex forms (whole court or field, all the players, all the rules).

The second type of popular sport is net activities. Volleyball, tennis, and badminton are examples of net activities. In net activities players do not share space. The object in net activities is to score by making the other team miss the ball. Offensive and defensive strategies involve learning how to defend your own space and learning how to make the opponents miss the ball. Offensive and defensive strategy for net activities consists largely of the following:

- **Offensive** strategy for net games
  Place the ball on the opposite court in a space not defended well by the other team.
  Use an offensive difficult-to-return hit (e.g., badminton smash, volleyball spike, tennis smash).
  Use a change-off hit (e.g., drop shot, dink) when the other team expects one of the hits just mentioned above.
  Change the direction or level of the ball.
  Play to an opponent's weakness.

- **Defensive** strategy for net games
  Defend the space.
  Anticipate where the ball will be placed.
  Block offensive shots.

Students should be able to use offensive and defensive strategies of games in stage three under less complex game situations in which the focus of the activity can be the basic strategies. The simplest condition for most sports activities is a one-on-one situation (two-on-one when the control of the skill action is difficult, as in soccer). It is at this simplest level that strategies are introduced. As is the case with invasion games, the development of skill in net games takes place from simple to complex. Students in one-on-one play in volleyball can begin to develop offensive strategies. As more players are introduced, the students are helped to understand how to relate what they do to additional players. In volleyball, for instance, two people on a court

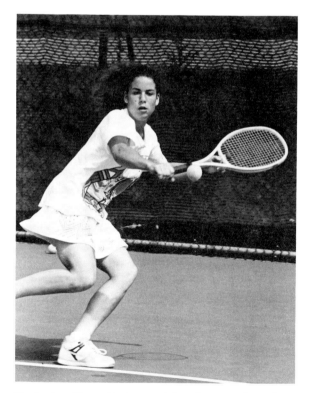

Students will need help practicing the execution of a strategy. (Courtesy SIUE Photo.)

requires that players know how to share space. The front line player in an up-and-back position must be helped to know how to open up (turn sideways as the ball comes overhead) and how to make the discrimination of what to let pass overhead.

Complexity is developed in stage three by adding people (in both offensive and defensive roles), boundaries, scoring, and rules for the conduct of the activity. As another element of complexity is added, students are helped to adjust their responses to what is added. Complexity is added very gradually.

Recently several physical educators, both in the United States and in England, suggested that students should start learning how to play games with stage three, not stages one and two (Spackman, 1983; Lawton and Werner, 1989). The assumption is that it is the strategy that is in fact the meaningful part of the game and that students will develop the skills out of a need for them. For instance, students will learn about moving a badminton opponent around a court and will learn how to use an up-and-back strategy without ever having to know that one shot may be called a *drop* shot and the other a *clear* or *smash*. The teacher can intervene to help students refine skills when the students are ready. Students in soccer will learn the game in very simple conditions but will again start with the strategy without an emphasis on how to dribble or how to pass or how to shoot.

The games strategy approach to teaching games has much in common with cognitive strategy approaches to learning discussed in Chapter 2. It is another way of looking at how to approach a content area. In the absence of research support for either a skills-to-strategy approach or a strategy-to-skills approach, teachers should keep an open mind and try both approaches with their classes.

Stage Four

There is no exact point where stage three experiences end and stage four experiences begin. Stage four experiences are complex. Stage four includes not only the full game, but also those experiences that are modified to help students reach that point. For most games stage four begins when offensive and defensive players become specialized. Players are added, most skills are used, and the conduct of

the game becomes more complex (e.g., rules for starting, procedures for rule infractions, scoring, and out-of-bounds play are added).

When students reach stage four, it is assumed that fairly high levels of individual skills have been established and that students have acquired basic games strategies used in simplified game conditions. For example, it is assumed that students can defend against an offensive player individually and with others in basketball or that they can place the ball away from an opponent and defend their space in a net activity.

A key aspect of conducting stage four activities in a meaningful way is the concept of *keeping the game continuous*. If a rule or part of a game performed in a certain way slows down the continuous flow of the game, the game should be modified to keep it continuous. If students cannot use all the players on a team, the number of players should be reduced. Examples of game modifications include eliminating free kicks or foul shots, replacing the serve in volleyball, batting in baseball with a throw or batting off a tee for some players, starting a game from an out-of-bounds play, and reducing the size of the playing field.

Positive examples of modifications

Basketball	Four-on-four games with no dribbling
	Five-on-five games with no foul shots or jump balls
Soccer	Seven-on-seven games; all the rules
	Eleven-on-eleven games; no out-of-bounds plays, corner kicks
Volleyball	All the rules; two players on a side must touch the ball
	Four-on-four games; modified space
Tennis	Smaller courts; all the rules
	Game started with a courtesy serve

The teacher who chooses to use a stage four game in a lesson does not give up the role of the teacher. The object is to teach students how to play the game well, not merely to let them play when they reach this level. A stage four task is an application task that can be extended by making the play more difficult or less difficult. The teacher should also refine students' performance through the use of refining tasks and a clear focus for their play.

EXAMPLE: I will be looking for the defensive players to open up the space in your games today. Every time I do not see a good use of space on the part of the defense, I will stop the game.

Sometimes teachers hesitate to modify games or change the rules because the game itself is sacred. Unskilled soccer players who cannot get the ball to the wing are not really playing the game the way it should be played. A tennis game that begins and ends with the serve is not tennis. A basketball game that involves one player dribbling down the court to shoot and others attempting to rebound so that they can do the same is not basketball.

Considerations Using the Games Stages

Like any conceptual framework for teaching, the games stages should be used and not abused. Some key ideas regarding the stages should be considered when planning curriculums and lessons.

1. **Students do not leave one stage when they are ready for another.** It is not possible to master a stage. Minimal levels of competency must be obtained before students can be successful with experiences at a higher level, but even varsity basketball practices include experiences at all stages, with an emphasis on stages two and three.

2. **The most neglected stages of development of games skills in physical education programs have been stages two and three**. If the skills developed in stages two and three in Table 12-1 (pp. 247-249) are examined, it can be seen that the essential aspects of both skills and game strategies are best taught at these levels. It is not uncommon to see units of instruction established that move directly from stage one to stage four. The result is always the same—play is not continuous, and the skills seem to fall apart. If teachers would analyze the demands of games and then gradually increase the complexity of those demands as students are ready, students would be more successful and would be able to play the game. A volleyball game in which the receiving team backs out of the way of the ball as it comes over the net cannot do much to increase students' approach tendencies toward volleyball.

3. **You can determine the skills students need to play the game by analyzing how skills are used in a game and what strategies are involved**. You can determine progressions for developing skills and strategies by gradually adding complexity from the very simplest conditions to gamelike conditions.

◆ MOVEMENT CONCEPTS

Concept teaching in physical education has received a great deal of attention in recent times. The *Basic Stuff* series developed by the National Association for Sport and Physical Education (1981, 1986) is a set of books that both describes the important concepts that students in physical education should be taught and provides suggestions for how to teach these concepts. Concepts are cognitive ideas. Often teachers choose to teach content they hope will transfer to other similar situations. Teachers hope that if they teach the overhand throw pattern, what is learned will transfer to skills such as the volleyball serve, overhead smash, or javelin. Teachers hope that if students understand how to receive force in one situation, they will be able to use that information in other situations requiring receiving force, such as catching, collecting a soccer ball, or landing from height. The ability to transfer learning from one situation to another is essential to both independence in learning and problem solving.

Many concepts that are related to movement would be valuable to the learner if taught to the level of transfer. The term **movement concept** is used in this text to refer to ideas that have transfer value. Movement concepts in physical education can be a label for a group of motor responses, such as catching, throwing, or traveling, that are actually a label for motor skills that can be done in different contexts. For example, throwing can be baseball, softball, whiffle ball, or bowling. Movement concepts can also be movement-related ideas and principles that are cognitive in nature that can be applied to a variety of contexts. Six categories of movement concepts useful in physical education are considered in this text as follows (these concepts are listed with examples in Table 12-2):

TABLE 12-2	Movement concepts	
Concept type	**Content area**	**Specific example of a concept**
Action words	Traveling, balancing, sending, striking, throwing, turning, rising	Balance: Increasing the size of the base stablizes a movement.
Movement qualities	Quickness, directness, levels, directions, bound movements, pathways, body awareness, sudden and sustained movements	Sudden and sustained movements: Contrasting types of movement are part of expressive experiences. An appropriate effort quality must be selected for skill movement.
Movement principles	Follow-through, weight transference, spin, stability, force production, force reduction	Force production: The more body parts involved in an action, the greater the force.
Movement strategies	Offensive strategies, defensive strategies, cooperative strategies, adjustments to relationships with others	Relationship with others: A ball should be passed ahead of a moving receiver.
Movement effects	Relationships of exercise to heart, muscular strength, endurance, flexibility	Strength: Muscular strength increases with increases in the work load or the duration of activity.
Movement affects	Relationships of participation in experiences to feelings, expression, social behavior, teamwork, sportsmanship	Feelings: People perform bettter when teammates are supportive.

- Action words
- Movement qualities
- Movement principles
- Movement strategies
- Movement effects
- Movement affects

Concepts are taught appropriately when students can discriminate when to transfer the idea to a new situation and when not to (Merrill, 1971). Movement concepts are used to a greater or lesser extent as the content of physical education, depending on the curricular and philosophic orientation of the program. Movement concepts as content in physical education have the potential to deal more broadly with the subject matter of physical education and achieve long-term curricular goals.

Teaching for appropriate transfer of skills, attitudes, and knowledge requires different kinds of processes than teaching for the specific instance. It also requires a high integration of curricular and instructional planning. Every instructional lesson must be viewed as a part of an integrated whole. Teaching for transfer of a concept from one situation to another takes time—time to plan both curriculum and instruction in a carefully integrated manner and time to teach students.

Movement concepts as content in physical education are most likely not as familiar as physical fitness or motor skills. For this reason, six types of movement concepts have been identified and will be explained with a description of the intent of instruction in that concept. It must be remembered that the division between these content areas is not always clear in a real teaching situation. Instructional goals are complex, often multifaceted, and interrelated. This section is followed by a discussion of how to teach movement concepts.

Action Words

Action words are broad categories of movements that include many different specific responses. The terms *balancing*, *traveling*, *striking*, *rising*, *receiving*, and *turning* are action words that are concepts because the action can be performed in many different ways and in many different contexts. A person can balance on one foot, two feet, or a head and two feet. A person can travel by skipping or running using the feet or by rolling or cartwheeling using other body parts. We give specific names to some responses within a concept, such as a headstand or forehand tennis stroke. Some responses we do not have names for, such as a balance on one hand and two feet. As concepts, action words include not only the responses for which there are names, but also all responses possible that fit the definition of the concept.

Teachers who use action words that are concepts as the content rather than just the specific responses that constitute that concept do so for several reasons. First, they assume that there is value in performing the action in a variety of ways, including ways for which there may not be labels. Second, teachers who use action words teach for what is common and important in the concept. For example, what is common and important in all types of jumping actions is the flexion and the powerful, force-producing extension that follows. As the teacher expands the number of ways in which students jump and produce elevation, the focus on flexion and extension remains constant. The teacher wants this ability to transfer to any jumping situation the student encounters (e.g., high jump, long jump, hurdle).

The process in teaching action words requires that the teacher continuously expand the number of ways students experience the action while holding constant the focus on what is important in skillful performance.

EXAMPLE: Teacher A has decided to teach the concept of striking. He gives his students many experiences striking objects with different parts of the body and with different implements (e.g., rackets, bats, sticks). He teaches his students what is important to all striking activities, such as

where force is applied to direct the object. He provides new experiences and asks students to apply what they have learned. He continuously reinforces major ideas related to striking in all student striking experiences throughout his program.

Movement Qualities

Another way of looking at movement responses is to organize them by the quality of the movement they share. Movement qualities are classes of movement responses that share a movement quality. Words that describe the spatial aspects (level, direction, pathway, plane), effort aspects (time, weight, space, flow), or relationship aspects (matching, leading, cooperating) of movement are movement concepts that in a broad sense are qualities of movement. Most of the more current movement quality concepts used in programs come from the descriptive analysis system of movement developed by Rudolf Laban (Logsdon et al., 1984). Content in physical education classes can be levels of movement, sudden and sustained movement, or leading and following relationships. The broader categories of body awareness, space awareness, effort, and relationships can also be categorizing concepts to be taught as content.

Most teachers who teach content organized as movement qualities believe that a physically educated person should have a broad range of experience with these qualities and should be able to transfer the use of the quality to new, appropriate situations. For example, if students have had experiences stretching, they should be able to reproduce the feeling of the stretch for skills such as the handstand or tennis serve. Students who have experience with light touch should be able to understand what is required in a basketball lay-up or a volleyball dink. Teaching movement qualities develops both a cognitive and psychomotor movement vocabulary that students can draw on in future learning as they experience the effect of the quality studied on their movement and develop a kinesthesia for the quality.

Movement qualities are used extensively in dance instruction, in which the teacher is likely to see students working on slow, sustained movement or quick, sudden movement as the actual content. The process of development is similar to action words in that the teacher continuously expands the number of ways the student actually experiences the movement quality. What remains constant is the emphasis on the student accurately producing the quality as the type of action changes.

EXAMPLE: Teacher B has organized her lesson around spatial relationship concepts. Students explore the different directions they can move and contrast that with the idea of pathways, levels of movement, and actions of single body parts. Teacher B wants to help the students build a vocabulary for describing how movement uses space and also wants the children to become aware and proficient in using space.

Movement Principles

Movement principles are a broad category of concepts that include principles governing the efficiency and effectiveness of movement. Ideas such as (1) the relationship of weight transfer or follow-through to force production and (2) the effect to top spin on the flight of a projectile, as well as ideas related to stability and balance, are movement principles that can become the content of a lesson rather than a by-product of other lesson focuses. The intent in teaching movement principles is to have the students generalize to new experiences where the principles are useful in assisting the beginning stages of the learning process.

The process involved in teaching movement principles can vary from one situation to another. What is most often common in all good teaching of principles is the process of defining the principle, providing examples and negative examples, and providing opportunities for students to apply the principle. It is possible to teach an entire lesson on a movement principle, which allows time for full development. Usually, however, principles are integrated into lessons with other objectives, which makes full development difficult and the need for constant reinforcement through other applicable experiences critical. Teaching that leaves learning at a cognitive level is not sufficient.

EXAMPLE: Teacher C is teaching a lesson in which the primary focus is balance. She wants students to understand what makes a balance more stable (e.g., having a low or wide base of support; keeping the center of gravity over the base of support). Students explore a variety of balances in gymnastics and other sport settings, trying to increase and decrease stability in different ways. Teacher C wants the students to be able to make themselves more stable when they need to be and less stable when quick movement is desired. Teacher C will reinforce the experiences students have in balance throughout her program.

Movement Strategies

Movement strategies are ideas related to how movement is used in cooperative and competitive relationships with others. Movement strategies involve such ideas as passing ahead of a moving receiver, adjusting dance steps as a leader or follower, and defensively placing oneself between the goal and the ball. Movement strategies are adjustments individuals must make in their movement when they are engaged in experiences with others.

As was discussed in the section on the games stages, all keep-away activities share common strategies, as do all net activities. Teachers who teach strategies as concepts do so with the intent that the strategies will transfer to different experiences. Teachers who teach strategies as concepts common to many game forms rather then one specific sport do so with the intent that students will be able to transfer these strategies appropriately (e.g., hitting the tennis ball to an open space just as one hits the volleyball to an open space; zone defense in soccer, basketball, and football). Transfer will occur more easily if the concept is defined and if many different opportunities are given students to apply the concept appropriately.

EXAMPLE: Teacher D is teaching a unit on net activities. Teacher D hopes to teach (1) offensively placing the ball or shuttlecock in the opponent's open space, (2) defensively returning to the center of one's own space after each play, and (3) offensively changing the direction and force levels of placements in the opponent's court. Students begin a one-on-one situation with an easy striking skill (paddles and a foam ball) in a limited space. Students experience the strategies with and without implements and gradually move into specialized sport forms. The strategies are kept consistent as students experience different sport forms through the curriculum.

Movement Effects

Movement effects are concepts related to the effect of movement experiences on the performer. The effect of vigorous exercise on the heart and the types of exercise that produce muscle endurance, strength, and flexibility are all movement effects concepts. Ideas related to exercise physiology are primary sources of movement effects concepts.

When a movement effect is the concept to be learned, the intent is that students are able to apply the concept to new experiences. If students fully understand the effects of vigorous activity on heart rate, they should be able to describe and design the kinds of activities that have the potential to decrease resting heart rates. Students who think that jogging is the only exercise that can be used in a training regimen to improve cardiovascular endurance have undergeneralized the concept. Complete concept development means that students can discriminate those experiences that have the potential to improve heart-lung functioning from those that do not.

The process involved in teaching principles of movement effects is again one that begins by defining the concept and helping students to understand the principles involved. It is followed by helping the students to generalize that principle to all applicable situations.

EXAMPLE: Teacher E has decided to teach the concept of flexibility. He wants students to be able to apply the principles of flexibility to a variety of joints. He brings in a visual aid of the shoulder joint and points out opposing muscle groups. Teacher E then talks about how flexibility is developed over a joint and the result of flexibility exercises on the muscles and tendons. Initially, several exercises for several joints are given to the class to illustrate how best to increase flexibility in a joint. Then students assess their own levels of flexibility and are asked to design two different exercises for each joint identified by the student as needing an increased range of motion. Teacher E assesses the accuracy of the students' choices of exercises, and students begin a personal program to improve flexibility.

Movement Affects

Movement affects are a special classification of concepts that focus exclusively on the affective area of human development. Movement affects concepts are related to expressiveness, the joy of moving, fair play, teamwork, feelings that describe why people move, and the effects of movement on affect. When movement affect is a primary goal of instruction, the intent of the teacher is to develop some aspect of feelings, attitudes, or social relationships that will transfer to other movement experiences and, most of the time, to student behavior in general. A continuous goal of all physical education programs is a positive attitude toward activity. Movement affects as a specific content focus go beyond just making learning motor skills a positive, successful experience. The major content focus of lessons is affective rather than psychomotor.

Teachers may want to teach expressiveness or fair play specifically. They may want to put students in tune with how they feel as a mover in different situations, such as winning and losing in risk-taking activities; in movement that demands light, sensitive movement responses; and in movements that use much space.   When an affective concept is taught, experiences are designed specifically to develop affective behaviors.

Teaching concepts related to movement affects requires that students understand and, more important, "feel" or have an attitude toward that concept. Teaching affective concepts directly means that student feelings, attitudes, and social relationships—not just behavior—must receive attention.

EXAMPLE: Teacher F has decided that he wants his students to get in touch with their feelings about themselves in different movement qualities. He chooses to teach a dance lesson that focuses on contrasting light and indirect movement with direct and strong movement. He knows that some students will have difficulty with the feelings elicited in moving lightly and indirectly (floatinglike movements). He also knows that some students will have difficulty moving with very strong, direct movements (punching movements). He begins his lesson by describing and defining these ideas by taking students through examples of both kinds of movements. He then asks them in a variety of tasks to explore ways in which they can use these qualities with other actions and with other body parts. He then works on having the students build sequences that will contrast the two qualities. At the end of the lesson Teacher F takes time to discuss with the students their feelings in this experience and their preferences for one or the other quality.

Teaching Movement Concepts

Although the primary value of teaching concepts is their transfer to different contexts, teachers can have different intentions in teaching concepts. Some of these objectives are described below:

1. They can intend that a student *know* a concept and be able to reproduce it on a test when asked (e.g., knowing that it is necessary to step forward on the opposite foot).
2. They can intend that a student comprehend the concept and thus be able to use it in the specific context in which it is introduced (e.g., producing force in throwing).
3. They can intend that a student be able to apply the concept to a given situation (e.g., giving an example of how force can be produced in the tennis forehand).
4. They can intend that a student be able to apply information to new movement experiences when not focused on the concept (e.g., stepping forward when learning a new skill without being told to do so.)

You will recognize that each of these intentions is a different level of cognitive learning (from Chapter 11 on planning) and that defining the concept in example number 1 is the easiest level to attain. Using the information in new contexts when not cued to do so is the most advanced level of concept learning. However, many levels of intent probably are missing from this list. The important point is to recognize that there is a real shift from knowing a concept in a cognitive sense and being able to use a concept behaviorally.

Concepts can be taught at any of these levels and many other levels in between. The word *concept* is cognitively oriented, and in many cases physical educators have intentionally designed programs to develop cognitive abilities in relation to these concepts. In some cases, however, physical educators have taken a cognitive idea whose value is its effect on performance and left it at the cognitive level. The value of a cognitive idea in physical education rests with its ability to be applied by the student to a psychomotor concern. The value of concept teaching in physical education is the effect the concept has on what the student *does* rather than on what the student *knows*.

Chapter 2 discusses what we know about transfer of learning from one motor skill to another. Generally, the ideas related to transferring cognitive information are similar. The more a new situation has in common with a situation already experienced, the more likely transfer will be. Researchers who take a cognitive perspective on transfer stress the role that cognitive memory structures play in transfer. Past learning is organized into memory structures, which are retrieved when the individual is faced with new learning situations. Knowledge learned in one context can be retrieved for use in another context when the individual sees relationships between information already stored and new experiences. Using this perspective, a primary role of the teacher is to help the learner organize and structure experiences so that information can be retrieved for new situations. This means the teacher must relate new experiences to previous ones and try and help the learner see more holistic perspectives on what is learned (how it is useful and in what contexts it is useful).

At one level the process involved in teaching a concept is easy. All that is required are the following actions:

- Define the concept for learners.
- Teach the critical features of the concept.
- Apply the concept to many examples (examples both where the concept is applied appropriately and where it is not).
- Give the student many opportunities to use the concept appropriately in different contexts.
- Reinforce the use of the concept throughout the program when appropriate.

Obviously concept learning is not that easy, and, in reality, we have only best guesses about how to help students learn a concept to the point at which they can actually apply that concept to all applicable situations on a regular basis. What follows is a discussion of how this might occur.

Defining the concept with students.
Because concepts are ideas and not a label for a single concrete response, students must be given a clear idea of what is and what is not the concept. The idea of the concept of "truck" will illustrate the point. Children learning about differences among trucks, cars, vans, and buses often confuse them because whether something is really a truck or a van or a car depends on more than one criterion. They learn to distinguish differences through many examples that allow them to discriminate the critical features of a concept. Although the concepts that you will teach will be more difficult than merely learning how to discriminate the idea of a truck, the process is the same. The first step for a teacher is to be very clear about the critical features of the concept. Table 12-3 defines several examples of concepts from each category of concepts and their critical aspects.

Once teachers ares clear about the concept, they can begin to help define it for students. Teachers can define the concept for students verbally and ask students to provide examples of the concept to check their understanding.

EXAMPLE: "We make our bodies move in two ways: (1) by flexing our muscles and then extending them and (2) through a process of rotation. This is flexion and extension of the legs. This is flexion and extension of the arms. This is rotation. If I want to produce more force in a skill that needs force, I will have to increase the degree to which I flex and then extend and/or rotate. I will need to make the movement 'bigger.' Who can name a movement that needs a lot of force? Okay, everyone stand up and show me how you might do that movement with a little force. Now show me how you might increase the force used in that movement? How did you make it bigger?"

Students can also be asked to give examples first

TABLE 12-3	Identifying critical aspects of concepts			
Concept	**Definition**	**Examples**	**Nonexamples**	**Critical aspects**
Force reduction (movement principles)*	Force is reduced by receiving force over a greater distance.	Bunt a baseball. Catch a ball. Roll. Bend knees when landing from height.	Allow caught ball to bounce out of the hand. Strike a ball rather than bunting. Land from height with the knees straight.	Reach with a body part to absorb force. Move with object in line of direction until force is reduced. Create maximal distance to receive force.
Strong movement (movement quality)	Strong movement is movement that has an inner quality of strength and tension; it is more isometric in nature.	Perform any action of the body or its parts, at any speed, whether stationary or traveling, that has an inner tension. Take a firm action or assume firm position.	Perform any action or assume any position of the body or its parts, at any speed, whether stationary or traveling, that has a light, loose, buoyant tension.	Be aware that inner tension can be experienced without the action accomplishing forcefulness. Use strong movement as preparation for forceful application of force. Be aware that strong movement is important to the forceful application of force.

*See p. 263 for a developmental analysis of this movement principle. *Continued.*

TABLE 12-3	Identifying critical aspects of concepts—cont'd			
Concept	**Definition**	**Examples**	**Nonexamples**	**Critical aspects**
Productive partner relationships in manipulative skills (movement affect)	Partners are responsible for challenging each other within personal limits, and the task is set by the teacher.	.If the teacher asks students to receive the ball at different levels, the throwing partner sends the ball to challenging levels within the ability of the receiver.	If the teacher asks students to receive the ball at different levels, the throwing partner sends the ball to levels that are too easy or too difficult for the receiver.	Each partner is responsible for working with the other partner at an appropriate level of work. Each partner must make a decision about appropriateness and work within those limits.
Rolling (action word)	Rolling is transferring weight to adjacent parts of the body excessively to reduce force by rounding those parts.	Do forward rolls. Do shoulder rolls. Do rolls that are initiated with any part of the body.	Allow the body to go flat. Use steplike actions. Slide.	Round parts and take weight successively. Guard action with the hands. Assume rounded body shape.
Offensive strategies in net activities (movement strategy)	Offensive play in net activities consists of (1) placing the ball in a space in the opponent's court where the player is not, (2) changing the direction of the oncoming object to make opponent move maximal distance, and (3) changing the force of the oncoming object.	Place to corners when defensive player is in center. Use a drop shot or a smash in tennis or badminton effectively.	Return the object (1) from the same direction, (2) to the opponent, or (3) with anticipated force level.	Anticipate where opponent will be on court. Look for the largest and most distant space to place object. Use changes in force level as unanticipated moves.
Development of muscular strength (movement effect)	Muscular strength is developed using the principle of work overload by increasing either the number of repetitions over time or the intensity of work load.	Lift weights (gradually increasing repetitions or size of weight). Do push-ups (increasing number of repetitions).	Lift weights (keeping repetitions and size of weight constant). Do push-ups (keeping number of repetitions constant).	Identify duration and work load and gradually increase them.

and then to define the concept more specifically.

EXAMPLES:
- "Who can tell me how to make your heart beat faster?"
- "What is a locomotor movement?"
- "How do we make a ball go further when we are throwing?"

Verbal definition alone without concrete examples is appropriate for concepts students have already experienced. It is usually not effective with young children who are still in the concrete stages of cognitive development or for any learner who lacks experience in the concept to be discussed.

Most teachers find that concepts must be defined in an experiential way. Students can be led through an example of the concept or a use of the concept (e.g., striking, traveling, cardiorespiratory exercise, flexibility), and then the teacher can talk about the experience in terms of the definition and critical ideas of the concept. Frequently, more than one example is necessary. In the examples just given the teacher would lead the group through many examples of increasing force in a movement, such as throwing, jumping, striking, and skipping. Examples of what is *not* the concept often help to define the concept by providing contrast, as illustrated in the following examples:

EXAMPLES:
- The teacher wants children to understand the concept of general space as defined by the basketball court lines in the gymnasium. She describes the boundaries and then asks the students to find a place to stand in general space. Students are then asked several times to find a different space. Finally, the students are asked to find a space not in the defined area.
- The teacher defines the concept of zone defense as guarding *space* rather than the *person*. He places students on a basketball court around the key and demonstrates areas for which students are responsible. Students are then instructed to shift with the position of the ball. Next, the teacher arranges the group in a different spatial pattern and asks the students to apply the same idea to the new situation.

The examples a teacher uses in concept definition are critical to student understanding. They must be a representative sample of possibilities. If the teacher selects examples that all share another similar characteristic in addition to the concept characteristics, students are likely to *undergeneralize* the concept (e.g., if every example of a fruit is red, children will think all fruit has to be red). If the teacher in the first example chose for demonstration purposes students who responded correctly inside the line but who were all on one side of the basketball court, students would be apt to think that general space meant being in a space on that one side of the court. If the teacher in the second example had used only one arrangement of people, students would probably think that zone defense was that single arrangement of people. As it is, the teacher in the second example has narrowed the application of the concept to basketball, and it is unlikely that students will be able to transfer the idea of zone defense to other appropriate activities, such as soccer, field hockey, or football, without additional help. What should be clear from this discussion is that teachers may narrow the applicability of a concept or the chance of transfer of the concept to a wider representation of contexts by the examples they choose.

Often, using an example of the opposite of a concept can help students to define concepts, particularly concepts that are broadly applied. Students can be helped to understand what traveling is if they know what traveling is not. They can be helped to understand teamwork if they understand what teamwork is not. These examples should be well selected and few in number so as to critically define the concept for students.

Expanding responses of students. Often teachers will want to expand or extend the applicability of a concept that is learned in one context to another. The intent is to help students apply the concept to a representative sampling of the experiences to which the concept is to be transferred. If traveling is to be defined as any action that moves the body from one place to another by using the feet or other body parts, including such motions as rolling, swinging, and sliding, a wide range of sample experiences must be provided. If cardiorespiratory endurance can be increased by manipulating the load, intensity, and duration of many different kinds of exercise, students must have an opportunity to apply these critical ideas to a representative sampling of activities (not just jogging).

The teacher can choose either to guide or to direct the exploration and application of experiences. As a teacher, I can give students the experiences and ask them to apply the principles, or I can ask students to select the experiences themselves and then apply the principles. In teaching the concept of striking, for example, the teacher can lead students through striking with each part of the body or the teacher can ask the students to strike balls using different parts of their bodies. You will recognize that the choice the teacher is making in this instance is one of teaching strategy—whether to guide the exploration or to give students responsibility for selection of responses. The same choice is open to teachers when working with action word concepts (e.g., striking, throwing, spinning), more cognitively oriented concepts (e.g., flexibility development, force production), or affectively oriented concepts (e.g., teamwork, leadership, positive social interaction).

EXAMPLE: The teacher has worked with students on the concept of flexibility and has given the students several critical aspects of the development of flexibility for a particular joint. The teacher can then either go through several joints with the students to ensure they can apply the concept or ask the students to take the critical features of the concept and apply them to a joint of their own selection.

The process of expansion is often assisted by narrowing choices initially and then expanding them later. This statement seems contradictory, but consider the results when a teacher says, "Write a composition on anything you want," and the idea of restricting or narrowing choices can be appreciated. Choices can be narrowed by such directives as the following:

- "Balance on three parts of your body."
- "Select activities you would do every day to set up your own cardiorespiratory endurance program."
- "Let's work on being supportive to our classmates when they are having difficulty."
- "Choose a throwing action to show that you

understand how weight can be transferred to produce force."

Narrowing choices ensures experience with a representative sample of behaviors and also assists students with the process of application.

A word about quality. As was discussed in the beginning of this section, the value of teaching concepts is their application to behavior. Sometimes teachers become so absorbed in expanding responses, they neglect the quality of the response. Exercises that are done incorrectly, balances that are not held, movement responses that apply principles inefficiently, or strategies that are performed incorrectly are not useful and defeat the purpose of development. It is not enough to "know" concepts in a cognitive sense; their value is their skilled application to experience.

To refine the responses of students, the teacher must establish criteria for good performance and hold students accountable for the criteria established. Teaching concepts is easier if the teacher establishes criteria in advance through planning. An example of a developmental analysis for a lesson on the concept of force reduction is provided in Table 12-4.

If good balance is defined as holding an extended position still for 6 seconds, student responses should be still and extended regardless of whether the bal-

Never before have so many adults been involved in activity. (Courtesy SIUE Photo.)

TABLE 12-4	**Force reduction: manipulative objects**	
Extension	**Refinement**	**Application**
Toss a ball into the air and receive it so that it makes no noise in the hands.	Reach to receive. Move down with object until the force is reduced.	Toss ball as high as possible and still receive it with "soft hands."
Identify concept (force is reduced by giving with it).	Create maximal distance to receive the force.	Come as close to the floor as possible before stopping the ball.
Receive thrown balls of different types (e.g., footballs, basketballs, softballs).	Place body parts directly behind object to receive the force.	Go as long as possible with partner without any sounds being made by hands.
Receive self-tossed balls.	Adjust hand placement to the level of the ball and shape of object.	Go as far away as possible from partner and still maintain quality of catch.
Receive balls from different directions. Receive balls from increasing distances and force levels.	Move to get behind object.	
Receive ball both while stationary and moving.	Anticipate where ball will land.	Same as all of above with the adjustment of an implement.
Receive manipulatable objects with implements (e.g., scoops, lacrosse sticks, hockey sticks, bats).	Same as all of above with the adjustment of an implement.	
Receive objects at increasing distances and force levels from a partner. Receive objects while both stationary and moving.		

ance is on two feet or two hands. If a good spot in general space is away from equipment, students should be held accountable for selecting a good spot. Even when responses are varied and are chosen by students (e.g., "Choose a throwing pattern you can use to demonstrate transfer of weight"), students still need to be helped to throw well in whatever patterns they choose. The cognitive idea is not enough by itself.

Critical ideas are inherent in many concepts that are actually transferred from one experience to another. These critical aspects are almost always part of concepts that belong to the movement principles, movement strategies, movement affects, and action words categories. Sometimes a single critical idea, such as "increasing the base of support increases sta-

bility," is all that the teacher wants to develop. As described in the following examples, however, several critical aspects are inherent in most concepts:

Concept	Critical Aspect
Striking	Follow through in line of direction. Move to get under or behind ball. Make striking surface as flat as possible.
Force reduction	Extend to meet an oncoming object. Increase time and space of receiving Gradually give with the object.
Cardio-respiratory endurance	Principle of overload. Increase heart rate through interaction of intensity, load, and duration of activity.

In one sense, critical aspects (features) are the "how to do" the concept being taught. If the concept is how to improve cardiorespiratory endurance, the critical aspect is the information that is actually used to improve cardiorespiratory endurance (e.g., overload). The critical aspects are actually subconcepts or principles that govern how the concept is used. They are, in effect, what the teacher hopes will transfer when students decide how to approach a new striking skill, how to receive force, or how to select experiences that will improve cardiorespiratory endurance.

Critical ideas or aspects are determined by the teacher before deciding how to develop the material for students. Along with the definition of the concept to be learned and the examples, identification of the critical ideas inherent in a concept prepares the teacher to do a developmental analysis of the concept for teaching.

Concepts that are to be transferred to a more limited range of context (e.g., zone defense to basketball; weight transfer to tennis) require only that the teacher have the students apply that concept to a particular setting. Concepts that are to be transferred to new and unidentified experiences require a lengthy process of development. Concepts used in this way must be taught for transfer. Use of these concepts must become automatic in the student's behavior. Because concept teaching developed to this level is lengthy and time consuming, teachers must carefully select the concepts they want to teach in this manner.

◆ CONTENT-SPECIFIC PEDAGOGY
Fitness

It is not difficult to understand how to make students fit from a conditioning perspective. All of you have had course work that has taught you the principles involved in developing cardiorespiratory endurance, strength, muscular endurance, and flexibility. What is not as clear is how to incorporate fitness into physical education curriculums and how to ensure that students will engage in an active lifestyle as students or as adults.

The NASPE Outcomes document (1992) describes very specifically the fitness goals inherent in a program to physically educate the youth of our country. Although many of the goals are directly related to valuing an active life-style and the health benefits from activity, several goals are specific to the fitness area:

- Assesses, achieves, and maintains physical fitness
- Designs safe, personal fitness programs in accordance with principles of training and conditioning
- Understands that wellness involves more than being physically fit
- Identifies the benefits, costs, and obligations associated with regular participation in physical activity
- Participates in health-enhancing physical activity at least three times a week
- Respects the role that regular physical activity plays in the pursuit of life-long health and well-being

What should be clear from the goals just described is that the goals span all three domains. Students should be fit, maintain fitness, have knowledge related to fitness, and, most of all, value fitness in their lives. The ultimate goal of physical education is an active life-style that goes beyond narrow perspectives of physical fitness easily attained with conditioning. Although there have been suggestions at times that fitness should replace sport and movement activities as a primary perspective for physical education, the perspective taken by this text is that we have a better chance of accomplishing our long-term goal of an active life-style with a balanced program.

Incorporating fitness into programs and teaching fitness are two of the most difficult aspects of program design for several reasons:

1. Many programs do not have the time to develop fitness, much less maintain it.
2. Many older students do not enjoy working hard physically, no matter how much we justify it on the basis of health.
3. Fitness gains are short lived—unless you maintain a level of activity, you are likely to lose it.
4. Teaching for specific cognitive and affective goals has not been a strong suit of physical education teachers.

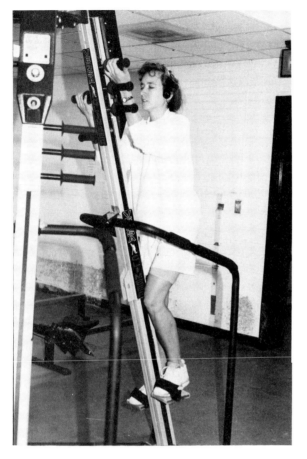

Students can develop their own fitness programs. (Courtesy SIUE Photo.)

In spite of the problems associated with fitness in the curriculum, most teachers value its inclusion and most teachers want a balanced program. Although the focus of this text is not a curricular focus, the following curricular alternatives for including fitness in programs are briefly described (Rink, 1992) so that their implications may be discussed.

Choose several grades throughout the curriculum that will focus primarily on fitness. Rather than doing a small amount of work in fitness every year, teachers should target particular grades and do a good job in fully developing work in fitness in all three domains for those years.

Planning and instructional implications: Physical education curriculum would have to be planned on a K-12 basis (e.g., fourth, eighth, and tenth grade fitness emphasis). The knowledges, skills, and attitudes appropriate for each level would be clearly described. Teachers would design an entire year or a large part of the year to meet these objectives. Sport skills would not be ruled out but would be taught with a fitness concept focus, as well as designed to meet primarily fitness objectives. Teachers at all three levels would have to teach skills, knowledges (including concepts), and attitudes. Having a full year to focus on fitness would allow the teacher to continuously reinforce concepts and to fully develop ideas, as well as have enough time to expect students to show achievable conditioning gains and attitude development.

Use school time other than physical education time. In this model the physical education teacher is responsible for the program but the implementation of the program takes place in the classroom in the case of elementary schools, or before school, after school, or at lunch times. School equipment and facilities are opened up to students as a "fitness center."

Planning and instructional implications: In this model the physical education teacher would teach students exercises and conditioning routines capable of being implemented by the classroom teacher or by the student independently. The teacher would use class time primarily to develop skills, attitudes, and knowledges necessary for the program conducted outside of class time.

Approach fitness as a health maintenance behavior. Sometimes this approach is called the "brushing your teeth" approach to fitness. Students may not enjoy sweating and working hard, but it is something that they must learn to include regularly in their lives. Few of us get any particular enjoyment from brushing our teeth, but we do it anyway because we were made to do it as children and value it as adults. Programs of this nature can be conducted as part of class, as part of school requirements, or as independent programs with accountability for student progress (you do not graduate unless you reach your fitness goals). The emphasis here is primarily on giving students the skills to view fitness as a health maintenance behavior. Conditioning aspects would be stressed.

Planning and instructional implications: In this model the teacher's role affectively is not necessarily to try to convince all students that they will like what they are doing (develop internal motivation), but that it is critical that they do it. Although the goal remains to internalize the value of fitness for the student, the teacher is not opposed to using external rewards to get students to do what they may not be ready to value. Implementation requires individualized realistic goals for each students and accountability mechanisms for monitoring student progress.

Choose motor skill activities that also have a high fitness value. Using this approach teachers would select the activities and sport skills they include in their programs primarily on the basis of their contribution to fitness objectives. Activities with little fitness value in the narrow sense, such as football, archery, golf, and table tennis, would not be included.

Planning and instructional implications: The teacher who chooses activities for their fitness value must decide either (1) to conduct the activity to help students to be skilled in the activity so they have the skills to want to participate or (2) to use the activity for its fitness potential and not necessarily be concerned with skill development (aerobic volleyball or basketball). The choice is basically between developing and maintaining fitness of the students at the time the activities are offered or building skills that can be used later to maintain and develop fitness. Generally the teacher will do skill development, which is not likely to result in immediate aerobic benefits, and also include in each lesson long periods of aerobic activity.

Design instruction in motor skills to include vigorous activity. In lesson planning teachers would

ensure that at least a part of the instructional lesson, regardless of content, included a significant amount of vigorous activity.

Planning and instructional implications: Many times teachers who are trying to engage students in vigorous activity for a part of every lesson believe that they must resort to learning experiences that are different from the lesson content. Teachers who are the most successful in using class time effectively to accomplish both fitness and content objectives practice the content of the lesson in a way that also contributes to fitness goals. Remember, even archery and golf can be aerobic activities if that is your aspiration.

Keep fitness days and motor skill days separate in the program. Schools that have 5-day-a-week programs have the option of dividing the week into very distinct emphases. Most commonly this becomes: M/W/F—motor skill; and T/Th—fitness, throughout the year.

Planning and instructional implications: Planning for both emphases would be primarily separate. Because the fitness program would run for the entire year, the activities and teaching emphasis in the year's program would need to change. Students should not be expected to do the same thing 2 days a week for the entire year.

Summary of teaching considerations—fitness. Each of the program orientations just described have both advantages and disadvantages. What all of these approaches to putting fitness into a program have in common are the following:

- A need for long-term planning
- A need to teach cognitive material for learning and to teach concepts to a level of transfer
- A need to teach values and attitudes
- A need to develop management skills with students to the point where self-direction and independent work are possibilities

■　■　■

The goal of all of these approaches is for students to value fitness and to have the skills to develop

BOX 12-2

Basic Considerations for Teaching Fitness

1. Decide on what you goals are and what approach you will use over a K-12 perspective.
2. Individualize programs by using preassessment to set personal student goals and postassessment to monitor the development of those goals.
3. If program time is limited, find ways to use time outside of class for development and maintenance of conditioning.
4. Focus on more than one aspect of fitness in a class period (exercise for a whole class period in one component is difficult).
5. Ensure that exercises are being done correctly. Keep up to date with the latest information on "best" ways, as well as harmful exercises.
6. Find ways of organizing the class so that there is maximum activity.
7. Teach the "why" as well as the "how" of fitness.
8. Make your goal student independence, as is appropriate for age level.
9. Keep parents and students informed on progress.

their own fitness programs (to be independent). Learning experiences in fitness must be carefully selected so that they contribute to these goals rather than ensure that the student will not participate when given the choice. The most successful programs have been those that have been personalized (students select personal objectives) and those in which students have been given choices (options in how to achieve goals). Some basic considerations for teaching fitness are presented in Box 12-2.

Dance

Many forms of dance are taught through physical education. At the elementary grades, rhythms, folk and square dance, and creative dance are most popular. At the secondary level, aerobic dance, folk and square dance, and modern, jazz, and other forms of contemporary dance are popular. Content-specific pedagogy is involved for each of these forms. There

are also some general ideas relative to teaching dance that teachers should consider in their planning. The suggestions that follow are divided into two sets. The first set describes those ideas most appropriate for direct instruction (Box 12-3, p. 268). The second set is primarily for creative dance forms (Box 12-4, p. 269). Many teachers will include aspects of both in the same lesson and unit.

Gymnastics

Gymnastics in physical education is usually taught either as Olympic gymnastics or as educational gymnastics. Because most teachers who teach Olympic gymnastics intend that the student be able to do a demonstrated movement skill, direct instruction is usually the primary way in which instruction is delivered. In educational gymnastics the teacher works with concepts. The teacher intends that the learner apply the concepts to a student-selected appropriate response (Box 12-5, p. 270). For educational gymnastics the previous section on concept teaching is particularly relevant.

Outdoor Pursuits

Many high school programs have begun to include outdoor pursuits in their programs. It is not uncommon to see programs that include kayaking, orienteering, skiing, bicycling, canoeing, sailing, ropes courses, and many other kinds of activities. Students really enjoy these activities, and they are activities that can be easily pursued in most areas as adults. All of these activities require training beyond what most of you will receive in your undergraduate programs. Most require certification in order to teach them in a safe way. You should not attempt to teach these activities unless you have been properly trained to do so. Many communities have facilities and equipment available that they are willing to loan. Likewise, many adults with expertise will donate their time to help you with classes and trips. See Box 12-6 (p. 271) for guidelines to follow when teaching outdoor pursuits.

BOX 12-3

Teaching Considerations: Dance (Direct Instruction)

1. When teaching a step pattern to students, have all students face the same direction. Give students enough room to move so that if one student makes a mistake, other students are not on top of him or her.

2. Change your teaching position so that the students who are in the front of the group and closest to you are not *always* in the front: either have students face where you are but change where you are so that other students have a chance to get closer to you, or rotate the students.

3. Use command teaching to walk students through a dance step with very clear cues. Cues can indicate the following:
   Which foot to use (right, left, right, right)
   Which direction to go (back, side, forward)
   How the rhythm is performed (quick, quick slow)
   The numerical beat (1-2-3, 1-2-3)
   A combination of above (side 2,3, back 2,3)

4. When teaching a specific step pattern that you want students to "copy," face the group and mirror the image (you go *right* where the directions say *left*). Tell the students you are going to do this so that some students do not attempt to use the exact foot or hand that you are using.

5. When teaching a dance with steps that are performed to specific music, if possible, students should see the dance performed to the music. If this is not possible, they should see the steps performed to the music at correct speed before trying to learn the dance. Videotapes are now available for many dances and for many dance forms. These should be used. Learners need to see the whole dance with the music.

6. Teach the steps of the dance individually before putting the steps to organizational patterns of the dance (e.g., alone before partners; partners before circles). Use the names of the step patterns of dances so that they may transfer to other dances using the same pattern.

7. If dances have a chorus or repeatable section, teach that first and then all the other parts of the dance.

8. Walk the students through a step pattern at a slow speed using verbal cues or a rhythmic instrument.

9. For complex step patterns, give students time to self-pace practice (do it in their own time without your cues).

10. Repeat patterns until they are really learned and the students are comfortable with them.

11. Do not move on unless almost all of the students have the pattern. Pair up slower students with more skilled tutors to work on a one-on-one apart from what you are doing.

12. Gradually increase the speed of performing a step pattern until it becomes consistent with the music. Add the music for practice of a part of the dance as soon as students can perform the step pattern with the music. Do not wait to add the music until all the parts of the dance are learned.

13. Use a variable-speed record player to adjust students' first experiences with the music to a slower speed if necessary. Maintain teacher verbal cues through initial practices and gradually withdraw them.

14. Build new parts of the dance on parts already learned. For example, if you start with part A and have practiced it to the music, after learning part B, do parts A and B together.

15. Once students have learned a dance, let them do it enough so that it becomes enjoyable to them. Plan on including the dances students know in other lessons.

16. For young learners, do not insist that partners be composed of one girl and one boy.

BOX 12-4

Teaching Considerations: Dance (Creative)

1. For beginning learners, add structure to initial experiences. It is difficult to be creative when students have yet to develop responses. Give the students a movement response and then help them explore variations in use of the body and its parts, spacial dimensions, effort actions, and relationships.

2. Keep movement sequences short, so that fast movement will not be interpreted as running around the gymnasium. Use percussion instruments or paced signals to help students mark time (e.g., you want the students to rise slowly from a low-level position to an extended position at a high level. Give them eight counts to get there so they can begin to understand phrasing of movement; if you want to contrast this with an explosive movement, give a hard beat of the drum to be explosive). Withdraw the help of the percussion instrument after students have explored the sequence enough to self-pace the movements.

3. Do not call on students to demonstrate unless you are absolutely sure that their efforts will be received positively by other students and will not destroy the involvement of the student who is doing well.

4. Encourage exploration and variety in responses by helping students to vary the body parts they use, the actions, the levels of the movement, and the force (weight), speed, and direction of the movement.

5. Early on, teach beginners to sequence their movements with a clear beginning and clear ending.

6. Do not be reluctant to demonstrate examples of what you mean.

7. Make lessons more relevant to learners by mixing work with pure movement concepts (body, space, effort, relationships) with more concrete ideas and expressions, such as action words, poetry, sport skills, conflict, art).

8. Give lessons an identity of their own with material to explore and an opportunity to practice and perfect a response.

9. Do not hesitate to suggest ways in which students might improve their responses by making what they do more clear, by using smoother transitions, and by presenting more interesting use of the body and movement quality.

10. Ensure positive reinforcement to learners for responses that are uncommon. Positively reinforcing a particular response is likely to send the message that it is the particular response that is good and not necessarily the uniqueness of it.

BOX 12-5

Educational Gymnastics

1. Gymnastics is primarily a safety problem when students are asked to try and perform skills that they should not be working with. Many students do not have the prerequisite physical abilities for Olympic gymnastic skills, which require high degrees of upper body strength, abdominal strength, and flexibility. The teacher can choose to develop the prerequisites or modify downward the expectations for performance.

2. Students should be taught early on how to manage and control the weight of their own bodies for safety. Students should be taught how to place body parts on equipment and mats and should not be permitted to throw body parts down on a mat. Crashing is not acceptable. Students can be taught how to come down safely from inverted positions.

3. Gymnastics units must be individualized so that there are different expectations for different students. Students should not be put in the position of trying skills that they are not ready to perform.

4. Students should be encouraged to demonstrate good form in what they do. It is not sufficient to get through a movement. It is better to do a simpler skill with good form than to move unsafely through a skill they cannot control.

5. Station teaching is useful for large apparatus work when skills have already been introduced on different pieces.

6. The use of spotters depends primarily on the age of the student and the difficulty of the skills being performed. Teachers should plan on spotting all aerial movements. Spotting is a skill, and spotters are not always necessary if students have been taught how to manage and control their bodies and are not put in positions where they are asked or feel pressured to do skills that they are not yet ready to do.

7. Young students should be requested to rest off the equipment and mats when the teacher is talking. The temptation to be off task on mats or equipment is more than most young children can handle.

8. Students should be encouraged to bring their movements to a close when the teacher asks them to stop. Some movements are dangerous if abruptly stopped in the middle.

9. For Olympic gymnastics it is sometimes helpful to provide students with checklists of skills in progressive order of difficulty. The teacher may want to evaluate students' success in a skill before they can move on to another skill.

10. Teachers should take advantage of videotape and other visual means of giving students the idea of skills and evaluating students' progress.

11. Teachers should build gymnastics units to a culminating experience even if the culminating experience is a class videotape of what the students have been able to accomplish. Gymnastics is performance oriented, and students will be more highly motivated if they are working toward something.

BOX 12-6

Guidelines for Teaching Outdoor Pursuits

1. Plan on spending at least the first instructional period in the classroom with many visual aids to teach safety. Do not waste time going out to a lake, course, or other area only to sit students down and talk to them for the entire period.
2. Beginning lessons are difficult because safety is such a strong aspect of most of these activities. Be creative about ways to involve students actively while they are learning how to be safe.
3. Do not tolerate any breach of safety rules for any reason.
4. Keep the numbers small in these classes. It is better to have a small group for a shorter period of time than a larger group for a longer period of time. This is because it is difficult to keep large groups safely involved.
5. Teach the basic concepts of these activities and reinforce them as the progression moves from simple to complex.
6. Encourage students to become involved in community opportunities in the activity.
7. Include at least one trip to a nearby site. Spend some time acquainting students with what is available to them in their own area, as well as the surrounding area.
8. Bring in adults from the community to talk to the students about what they have done with the activity.

SUMMARY

1. Teachers have a moral obligation to teach tolerance and to develop a sensitivity for the rights and feelings of others.
2. Teachers should become aware of their own values and attitudes in respect to students who are different from themselves.
3. Building a climate for inclusion in physical eduction starts with the teacher. Student gender, race, culture, socioeconomic position, and physical abilities are all concerns that should be attended to in today's society in respect to equity issues.

4. When the content to be taught is a complex game, with many different skills used in offensive and defensive relationships with others, the complexity of interrelationships between skills and the use of those skills must be considered. There are four stages in the development of a complex game, which progress from the development of mastery and control of the object to the use of skills in complex offensive and defensive arrangements.
5. A movement concept is a label for a group or class of motor responses or movement ideas that share similar relationships.
6. The intent in teaching movement concepts is transfer of learning from one situation to a new situation.
7. Movement concepts can be action words, movement qualities, movement principles, movement strategies, movement effects, and movement affects.
8. Movement concepts are taught by defining the concept for learners, providing many examples and opportunities to use the concept, and reinforcing the use of the concept in new situations.
9. Teachers who want to include fitness in their programs must first do long-term planning to decide what they really want to teach and the best way to teach fitness in a K-12 program.
10. Teaching dance, gymnastics, and outdoor pursuits requires some very context-specific pedagogy that should be considered when approaching these content areas.

CHECKING YOUR UNDERSTANDING

1. What can teachers do to make themselves aware of their own attitudes and prejudices toward different students?
2. Why are equity issues important in physical education, and how can teachers develop a climate for inclusion in their classes?
3. Name several things that you do that might send the wrong messages to students regarding gender issues.

4. What can a teacher do to be effective working with students of different cultures, disadvantaged students, and students with disabilities?

5. Choose a team sport, and make a list of four major tasks that might be included under each of the games stages.

6. Choose two skills from a team sport, and describe how these skills are used in a game situation.

7. List two different concepts under each of the major kinds of concepts typically included as content in physical education.

8. For one of the concepts listed above describe the procedures you would use to teach that concept for transfer to a unique situation.

9. Describe five different ways a teacher might use to include fitness in a physical education curriculum.

10. List eight ideas that the teacher should consider when teaching each of the following:

>   Folk dance
>   Creative dance
>   Gymnastics
>   Outdoor pursuits

REFERENCES

Casanova U: Ethnic and cultural differences. In Richardson-Koehler V, editor: *Educator's handbook: a research perspective*, New York, 1987, Longman.

Lawton J, Werner P: A program of badminton/net games which emphasizes tactical awareness, *Physical Educator* , Spring, 1989, pp. 99-106.

Logsdon B et al: *Physical education for children: a focus on the teaching process*, Philadelphia, 1984, Lea & Febiger.

Merrill DM, editor: *Instructional design: readings*, Englewood Cliffs, NJ, 1971, Prentice-Hall.

National Association for Sport and Physical Education (NASPE): *Basic stuff series*, Reston, VA, 1981, American Alliance for Health, Physical Education, Recreation & Dance.

National Association for Sport and Physical Education (NASPE): *Basic stuff series II*, Reston, VA, 1986, American Alliance for Health, Physical Education, Recreation & Dance.

National Association for Sport and Physical Education (NASPE): *Physical education outcomes*, Reston, VA, 1992, American Alliance for Health, Physical Education, Recreation & Dance.

Rink J: Fitting fitness into the curriculum. In Hohn D, Pate R, editors: *Fitness in physical education*, Champaign, IL, 1993, Human Kinetics Publishers.

Schloss P, editor: Integrating learners with disabilities in regular education programs, *Elementary School Journal* 92:3, 1992.

Spackman L, editor: *Teaching games for understanding*, Cheltenham, England, 1983, Curriculum Development Center, College of St. Paul and St. Mary.

University of South Carolina, Publication of the Department of Student Life, Office of Minority Affairs, 1992.

SUGGESTED VIDEOTAPE

A videotape entitled *The Games Program in Physical Education* is available. It describes the games stages in this chapter. The tape was professionally produced and is available for a small service charge from:

>   The NASPE Media Center
>   Physical Education Department
>   University of South Carolina
>   Columbia, SC 29208

Observation and Analysis of Instruction

❖ ❖ ❖ ❖ ❖ ❖ ❖ ❖ ❖ ❖

OVERVIEW

Growth as teachers depends largely on the ability of teachers to objectively evaluate what they do and the effects of what they do on students in the instructional process. To improve teaching, teachers must make judgments on the teaching/learning process using meaningful, valid, and reliable information. Collecting information is facilitated by looking at the right things in the right way. The purpose of this chapter is to help the teacher understand the process of collecting information on instruction that will provide meaningful data from which to make judgments about relationships in the instructional process.

❖ ❖ ❖ ❖ ❖ ❖ ❖ ❖ ❖ ❖

CONCEPTS

- **Why collect data on teaching?**

- **Definition of systematic observation and analysis**

- **Process of systematic data collection and analysis**
  Deciding what to look for
  Choosing a method or tool to collect information
  Learning how to use an observational tool
  Collecting data
  Analyzing and interpreting the meaning of data
  Making changes in the instructional process
  Monitoring change in teaching

TEACHING is complex. Each teaching moment presents a very different set of variables that must be considered before teachers act. The very complexity of teaching has led some to conclude that good teaching cannot be defined. If good teaching cannot be defined, any teacher decision is as good as any other teacher decision. Obviously, the first part of this text concludes just the opposite. Although different teaching behaviors can perform similar instructional functions (i.e., different teaching behaviors can act in the same way), the decisions teachers make and what teachers do result in different student behaviors, different learning environments, and different learning outcomes in different teaching settings.

Teaching is a set of complex open skills. Some teachers bring to the teaching profession skills they have developed through other life experiences. Some teachers have to work hard to establish even basic instructional skills. All teachers should continue to develop their teaching skills throughout their careers as teachers. Learning how to teach does not end with graduation. In a very real sense, graduation and the first teaching job are the beginning of a teacher's growth. Continuing growth as a teacher depends largely on the ability to do the following:

- Reflect on relationships between what you do as a teacher and the effects of what you do on students in relation to your teaching goals.
- Collect information on the teaching/learning process that will help you make judgments about what is occurring.
- Use that information to make changes in what you do.

The last chapters in this text are designed to help you collect information on the teaching/learning process through the use of both systematic observation and qualitative methods that will help you analyze your own teaching and the effects of your teaching. The purpose of collecting this kind of data is to help you improve your own teaching. Teachers will be observed and analyzed by others while student teaching and throughout their teaching career. Supervising teachers, cooperating teachers, school principals, and other professionals will observe and analyze your teaching in both evaluative and nonevaluative ways. In some states teaching certification is determined by an evaluation of teaching skills done through observation. Teachers should become familiar with the observation and analysis of teaching in this context as well. The focus in this chapter is on the use of systematic observation and analysis for self-improvement.

◆ WHY COLLECT DATA ON TEACHING?

Teachers can learn a great deal about teaching through experience alone. There are, however, problems with a learn-through-experience model of improving teaching skills. First, many teachers do not learn through experience—if this were the case, every teacher with 10 years of experience would be a good teacher, and this is obviously not so. Second, by changing what they are doing on a trial-and-error basis, many teachers make the wrong change for the wrong reason. For example, a beginning teacher might conclude, "Students who are responsible for setting out apparatus and working in small groups independently fight with each other." As a result of this conclusion, the teacher might then decide to take all the responsibility for setting out the equipment. The problem, however, is not in the students but in the way in which the teacher taught students to take responsibility. When trial and error is used, teachers often make decisions based on insufficient information and with less than a total perspective. Teachers who begin with strong expectations for themselves and their students and who objectively analyze the instructional process in terms of these expectations are in a better position to guide the instructional process in the intended direction.

It is difficult when teaching to be aware of what is actually happening in the class. Teachers are so immersed in what they are doing that they are unable to take in all that is going on around them, much less bring all they are doing to a conscious level of awareness. Teachers who are **reflective** (i.e., they take time to consider what they did and the effect of what they did on students in relation to their goals and objectives) will continue to grow and improve. Reflective teachers ask why things work and why things do not work. Reflective teachers continuously search for better ways to do things. They have high expectations for both themselves and their students.

Teachers also need the opportunity to get feedback from others and to have others or themselves look at their teaching in a more objective way with an open and probing mind. Most teachers seeking to improve skills or to solve instructional problems would benefit from opportunities to both reflect on what they are doing and collect objective information on what they are doing and the effects of what they are doing. Long-term development of teaching skills depends on such a process.

◆ THE PROCESS OF REFLECTION

Few teachers enter the teaching profession without a commitment to helping people in some way. When you decided to become a teacher, each of you had a vision of trying to positively contribute to the development of youth. You wanted to make a contribution. You wanted to make the world a better place. As you learn how to be a teacher and as you gain experience being a teacher, the goals you have for your role as a teacher will become more developed and in some cases modified. You should not lose your vision of the potential contribution of teachers to affect the lives of students entrusted to you. Teachers *can* make a difference. With time, many beginning teachers become cynical about their potential to effect change in positive directions. This is sometimes caused by unrealistic expectations for themselves in particular settings, but it is also sometimes caused by a lack of patience and an unwillingness to take students from where they are to where teachers think they can be. Growth depends on the ability to work with issues related to *how* to get to where you want to go.

The process of reflection is a process of clarifying your goals as a teacher and sorting out how to best accomplish those goals. Consider the experience of Kathy, which is presented in Box 13-1.

Teaching is a process that requires vision and skill. Reflective teachers continuously assess the relationship between what they do, why they are doing it, and the effectiveness of what they are doing. Kathy needed to gain control of her classes. To do this, she realized that she was going to have to be

BOX 13-1

Example of Process of Reflection

Kathy came into teaching because she had very positive personal experiences in physical education and athletics. Kathy had a teacher/coach who took a personal interest in her and always seemed to know what to say and do to help Kathy be the best athlete she could be and also be the best person she could be. Kathy's coach helped her to be supportive of others and to be a positive leader. Kathy's coach also helped her to sort out what was really important in life and to put athletics in perspective.

Kathy's beginning teaching experiences were in a low socioeconomic community. She began her school year wanting to make a contribution to her students, who she believed really needed a positive role model and someone to help them build self-esteem. Within a very short time Kathy's classes were out of control— chaos prevailed. Kathy spent several months convinced that she had made a mistake going into teaching and questioned her vision of a better world. When she returned for her second year, Kathy began a new strategy. She decided that her vision was not wrong but that her methods of getting to her vision were inappropriate. Kathy began assessing the effect of her teaching on students. She did this both formally, by videotaping what was happening in her classes and collecting some objective data, and informally, by judging what was working and what was not working. She did this during her classes, as well as after her classes, sometimes just pulling herself away from what was going on in her class to take 30 seconds to ask herself what was happening and why. When she found things that did not work, she asked why and remained open to the idea that she was largely responsible when things did not work. Kathy did not lose her vision, but she decided to make her behavior more appropriate for where the students were in relation to that vision. She gained patience. She stayed at the same school for 7 more years and in that time was able to move her classes to many aspects of self-control that were part of her vision. Although she was not able to reach all students, she made a major impact on the lives of many.

much more structured in her teaching than she really wanted to be. Kathy had the skill to add and remove structure as needed. Because Kathy had a vision of her potential contribution to a "bigger" picture, she was not satisfied with just having control and was able to gradually remove the structure.

Reflective teachers spend a great deal of time assessing their teaching. Sometimes this is done informally without the need to collect more objective information, and sometimes it is necessary for the teacher to collect more objective information on what he or she is doing. The process of collecting more objective information is usually called **systematic observation**.

◆ DEFINITION OF SYSTEMATIC OBSERVATION AND ANALYSIS

Systematic observation and analysis of instruction is a process of collecting objective information on the instructional process and analyzing that information in a meaningful way. This information is usually collected by a live observer or by using audiotapes or videotapes. Information can be collected on any phase of the instructional process, including some of the following:

- The type and quality of teacher feedback
- The amount of instructional time spent organizing a class and/or how this is done
- The amount of appropriate practice time students actually get
- The progressive sequence of the teacher's tasks
- The amount of decision making permitted students
- The teacher's primary role during activity time
- Student off-task behavior

Sometimes tools are used that collect information on many different instructional events simultaneously, such as on-task behavior of students and teacher feedback. Sometimes only one event is described. To collect accurate data, observers must be trained to use these tools. After data are collected, they are analyzed to determine the appropriateness of the instructional events observed to the setting in which they occurred.

Change is recommended if needed. *Determining the appropriateness of behavior and recommending change are the most difficult analytic skills to develop.* For example, assume that a teacher analyzes a lesson and determines that students are actually getting to practice skills only 30% of the time. First, the teacher must decide if this is appropriate and, if not, why such a low practice time is occurring. Possible problems may be instructional arrangements, management time, or too much time spent lecturing. A second observation and analysis might need to be done to determine the cause of the problem. After the problem is initially determined, the teacher must set goals and make changes to correct the problem. The teacher should also monitor the degree of change through a series of later observations.

◆ PROCESS OF SYSTEMATIC OBSERVATION AND ANALYSIS

Improving teaching skills depends largely on becoming aware of instructional events and the relationships between these events, deciding on the appropriateness of what is occurring, making change, and monitoring that change. This process is aided through systematic observation and analysis procedures. The major steps used in systematic observation and analysis for the improvement of teaching skills are presented in Box 13-2. A detailed discussion of the steps follows.

BOX 13-2

Using Systematic Observation

---

1. Decide what to look for
2. Choose an observational method or tool to collect information
3. Learn how to use an observational tool
4. Collect data
5. Analyze and interpret the meaning of data
6. Make changes in the instructional process
7. Monitor change in teaching

Deciding What to Look For

When teachers are preparing for the profession, their instructors and supervisors, to a large extent, select what they are to observe in their teaching and help them to analyze what is good and what requires change. Practicing teachers, however, must make these judgments based on their knowledge of effective teaching and their instructional goals in a particular teaching setting. This chapter presents some useful tools for looking at teaching behavior and instructional events.

The selection of what to look at in teaching depends on where teachers think they may need improvement based on their observations of the outcomes of their teaching. The analysis begins with defining the problem and seeking possible solutions. Box 13-3 (p. 278) presents some questions about outcomes and possible related dimensions.

This list is by no means complete, but it should help teachers begin the analytic process. Teachers may want to verify the problem through observation that specifically focuses on the dimension identified. Determining possible causes of problems is not easy and requires a great deal of reflection on the part of the teacher. It will be noted that few of the causes just listed are directly attributable to students. The teacher is in control of the instructional process and should be able to adjust that process to students' needs. Comments such as the following may very well be true, but offer little help in solving the problem:

- "The students weren't listening."
- "Students don't have the arm strength."
- "The students in this class never do what they're told."

Teachers should think in terms of how their teaching can change student behavior in a positive direction. Teaching decisions must be based on their appropriateness for specific teaching conditions. Once possible causes are identified, data are systematically collected to determine whether a particular cause is contributing to the problem in any way. This is the developing-an-awareness stage.

Once the data have been collected, teachers can decide whether the teaching behavior is appropriate for the group of students with whom the teacher is working. Before data on problems, causes, and possible solutions can be collected, however, a tool for observation must be chosen.

Choosing an Observational Method or Tool to Collect Information

Once the teacher has decided what to look for, a method of collecting data must be selected. Similar kinds of information can be collected in different ways. The decision of what method to use or what tool to use depends primarily on what kind of data the teacher is looking for and the practicality, reliability, and validity of the instrumentation.

It is possible to collect information on an informal basis by looking at a videotaped lesson or listening to an audiotaped lesson and making a few notes on the instructional behavior or instructional event being examined. This procedure is valuable, particularly if time is important and if teachers are not sure exactly what behavior they are interested in focusing on. For example, a teacher who is trying to determine causes of off-task behavior might isolate an incident of off-task behavior in some students and begin zeroing in on the possible causes by reviewing the events leading up to that behavior. Although this analysis is not aided by specific instrumentation, it is systematic. The teacher might identify several plausible causes, including teacher clarity of task presentation, organizational clarity, and teacher positioning. Next, the teacher might choose a specific instrument to isolate these causes and study them in more detail.

Most instructional analysis is aided by using a specific tool to look at specific instructional events. These tools must be selected with care if the information recorded is to be useful. **Observational tools** are valuable to the extent that they do the following:

- Provide information important to the question being asked
- Are practical in nature
- Provide objectivity by inferring as little as possible about the behavior being studied
- Can be used reliably
- Collect valid data

BOX 13-3

Questions About Outcomes and Possible Related Dimensions

Question	*Possible related dimensions*
Is the teacher getting the kind of quality being sought for in student responses?	Lack of practice time; inappropriate development of material; inappropriate quantity and quality of feedback; inappropriate cue selection; low student motivation
Is the teacher spending a lot of time managing after students begin working on a task?	Poor task clarity; inappropriate environmental arrangements; inappropriate tasks
Does the teacher's feedback tend to be general in nature?	Lack of knowledge of the subject matter; failure to plan specifically; inappropriate teaching roles during activity
Do students fail to work within the dimensions of the task?	Poor task clarity and cue selection; inappropriate tasks; inconsistent monitoring; inappropriate degree of task structure
Do some students fail to become involved?	Need for task modification; inappropriate environmental arrangements; unclear teacher expectations; poor class social interaction
Is the teacher's practice time limited?	Inappropriate use of student time; inappropriate use of teacher time; inappropriate practice organization
Do management transitions consume more time than they should?	Unnecessarily divided management tasks; student inattention; overly complex organization relative to practice time; failure to teach frequently used routines
Does student on-task behavior decrease with time spent on task?	Unchanging task focus; inappropriate tasks; inappropriate teaching roles during activity
Does the teacher feel like a police officer in the classroom?	Unclear teaching expectations; inappropriate degree of structure; inconsistent monitoring; inappropriate content
Are students not successful with the task?	Inappropriate tasks; inappropriate task presentation; inappropriate feedback; lack of practice time
Do students fail to respond creatively when asked to?	Poorly defined concept; feedback inconsistent with creativity; nonsupportive environmental arrangements; poor class social interaction

---

Each of these dimensions are discussed separately to provide a guide to the teacher in selecting and using observational tools.

Importance of data to question being asked. The young science of teaching analysis tends to use tools simply because they exist and to ignore the meaning of the data after they have been collected. The tool selected for use should be relevant to the question being asked about the teaching. Teachers should know in advance why the behavior they are looking at is important and how it functions in an instructional setting.

If a tool is not available that specifically meets the needs of the teacher's observation, the teacher is encouraged to design one. This section describes the criteria for good tools and should help the teacher think about how to begin designing a tool. Teachers will also find it helpful to become familiar with the tools discussed in Chapter 14.

Practicality of the observational tool. *Practicality* involves primarily the amount of time needed to learn how to use an observational tool, the complexity of the data-gathering procedures, and the ease of data analysis. For teachers who are engaged in self-improvement, practicality is a very real concern.

In general, the more data collected at one time and the more high-inference the behavior being studied, the more time it takes to learn to use a tool. The Observation System for Content Development in Physical Education (OSCD-PE) (Rink, 1979) simultaneously records information on more than 50 different instructional behaviors and events. Much of this text is based on data accumulated with the instrument. However, it takes about 40 hours to learn how to use OSCD-PE reliably, and each lesson coded using this instrument takes several hours to analyze. The instrument is a valuable research tool but is not practical in its entirety for teachers doing self-analysis. The instruments described in Chapter 14 were selected with practicality in mind.

Low-inference versus high-inference observational tools. High-inference tools require much more observer judgment than do low-inference tools. It is obvious that tools that require observers to infer little from the behavior they are recording produce the most accurate data. Observers looking for the occurrence or nonoccurrence of demonstration in a lesson do not have to make many inferences based on what they see. Observers looking for accurate demonstrations must use their judgment a great deal more. To define "accurate," criteria must be established that can be judged through observation, and observers must be consistent in using the established criteria. Criteria for accuracy of demonstrations might include the following:

- Uses the whole action
- Uses accurate speed
- Uses accurate flow of the movement
- Includes implements or objects appropriately
- Ensures that conditions of demonstration reflect conditions in which the skill will be used

The purpose of this discussion is not to discourage teachers from looking at behaviors that are hard to make judgments about, but to encourage them to establish criteria for what they are looking at. The criteria teachers select must be put in directly observable terms so that difficult judgments are made as low-inference as possible. Teachers want the information they collect to be useful. It can be useful only if they can be reasonably sure that the information reflects what really happened.

Reliability of the observational tool. The term **reliability**, when used in conjunction with observational tools, can have several meanings. First, it refers to whether the tool can be used to observe accurately. To observe accurately, the observer must code or record a behavior, such as positive feedback, each time it really appears and not when it does not appear. *Accuracy* is usually determined by comparing the observations of one observer with those of another observer who is considered to be an expert. When no expert is available, reliability is usually determined by *agreement* between more than one observer on the same event (Frick and Simmel, 1974). (Agreement between observers is usually called **interobserver agreement**.) Accuracy also depends on the observer's ability to be *consistent* (i.e., to code the same behavior in the same way more than once). Would an observer code the same lesson the same way on different days? (Agreement of one observer with himself or herself is usually called **intraobserver agreement**.)

Reliability is a function of an observational measure and not an observational tool in its entirety (Rowley, 1976). In other words, a particular observational tool may enable the teacher to observe some events reliably and not others.

To use observational tools to collect information, teachers should test themselves to see if they can observe reliably what they are looking at. Many sophisticated means of testing reliability are available for research purposes. For a teacher seeking improvement in teaching skills, one of the easiest ways to compute reliability is through the use of simple percentage of agreement. Simple percentage of agreement is computed with the formula presented in Box 13-4 (p. 281).

Researchers use varying criteria for reliability, depending on the sophistication of the tool. For purposes of self-improvement, the reliability of the tools teachers use should be at least 70%.

Validity of the observational tool. The term **validity** refers to the degree to which an observational tool measures what it purports to measure.

Validity is critical in choosing an observational tool. For example, to look at the amount of **personalizing** a teacher did with students, personalization might be defined using the following behaviors:

- Teacher calls students by name.
- Teacher touches students.
- Teacher refers to experiences students have inside and outside of class.

A system could be designed that counted the number of times teachers exhibited these behaviors. It could then be said that teachers who exhibited more of these behaviors personalized more with students than teachers who engaged in these behaviors less frequently. However, is this necessarily true? Are there other ways teachers personalize? Is every time a teacher calls a student by name a valid example of personalizing?

Validity is very difficult to measure. Validity could be added to the behaviors just described by attaching some conditions to the behaviors (e.g., teacher touches student with *intent* to personalize). Another category could be added to record unpredicted incidents of teacher personalization. Attaching conditions to the behaviors and allowing observers to make judgments about events could add to the validity of what is described. In many cases, however, these changes would also decrease the reliability of the information collected.

It should be apparent by now that it is difficult to design instrumentation that is both valid and reliable. Reliability is a major factor in validity. If the data are reliable but do not validly reflect what is being looked at, the data are not useful. On the other hand, valid data that are not reliable are of no use either. Sometimes it is worth sacrificing some reliability if this enables the observer to look at events in teaching that are very difficult to observe. Nevertheless, *observers should strive for both valid and reliable data.*

Learning How to Use an Observational Tool

To collect reliable and valid information about their teaching, teachers must be skilled in the use of the instrument they choose. If the data are to be used exclusively for a teacher's own personal improve-ment, it is not as critical that the teacher agree with other observers on what is and what is not a described behavior (interobserver agreement). What is critical is that the teacher agree with himself or herself (intraobserver agreement).

Before teachers begin using an observational tool, they must define the instructional events they want to collect information on and be able to give numerous examples of these events. For example, assume a teacher wants to observe the off-task behavior of students who are practicing throwing both ground-level and high fly balls to a partner. Which of the following events would be considered off-task behavior?

- Partners are standing next to each other chatting.
- Partners are using high fly balls only.
- One partner makes no attempt to catch the ball but backs out of the way.
- Partners are too far from each other to catch the ball before it bounces.

Whether the teacher considers these events off-task behaviors is determined by the teacher's definition of off-task behavior and by the specific ground rules chosen for applying that definition. There are few absolutely clear, black-and-white instructional events. The difficulty of observation is to decide which events, out of all those events that fall into the gray area of decision making, the teacher will focus on.

Teachers can improve their reliability in the use of an instrument by anticipating gray areas in advance and designing a set of ground rules for making decisions about these events. Throughout the data collection, they will need to revise their own definitions or reexamine the instrument definitions to observe reliably and accurately.

Once teachers have defined the behavior they want to observe and have chosen the events they will collect data on, they must practice using the observational tool. There is no substitute for practice. After teachers begin to get some consistency in their observations, they must check their reliability. This can be done by using the instrument on a representative sample of their teaching or on another's teaching in a similar environment. The same lesson should be coded twice, and the reliability should then be computed using the percentage-of-agreement formula

BOX 13-4

Formula to Compute Simple Percentage of Agreement

$$\text{Percentage of agreement} = \frac{\text{Number of agreement}}{\text{Number of agreements} + \text{Disagreements}} \times 100$$

In simple observational systems, such as determining the time spent in activity, the agreement between two observers might be computed in the following way:

Observer 1 = Activity time of 35 minutes
Observer 2 = Activity time of 45 minutes
Agreement = 35
Disagreement = 10

$$\text{Percentage of agreement} = \frac{35}{45} \times 100 = 77.77\%$$

If working with a 10-category system, the scores for two observers would be described as follows:

Category	Observer 1 Number of behaviors	Percentage of behaviors	Observer 2 Number of behaviors	Percentage of behaviors
1	28	18	15	10
2	18	11	16	11
3	3	2	7	5
4	30	19	29	20
6	16	10	13	9
7	18	11	22	15
8	18	11	22	15
9	6	4	3	2
10	4	3	4	3
TOTALS	159	100	147	100

The column labeled ''Number of behaviors'' represents the number of times each observer recorded a behavior in each of the categories. The column labeled ''Percentage of behavior'' gives the percentage of the total number of behaviors represented by each category.

To compute percentage of agreement for a system such as this, the difference in percentages between the two observers for each category is recorded. For this example the computation would be as follows:

Category	Percentage difference between observers
1	8
2	0
3	3
4	1
5	0
6	1
7	4
8	3
9	2
10	0
	22% Disagreement

Percentage of agreement is computed by subtracting the total disagreement from 100:

$$\text{Percentage of agreement} = 100 - 22 = 78\%$$

described in Box 13-4. At least one full lesson should be used to determine reliability. Teachers should work with the use of the tool until they have achieved a percentage of agreement of at least 70%.

Collecting Data

One problem teachers face in the schools is how to collect information on their teaching while they are teaching. Several alternatives exist for the teacher who is really interested in self-improvement:

- Using audiotape lessons
- Using videotape lessons
- Asking colleagues for help
- Asking students for help

Using audiotape lessons. Many teaching behaviors can be observed through the use of audiotape alone. *Audiotape* offers several advantages over other ways of collecting information. The teacher does not have to depend on anyone else, and the equipment is readily available and inexpensive and can be used over and over for different purposes.

It is recommended that the teacher wear the tape recorder when recording. It is possible to place a recorder somewhere in the gymnasium and record much of what is going on, but the quality of the recording is not very satisfactory. Knapsacks, jackets with large pockets, or belts to which recorders can be attached can be used to hold recorders if more specialized equipment is not available. Microphones can be clipped or pinned to clothing, but most built-in microphones also do a good job.

Audiotape is useful for many instructional events at which it is not necessary to collect visual data. Even when videotape or other tools are used to collect data, it is highly recommended that teachers use audiotape on a continuous basis to listen to their teaching.

Using videotape lessons. Some instructional events require the visual observation of the activities of students and teachers. For example, data on teacher positioning, accuracy of teacher feedback, or student movement responses to tasks cannot be obtained by audiotape. *Videotape* is extremely use-

ful because the teacher can observe the results of behavior on student work and can replay the tape to look at many different dimensions of teaching.

Camcorders have made videotaping much more convenient. Most schools have videotape equipment available, and all teachers should be familiar with the operation of this valuable tool. Some schools have personnel assigned to help teachers use the equipment or to do the actual taping. If no other assistance is available, an older student who is not participating can be asked to run the camera or teachers can leave the camera set up in a corner of the gymnasium with the lens on wide angle.

One word of caution on the use of videotape—the microphones on some cameras are not sensitive enough for large gymnasiums, particularly when the gymnasium is noisy. Whenever possible, cordless microphones, which have also become much less expensive recently, should be used with the videotape equipment.

Asking colleagues for help. It is possible for teachers to improve their own teaching without the assistance of others, but it does help to have others interested in what the teachers are doing. Data collection is easier when more than one teacher is interested in improving teaching skills through systematic means. Working with other teachers also provides a needed support system and another set of eyes for analysis.

Teachers tend to be defensive about their teaching, and this inhibits shared work to improve teaching. Defensive positions stem primarily from a feeling that one is not as good as one should be. Perhaps it would help to know that all teachers can profit from efforts to improve their teaching skills. Even a teacher's superiors and supervisors (I include myself) are much better at describing what is wrong than they are at actually doing what should be done.

Asking students to help. Students can be taught to use simple observational systems and to run equipment, and most are delighted to be asked. Students who have free time during the school day or who are not participating can be valuable observers for many behaviors and instructional events. *Students should not be removed from class time*, however, to perform this function.

Analyzing and Interpreting the Meaning of Data

Most of the tools described in this text are nonevaluative tools. They help to describe what occurred but do not tell the teacher if what occurred was good or bad. *Evaluative judgments* must be made using information on the following:

- The conventional wisdom of the field of teaching
- The teacher's own instructional goals
- Information on the students
- The specific teaching situation of the lesson

For example, suppose a teacher's analysis shows the class receiving only 30% practice time. How would these data be interpreted? There are tolerable limits for some instructional events beyond which no lesson should go. For example, activity time should probably never fall below 50% under any circumstances, and in most cases, although not all, it should be higher. If new material is being introduced or the teacher is working on management skills or affective concerns, there is reason to consider lower activity levels appropriate.

Most teaching behaviors have desirable limits for specific situations. The degree to which a teacher is working within these limits must be interpreted by the teacher based on the data collected. For example, a teacher working with students in game strategies should have a high percentage of feedback to students related to the strategy and not the mechanics of the movement. A high percentage of feedback on mechanics may indicate that students are not ready for a stage three games experience.

Interpreting the meaning of the data obtained through observation and deciding on the appropriateness of the behavior described test the analytic skills of even the most competent researcher. The process is an exciting one, however, and provides teachers with valuable insight not only into their own teaching, but also into the instructional process as a highly interdependent set of instructional events.

Decisions about the appropriateness of teaching behavior are best made over many lessons. Teachers need the freedom to respond to the day-to-day needs of learners in a class. If, however, patterns of behavior are identified over several lessons that clearly describe teaching behaviors that are beyond desired limits, there is cause for concern (i.e., little feedback, little activity time, a great deal of off-task behavior, little demonstration).

Making Changes in the Instructional Process

Making a change in teaching is not easy, even when teachers identify the change they want to make and are fully aware of what they are doing. Most likely they have been doing what they are doing for a long time, and the behavior is a natural one for them. New behavior does not feel natural and may even feel awkward at first.

Change can be made easier by initially limiting expectations and setting temporary goals that will help teachers on their way to a larger goal. For instance, if teachers are not accustomed to giving specific feedback, they might begin with a small ratio of specific to general feedback and then gradually increase it.

Change can be expedited if teachers do not try to change more than one process teaching behavior (i.e., one that occurs during instruction). It is difficult to keep track of more than one process variable because teachers must remain conscious of their behavior and teach at the same time. Changing their behavior takes much effort and a willingness to tolerate initial frustration if they are not able to immediately accomplish what they set out to do.

Monitoring Change in Teaching

After teachers decide to change teaching behavior, they should verify that change through additional observations of their teaching. It is possible to think that a change has occurred when, in reality, it has not occurred to any great extent. Teachers who have fully developed an awareness of their behavior usually do know the extent of the changes they have made, but few teachers can remain aware for long periods of time. New teaching behaviors, like new motor skills, must be practiced until they become automatic. To that end, checking the progress of change is necessary.

SUMMARY

1. Reflective teachers maintain a vision of their contribution and seek ways to make that vision work.
2. Growth as a teacher largely depends on (1) the ability to observe, analyze, and make judgments about what is occurring in the instructional process; and (2) the ability to use that information to make changes in teaching behavior.
3. Systematic observation and analysis of instruction is a process of collecting objective information on the instructional process and analyzing that information in a meaningful way.
4. The process of systematic observation and analysis of instruction consists of the following:
   - Deciding what to look for
   - Choosing an observational tool
   - Learning how to use an observational tool
   - Collecting data
   - Analyzing and interpreting the meaning of data
   - Making changes in the instructional process
   - Monitoring change in teaching
5. Deciding what to look for is one of the most difficult aspects of evaluating instruction.
6. Observational tools are valuable to the extent that they:
   - Provide information important to the question being asked
   - Are practical in nature
   - Provide objectivity by inferring as little as possible about the behavior being studied
   - Can be used reliably
   - Collect valid data
7. Learning how to use an observational tool reliably takes a great deal of practice.
8. Observational data that have been collected should be interpreted in terms of the context of the situation.

9. Only a few teaching skills should be selected for change at any one time.
10. Change in teaching behavior should be monitored over time.

CHECKING YOUR UNDERSTANDING

1. What is reflective teaching?
2. What advantages does systematic observation of instruction have over less formal means of evaluating teaching?
3. What steps should a teacher follow who wants to use systematic observation and analysis to make a change in the instructional process?
4. What characteristics does a good observational tool have?
5. How are the validity and the reliability of an observational tool related?
6. Determine the percentage of agreement between the following two observers, noting the number of times a behavior occurs in a physical education class:

   Observer 1 = 10
   Observer 2 = 13

7. Determine the percentage of agreement between the following two observers viewing the same videotape lesson:

Category	Observer 1	Observer 2
1	60	50
2	30	2
3	10	20
4	5	15
5	40	30

8. How can teachers working in the public schools collect data on their own teaching?
9. Once teachers decide to make a change in their own teaching behaviors, what kind of goals should be set and how do the teachers go about making change?

REFERENCES

Frick T, Simmel MI: *Observational records: observer agreement and reliabilities.* Paper presented at the annual meeting of the American Psychological Association, Chicago, April 1974, Eric Document Reproduction Service No. Ed-977 375.

Rink J: *Development of a system for the observation of content development in physical education,* unpublished doctoral dissertation, The Ohio State University, 1979.

Rowley G: The reliabilities of classroom observational measures, *Amer Educ Res J* 13(1):51-59, 1976.

SUGGESTED READINGS

Darst P, Zakrajsek D, Mancini V, editors: *Analyzing physical education and sport instruction,* Champaign, IL, 1989, Human Kinetics Publishers.

Metzler M: *Supervision for physical education,* Champaign, Il, 1990. Human Kinetics Publishers.

Tools for the Analysis of Instruction

❖ ❖ ❖ ❖ ❖ ❖ ❖ ❖ ❖ ❖

OVERVIEW

In Chapter 13 the process of improving teaching was discussed with the intent to provide a rationale for teachers to continuously reflect on and collect information on their own teaching for the purpose of self-improvement. The purpose of this chapter is to provide the teacher with a sample of basic tools that can be used to collect information on fundamental teaching skills. The second part of this chapter describes alternative methods and techniques for the observation and analysis of instruction that may be used to modify or develop an instrument to collect data on teaching.

❖ ❖ ❖ ❖ ❖ ❖ ❖ ❖ ❖ ❖

CONCEPTS

- **Observational tools**
  Student motor activity: ALT-PE
  Student use of time
  Content development: OSCD-PE
  Teacher feedback
  Student conduct
  QMTPS: combination instrument
  Teacher movement and location

- **Techniques and methods of observation**
  Systematic observation methods
    Intuitive observation
    Anecdotal records
    Rating scales
    Event recording
    Duration recording
    Interaction analysis
    Interval recording
    Time sampling
  Qualitative methods of collecting data
    Observation
    Interview
    Questionnaire

O VER the years teachers and researchers have used a variety of observational instruments to help them record, analyze, and make judgments about the teaching/learning process. Each of these instruments can reveal only a very small part of the reality of a very complex and interrelated process. An observational tool or other method of collecting data on teaching is like a lens or filter on a camera. In selecting the lens or filter to be used and pointing the camera in a particular direction, the photographer chooses not only what is seen but also what is not seen. A lens pointed in one direction cannot see what is outside the limitations of that lens. Tools and other data collection techniques are designed to assist the observer and are useful only to the extent that the observer can put the data obtained back into the context of the whole. The data collection techniques can *reveal* what is, but they cannot put a value on what is.

Different methods of collecting data produce different kinds of data. The same instructional phenomenon can be looked at using different methods and techniques that vary in the amount of information obtained and the degree of specificity of that information. Teachers who understand observational techniques and other methods of collecting data on teaching have more flexibility in designing original tools or in adapting existing tools to their own purposes.

This chapter is designed to assist teachers in choosing an observational tool and technique appropriate for the part of the teaching/learning process they want to view in more detail. The chapter begins with a presentation of several established instruments that look at common areas of investigation in the teaching/learning process and ends with a discussion of observational methods and techniques for the analysis of instruction.

◆ OBSERVATIONAL TOOLS

Many different observational tools already exist that have been used to collect information on different aspects of the teaching/learning process. Many of these tools were designed for research purposes and are not practical for the teacher whose purpose is self-improvement. Seven tools are presented in this section. They were selected to represent both important dimensions of the teaching/learning process and different observational methods. Category definitions are provided for the tools, but in some cases the definitions are not sufficient to fully communicate the intent of that category. Researchers use manuals that give many examples of each category. However, even without more elaborate examples, teachers will be able to use most of these systems with some degree of reliability. It is suggested that teachers keep a **decision log** of examples they have difficulty with as they are learning to use a system. This will enable teachers to set ground rules for using the instrument in their particular situations.

Student Motor Activity: ALT-PE

Academic Learning Time-Physical Education (ALT-PE) was developed by Siedentop and the graduate students at The Ohio State University (Metzler, 1979; Siedentop et al, 1979; Siedentop et al, 1982). The instrument was designed to measure the portion of time in a lesson that a student is involved in motor activity at an appropriate success rate. The total instrument is capable of describing both the context of physical education lessons in which the total class is involved and the type of motor involvement of a selected sample of students. Several different types of observational methods can be used with ALT-PE. The small portion of the full instrument presented here provides information on motor activity only. The reader is encouraged to consult the ALT-PE manual for the more complete instrument and other types of methods.

Purpose. The purpose of this instrument is to describe the amount of time students are engaged in motor activity at an appropriate level of difficulty. See Box 14-1 (p. 288) for category definitions.

Recording procedures. Four different observational methods are available to collect ALT-PE data on the categories just listed. These procedures follow:

BOX 14-1

Category Definitions for Student Motor Activity: ALT-PE

Motor appropriate (MA). The student is engaged in a subject matter–oriented motor activity in such a way as to produce a high degree of success.

Motor inappropriate (MI). The student is engaged in a subject matter–oriented motor activity, but the activity or task is either too difficult for the individual's capabilities or so easy that practicing it could not contribute to lesson goals.

Motor supporting (MS). The student is engaged in subject matter–oriented motor activity with the purpose of assisting others to learn or perform the activity (e.g., spotting, holding equipment, sending balls to others).

Not motor engaged (NM). The student is not involved in subject matter–oriented motor activity. This category can be further described in terms of what learners are doing when they are not motor engaged as follows:

> **Interim (I).** The student is involved with a noninstructional aspect of the ongoing activity.
>
> **Waiting (W).** The student has completed a task or motor response and is waiting for the next opportunity to respond.
>
> **Off-Task (OF).** The students are not doing what they are supposed to be doing at the time.
>
> **On-Task (OT).** The student is appropriately engaged but not in a subject matter–related motor response.
>
> **Cognitive (C).** The student is appropriately involved in a cognitive activity.

Interval recording. Short intervals (usually 6 seconds) of alternating observing and recording can be used for one student or an alternating sample of students (typically three students are used). Usually a prerecorded audiotape is employed to signal the beginning and end of an "observe 6 seconds and then record 6 seconds" format. During the observing interval, the observer watches one student. At the recording interval, the observer decides whether the student is engaged in motor activity. If the student is engaged in motor activity, the observer classifies that engagement as being either MA, MI, or MS. If the student is not engaged in motor activity, the observer continues to define the behavior in terms of the categories I, W, OF, ON, or C. Data can be presented as a percentage of each category. A typical recording sheet for this instrument is described in Figure 14-1. Only the learner involvement categories are used. Context level is not used.

ALTERNATIVE RECORDING PROCEDURES:

Group time sampling. Every 2 minutes the observer scans the group (15 seconds) and counts the number of students engaged at an appropriate level of motor activity (MA). Data can be presented as an average for the class.

Duration recording. The observer monitors a single student using a time line to categorize into the four categories what the student is doing the entire period. Another alternative is to measure just MA time—starting a stopwatch when the student is appropriately engaged and stopping the watch when the engagement stops. Total MA time for the lesson can be presented as a percentage of total lesson time.

Event recording. The observer counts the number of practice trials at an appropriate level of difficulty (where discrete trials are inherent in the activity). Data are presented as MA trials per minute or per larger unit of time.

Figure 14-1 describes a typical recording sheet for collecting ALT-PE data on engagement level only using the interval method of recording. In summarizing the data, the teacher counts the number of intervals scored in each category for each student observed. The critical variable here is the number of intervals the student is engaged at a motor-appropriate level of involvement. To make this meaningful, the number of motor-appropriate intervals (MA) is expressed as a percentage of the total number of intervals recorded for a student.

Interpreting data. The average ALT-PE motor-appropriate categories for physical education classes lie somewhere between 15% and 25% (Parker, 1989). This is not particularly good. If motor-appropriate time is highly related to learning,

ALT-PE coding sheet

	1	2	3	4	5	6	7	8	9	10	11	12	13	14	15	16	17	18	19	20	21	22	23	24	25	26
C																										
LI	W	W	C	C	ON	ON	ON	OF	MA	MA	MA	MA	MA	C	C	MI	MI	MI	MI	OF	I	I	W	C	C	C

S #1

	1	2	3	4	5	6	7	8	9	10	11	12	13	14	15	16	17	18	19	20	21	22	23	24	25	26
C																										
LI	W	W	C	OF	OF	OF	OF	OF	ON	ON	MA	MA	MA	C	C	C	MA	MA	MA	MA	I	I	W	C	OF	C

S #2

	1	2	3	4	5	6	7	8	9	10	11	12	13	14	15	16	17	18	19	20	21	22	23	24	25	26
C																										
LI	W	W	C	OF	ON	ON	ON	ON	ON	MI	MI	MI	MI	C	C	MI	MI	MI	MI	MI	I	I	W	C	OF	C

S #3

	1	2	3	4	5	6	7	8	9	10	11	12	13	14	15	16	17	18	19	20	21	22	23	24	25	26
C																										
LI	MA	MA	MA	MA	MA	MS	MS	MS	I	I	W	C	C	OF	OF	MA	MA	MA	MA	MA	MC	I	W	W	C	C

S #1

	1	2	3	4	5	6	7	8	9	10	11	12	13	14	15	16	17	18	19	20	21	22	23	24	25	26
C																										
LI	MA	MA	MI	MI	MI	MS	MI	MS	I	I	W	C	C	C	C	MA	MA	MA	MA	MA	MA	I	W	W	C	C

S #2

	1	2	3	4	5	6	7	8	9	10	11	12	13	14	15	16	17	18	19	20	21	22	23	24	25	26
C																										
LI	MI	MI	MI	MI	MI	MI	MS	MI	I	W	W	C	C	C	C	MA	MA	MA	MA	MA	MC	I	W	W	C	C

S #3

Context level

General content	SM knowledge	SM motor
Transition (T)	Technique (TN)	Skill practice (P)
Management (M)	Strategy (ST)	Scrimmage/routine (S)
Break (B)	Rules (R)	Game (G)
Warm up (WU)	Social behavior (SB)	Fitness (F)
	Background (BK)	

Learner involvement level

Not motor engaged	Motor engaged
Interim (I)	Motor appropriate (MA)
Waiting (W)	Motor inappropriate (MI)
Off-task (OF)	Supporting (MS)
On-task (ON)	
Cognitive (C)	

FIGURE 14-1
Example of ALT-PE data using interval recording.

teachers should strive for the highest possible level of motor-appropriate time.

ALT-PE is considered by some authors to be the single best predictor of teacher effectiveness in physical education (Siedentop et al, 1979). A study done by Silverman (1991) showed a relationship between high levels of student engagement and student learning. It is reasonable to assume that the student who is engaged more at an appropriate level of difficulty in motor activity will learn more. Although there are problems with the application of this idea to different physical education settings, it has a great deal of logical support and is, at minimum, a necessary but not a sufficient condition for learning.

Student Use of Time

Purpose. The purpose of this instrument is to describe how students spend their time. See Box 14-2 for category definitions.

Recording procedures. Several alternatives are available for recording how students spend their time. Duration recording can be used by employing a time line or by placing real time into the appropriate categories. When 51% of the students change what they are doing, the observer notes the time and

---

BOX 14-2

Category Definitions for Student Use of Time

Management organization (MO). Students are engaged through activity or listening with organizational arrangements for people, time, equipment, or space that support lesson content.

Management conduct (MC). Students are engaged through activity or listening with functions that direct or maintain the expectations for conduct.

Activity (A). Students are motorically engaged in the lesson content.

Instruction (I). Students are receiving information on the lesson content.

Off task (OT). Students are not engaged as directed by the teacher.

---

marks a recording sheet. The most common method of using this type of instrument is to use interval recording (note on the recording sheet what is happening every 10 seconds). In either case the total group or a single student can be observed. Data can be analyzed in terms of the percentage of total time devoted to each of the categories.

The simplest form of this instrument is to select three categories of engagement (instruction [I]; activity [A]; and management [M]) and to code one of the three every 10 seconds on a time line. If the category changes within the 10-second interval, the observer must make a judgment regarding which category best describes that 10-second interval. An example recording sheet is provided in Figure 14-2.

Interpreting data. Although activity time is not as specific a measure of appropriate motor-engaged time as ALT-PE, activity time will give the teacher a measure of a student's opportunity to practice or to learn motor activity. High levels of activity time are desirable, and the level should probably never fall below 50% of total time in a physical education class. The use of the other categories will give the teacher an indication of where the time that decreases activity time is being spent. These other areas then can be decreased if needed. Large blocks of management or instructional time consistently over a period of lessons should be avoided.

Content Development: OSCD-PE

The Observation System for Content Development-Physical Education (OSCD-PE) (Rink, 1979) was developed to look at the way teachers develop the content of their lessons. It is a sophisticated interaction analysis tool with many facets. One of the pieces of information it collects is a description of task sequences in terms of their development focus in a lesson. That small part of the instrument is included here.

Purpose. The purpose of this instrument is to describe the way content is developed in a physical education lesson in terms of the focus of the motor task. See Box 14-3 for category definitions.

CODING DIRECTIONS: The observer codes either M (management), A (activity), or I (instruction) directly on the time line to indicate what the student is doing. Each block represents 1 minute divided into six 10-second units. It is necessary to indicate a change only from one category to another category.

Total number of 10-second intervals _108_
Total M _24_ % M _22_
Total A _63_ % A _58_
Total I _21_ % I _19_

FIGURE 14-2
Duration recording sheet (student time expenditure).

Recording procedures. Several observational methods are available as alternatives for describing content development through the task focus. The first and easiest to use is event recording. When the teacher gives a task, the observer determines the type of task and places a point on the polygraph in sequence (Figure 14-3, p. 292). If information on how long students work with a task focus is desired, duration recording can be used to record how much time is spent on each task. The observer starts a stopwatch when a task begins and stops the watch when a task ends. This information can be recorded next to the designated category of the task.

BOX 14-3

Category Definitions for Content Development: OSCD-PE

Refining task. A refining task seeks to qualitatively improve the way in which students are performing a previous task (e.g., "This time work on getting your toes pointed").

Extending task. An extending task seeks a variety of responses or adds complexity or difficulty to a previous task.

Applying task. An applying task asks students to use their motor skill in an applied or competitive setting (e.g., "How many times can you toss the ball up into the air without losing control of it?" or "Today we are going to play softball").

Informing task. An informing task states or presents a motor task that is not an extending, refining, or applying task. This task is usually the first task and merely describes what the students are to do.

Repeat Task. A repeat task is the same task as the previous task with no changes.

Interpreting data. Some teachers are able to develop content with students by refining or changing the task on an individual basis. In large classes characteristic of most physical education settings, this is not possible and the focus given tasks presented to the entire class becomes very important.

There is no ideal sequence in which tasks should be presented. However, if teacher lessons continuously lack refining and extending tasks or if they move quickly from the informing task directly to the applying task, the appropriateness of the way the content is developed is questionable. In the example lesson in Figure 14-3 you will notice that the sequence of tasks the teacher developed used refining, extending, and applying tasks. In this particular lesson there are more refining tasks, but all lessons do not have to have such a high percentage of refining tasks.

Teacher Feedback

Teacher feedback has been the focus of many different observational tools. Fishman and Tobey

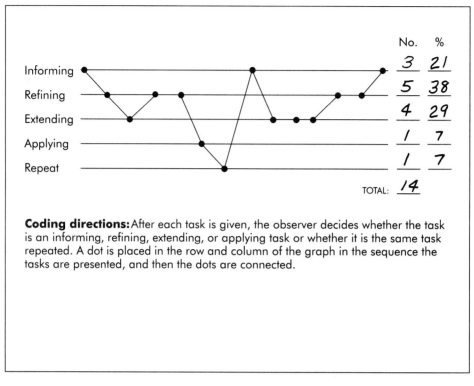

FIGURE 14-3
Task focus recording sheet (content development).

(1978) developed an instrument that describes in relative detail six different dimensions of augmented feedback in physical education lessons. Systems designed for research purposes by students at The Ohio State University used simple event recording to classify feedback into different categories (Dodds, 1973; Stewart, 1983). The tool presented here is a modification of these event-recording systems. The reader should consult Chapter 8 for other possible dimensions of feedback that may need to be included.

Purpose. The purpose of the teacher feedback instrument is to describe the kind and frequency of feedback given to students in a physical education lesson. See Box 14-4 for category definitions.

Recording procedures. Event recording is the best method of collecting this information. A sug-

gested recording sheet is provided in Figure 14-4 (p. 294). In this recording sheet, only the type of feedback, target of feedback, and the positive/negative aspects of feedback are recorded. If other aspects of feedback just described are to be included, they must be added to the recording sheet. Each time a feedback statement is given, the observer puts a slash in the appropriate category. Data are analyzed in terms of the amount of feedback given in a particular lesson (divide the number of feedback statements by the number of minutes to produce a rate per minute [RPM] score). Data are also analyzed in terms of a percentage of feedback for each of the concepts of the instrument (e.g., for the target of feedback the percentage of feedback statements falling into individual, group, and class).

Interpreting data. For the most part, it is desirable to have feedback that is more specific than gen-

---

BOX 14-4

Category Definitions for Teacher Feedback

Target

Class. Feedback directed to the whole class.
Group. Feedback directed to more than two students.
Individual. Feedback directed to one or two students.

Type

Evaluative. Feedback that makes a judgment about past performance.
Corrective. Feedback that suggests how future performance can be improved.

Level of specificity

General. Feedback that is evaluative but does not include information on why the judgment was made (e.g., "Good job").
Specific. Feedback that is evaluative and includes information on why the evaluation was made.

Positive or negative

Positive. Feedback that is expressed positively in terms of what the student did right or should do correctly.

Negative. Feedback that is expressed negatively in terms of what the student did or should do (e.g., "Don't step into the swing" or "That's not quite right").

Context of feedback

Skill. Feedback is related to the substantive part of the lesson.
Behavior. Feedback is related to management (either organization or conduct of the students.

Congruency

Congruent. Feedback is directly related to the focus the teacher has given a task (e.g., the teacher has asked the students to get under the ball and the feedback statement is "Tommy, you are really getting under the ball").
Incongruent. The feedback statement is not related to the specific focus the teacher has given for a task, no matter how appropriate that feedback statement may be (e.g., the teacher task is to get under the ball; the teacher feedback is "Try to get your elbows out to receive the ball").

---

eral; more positive than negative; more corrective than evaluative; and more congruent than incongruent. The results of research on the specific role of feedback in learning motor skills in a group instructional setting have not been consistent. This is probably because it is very difficult to describe the appropriateness and accuracy of feedback for different learners in different contexts. Value judgments that are placed on the desirability of feedback stem largely from data generalized from other teaching settings and from theoretic support. Feedback also plays a major role in monitoring student performance and maintaining student focus.

Data must be interpreted in context. For example, it may be inappropriate to give much individual feedback in a creative dance lesson. It may be very appropriate to give much individual feedback in a lesson using manipulative skills in which the students are reviewing or practicing what they have already learned and the teacher is free to work with

individuals. Collecting data on teacher feedback can describe what the teachers are doing. The teachers must interpret the appropriateness of what they are doing for the lesson they have taught.

Student Conduct

Student conduct is sometimes referred to as *student behavior* (behavior meaning the appropriateness of the way students conduct themselves in a setting). This instrument is another modification of information available from OSCD-PE (Rink, 1979). It is based on the assumption that it is important to know how teachers develop and maintain appropriate behavior in their classes.

Purpose.   The purpose of this instrument is to describe how teachers structure, direct, and reinforce their expectations for the appropriate behavior of students. See Box 14-5 (p. 295) for category definitions.

FIGURE 14-4
Teacher feedback coding sheet.

Recording procedures. The observer records three dimensions of the manner in which the teacher deals with the conduct of students: the type of language communication; when the teacher's behavior occurred; and whether the behavior is positive or negative. Event recording is the most useful observational method for this system. Every time a conduct-related teacher behavior occurs, it is classified into one of the boxes illustrated in Figure 14-5 (p. 296). To do this, the observer must first decide whether the behavior is **structuring** (making clear expectations), **soliciting** (requesting an immediate response), or **appraising** (sharing a value judgment about behavior with students in relation to student conduct). If the teacher behavior occurred before any student conduct behaviors, it is considered **preventive**. If it occurred after student conduct problems, it is considered **corrective**. The third decision is to decide whether the behavior is expressed positively in terms of what students should do or did, or negatively, in terms of what students should not do or did. A recording procedure that uses codes for each of these categories and maintains the sequence of events may be useful also.

BOX 14-5

Category Definitions for Student Conduct

Type of communication

Structuring. Structuring is any teacher verbal behavior (except an appraisal) that communicates information on the manner in which students are to conduct themselves but does not expect an immediate response (e.g., "We're going to *walk* over to get our equipment today").

Soliciting. Soliciting is any teacher verbal or nonverbal behavior that communicates information on the manner in which students are to conduct themselves and expects an immediate response (e.g., "Stop fighting" or "Put the balls *inside* the hoop"). Soliciting is a teacher reaction to student behavior. A negative solicitation for students to stop what they are doing is called a *desist* behavior (Kounin, 1977).

Appraising. Appraising is any teacher verbal or nonverbal behavior that makes a judgment about the way students have conducted or are conducting themselves (e.g., "I like the way Sally is sitting quietly waiting to begin").

When the behavior occurred

Preventive. Preventive behaviors are any structuring, soliciting, or appraising conduct comments by the teacher that occur *before* there is evidence of a need for that behavior (e.g., "Before you start, remember you are working quietly and in your own space").

Corrective. Corrective behaviors are any structuring, soliciting, or appraising conduct comments by the teacher that occur after there is evidence of a need for that behavior (e.g., "Don't pick at the foam of the balls").

Positive/Negative

Positive. Positive behaviors are any structuring, soliciting, or appraising behaviors by the teacher that are not put in a negative framework (e.g., "Tommy, get back in line").

Negative. Negative behaviors are any structuring, soliciting, or appraising behaviors by the teacher that are explicitly put in a negative framework (e.g., "Don't get out of line" or "You're behaving like 2-year-olds").

Interpreting data. Many times students in physical education classes learn how to behave by making mistakes and being corrected on these mistakes. In Figure 14-5, the teacher plays primarily a corrective role in handling student conduct. A better way for teachers to communicate their expectations for behavior is to make those expectations clear ahead of time (structuring and preventive) and positively. Teachers often omit structuring behavior when handling the conduct of students—whether before there is a problem or after there is a problem.

Soliciting directives to students on conduct (most often used to desist behavior) work when it not overused and abused. Directives are abused when students are not told in advance what the expectations for behavior are and when the same behavior is continuously the content of a directive (i.e., when the

teacher nags). Positive directives are usually more appropriate than negatively stated ones and achieve the same purpose.

Appraising behaviors, frequently used with young children to reinforce expectations, are effective. Chapter 3 discusses their use and value from a research perspective. Teachers may also want to include in their description whether the behavior is directed to the class or to individuals. Most teachers structure behavior through the class and deal with problems individually.

In the example data in Figure 14-5 the teacher spent much time dealing with behavior problems—primarily telling students not to do something. Unfortunately, most of the time was spent trying to correct problems after they became problems, and little time was spent trying to prevent problems by clarifying expectations for behavior ahead of time.

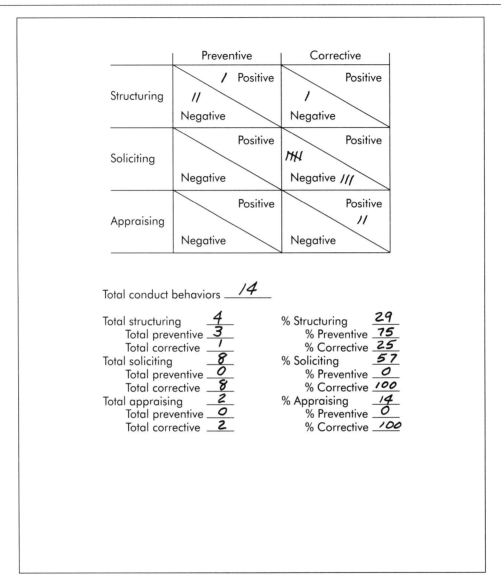

FIGURE 14-5
Student conduct recording sheet.

Qualitative Measures of Teaching Performance Scale (QMTPS)

Purpose of the instrument.   The Qualitative Measures of Teaching Performance Scale (QMTPS) (Rink and Werner, 1989) was designed to collect data on several instructional variables at the same time. The major constructs of the instrument are the following:

- Type of task (informing, refining, extending, repeating, applying)
- Task presentation (clarity, demonstration, appropriate number of cues, accuracy of cues, qualitative cues)
- Student responses appropriate to task focus
- Teacher specific congruent feedback

See Box 14-6 for category definitions.

BOX 14-6

Category Definitions for the Qualitative Measures of Teaching Performance Scale

Type of Task

Informing. A task that names, defines, or describes a skill or movement concept with no focus other than just to do it. It usually is the first task in a sequence of tasks.

Refining. A task that qualitatively seeks to improve motor performance. Usually this type of task focuses on improving the mechanics of a skill or tactical/strategic aspects of play.

Extending. A task that quantitatively changes the original task content by manipulating the level of difficulty or complexity of conditions under which the task is performed or that seeks a variety of responses.

Repeating. A simple repetition of the previous task with no changes.

Applying. A task that focuses the purpose of student performance outside the movement itself. It is usually competitive or self-testing in nature.

Task Presentation

Clarity. Teacher's verbal explanation or directions communicate a clear idea of what to do and how to do it. This judgement is confirmed on the basis of student movement responses to the presentation and is relative to the situation.

Yes - Students proceed to work in a focused way on exactly what the teacher asked them to do.

No - Students exhibited confusion, questions, off-task behavior, or lack of intent to deal with the specifics of the task.

Demonstration. Modeling desired performance executed by teacher, student(s), and/or visual aids.

Yes - Full model of the desired performance.

Partial - Incomplete model of task performance exhibiting only a portion of the desired movement.

No - No attempt to model the movement task.

Appropriate number of cues. The degree to which the teacher presents sufficient information about the movement task without overloading the learner.

Appropriate - Three or fewer new learning cues related to the performance of the movement.

Inappropriate - Either more than three or no new learning cues related to the movement.

None given - No attempt at providing learning cues was made.

Student responses appropriate to the task focus. The degree to which student responses reflect the intent to perform the task as stated by the teacher.

All - No more than two students exhibited inappropriate responses.

Partial - Three or more students exhibited inappropriate responses.

None - No students exhibited appropriate behavior.

Teacher specific congruent feedback. The degree to which teacher feedback during activity is congruent with (matched to) the focus of the task.

Yes - More than two incidences of congruent feedback.

Partial - One or two incidences of congruent feedback.

No - No congruent feedback was given.

Recording procedures. QMTPS can be used live, but it is easier to do the observation with this instrument if videotape is used. A typical recording sheet for this instrument is described in Figure 14-6 (p. 298). The observer stops the tape after each movement task is given by the teacher. The observer then makes a decision regarding the type of task and all of the task presentation categories. The tape is continued and then stopped again after the teacher indicates that time for practice of that task is over. At this time the observer codes the student responses and feedback categories of the instrument.

Interpreting the data. To analyze QMTPS data, the observer adds the number of tasks. Each dimension of the instrument (e.g., type of task, clarity, demonstration) is then analyzed in terms of the percentage of the total tasks that are categorized a particular way. In the data expressed in Figure 14-6, for instance, only 2 of the 12 tasks are presented with a demonstration (17%). In most of the constructs of the instrument, category number one is a more desirable category. A higher percentage of tasks in this category should reflect a more skilled teacher. As in all instruments, however, the data must be inter-

Qualitative measures of teaching performance scale

Name of teacher __M. Martins__   Name of coder __C. Fry__

Focus of lesson __Throwing - 2__   Lesson number __2__

Number	Type of task	Clarity	Demonstration	Number of cues	Accuracy of information	Qualitative information	Student response appropriate to the focus	Specific congruent feedback
								Presentation of task
1	I	1	1	1	1	2	2	2
2	E	1	2	2	1	2	1	3
3	R	2	2	1	1	1	3	2
4	R	2	3	3	3	2	3	1
5	E	1	3	3	3	2	3	2
6	E	1	1	2	1	2	3	1
7	R	2	2	2	1	1	3	2
8	RE	1	3	1	2	2	3	2
9	A	2	3	2	2	2	3	2
10	RE	1	3	1	1	2	3	2
11	R	1	3	3	3	1	3	2
12	E	1	2	3	3	2	3	2
13	R	1	3	3	3	2	3	1
14	A	1	3	3	3	2	3	1
15	A	1	3	3	3	2	3	1
Totals		1.11 / 2.4	1.2 / 2.4 / 3.9	1.4 / 2.4 / 3.7	1.6 / 2.2 / 3.7	1.3 / 2.12	2.1 / 3.13	1.5 / 2.9
Percent for each category		1.73 / 2.27 / 3.60	1.27 / 2.27 / 3.47	1.40 / 2.13 / 3.47		1.20 / 2.80	1.7 / 2.7 / 3.86	3.1 / 1.33 / 2.66
Percent most desirable		73%	27%	40%		26%	7%	33%

Type of task
 I-Informing
 R-Refine-quality
 E-Extend-variety
 Re-Repeat-repeat same task
 A-Apply-self testing

Clarity
 1-Yes
 2-No

Demonstration
 1-Full
 2-Partial
 3-None

Number of cues
 1-Appropriate
 2-Inappropriate
 3-None given

Accuracy of information
 1-Accurate
 2-Inaccurate
 3-None given

Qualitative information
 1-Yes
 2-No

Student responses
 1-All
 2-Partial
 3-None

Specific congruent feedback
 1-Yes
 2-Partial
 3-No

FIGURE 14-6

Qualitative measure of teaching performance scale.

preted in the context of the lesson.

It is also possible to calculate a total QMTPS score by adding the percentage score for the most desirable categories for each concept and dividing by the number of concepts. We have found in our work with teachers that if the total QMTPS score falls below 50%, a teacher usually has instructional communication problems that need to be addressed. It is not possible, or perhaps even appropriate, for teachers to always score in the most desirable category every time they present information to learners. Teachers should, however, try to attend to these communication indicators in their teaching.

Teacher Movement

Purpose of the instrument. The purpose of this instrument is to determine teacher movement throughout the class. Teachers who move to different parts of the gymnasium or play space during a class can better monitor and relate to all students than teachers who tend to stay in one area or move to only selected areas of the play space.

Coding procedures. There are many ways that information can be recorded on where a teacher moves during a lesson. One of the most useful is described in Figure 14-7. To use this recording sheet the observer starts with the box in the top left corner that represents the play space. If the play space in use is shaped differently, it would be appropriate to draw different boxes. Each of these boxes represent 5 minutes of time. The observer merely draws a connecting line to where the teacher moves in the box as illustrated.

Interpreting the data. Although it is sometimes appropriate for a teacher to spend a longer amount of time in one area than another, the overall pattern of the teacher's movement throughout a play

Observation of teacher movement

Teacher _F. Razor_   Date _4/21_

Lesson content _dance_   Observer _Jackie_

Grade level _7_

Coding direction: Each box represents 5 minutes of class time. Draw a continuous line indicating the teacher's movement through the area for each 5-minute time interval. Analyze each of the 5-minute time segments to assure that the teacher is getting to all of the areas of the facility where the students are working.

FIGURE 14-7
Observation of teacher movement.

area should reflect an attempt to move to all areas of the play space. Students soon learn where they can go to "hide" should they want to if teachers consistently fail to get to particular areas of the play space.

◆ TECHNIQUES AND METHODS OF OBSERVATION

Different types of observational techniques and methods will give the observer different types of information. Observers can sit down with a blank sheet of paper and record what is interesting to them. They can decide to look for a specific behavior or set of behaviors and either count the number of times a behavior occurs or merely record that a behavior (e.g., feedback) did occur. They can use a stopwatch to record how long a particular instructional characteristic (e.g., activity time) occurred. Observers can also categorize behaviors (e.g., types of feedback), relate one behavior to another (e.g., teacher feedback to student response), or use a time-sampling technique to record only at particular intervals or times. These are all different methods and techniques available to the teacher for recording observational data on teaching.

Each observational method and technique has both advantages and disadvantages and is useful for different purposes. The methods and techniques vary in their practicality and in the ease with which both valid and reliable data can be obtained. There is no one best method of recording observational data.

Intuitive Observation

An intuitive method of observation is not a systematic method. The observer does not go into an observation with the intent to look at anything specific or to record what is seen in any formal sense. An observer using an intuitive method of observation makes conclusions without collecting specific information. Most teaching is observed in this way.

Use. Observers who use an intuitive method of observation rely on their own judgment of what is seen to draw conclusions about what has occurred and the value of what has occurred. A supervisor who jots down notes with comments such as "orga-

nized well" or "needs to circulate more among the students" or "task presentation unclear" is using an intuitive method of observation. Figure 14-8 is an example of an observational record done on an intuitive observation. This information is usually shared with a teacher in verbal or written form.

Strengths and weaknesses. Because intuitive observations are not done systematically, the probability of arriving at invalid and unreliable conclusions is very high. The more experienced the observer, the less probability this will occur, but even two experienced observers will rarely come to the same conclusion or select the same behaviors to look at in more detail.

The strength of intuitive observation is that this method can begin to isolate glaring problems in the process and is therefore useful when more specific events have not been identified as being important to look at. The observer is free to consider the whole range of instructional events. Even when more specific tools are used, much insight into the instructional process is obtained by observers who are free to view all instructional events in the context in which they occur and who do not go into an observation with tunnel vision.

Intuitive observation requires no formal training in a specific tool or data analysis. This makes it very practical and appealing. However, because data are not collected in any systematic way, recording the progress of the teacher over time is difficult. For example, if an observer notes that the teacher "does not give much specific feedback," it is difficult to determine whether improvement occurs in the next observation because insufficient information was collected.

Application. Intuitive observation is most useful when specific events or behaviors have not been determined as being important to look at. Many teachers who have not recorded or listened to their teaching should initially just listen or view their teaching without looking for specific things. They can then take notes on what they want to view more specifically with a more systematic tool.

Intuitive observation is also useful for generating

Teacher _Sally Jones_   Lesson content _Tossing and catching_

Class and grade level _3rd Mrs. Steele_   Date _Nov. 3_

Observer _Mr. Fields_

Teacher strengths

- Delivers tasks clearly
- Tasks are appropriate for group
- Equipment arrangements planned for

Teacher weaknesses

- Doesn't wait for student attention before speaking
- Lets tasks deteriorate into unproductive behavior before refocusing
- Little specific feedback

FIGURE 14-8

Intuitive observation recording sheet.

hypotheses. Teachers who have identified global problems in their teaching (e.g., off-task behavior) may want to view their teaching more globally at first to begin to determine possible causes. Those hypotheses can then be tested with more specific observations using a systematic tool.

Anecdotal Records

The observer doing an anecdotal record establishes broad categories of concern and then takes notes on everything that happens related to those categories. Notes are usually kept in the form of a log into which *nonevaluative* statements are made describing what is occurring.

Use. The anecdotal record provides an actual description of events. In the teaching/learning process the anecdotal record can be used to describe what teachers do, what students do, or the relationship between what teachers do and students do. Figure 14-9 is an example of an observation that focuses on the interaction between the teacher and the individual student. It is important in doing an anecdotal record to record events objectively without evaluating whether what occurred was good or bad. Judgments about events are made only after the anecdotal record is complete.

Strengths and weaknesses. The anecdotal record is very useful for collecting a great deal of valid and reliable data on events in the teaching/learning process. Because data are not organized into preconceived categories or lists of occurrences, the data represent what actually happened and can be analyzed from different perspectives. This eliminates the danger of important context being lost in the recording procedures.

Anecdotal records are not highly systematic. There is the danger of different observers recording different information on an occurrence. However, more highly trained observers learn to record objectively and in great detail. Thus the method can be a reliable and valid way to collect information.

The major disadvantage of anecdotal records is the amount of information that must be recorded at great length and then analyzed. The usefulness of

anecdotal records is the detail. Sorting out the detail into meaningful information after an observation takes time and sensitivity to that data.

Anecdotal records at first appear to be simple. Learning to observe without bias and without being evaluative, however, is more difficult than most people realize.

Application. Anecdotal records are useful for collecting data before hypothesis generation. This means that teachers can view in detail the behavior of a student, their own behavior in a specific situation, or their interaction with the student to try to generate hypotheses about that behavior. For example, a teacher might ask the following questions:

- "What does the single student experience in my class?"
- "How do my students interact with each other?"
- "How do my students respond to my individual attention?"
- "How do I respond to student inattention? Off-task behavior? Student unskilled responses? Student skilled responses?"

These and other questions might cause teachers to observe their lessons using an anecdotal record. The question would serve as the focus for what is recorded. The observer would record all the behavior of the student to answer the question of what the single student experiences in the class. The observer would record all, or as much as possible, of the interactive behavior of student to student to answer the question of how the students interact with each other.

After the anecdotal record is complete, the teacher looks at and tries to understand what actually happened and possible relationships between what occurred. The teacher can test those relationships with a more specific observational tool or can make a judgment that change is needed, with some insight into what needs changing.

Anecdotal records are useful to teachers when the specific behavior important to a question cannot be anticipated in advance. For instance, teachers could try and predict all the things students could possibly experience in a physical education class and make a list of those behaviors. Teachers could then simply check that list every time a student did something on

Student _Vickie S. Age 12_   Lesson content _Gymnastics_

Teacher _Tim C._   Observer _T. Pine_

Date _3/5_   Time _3rd Period_

Vickie waits for the teacher to begin by sitting attentively. At the start of instruction Vickie turns to a neighbor and comments that she can't wait for class to be over. The teacher continues instruction on the handstand and asks students to get a partner. Vickie slides close to Sharon. The teacher asks partners to find a mat. Vickie and Sharon are the last to get up and find a mat on the outskirts of the play area. They both lie down flat on the mat. The teacher instructs the class to begin. Vickie and Sharon rise slowly. Vickie puts her hands and knees on the mat and stays in that position. The teacher comes over and asks Vickie to see if she can get her legs up. Vickie raises her seat and gets ready to lift one leg. The teacher turns and goes to a new student. Vickie goes back to the hands and knees position and stays there until the next skill is presented.

FIGURE 14-9
Anecdotal record recording sheet.

that list. However, teachers risk not including some important behaviors if they try to anticipate in advance what will occur. The list may not exhaust all possible behaviors. The anecdotal record ensures that this does not occur, since the behaviors are not classified until after they have been recorded. After many anecdotal records on the same question, teachers may then be better prepared to design more specific instruments that cut short recording and analysis time and enable comparison of lessons to be made.

Rating Scales

Of all the observational techniques available to look at teaching, the reader is probably most familiar with the rating scale. The rating scale divides a phenomenon to be observed into either qualitative or quantitative levels (e.g., always, sometimes, never; poor, fair, good, excellent).

Use. Rating scales are used when specific behaviors have been identified as being important to look at and when specific levels of those behaviors can be described. Rating scales attempt to quantify data. This means that they look at the quality of an event and assign it a level or number. Figure 14-10 is an example of a rating scale used to describe skill performance in volleyballl.

Strengths and weaknesses. Rating scales are deceptively simple. They are easy to design but very difficult to learn how to use well enough to collect reliable data. For instance, consider the difficulty of learning how to classify student responses into the levels "highly skilled," "average skilled," and "poor skilled" or classifying teacher cues as "appropriate," "somewhat appropriate," or "not appropriate." To use either of these scales reliably, a great deal of effort must be put into definitions and specific criteria for each level. Observers need much training to learn how to use the system reliably.

The problem with rating scales is that they usually are abused. They are often used without the benefit of careful definitions or adequate training in the use of those definitions. In such cases they are nothing more than subjectively quantified and have little value.

Rating scales are useful for studying qualitative dimensions of behavior that other observational methods do not handle well. If it is used carefully and with attention to reliability, the rating scale can be an extremely useful method.

The teacher who wants to design a rating scale should select the dimension to be studied and the number of levels of that dimension that need to be discriminated. It should be remembered that the more levels there are, the more difficult it is to discriminate those levels reliably. Each level should have carefully designed definitions that clearly delineate one level from another. The rating scale should be practiced in each setting for which it is going to be used and modified where necessary. Use of the tool should be practiced until it can be used reliably.

Application. Rating scales are useful for qualitative dimensions of behavior (i.e., when it is not sufficient just to know whether a behavior occurred or did not occur). Appropriateness of teacher or student behavior, skill levels of students, creativity of response, quantity of response (e.g., number of student practice attempts), or form characteristics of a skill response are all instructional events for which a rating scale could be useful. Rating scales are most useful for discrete, observable behavior. Global evaluations of broad and complex phenomenons are not useful.

The rating scale is useful for monitoring behavior. Averages for each lesson can be determined, and the progress of the teacher or students can be determined over time. Because rating scales are very practical instruments, they have a great deal of appeal to teachers who are attempting to evaluate large numbers of students quickly. Because teachers must observe each student, although for a limited amount of time, rating scales can be a useful tool, particularly for formative evaluation.

Event Recording

Event recording is one of the most-used observational methods in teaching. Event recording determines the occurrence or lack of occurrence of the behavior or event being observed. Observers check when a behavior, such as demonstration, occurs.

Name of student	Forearm pass	Overhand pass	Serve	Game play
D. Dasilva	2	2	3	
K. Kirtes	1	2	2	
L. Moley	2	3	3	
J. Nelson	3	3	3	
V. Niles	1	1	1	
P. Pope	2	2	3	

Forearm pass

1 — Cannot receive a serve and direct it with any accuracy
2 — Receives a serve most of the time and directs accurately
   sometimes
3 — Receives and directs the serve most of the time

Overhead pass

1 — Cannot convert a ball over the net or a forearm pass to an
   overhead pass and direct it with any accuracy
2 — Can convert a ball to a pass and direct it with accuracy some
   of the time
3 — Converts and directs a pass accurately most of the time

Serve

1 — Cannot get the ball over the net
2 — Gets the ball over the net some of the time
3 — Gets the ball over the net most of the time

FIGURE 14-10
Rating scale.

Usually, the frequency of that event is determined by counting the number of times the behavior occurs in a lesson.

Use. Event recording is used when the occurrence or lack of occurrence of a behavior is important to know or when knowledge of frequency of a behavior is important. Behaviors can be important because they positively influence learning (e.g., feedback) or because they negatively influence learning (e.g., criticism or conduct interactions between the teacher and student).

Usually, several behaviors or different dimensions of the same behavior are recorded at one time. Figure 14-11 (p. 306) is an example of an event recording sheet that not only records the occurrence of feedback, but also begins to sort the feedback behavior of the teacher into types of feedback. This

Teacher _H. Shots_   Lesson content _Softball_

Observer _R. O'Hara_   Date _5/2_

Task number

Target of feedback	1	2	3	4	5	6	7	8	9	10	Total	%
Class	✓										____	____
Group											____	____
Individual		✓	✓	✓	✓						____	____
Positive or negative											____	____
Positive	✓			✓							____	____
Negative		✓	✓								____	____
Specificity											____	____
General	✓			✓							____	____
Specific		✓	✓								____	____
Type of feedback											____	____
Evaluative	✓			✓							____	____
Corrective		✓	✓								____	____
Not applicable											____	____
Congruency with cues											____	____
Congruent		✓	✓								____	____
Incongruent											____	____
Not applicable	✓										____	____

Length of lesson in minutes _____

Rate per minute of feedback _____

FIGURE 14-11
Event recording sheet (teacher feedback).

information can then be converted into a total number of behavior occurrences or, if comparisons between lessons with different time allotments are needed, into a rate per minute. Teacher or student behaviors can then be monitored to determine whether they have increased or decreased with each lesson.

The teacher who wants to design a system using event recording must carefully define each behavior being observed and practice using that definition reliably over any contexts in which the system applies.

Strengths and weaknesses. Event recording is systematic and can result in valid and reliable data. The only observer judgment that needs to be made is whether the behavior occurred. This makes event recording very practical to use. The difficulty of obtaining reliable data increases with (1) the number of different behaviors observed at any one time and (2) the amount of observer inference required to make judgments. Teacher demonstration is a fairly easy behavior to discriminate. Student off-task behavior requires more inference. The appropriateness of the teacher's task requires even more inference.

The reliability of event recording can be increased with careful definitions and much practice in discriminating when the behavior occurs and when it does not. The validity of event recording rests with the appropriateness of the definitions used to discriminate the behavior. For instance, if nonverbal behavior is excluded from teacher feedback, the feedback behavior of a teacher who gives a thumbs-up signal to a student is eliminated. Therefore the information on teacher feedback does not reflect the reality of the situation and is less valid to any description of feedback.

Application. Event recording is useful to observe any event or behavior for which quantitative information on an occurrence is useful. If the question "How much?" is asked, event recording is a useful choice of methodology.

Event recording has been used by many developed observational tools for teaching, as were described in the first section of this chapter (teacher feedback, type of task, student conduct). Because event recording does not deal well with context or appropriateness, teachers should use event recording with care. Just knowing that the teacher has a high rate of feedback or uses demonstration frequently may be of little value if the feedback is not appropriate or if the demonstration is not accurate. Likewise, simple event recording does not deal well with relationships between different kinds of behaviors. The sequence of events and the events that preceded or followed a tallied behavior are lost.

Duration Recording

Duration recording is an observational technique that provides information on the use of time. This technique can answer the questions of how time is spent or how much time is used for specific dimensions of the teaching/learning process.

Use. The basic tool in duration recording is a stopwatch. Observers keep track of when an event occurs and when it ends. Time for that event is then summed to get a total for a lesson or unit.

Duration recording has been used successfully to record how students spend their time. Exclusive categories (e.g., listening, waiting, being organized, receiving behavioral instruction, making a skill attempt, playing a game) are part of many tools that have looked at how students spend their time.

Figures 14-12 (p. 308) and 14-13 (p. 309) illustrate two methods of duration recording. The first uses a time line and the other keeps track of actual time spent. When using a time line, the recorder codes on the time line when an event occurs and when it ends. The advantage of the time line is that the relationship between the sequence of events is preserved.

Sometimes the sequence is unimportant, and the teacher may be interested just in how much time is spent doing what. Figure 14-13 illustrates how the teacher can keep track of time spent on different stages of game play in a unit.

Strengths and weaknesses. Duration recording can result in both valid and reliable data with little effort and training. Most events for which time

Coding directions: The observer indicates on the time line (each large block represents a minute) when the student is engaged in the following activities:

	Time	
	Minutes	%
M = Management	3	11
W = Warm-up exercise	4	14
L = Listening	10	36
S = Practice skills	11	39
G = Game play	0	

FIGURE 14-12
Duration recording sheet (time line).

Teacher __T. Mand__   Lesson content __Basketball__

Lesson number __6__   Date __1/3__

Observer __R. M.__

Time spent in stages of game play   **Total time   %**

Stage one _30", 45", 20"_   __95"__   __5__

Stage two _60", 80", 120", 123"_   __383"__   __21__

Stage three   __0__   ____

Stage four _22"_   __1320"__   __73__

Lesson beginning time __10:45__   Total lesson time __1798"__

Lesson end time __11:30__

Coding directions: The observer starts a stopwatch every time the students begin work in one of the four stages of game play. The watch is stopped when work in that stage concludes. The amount of actual time spent at each stage is recorded on the appropriate line. At the conclusion of the lesson, the amount of time spent at each stage is totaled and divided by the total lesson time to get the percentage of time spent at each stage.

FIGURE 14-13
Duration recording sheet (real time).

data are useful are relatively easy to define and to discriminate in an instructional setting. This keeps training time at a minimum.

Duration recording is useful only for large global ideas that occur for long periods of time. If behavior changes quickly, there is little point in trying to record it using duration recording. The more frequent the changes in behavior being recorded, the more difficult it is to get reliability and the less practical duration recording becomes as a technique. For instance, teacher feedback takes, on the average, 5 seconds and would not be a good choice for duration recording.

As with other observational methods for looking at specific behavior, definitions must be established for the occurrence or lack of occurrence of an event when duration recording is used. When looking at broad categories of events, it is sometimes difficult to anticipate all cases of occurrence or lack of occurrence (e.g., how many students have to be active for activity time). Practice using the definitions in a variety of situations will help uncover problem areas and will enable the observer to collect valid and reliable data.

Application. Duration recording is most useful for looking at how students or teachers spend their time. Such questions as how much time a teacher spends observing, giving directions, dealing with problem behavior, or organizing for activity are handled well by duration recording. Questions on student use of time, particularly those behaviors related to actual appropriate practice time, maximum vigorous activity in relation to fitness activities, and other student behaviors are also appropriately handled by duration recording.

Interaction Analysis

Interaction analysis is the most sophisticated observational method discussed thus far. An interaction analysis observational system generally records both teacher and student behavior as it occurs in sequence. Behaviors are usually classified into inclusive and exclusive categories. This means that any behavioral event can be classified into only *one* of the system's major categories. The result is a record of the scope and sequence of events seen through the categories used to describe behavior.

Use. Most instruments in physical education that could be classified as interaction analysis systems have their root in classroom observational tools. Flanders Interaction Analysis System (FIAS) (Flanders, 1960) begot Cheffers Adaptation of Flanders Interaction Analysis System (CAFIAS) (Cheffers, Amidon, and Rodgers, 1974); the Observation System of Instructional Analysis (OSIA) (Hough et al, 1975) begot OSIA-PE (Olson, 1979). OSCD-PE (Rink, 1979) is also an interaction analysis system used for research purposes. The heavy reliance of classroom teaching on the verbal interaction between students and teachers and the relationship between their behaviors led to the popularity of the interaction system. For obvious reasons, most physical education instruments of an interaction type have been adapted to include motor responses or nonverbal components.

Teaching is basically an interactive process. Because interaction systems preserve relationships between behaviors, they more clearly reflect this interactive nature. Most interaction analysis systems have clearly defined categories. Observers make a decision regarding into what category a behavior falls. Most systems record behavior when a change in category is noted or at very small intervals of 3, 5, or 10 seconds when behavior does not change categories. The teacher is usually the source of most behavior categories, but in many systems student behavior as interaction occurs is recorded as well. A recording sheet for OSCD-PE is provided in Figure 14-14 so that you may be familiar with the type of data that is possible using interaction analysis.

What emerges from an interaction analysis observational record is not only the frequency and occurrence of events, but also sequences of behavior patterns. These sequences are called *chains*, or in some cases *episodes*, of behavior.

Strengths and weaknesses. The strengths of interaction analysis systems are their inclusive nature and their preservation of both the scope and sequence of events. Because all behavior is coded in

Page No. _____

I. D. *Jr. High Co-ed tennis*   Date _____   Coder _____

Description of content *forehand/backhand tennis — individual skill*

Arrangement of equipment *1 court, balls and rackets for every student*

C	I	G	I/C
36			
36			
16			
		36	
		36	
		36	
36			
31			
31			
		36	
		36	
15			
31			
31			
36			
36			
		916	
		26	
16			
	31		

C	I	G	I/C
		31	
			40
			41
			12
			12
12			
			(42)
			12
			12
			12
			42
			12
			12
16			
16			
31			
32			
(32D)			
32			
(42)			

C	I	G	I/C
32			
(42)			
12			
			822
42			
42			
32			
16			
			12
			41
			12
			11
			12
			20
			42
16			
			12
36			
			12

(T) teacher   (1) soliciting   (1) informing   (C) class   (51) indirect-overt
(S) student   (2) responding   (2) refining   (I) individual   (52) indirect-covert
(O) other   (3) initiating   (3) extending   (G) group   (60) noncontributing
            (4) appraising   (4) applying   (I/C) individual
                                  (5) conduct   (nonprivate)
                                    (6) organization

FIGURE 14-14
OSCD-PE recording sheet.

some way on the dimensions studied, there is little chance of leaving out large pieces of meaningful data on a facet being described. Because the sequence of events is preserved, the relationship between events can be analyzed (e.g., whether long periods of teacher directions create management problems).

The meaningfulness of the categories themselves to the desired information is the most critical part of this or any tool. It is unlikely that a sophisticated interaction analysis tool that categorizes only teacher questions and student responses will be helpful in settings where little or no teacher verbal questioning occurs. The categories must be relevant to the questions being asked.

The largest weakness of interaction analysis systems is their practicality. It takes a long time to design mutually exclusive and inclusive categories for even the simplest dimension to be studied. Because coding is rapid and inclusive, it takes a long time to learn how to use most interaction analysis systems reliably. OSCD-PE (Rink, 1979), for example, takes 40 hours to learn how to use for research purposes.

Application. Because of their complexity and the amount of time needed to design and to learn how to use interaction analysis systems, most of these systems are not suitable for the teacher whose purpose is self-improvement. The interactive nature of teaching, however, can best be described with interaction analysis tools, and it may be worth the time to learn how to use them. Relationships in physical education that involve teacher behaviors and student responses to that behavior, as well as student behaviors and teacher responses to that behavior, are *very* important relationships. Interaction systems designed so far deal very well with verbal interactions, but few handle student motor responses with sufficient detail to be meaningful. The difficulty of categorizing student movement responses in a way to collect reliable data has inhibited this investigation. This is a significant need in the field if the interactive nature of teaching physical education is to be investigated. Interaction analysis methodology is a strong possibility for uncovering some of these important relationships.

Interval Recording

Interval recording is a technique used for sampling behavior. An observer watches carefully for a set time period and then makes a decision on which category of a predetermined set of categories best describes what was observed. Most interaction analysis systems record continuously in their 5-, 3-, or 1-second intervals. Interval recording systems alternate recording and observing intervals of time. Sometimes the recording interval is the same length as the observing interval, and sometimes it is different. ALT-PE (see pp. 288-289) is an example of an instrument that uses interval recording.

Use. Interval recording can be used when it is not likely that more than one category of behavior will be exhibited in one observation interval. Obviously, the length of the interval is a critical decision when designing an interval recording system. An appropriate interval for what is being looked at ensures that not more than one type of behavior will be categorized in one interval.

In interval recording the observer must be able to keep pace with time. Sometimes stopwatches are used for this purpose, and sometimes a prerecorded cassette tape with signals to record or observe are used when appropriate. Interval recording is useful for determining how teachers and students are spending their time (e.g., what skills students are working on; on-task and off-task behavior of students; what teachers are doing during instruction).

Strengths and weaknesses. Generally, the shorter the interval, the more valid and reliable the data will be, up to a point. Observers are limited in the time it takes them to discriminate and record behavior. There also seems to be a naturally occurring time for most behaviors in a physical education setting. This is about 3 to 5 seconds for the most discriminating systems. If the observer is interested in how much time is being devoted to particular skills in a lesson or parts of a lesson, it is reasonable to assume that a very large interval can be used without sacrificing a great deal of validity.

When observe and record intervals are alternated, the result is a time sample of what actually occurred.

Behaviors that occur during the recording interval obviously go unrecorded. Whether data that reflect the reality of the lesson are obtained depends on what is being looked at. Some time samples are every 5 or 10 minutes. If teacher questioning is being looked at with this time sample, valid data might not be obtained. Before a time sample is used, data should be collected both on entire lessons and on the time sample chosen. If the data collected by the two methods result in the same percentage for each category, the time sample chosen most likely is a valid representation of the lesson.

It is difficult to measure the reliability of interval recording systems that alternate observing and recording intervals without having some way to ensure that all observers are observing and recording at the same time. Observers can sit together and signal each other, or cassette-recorded cues can be used for this purpose. Videotapes with time clocks on them are also useful for this purpose.

Application. Interval recording done with small units of time enables the observer to continuously record behavior. The smaller the time interval and the more discriminating the possible categories into which behavior is classified, the more complete will be the description of what actually happened in any lesson.

Interval recording can be used in much the same way as duration recording when more specific descriptions of how time is spent are needed. What the teacher is doing (e.g., lecturing, organizing, demonstrating, giving feedback, working on conduct, observing, personalizing) can be discriminated at any level of specificity desired. The teacher's position in the gymnasium and nonverbal behavior can also be accurately described using an interval recording system.

When categories of different kinds of teacher or student behavior are important to describe, interval recording is a good choice. The more discriminating the categories, the smaller the interval necessary and the less practical the instrument becomes in terms of the time needed to develop, learn to use, and analyze the data of the instrument. If behavior is recorded sequentially rather than tallied, information on sequence can be obtained.

Time Sampling

Time sampling is another observational technique similar to interval recording. In time sampling the observer at periodic intervals makes a decision on an instructional event. Usually the intervals are longer than interval recording and sometimes as long as 10 or 15 minutes.

Use. Time sampling is used to observe instructional events that do not change quickly. For example, it has been used to spot check the number of students participating in activity at any one time (Dodds, 1973). Every 2 to 3 minutes, the observer counts the number of students not active or not appropriately engaged in activity. Time sampling is also useful for looking at the amount of time spent in different content areas of a lesson or in determining teacher positioning.

Strengths and weaknesses. Time sampling enables the observer to collect useful information in a very short time. Because time sampling uses so little observer time, the observer is free to use other observational methods to look at other instructional events. When definitions are clearly written and appropriate, time sampling can yield highly reliable and valid data.

Time sampling can be used only for behaviors that do not change quickly. For example, it is useless to use time sampling as a method of getting information on teacher feedback. Feedback occurs frequently at certain times in a lesson and not at all at other times. The behavior chosen must overlap the time periods chosen to sample. Again, the smaller the interval of time, the less likely the results are to reflect a sampling error.

Application. Time sampling is a very useful method of observation when the information desired is on instructional events or characteristics that appear distributed through a lesson. Because time sampling requires so little observer time, it is a useful technique for teachers while they are teaching to keep track of what students as a whole are doing, as in the spot check, or what individual students are doing. Content of lessons can also be recorded using time sampling. How much time is actually being spent on different skills or different stages of skill development thus can be determined.

Teachers who want to use time sampling should do the following:

- Determine the instructional event they want information on.
- Decide how they want to discriminate the dimension being studied (e.g., event, category, rating scale).
- Determine the appropriate interval to collect valid data on that dimension.

The appropriate interval can be determined by starting with very small time units and increasing the time unit only to the point where the sample sheet reflects what actually occurred in the lesson.

◆ QUALITATIVE METHODS OF COLLECTING INFORMATION

Over the past decade researchers have turned to qualitative methods of data collection to get information on the teaching/learning process. Qualitative techniques of data collection differ significantly from the tools and techniques thus far described in this chapter. Qualitative techniques are used to answer different kinds of questions. Whereas systematic observation techniques are designed to help answer questions about what has actually occurred in the teaching/learning process from an observer's perspective, qualitative techniques are designed to answer questions regarding the meaning of events to the participants. What teachers are thinking about, how students feel about what they are doing, what students like to do and do not like to do, how participants interact with each other and with different approaches to a lesson or different content are questions that are appropriately answered with qualitative techniques and methods of data collection.

To answer these questions, researchers depend on observation that has its intent to describe what is happening without trying to create categories in advance. Themes and ideas emerge from the data after rich descriptions of what is happening are recorded in a nonevaluative way. Box 14-7 describes

an event recorded descriptively. Qualitative techniques also include extensive interviews with participants about events.

Although qualitative research is not easy to do and a great deal of training and time is needed to gather useful data for the researcher, qualitative techniques are very useful for teachers who want to gain insight into their own teaching and what is going on in their gymnasium that may not be readily apparent.

The Teacher as the Participant Observer

Insightful and reflective teachers are more aware of what is going on in their classes than teachers who are not reflective and do not seek to understand the meaning of what is going on.

Because of their responsibility for the conduct of a class, it is difficult for any teachers involved in instruction to focus on individuals or interactions in an environment for a long enough time to be able to understand their meaning. Watching videotapes of classes can be a great source of information for teachers. Teachers who use videotape on a continuous basis are amazed by all that is going on in their classes that they "missed" while they were teaching the classes.

Many questions are suitable for descriptive observation by the teacher, including the following:

- How do boys and girls interact in my classes?
- Who are the students who seem to be "in charge?" Left out? Nonparticipants?
- How do students of different cultural or racial origins interact with each other?
- How do students respond to different content areas?
- What do I do that affects the motivation levels of my students?
- How do students respond to success or failure?

To gain insight into these kinds of questions, the teacher chooses to focus the observation on one of these broad areas. In viewing the videotape, the teacher then describes in as much detail as possible what was going on in the class. An example of an exert from a descriptive record of a ninth grade class focusing on the interaction of black and white students within one class is presented in Box 14-7.

The teacher who recorded this scene will gain

Excerpt From a Descriptive Record

The teacher called the students to the center of the gymnasium for task instructions after the warm-up. Although students were assigned areas for the warm-up that did not divide the races, students chose to sit next to other students of their own race as they sat down by the teacher. Boys and girls were mixed within the black and white groups. No interaction took place between the races during the teacher's instructions. The teacher asked the students to divide into groups of four students. After several initial groups were formed that were all black and all white, it became evident that two black students and two white students were going to have to work with each other. Disappointment was evident on the faces of all these students. The teacher did not acknowledge the problem, but motioned to the two groups of two to form a group of four. Other groups began their work on the task immediately when they had collected their equipment. The mixed group failed to get their equipment and just stood without acknowledging each other. The teacher motioned to one of the black students to go get the equipment and get started. After the equipment had been obtained, the group's practice was characterized as "going through the motions with little effort."

about something is to *ask* them. Although the interview has been used extensively by researchers to collect information on many different areas, teachers have not recognized the immense value of this technique for helping them to understand the perspective of the student. The interview is a very useful tool to gather data on student perspectives of what is going on in the gymnasium. Student interest, student needs, how students feel about the way a class is conducted, how students feel about other students in a class, what students identify as what they are learning or not learning, what motivates students, where students are in their understandings of important ideas, and why students feel and think the way that they do are some of the questions that can be addressed in the interview.

In a series of interviews with ninth grade students regarding their physical education experiences, a team of researchers learned a great deal, including the following:

- Many girls were afraid of the aggressiveness of boys in coed soccer classes.
- Students enjoyed an 8-week unit in a sport (units in their classes were usually 3 weeks) because they recognized that they learned more.
- Students had a clear idea of where they improved and where they did not improve.
- Attentive and on-task students were tired of having to be in classes with disruptive students.
- The students' enjoyment of their physical education classes was closely related to the friends they had in the class.

Teachers can use this type of information to help make physical education classes more meaningful to students.

Teachers do not have to be researchers to conduct an interview with students. Targeting students and asking them to stay a few minutes before or after class, during lunch breaks, or before or after school is one useful way to get started. It is not necessary for teachers to interview all students. Randomly sampling a class or sampling students who have different characteristics based on skill level, gender, race, age, etc. can help the teacher begin to get the student perspective.

great insight into race relations in her class. If she continues to record what is happening for other aspects of the class and in different classes, she will recognize that there is a problem and that perhaps her own teaching can affect that problem either positively or negatively. Descriptive observation does not put a value judgement on what is happening or tell the teacher what to do. Descriptive analysis can tell a teacher what is happening, and then the teacher can make a judgment about the need for change.

Interview Data

One of the easiest and most direct ways to collect information on what people are thinking and feeling

How to use the interview

Preparing for the interview. You should prepare for the interview by composing the questions you want to ask students. You may want to have some questions that are targeted and very specific to what you want to know that can be easily answered without a great deal of discourse, such as what the student's favorite activities are. You should also have follow-up questions to some of these more specific questions that will give the students an opportunity to tell you why they feel the way that they do or under what circumstances they feel the way they do (e.g., why is this your favorite activity?). The purpose of the interview is to understand not only what students think and feel, but *why* they think and feel this way. Open-ended questions will usually emerge more from more specific questions than they will from the teacher asking students why they like or do not like their physical education classes.

Structuring the interview. Because teachers are authority figures, it is more difficult for them to get students to respond openly to questions. Recognizing this, teachers must first make clear the purpose of the interview and put the students at ease about the way in which the teachers will proceed.

EXAMPLE: "Angie, I have asked some students from your class to come in and talk with me about their experiences in their class. I am doing this because I really want to know how you feel about what is going on. I know sometimes it is not easy to tell anyone how you feel, but I want you to know that it is really important to me to get honest and open answers from you. Nothing you tell me will be told to anyone else. I am going to use this tape recorder because I can't always write down all the information I need when you are talking. The tape will be erased after I listen to it."

Conducting the interview. After the student has been put at ease about what is about to occur, the teacher can begin the interview process in earnest. The following sequence of questions reflects a teacher trying to establish the student perspective of events that have occurred or are occurring in a fitness unit:

- "We have been doing fitness for 2 weeks now. What do you think about what we have been doing?"
- "You have said that you really don't like fitness; can you tell me why?"
- "Why do you not think you are good at it?"
- "Can you describe to me what happened when students laughed at you?"

Several important ideas are imbedded in this short sequence of questions. It is important to recognize that the teacher did not stop at the student's response that he was not good at fitness. Teachers should understand why students feel the way they do if the information is to be valuable in helping the teachers to make experiences more meaningful for students. To do this, the teacher used several techniques that helped draw out more useful responses:

- *Restatement*: Using the student's words and expressions so that the student will expand on the meaning of his or her response.
- *Pausing*: Using silence to allow the student time to collect his or her thoughts.
- *Asking for description*: Asking the student to describe in detail what he or she was thinking, feeling, or doing in an event.
- *Asking for meaning*: Bringing student responses back to what the ideas mean to the student, not just evaluative or factual information.

Recording information. If you want to collect more formal data, you should record verbatim what students say to your questions or use a tape recorder to go back to what students say to pull out important ideas. In most instances teachers do not have time to conduct formal studies of their classes but can accumulate a great deal of useful information by outlining major questions on a sheet of paper and filling in notes as students respond to those questions. These condensed notes are not as useful as verbatim transcripts of what occurred, but they eliminate the enormous amount of time spent transcribing and analyzing interview data that must be done by researchers. Condensed notes should, as much as possible, reflect what the student actually says and should not be translated at this point by the teacher.

Analyzing the interviews. After you have interviewed enough students to obtain a representative sample of your class, you should try to analyze in some useful way all the information the students gave you. Most people find it helpful to collect all the responses to one question and to look for "themes" or ideas that seem to represent the group or subgroups interviewed. When different ideas are expressed, it is useful to look for reasons why some students may feel differently than others.

The Questionnaire

Although not as useful for getting at the meaning of different perspectives, the questionnaire is a useful tool for the teacher to collect data on student attitudes, interests, and feelings about their physical education experiences. The most effective questionnaire with students are short ones. Students tend to be "turned off" by pages of questions, and it is unlikely that they will take the time and effort to answer them with enough thought for them to be useful. If teachers want much information, they will get better results if they do not ask all of their questions in one questionnaire. In fact, the simplest adaptation of the questionnaire is to give students only one question and several minutes to answer it. The following questions are examples of successful single questions used to obtain information on student experiences in a class:

- "What did you most like/dislike about class today?"
- "How could this class have better met your needs?"
- "What did you do today that you really did well?"
- "How did you feel while playing the game?"
- "How could you have been a better participant?"

SUMMARY

1. The same instructional phenomena can be observed with different observational tools and with different observational techniques.

2. An observational tool is like a lens on a camera—it determines what you see, as well as what you do not see.

3. Many different observational tools have been developed to look at teaching. These tools can be used in a flexible way, both in combination with other tools and with different observational methods. The tools described in this chapter allow the teacher to collect information on the following:
   - Student motor activity: ALT-PE
   - Student time expenditure
   - Content development: OSCD-PE
   - Teacher feedback
   - Student conduct
   - Teacher movement and location
   - Combination instrument: QMTPS

4. Intuitive observational procedures are not systematic. Observers make judgments without collecting data.

5. Anecdotal records describe in detail what an observer sees in a nonevaluative way. Data are sorted into meaningful information after they are collected.

6. Rating scales divide a phenomenon being observed into quantitative or qualitative levels. Rating scales that are used in a broad, evaluative way are of little value.

7. Event recording determines the occurrence or lack of occurrence of an event. Usually, the frequency of an event is also determined.

8. Duration recording determines the amount of time devoted to a particular behavior or instructional phenomenon. Duration recording can add up real time for an event or use a time line to determine the sequence and duration of events.

9. Interaction analysis is used to relate one behavior to another. Usually, spontaneous and continuous recording of categories is used. Interaction analysis is inclusive of all behaviors and preserves the scope and sequence of those behaviors.

10. Interval recording is a technique in which the observer watches closely and then records continuously for a specified interval of time.

11. Time sampling is a technique that allows the observer to sample the occurrence of a behavior that does not change quickly by observing at periodic intervals (e.g., every 10 minutes).

12. Qualitative methods, such as participant observation, interviews, and questionnaires, are useful for collecting data on the meaning of events to the participants.

CHECKING YOUR UNDERSTANDING

1. Identify the observational techniques or methods you might use to collect data on the following:
   - The type of feedback a teacher gives
   - The incidence of student off-task behavior
   - Time allotted to activity
   - The amount of lecturing a teacher does
   - What students like/dislike about their physical education class
   - The accuracy of a teacher's demonstration
   - Causes of off-task student behavior
   - The progression the teacher uses in terms of refining, extending, and applying
   - Major problems a teacher might be having in a class
   - Teacher enthusiasm
   - Teacher use of questioning

2. Design an observational system for a student and/or teacher behavior of your choice. Describe the type of observational method you will use, define your categories specifically, and state your coding procedures.

3. Use your observational system on a recorded lesson. Analyze and interpret your data. Evaluate your observational tool.

4. List the advantages and disadvantages of the following techniques and methods of observation:
   - Intuitive observation
   - Anecdotal records
   - Rating scales
   - Event recording
   - Duration recording
   - Interaction analysis
   - Interval recording
   - Time sampling

5. Design a set of interview questions that could be used by a middle school physical education teacher to collect information on student perceptions of their physical education class.

REFERENCES

Cheffers J, Amidon E, Rodgers, K: *Interaction analysis: an application to nonverbal activity*, Minnesota, 1974, Association for Productive Teaching.

Dodds P: *A behavioral competency-based peer assessment model for student teacher supervision in elementary physical education*, unpublished doctoral dissertation, The Ohio State University, 1973.

Fishman SE, Tobey C: Augmented feedback. In Anderson W, Barrette G, editors: What's going on in the gym? *Motor Skills: Theory into Practice*, 1978, Monograph 1.

Flanders N: *Interaction analysis in the classroom: a manual for observers*, Minneapolis, 1960, University of Minnesota Press.

Hough JB et al: *The observation system for instructional analysis* (Draft Papers 1-7). Unpublished manuscript, The Ohio State University, Faculty of Curriculum and Foundations, 1975.

Kounin J:*Discipline and group management in classrooms*, Melbourne, FL, 1977, RE Krieger Publishing.

Metzler M: *The measurement of academic learning time in physical education*, unpublished doctoral dissertation, The Ohio State University, 1979.

Olson J: *Adaptation of the Observational System for Instructional Analysis (OSIA) for use in physical education*, unpublished doctoral dissertation, The Ohio State University, 1979.

Parker M: Academic Learning Time-Physical Education (ALT-PE), 1982 Revision. In Darst P, Zakrajsek D, Mancini V, editors: *Analyzing physical education and sport instruction*, ed 2, Champaign, IL, 1989, Human Kinetics Publishers.

Rink J: *The development of an instrument for the observation of content development in physical education*, unpublished doctoral dissertation, The Ohio State University, 1979.

Rink J, Werner P: Qualitative Measures of Teaching Performance Scale (QMTPS). In Darst P, Zakrajsek D, Mancini, V, editors: *Analyzing physical education and sport instruction*, Champaign, IL, 1989, Human Kinetics Publishers.

Siedentop D, Birdwell D, Metzler M: *A process approach to measuring effectiveness in physical education.* Paper presented at the American Alliance for Health, Physical Education, Recreation, and Dance National Convention, New Orleans, March 1979.

Siedentop D, Tousignant M, Parker M: *Academic learning time-physical education: 1982 revision coding manual*, Columbus, OH, 1982, The Ohio State University, College of Education, School of Health, Physical Education and Recreation.

Silverman S: Research on teaching in physical education: review and commentary, *Res Q Exercise Sport* 62(4):352-364, 1991.

Stewart M: Observational recording record of physical education's teaching behavior (ORRPETB). In Darst P, Mancini V, Zakrajsek D, editors: *Systematic observation instrumentation for physical education*, West Point, NY, 1983, Leisure Press.

SUGGESTED READINGS

Anderson W: *Analysis of teaching physical education*, St. Louis, 1980, Mosby–Year Book.

Bogdan RC, Biklen SK: *Qualitative research for education*, Boston 1982, Allyn & Bacon.

Darst P, Zakrajsek D, Mancini V, editors: *Analyzing physical education and sport instruction*, ed 2, Champaign, Il, 1989, Human Kinetics Publishers.

Metzler M: *Instructional supervision for physical education*, Champaign, IL, 1990, Human Kinetics Publishers.

Spradley JP: *The ethnographic interview*, New York, 1979, Holt, Rinehart & Winston.

Glossary

Academic learning time The time a learner spends with the content at an appropriate level of difficulty.

Achievement theory A theory of motivation that emphasizes the idea that a person's motivation toward a particular goal is a function of the relative strength of both the desire to achieve and the tendency to avoid failure.

Adaptability of skill performance A quality related to the degree to which a performer can adjust movement performance to conditions surrounding performance.

Affective objective An educational outcome specified for the development of feelings, attitudes, values, and/or social skills.

Application A teacher move that communicates a concern for shifting the learner focus from *how to do the movement* to *how to use the movement.*

Associative phase The second phase in learning a motor skill, in which the learner can attend more to the dynamics of a skill.

Attention Alertness in a particular situation to selectively receive and process information.

Attribution theory A theory of motivation that emphasizes the important role of what people attribute success or failure to as a critical aspect of their approach to achievement-oriented tasks.

Authoritative management A perspective on classroom management that has as its goal student self-management, but releases control as students are ready.

Automatic phase The last phase in learning a motor skill, in which processing has been relegated to lower brain functions.

Behaviorism A psychology of human behavior emphasizing environmental contingencies.

Closed skill A motor skill performed in a fixed environment.

Cognitive objective An educational outcome specified for the development of knowledge and thinking-related processes.

Cognitive phase The initial phase of motor learning, in which the learner is engaged primarily in processing how the movement should be performed.

Cognitive theory A holistic perspective on learning, emphasizing problem solving, transfer, and creativity.

Cognitive theory of motivation A theory that emphasizes the subjective experience of the person as an explanation of behavior.

Congruent feedback Feedback on performance that is consistent with the immediate task focus and cues.

Content behaviors Those teaching behaviors that are directly related to the content of the lesson as opposed to the management of the lesson.

Content development The teaching process that takes the learner from one level of performance in a content area to another.

Context The specific situational conditions.

Continuous skill Skill that has arbitrary beginning and ending points, such as dribbling a basketball, swimming, and running.

Cooperative learning A teaching strategy in which learning tasks or projects are assigned to a heterogeneous group of learners to work cooperatively as a team.

Corrective feedback Feedback that gives the learner information on what to do or not to do in a future performance.

Cue for the response A learning cue that gives the learner information on the process/mechanical efficiency of the response.

Cue for use adjustment of the response A learning cue that gives the learner information on how to adjust the movement response to a different condition.

Cue for use of the response A learning cue that gives the learner information on how to use a movement in a particular situation.

Curriculum guide A plan for a program of study.

Developmental analysis An analysis of lesson content divided into a progressive assessment of extension, refinement, and application.

Direct instruction A highly structured, step-by-step, teacher-dominated, active style of teaching.

Discrete skill A skill performed once, with a clear beginning and end.

Distributed practice Practice of the same skill over more than one day.

Educational goals Broadly defined outcomes of an educational program.

Educational objective A specifically identified desired outcome of an educational program usually specified for affective, cognitive, and psychomotor areas of development.

Effective learning environment An environment characterized by high levels of student involvement in what is to be learned.

Effectiveness of skill performance A quality of a movement related to the degree to which the movement accomplishes its intent.

Efficiency of skill performance A quality of a movement related to the degree to which the movement is mechanically correct for a given performer and situation.

Environmental arrangements Organizational arrangements for people, time, space, and equipment.

Environmental design An approach to instruction that attempts to elicit good performance through the design of the task and environmental arrangements for the task.

Evaluative feedback Feedback that makes a judgment about past performance.

Expectancy effects The relationship between teacher expectations for behavior, the characteristics of the student, and the actual achievement of the student.

Feedback Feedback an individual receives as a result of a response.

Formative evaluation Assessment of progress toward a goal.

General feedback Feedback that acknowledges performance but conveys no specific information on performance.

Guided discovery A problem-solving teaching strategy in which the teacher leads students to a correct answer.

High-inference tools Those observation tools that require a great deal of observer judgment to use.

Humanism A psychology of human behavior emphasizing personal control.

Implicit curriculum What students learn or experience in school that is not expressed explicitly.

Indirect instruction A less structured learning environment in which the goals may not be explicit and a portion of instructional functions are transferred to the student.

Indirectly contributing behaviors Teaching behaviors that contribute only indirectly to lesson content by structuring or maintaining the learning environment.

Information processing As a learning theory, an emphasis on how learners select, interpret, use, and store information.

Interactive teaching A teaching strategy in which a teacher move is based on the immediate responses of students.

Intertask development A progression from one skill to another (e.g., volleyball underhand serve to volleyball overhand serve).

Intratask development A progression of experiences that are related to a single movement skill or idea.

Invasion games Those activities and sports that involve changing offensive and defensive roles in shared space according to who has the ball.

Knowledge of performance Information the learner receives on how the skill is being performed (mechanical or feeling of the skill).

Knowledge of results Information the learner receives on the extent to which a movement or skill has accomplished its purpose (e.g., whether the ball went into the basket).

Learning A relatively permanent change in behavior resulting from experience and training interacting with biological processes.

Learning cue A word or phrase that identifies or communicates to a performer the critical features of a movement skill or task.

Learning experience A set of instructional conditions and events that gives structure to an experience and is related to a particular set of teacher objectives.

Limited task A movement task that gives little choice to students in their response.

Low-inference tools Those observation tools that do not require a great deal of observer judgment to use.

Management Instructional behaviors related to structuring, directing, or reinforcing appropriate conduct, as well as arranging the learning environment (time, space, people, equipment).

Massed practice Repetitive practice of the same skill over time.

Motor program A memory representation for a pattern of movement.

Movement concept A label for a group of motor responses or movement-related ideas that share particular characteristics.

Movement task A motor activity assigned to the student that is directly related to the lesson content.

Need theory A theory of motivation that assumes that people act to fulfill needs.

Net games Those activities such as volleyball and tennis that involve alternating discrete skills, usually over a net.

Noncontributing teaching behaviors Teaching behaviors that make no contribution to lesson content.

Open skill A motor skill performed in an environment that is changing during performance.

Order In relation to classroom ecology—high levels of engagement in what the student is supposed to be doing and low levels of engagement in inappropriate behavior.

Organizational arrangements The arrangements teachers make for the organization of people, space, time, and equipment for a particular task or learning experience.

Peer teaching An instructional strategy that transfers the teacher's responsibility for instructional components to students, who function in the role of the teacher.

Perception The interpretation of sensory information at the cortical level.

Postlesson routines All of the routine events that take place in a class after the instructional lesson is concluded.

Prelesson routines All of the routine events that take place in a class before the onset of the instructional lesson.

Presage variables Factors that influence teaching and are related to teacher characteristics.

Procedures The customary method of conducting a class, particularly organizational procedures.

Proximity control Standing near or touching a student who may be disruptive, expressing a concern in the behavior.

Psychomotor objective An educational outcome specified for the development of physical abilities or neuromuscular skills of the learner.

Refinement A teacher move that communicates a concern for the quality of student performance, such as "Work to get your toss a little higher."

Reliability of observational tools The degree to which an observational tool/construct can be used both accurately and consistently to collect data.

Routines Established and customary ways of handling events that occur with great frequency in a class setting.

Rules Designated acceptable or unacceptable behaviors.

Scope and sequence of content What is to be learned and how what is to be learned should be organized for delivery to the learner.

Self-instructional strategies Teaching strategies that are designed to permit the student to function with a degree of independence from the teacher.

Serial skills Several discrete skills put together, such as a handstand into a forward roll.

Set induction That part of the lesson in which the teacher orients the students to what they will be doing, how they will be doing it, and why they will be doing it.

Specific feedback Feedback that conveys specific information to the learner on performance.

Station teaching A teaching strategy that arranges the environment so that two or more tasks are going on at the same time in different places.

Success rate The degree of success a learner experiences in learning.

Summative evaluation An assessment of the degree to which program objectives have been received.

Systematic observation and analysis A process of collecting objective information on the instructional process and analyzing that information in a meaningful way.

Target of feedback The individual, group, or class to whom feedback is directed.

Teacher-directed learning environment A highly structured learning environment in which most of the instructional decisions are made by the teacher, not the student.

Teaching function Those critical aspects of teaching that must be attended to regardless of the content or context of a lesson.

Teaching strategy A framework that arranges an instructional environment for group instruction.

Team teaching A teaching strategy in which two or more teachers share the responsibility for instructional functions for a given class.

Transfer of learning The influence on one skill of having learned another skill

Unlimited task A movement task that gives students maximum opportunity to respond in different ways.

Validity of an observational tool The degree to which an observational tool measures what it purports to measure.

Index